SPANISH DRAMA OF PATHOS

1750-1808

II. LOW TRAGEDY

SPANISH DRAMA OF PATHOS

1750-1808

BY

I. L. McCLELLAND

*Reader in Spanish in the
University of Glasgow*

IN TWO VOLUMES

II

LOW TRAGEDY

UNIVERSITY OF TORONTO PRESS

1970

Published in Canada and the United States by
UNIVERSITY OF TORONTO PRESS

Copyright © 1970 by I. L. McClelland

8020 1694 4

First published 1970

Printed in Great Britain by
Hazell Watson & Viney Ltd
Aylesbury, Bucks

CONTENTS

VOLUME II

LOW TRAGEDY

CONTENTS

vi

VOLUME II

Low Tragedy

Melodrama: A Compromise

ONE apparently respectable way of making *tragedia pura* emotionally contemporary, and therefore acceptable, was to present it in the freak-form of melodrama in which reason treads meaningly to music—often so meaningly, indeed, that treading itself becomes precarious. At first sight the relation between High Tragedy and the one-act melodrama, or drama with music, is not apparent, and the theme of Rousseau's *Pygmalion* which stimulated Spain to write melodramas is not a tragic one. But Rousseau's admirers had natural reasons for turning melodrama to tragic account. The dramatic use of incidental music and dumb posturing of more than life-size intensity is acceptable only in a context of fantasy, comic opera, or poetic tragedy. Pure fantasy seldom takes root on Spanish soil. The *zarzuela* left few vacancies for other light, operatic pretensions. And, in any case, the startling peculiarities of eighteenth-century melodrama had much to do with the epoch's natural sense of deep solemnity.

It was understandable that music, which sadly enough had now become the most acceptable feature of dramatic entertainment, should, in this century, have broken out of its normal bounds in the opera, serious or comic, to invade other forms of drama. Even so, the play with some kind of musical interlude was not new to Spain, France, Italy, or England. Music inserted into serious drama as relief, or to insinuate tense atmospheres and emotions, or, in comedy, to produce an air of madrigal light-heartedness, had been as common in Spain's dramatic prime as in England's, and at times seems to have had associations with popular miming.[1] But the vogue of the spectacular Italian opera,

1. See P. Ginisty, *Le Mélodrame*, Paris, 1910; F. Gaiffe, *Le Drame en France au xviiie Siècle*, Paris, 1910, pp. 238 ff; A. Nicoll, *A History of English Drama. 1660–1900,* vol. iii. Cambridge, 1952, pp. 97 ff; Cot. *Iriarte*, pp. 403 ff.

together with the eighteenth century's histrionic change of heart, had suggested new combinations of music and movement, of implied meaning and the spoken word; and the self-conscious *scène lyrique*, as conceived by Rousseau in *Pygmalion*, which was known for some five years before being performed in Paris in 1775, presented old features with a modern emphasis. In 1770 Ramón de la Cruz, who probably knew this work, and who already in 1757 showed a disposition to analyse the relationship of drama and music,[2] parodied what looks like an effect in melodrama in *La despedida de los cómicos*.

El teatro representa una soledad y sonando una sinfonía de flautas, y violines . . . sale Chinica muy triste y después que a compás de algunos suspiros, sin hablar, empieza a representar.[3]

In 1774 he produced a symbolical *sainete* in which characters, directed to rest in the shade of a tree, are lulled by 'un coro de violines expresivo del cansancio'.[4] These are precisely the forms of emotional expression which the melodramatists were to investigate.

Eighteenth-century melodrama, advancing, then, from the idea of sung words and of musical accompaniment to action and words combined, as in, for instance, Cañizares's 'melodrama', or 'zarzuela', or 'ópera scénica', *Angélica y Medoro*, of 1721, introduced music to accompany spoken words, with special atmospheric insinuation, or, more peculiarly, used it to accompany and underline dumb action or to fill pauses with meaning. This single-act, *escena lírica*, for one or two characters, often described as a drama 'con intervalos de música', or as an 'unipersonal', a 'diálogo', 'trílogo', or a 'melólogo', normally induced the very opposite feeling to the lyrical irresponsibility inspired by grand or light opera. Its atmosphere was close, dense, and heavy with meaning. The eighteenth century saw in it, as well as in opera, what the twentieth sees in serious ballet. Melodrama was talked about as if it were the perfect expression of pan-artistic mind.

At the same time many reputable critics were uneasy about it. They might glory in opera and admire restrained melodrama. But it was clear that the very nature of the new genre exposed it to abuse. Arteaga's

2. See *Quien complace a la deidad acierta a sacrificar. Nuevo drama cómico-harmónico*, Madrid, 1757. In the Preface Cruz considers the verisimilitude of having music interspersed with the spoken word.
3. There is a manuscript in the Biblioteca Municipal, Madrid.
4. See Cot. *R.X.*, p. 190.

complaints about the popular decorative excesses of opera are even more applicable to melodrama:

Il Cornelio, e il Racine del teatro lirico [i.e. Zeno and Metastasio] credettero, che l'eccellenza dell'opera italiana consistesse principalmente nella bella musica e nella bella poesia; si crede ora che il suo pregio maggiore consista nel favellar agli aocchi piuttosto che agli orecchi, e nell' interessare collo spettacolo e con le superbe comparse anzichè colla ben pensata modulazione e coi fiori della eloquenza. Siffatto principio avrà delle pericolose influenze sù tutto il sistema. . . .[5]

The new genre was never very clearly defined. At first, reviewers expected some part of it to be sung and criticized its authors for not knowing what they were about:

A este trílogo se da el nombre de melodrama; ¡otra confusión! Melodrama quiere decir verso suave, verso cantado, canto: y aquí no se canta nada; también a la ópera se llama melodrama; el segundo título de *con períodos de música* no explica más in menos.[6]

Soon a reviewer noted that audiences had quickly tired of monologues or dumb actions despite, apparently, the spectacular scenery with which these were presented, and that more dramatic forms, with dialogue, had been the inevitable consequence.[7] Even in 1796, by which time certain characteristics of the 'melodrama' had become fixed, critics were still puzzled:

. . . ¿qué nombre se la había de dar en nuestro teatro? Porque no siendo ópera porque no tiene más que alguna vez un poco de canto musical, le era impropio este nombre. Además hay sus intervalos de música instrumental para ayudar las expresiones de los actores, o en los intervalos mudos, o aun a veces representando: en donde se ve la imitación de los monólogos, o diálogos, o trílogos, etc.; por esta razón ya resultaba una pieza de un nuevo género compuesto de monólogos y algo de canto. ¿Cómo pues se ha de llamar? '*melodrama*': otra confusión, pues melodrama y ópera hasta aquí habían pasado por sinónimos; pero ella se había de llamar H o R pues llámese '*melodrama*', que importa poco que un nombre signifique lo que al autor de diere la gana.[8]

5. Esteban de Artega, *Le Rivoluzioni del teatro musicale italiano* . . ., Bologna, 1783–8, vol. ii, p. 165.
6. *Memorial literario*, December 1793. The writer is reviewing *Ariadna abandonada en Naxos*.
7. *Memorial literario*, September 1793.   8. Ibid., January 1796.

Yet, true as it was that the authors of melodrama were even more confused than the critics, they were obeying some dark instinct to experiment on the free literary commons where experiment was still possible. For, whatever 'melodrama' may eventually have meant to other countries, to Spain it was a logical, if temporary, solution to the problem of contriving an acceptable form of concentrated tragedy which all classes of playwrights now believed to be the most sublime aspect of drama. Primarily, for Spanish tragedians with nothing worth saying, it had the practical advantage of being short. A little thinking, a little reasoning on emotion, which in five acts looks as inadequate as it really is, can appear in a one-act setting to be selected from a bottomless store. Great tragedy should suggest that the author's thought is limited only by space. Each act should assert its dramatic values as being essential to the ultimate depth and power of the whole play. Spain's eighteenth-century tragedy had given the impression that four out of the five acts were written solely for the sake of appearances.

In the second place, the modification of classical tragedy through opera had foreshadowed this very solution. The austerity of Unities, the stark reasoning, had been eased, even for the purists, by the viewless pageantry of sound and a visible grandeur of scenery. The necessarily stilted posturing to music in tragic grand opera marks the first stage of consciousness in the history of modern melodrama. The psychological and atmospheric value of posture, as heightened by operatic singers, had become by the seventies an important consideration in theoretic histrionics. Diderot had been fascinated by potentialities of posture and developed his ideas on the subject in 1757, in *Les Entretiens sur le Fils Naturel*. The Riccobonis before him had studied the question exhaustively, and English players, intelligently observed by the elder, had practised insinuating poses in those Shakespearian soliloquies which put continental actors of later decades to the test. The Riccobonis had spoken of the new conception of the pause; and this tragic pause to music is the essence of eighteenth-century melodrama the authors of which did not know that they were substituting emotional atmosphere for pure thought, but believed that they were giving thought a sharper significance. Nevertheless, the undefined intention behind melodrama was to suggest, by making music project the brooding atmosphere of the pause, that the protagonist's thoughts lay too deep for words, and to guide the spectator, by posture or some economic pattern of movements, to sympathize with the emotional effects of the hero's full-length thoughts which he was keeping to himself. His reasoning, exteriorized in key speeches at intervals, is meant, between statement and implication, to be fully developed. Even more notably than grand opera this was to be, to all external intents and purposes, a form of High Tragedy, a form acceptable to the general public. Incidentally to the mediocre tragedian it was to mean a great saving in mental effort.

A significant fact about this genre in Spain is that while it provoked a certain amount of sarcasm, especially in its later stages, it was not so consistently ridiculed as the much less ridiculous tragedy proper. This is explained by the popular attraction of music which could cover a multitude of dramatic absurdities, and by the fact that for intellectuals the new melodrama had been established reputably by such enlightened progressives as Rousseau and his admirer Tomás de Iriarte. Also the new melodrama demonstrated so extreme an economy of technical means that it roused the curiosity, not only of those who approved of Unities on principle, but of those who sought novelty. Its sensational feature was the presentation of highly emotional and dramatic episodes by one, two, or three characters only. The curious went to the theatre to see how one actor could make a drama. They stayed because his posturing to music was satisfyingly dramatic and easy to understand. One-man plays roused the curiosity then that they sporadically evoke at the present day. They can encourage mere trickery; or they can be useful experiments in dramatic ways and means. On the whole, for the eighteenth century which had not yet learnt the tricks of peopling the stage with disembodied telephone-callers or of linking a single actor with the world of catastrophe by telegram and radio, they were more useful than vicious. At least they demonstrated that the Unities could have lively potentialities.

However, while the general public and many intellectuals took specialized melodrama very seriously: the former because it was sensational, the latter because it was an interesting experiment and did not transgress against book-logic, acute critics either amusedly reserved their judgement or were openly sarcastic. In *Dell'origine e delle regole della musica* of 1774 Antonio Eximeno, one of Metastasio's most intelligent Spanish admirers, who did not as yet clearly distinguish between the 'drama with music' and pure opera, nevertheless had grave misgivings about the popular spread of musical pieces and felt the necessity of insisting that not all drama is suitable for musical interpretation.[9]

L'instabile condizione dell'uomo non porta giammai le cose alla sommità della perfezione, se non per mandarle più precipitosamente in rovina. Il teatro in musica è uno spettacolo da darsi solamente da un Principe amante della Musica, e della magnificenza; me l'avidità dell popolo italiano per godere di si fatti spettacoli fece aprire i teatri da guadagno, ne' quali manca sempre da qualche parte il fondamento del teatro in musica, che è l'illusione.[10]

Santos Díez González approved of Iriarte's 'unipersonal' *Guzmán el Bueno* in 1791[11] chiefly, perhaps, because he approved of Iriarte[12] and because the national theme was 'regularly' and decorously presented. But Félix María de Samaniego saw in this *Guzmán* a dangerous Spanish precedent. Even allowing for the fact that he had already come into literary collision with Iriarte[13] and could hardly regard him disinterestedly, one must admit that his sneers at this new dramatic stunt, and his parody on it[14] were excusable criticisms of the genre's sensational inanities:

Apenas leí el *Soliloquio de Guzmán el Bueno*, exclamé: ¡perdidos somos! El maldito ejemplo de Pigmaleón, perdóneme su mérito, nos va a inundar la escena de una nueva casta de locos. La pereza de nuestros ingenios encontrará un recurso cómodo para lucirlo en el teatro, sin el trabajo de pelear con las dificultades que ofrece el diálogo. Cualquiera poetastro elegirá un hecho histórico, o un pasage fabuloso, o inventará un argumento; extenderá su razonamiento, lo sembrará de contrastes, declamaciones, apóstrofes y sentencias, hará hablar a su héroe una o dos horas con el cielo o con la tierra,

9. *Dell'origine e delle regole della musica*, Rome, 1774. See pp. 440 ff.

10. Ibid.

11. See his *censura*, dated 1791, of the Cádiz edition of 1790. '. . . y representándose en ella una acción ilustre, que nos trae a la memoria el amor a la patria, en que se distinguieron nuestros mayores, la hallo digna de nuestro teatro nacional.' The licensed copy is in the Biblioteca Municipal, Madrid.

12. He had recommended with tremendous enthusiasm the licence for Iriarte's *La señorita mal criada* (Madrid, 1788) in 1790, calling it 'digna de contarse entre las primeras que hacen honor al teatro español, y a la lengua castellana', and suggesting that not only should the licence be granted but that the author should be personally thanked 'por su celo, y aplicación en contribuir a la cultura de [los teatros] ellos'.

13. See Cot. *Iriarte . . .*, ed. cit., pp. 265 ff.

14. See 'Respuesta de mi Tío sobre lo que verá el curioso lector, publicada contra la voluntad de su merced, con licencia, 1792' in *Obras inéditas de D. Félix María de Samaniego. . . .*, Vitoria, 1866, pp. 218-19.

con las paredes o con los muebles de su cuarto; procurará hacernos soportable
tal delirio con la distracción de *allegro, adagio, largo, presto* con *sordinas* o sin
ellas; y se saldrá nuestro hombre con ser autor de un soliloquio, monólogo
o escena trágico-cómico-lírica unipersonal.[15]

Less prejudiced observers than Samaniego too, and all who could see
clear of aesthetic rationalism, soon realized that melodrama, even taken
in the original sense, was for the most part artistic fraud and humbug.
In 1793, when the new genre had got well into its stride, the *Memorial
literario* damned a typical example in a disgusted sentence:

> . . . Es una escena . . . para hablar mucho sin substancia entre los espacios
> músicos. . . .[16]

A valuable yet easily exaggerated feature of melodrama was its
development of histrionic art by studied posture, pause, and dumb
expressiveness, in other words, its application of Riccoboni's histrionic
theory. The less an author thought the more attention he gave to pantomime. So that interest in silent expression as a conveyer of what the
melodramatists hoped would be taken for complex thought soon
showed signs of becoming a histrionic mania. Perhaps Sheridan was
thinking of melodrama and its relatives in an episode of *The Critic* of
1779, where Lord Burleigh, parodying the new histrionic tendency,
demonstrates a process of complicated reasoning merely by the way
he shakes his head:

> *Sneer.* The devil! Did he mean all that by shaking his head?
> *Puff.* Every word of it—if he shook his head as I taught him.
> *Dangle.* Ah! There certainly is a vast deal to be done on the stage by dumb
> show and expression of face; and a judicious author knows how much he
> may trust to it.

By literary standards—we are not concerned with musical ones—no
melodrama ranks high as a work of art. But on this eccentric genre and
its three-act relation, the *drame*, was laid the onus of effecting the
change from old to modern expressions of tragedy. Purists could never
have engineered the transformation. Not even quotation from contemporary philosophers or conscientious exercises in the technique of
contemporary reasoning could make new tragedy look more new than

15. Op. cit., pp. 218–19.
16. See *Memorial literario*, December 1793. Part I, p. 399.

old. Often great changes in dramatic ideology are projected, like broad shadows on a screen, by writers who sense novelty but do not understand its philosophical significance. This is true of the melodramatists. Neither Rousseau nor Tomás de Iriarte, neither Diderot nor Comella, fully understood what he was doing when he projected posture and pause against a backcloth of tacit meaning. No eighteenth-century dramatist saw the full curve of rationalistic ideology of which he represented a section, for it reaches down to the present day. To appreciate the historical value of melodrama we must understand that, despite many appearances misleading to modern eyes, the ultimate aim of its authors was realism: a realism of exterior circumstances and of mental conditions, with their causes and effects, that had been teasing the intellects of the whole epoch, the ablest philosopher and the humblest scribbler alike. Eighteenth-, like twentieth-century philosophy, was so matter-of-fact, so closely concerned with the everyday behaviour of the common man that the common artist could be expected to grasp its incidental illustrations if not its connected thought. Unfortunately incidental illustrations of thought are apt to be confused by all but first-class artists with spasms of emotion, and the melodramatists, aiming at an artistic exhibition of pure thought, found themselves engaged instead in demonstrating the emotional moodiness which was merely accidental to the thought they meant to suggest. More pregnant with self-evident thinking is the pause as objectively understood by Ibsen and Chekhov. But to prepare for deep psychology through silence it was necessary to experiment with the technical nature and the emotional possibilities of silence. The experimental feature of melodrama in this technical sense gives it historical justification.

The prose *Pygmalion* of Rousseau considered from such an angle is extremely tentative. The story of the statue which came to life before its sculptor's eyes suggested little to the author's verbal imagination. He depended primarily for his suggestiveness on the inarticulated meaning of the musical intervals. It was to be a monologue in a context of musical and gesticulative insinuation. What this master, who was no master playwright, did not realize, however, was that a pause, set even to the best of music, could not sustain an atmosphere of imaginative meaning if the preceding monologue were not poetically suggestive. Rousseau's monologue is often merely exclamatory. Many of the musical intervals are engineered for convenience. For example, the exclamatory nature of the following detracts from the reflective atmosphere of a succeeding pause-to-music, making it seem artificial and even detached from its context:

Pygmalion. Que l'âme faite pour animer un tel corps doit être belle!

(*Il s'arrête longtemps: puis retournant s'asseoir, il dit d'une voix lente et changée:*)

Quels desirs osé-je former! quels voeux insensés! qu'est-ce que je sens? . . . O ciel! le voile de l'illusion tombe, et je n'ose voir dans mon coeur: j'aurais trop à m'en indigner.

(*Longue pause dans un profond accablement*)

Voilà donc la noble passion qui m'égare! c'est donc pour cet objet inanimé que je n'ose sortir d'ici! un marbre! une pierre! une masse informe et dure, travaillée avec ce fer! . . .

But it was the general form rather than the specific content of *Pygmalion* that proved influential, though doubtless there were those who regarded every word falling from Rousseau's pen as intrinsically sacred. One reason why the subject matter of this scene did not admit of close imitations would be that Rousseau's complete works, as Spell reminds us, were banned with renewed emphasis by the revised Index of 1790, although only after some five or six translations of *Pygmalion* had been put into circulation,[17] so that, while reproduction of the same theme was inadvisable, there was nothing to stop playwrights who knew *Pygmalion* from writing harmless parallels. Another reason, one suspects, was that Spain was not addicted by temperament to rarefied idylls like the story of Pygmalion. Still another was that, when once presented with the 'melodramatic' idea of *Pygmalion*, Spanish playwrights, even of mediocre calibre, were capable of turning it into something more alluring, more realistically suited to the tastes of the epoch than *Pygmalion* itself.

There is evidence that *Pygmalion* in French or Spanish, was known in Spain before 1788.[18] But the first published translation was made in verse by Francisco Durán in 1788 from a prose version supplied for the audience at the Caños where the original was presented in French.[19]

17. J. R. Spell, *Rousseau in the Spanish World before 1833*, pp. 117 ff.
18. Op. cit., pp. 120 ff.
19. Op. cit., p. 120. The verse translation is reproduced in Appendix A of Spell's study. See pp. 265 ff.

In the same year Juan Ignacio González del Castillo, the *sainetista*, appears to have produced another verse translation.[20] Durán's version probably keeps as close to the original as verse can keep to prose, and, on the unimportant occasions when the translator diverges, he generally changes to improve—not, of course, too difficult an achievement. In the idyllic circumstances of the scene, verse is more convincing than Rousseau's prose, and a notable feature of the translation is that the metres change sensitively with the speaker's mood, as, indeed, Spanish metres had always changed to suit a Spaniard's feelings. Here the translator was on surer ground than Rousseau whose prose tone cannot alter except in degrees of verbal exclamation. The following example, which begins in tones of busy harangue and changes to a Renaissance movement of reflection, is not ineffective:

> *Pigmalion Patéticamente.*
>> Y tú, suprema esencia, que te ocultas
>> a los sentidos y en el pecho brillas,
>> . . .
>> ¡Tú que recibes cultos obsequiosos
>> que los mortales todos te dedican,
>> y a quien no honra aquél que nada siente,
>> tu gloria aumenta con tus obras mismas!
>> Salva el sonrojo de la naturaleza,
>> sí, el baldón que la resulta evita
>> de que este perfectísimo modelo
>> sea imagen de cosa que no exista.
>> *Quédase abatido un rato, y al volver en sí, dice blandamente:*
>> ¡Qué inesperada calma!
>> Cuando mi sangre ardía
>> en una mortal fiebre,
>> mis miembros imprevisto aliento anima.

A similar instinct causes the translator to rearrange the fussy changes of mood directed by Rousseau into a more balanced shape of contrasted light and shade. Rousseau's vague, artificial scheme of emotional ups and downs as indicated by the order of these directions:

Longue pause dans un profond accablement . . . Impétueusement . . . Moins vivement, mais toujours avec passion . . . Transport . . . Avec un enthousiasme plus

20. See Spell, op. cit., p. 121. It figures in the *Índice general de los libros prohibidos . . .*, for the year 1793.

pathétique . . . Il revient à lui par degrès avec un mouvement d'assurance et de joie . . Ironie amère . . .

becomes more coherent, more dramatically defined:

. . . Se entrega a un abatimiento que le obliga a apoyarse en algo . . . Con ímpetu . . . afectuosamente . . . Fuera de sí . . . Patéticamente . . . Quédase abatido un rato, y al volver en sí dice blandamente . . . Irónicamente . . .

Clearly the translator's own imagination was working. He was at his worst in bringing Galatea to life. But so was Rousseau. Her dawning awareness of herself, which, as a Lockian degree of self-discovery, might have been subtly linked with the epoch's analytical self-consciousness, has an air of nursery finality, a game-like conclusiveness:

> *Galathée, se touchant encore.*
> C'est moi . . .
> *fait quelques pas et touche un marbre*
> ce n'est plus moi.

which was turned into Spanish with the clumsy grammar of:

> Esto es yo . . .
> Esto no es yo.

Even this form of drama could lend itself to ornamental rant, and Francisco Mariano Nipho in another translation of *Pygmalion*[21] swelled out the more inflatable passages with decadent images:

> *Pigmalión* Los pintores, poetas de la vista,
> los poetas, pintores del ingenio,
> ni me admiran aquéllos con sus rasgos,
> ni me hechizan los otros con sus versos . . .

But before the end of the eighties *Pygmalion* had already been imitated in a different kind of theme. González del Castillo, fired by the idea of posturing silences, and stirred by subjects more vital than mythology, presented his *Hanníbal* in Cádiz in 1788,[22] apparently inspiring Tomás de Iriarte, who heard of its success when he visited that region, to imitation.[23] *Hanníbal* is as good as Iriarte's later *Guzmán*,

21. See *Pigmalión, Monólogo patético, traducido del francés libremente y aumentado en verso castellano*, Madrid, 1790.
22. *Hanníbal. Scena lírica, original, en metro endecasílabo castellano, por . . ., para representarse el día 3 de diciembre del presente año de 1788*, Cádiz, 1788.
23. See Subirá, op. cit., pp. 243 and 251 ff.

in some features is superior to it. The explanatory 'movement' passing to retrospective description and leading on to present worries and moods of indecision:

> Mi mal es cierto . . . sí . . . yo soy perdido . . .
> Terrible multitud de gente, y armas
> se conduce a este sitio . . .
> Ea, pues, alma mía, ¿qué resuelves?

might come from any later melodrama. But González del Castillo, a better dramatist than Iriarte, had a keen sense of nervous tension to produce which, Hanníbal, hiding in a room containing nothing, so far as we can see, but a portrait and a jug of water on a table, keeps restlessly passing from one window to the other as a man in his physical and nervous circumstances naturally would. Even some of his more sensational behaviour is realistically accounted for by the menace he sees or frustratingly is unable to see through the window. The melodramatic mood of frenzied collapse, hinted at in *Pygmalion*, is more extreme in this atmosphere of claustrophobia and recalls *Le Fils Naturel*:

> *. . . mortal desesperación; se conduce y apoya la cabeza en un extremo de la escena. . . .*

Perhaps it is not meet in this otherwise economically contrived drama that he should die self-indulgently on the stage, for the play is less concerned with sights than with sounds and interior atmosphere. Thus when Hanníbal reasons himself into taking heroic poison, and brings himself through exclamations and points of suspension to his last agony, he is instructed to fall 'within' that the effect might be fully classical.

Iriarte, doubtless inspired by *Hanníbal* as well as by the more famous *Pygmalion*, could not, however, reach either González del Castillo's level of poetry, or his close suspense which a parodist, perhaps affectionately, ridiculed in *El Domingo*, a melodrama in a closed room containing nothing but a table and a jug of water. Thereafter the tendency was to furnish elaborately, even to the point of competing with the scenic effects of opera. Again, then, drama sold its power to *décor*.

In studying *Pygmalion* Tomás de Iriarte had the advantage of understanding the music in all its technical implications, and it is from his

knowledge of music that he is able to bring novelty to his own melodrama. In his poetic thesis *La música*, of 1779, he had tried to analyse
not only the emotive qualities of the movements of symphony and
their relation to different keys and instruments, but he had considered
the psychology of the musical pause and rest and had insisted that no
amount of technical knowledge could produce successful composition
in the absence of sensibility.

Since much of what he had observed in music coincided with the
histrionic experiments of his day, in which he was also interested, his
'melodrama', based on his experiences in both fields, was far more complex than that of Rousseau whose dramatic thinking was slighter. The
pause in music, with its atmospheric silence and insinuated rhythm,
was too close to the tense pause discussed by the Riccobonis and practised by Diderot and by French and English actors for the intelligent
Iriarte to overlook it.

> Muchas veces conviene que insinúe [La música]
> con las esperas y las pausas tanto
> como expresar pudiera el canto.
>
> . . .
>
> Pero silencios hay de dos maneras:
> Unos tienen tan breves duraciones,
> que el nombre se les da de aspiraciones;
> otros, que duran cláusulas enteras,
> se suelen distinguir con el de esperas:
> y como a notas vivas equivalen,
> logran en el compás justa cabida . . .

The musical movements, or moods, themselves constituted the very
essence of new melodrama and Iriarte derived intellectual pleasure
from his investigation of the technical ways and means of producing
various emotional effects, as in this short instance:

> Aquel modo menor que significa
> todo el afán que en la tristeza cabe,
> si se transporta a diapasón más grave,
> miedo, pasmo, horror también explica.[24]

In Canto IV he speaks of 'melodrama', the term being used by him

24. Op. cit., Canto II.

in its operatic senses, and he discriminates between melodrama, as a work of art, and its depraved imitations. Further, in discussing the effect on the audience of the overture and its relation to other parts of a melodrama, he shows that he can look at music from the standpoint of the stage. Instead of conventional musical movements unrelated to the psychological requirements of the opening and succeeding scenes of the opera, he asks for a sympathetic relationship of musical movement and dramatic mood:

> De este conjunto armónico el efecto
> no solamente debe
> aplacar el bullicio de la plebe,
> sino mover también algún afecto,
> o alguna imagen anunciar, no ajena
> de la que ofrece la primera escena.
> Muy pocos evitamos la censura
> de haber distribuido la obertura
> en tres partes de estilo diferente,
> y ninguna tal vez correspondiente
> al principio del drama,
> (abuso indigno de su antigua fama.)
> De un majestuoso Alegro precedido
> un moderado Andante,
> y seguido de un Presto tumultuoso,
> tiempo ha que de preámbulo ha servido
> a las quejas de triste naufragante,
> a los extremos de un galán dichoso,
> al combate, al solemne sacrificio,
> al festivo banquete, y al suplicio.

So Iriarte approached *Guzmán el Bueno*, his national *scène lyrique*,[25] with studied technical logic. His overture to the soldierly drama, which is reduced to the Unity of the Christian ramparts, is 'martial and loud', and the figure revealed on the stone bench as the curtain rises, is Guzmán in full armour. There he is to sit ensteeled in silence while the mettlesome music gradually diminishes to *piano* and comes to a stop. Even then he is told to let an interval pass before he speaks. When at

25. See *Guzmán el Bueno. Soliloquio o escena trágica—unipersonal, con música en sus intervalos.* Both music and words were composed by Iriarte. There is an undated edition in the British Museum. It was performed in 1791.

last he does so, he is to suit his voice to his previous attitude of thought on the bench, and speak in a 'grave and measured' tone. Thus far, then, the atmosphere of military crisis, with the High Command momentarily irresolute to heighten the tension, exemplifies Iriarte's principles admirably. One notes that Guzmán is not yet instructed to exteriorize his thinking with gesture. Iriarte had taste and restraint.

The hendecasyllabic opening speech sets a standard of bookish dignity which the hero is to observe throughout.[26] If we are disappointed that the literary content of this revolutionary experiment in form should sound, when separated from its music, like any other crucial speech of indifferent High Tragedy, we must remember that Iriarte was an unimaginative Arandan, artistically incapable of supplying the liberated power of ideas required by his liberal medium. Unfortunately literary form is easier to perceive and imitate than the ideas for which it is instinctively designed. Iriarte was conscious of the atmospheric, scenic, musical, and histrionic values of his experiment and could analyse them; he could appreciate and copy the rationalistic technique that would bring his hero to objective self-examination, and to an impartial weighing of alternatives; he could see how emotion might mislead the thinker into believing that reason was weighing down the scale on the side more convenient to him, and how an honest man could correct his misjudgement by sternly eliminating emotion from his calculations for the necessary period of decision, balancing the stark alternatives of reason one against the other. But taste, technique, and academic ideas without genius are vain in literature and Iriarte was typically Arandan in his uncreativeness.

Guzmán's mind sways between the two alternatives of duty to his son held as a hostage by the Moors, who threatened to put him to death if his father refused to surrender the city, and duty to his country. Prompted by the strategic music he doubts and wavers, lets his emotion confuse his reason, his reason conquer his emotion. He deals with the depression produced by his decision to sacrifice his son with gradually strengthening resignation. But he is full of words, not thoughts; of words that all Arandan heroes use. Music cannot free him from their stereotyped eloquence. When his dramatic mood changes he forces it upon the audience by dint of verbal repetition:

26. See note 1, page 569.

Guzmán ¡Ah, Guzmán infeliz!...
¿Cuándo tal sobresalto has padecido,
augustia igual, tormento semejante?
. . .
Cobrando espíritu
¿Arrepentirme yo? ¿De qué?...
. . .
Con aflicción
Mas ¡ay! mueres cautivo,
mueres en tierna edad, solo, indefenso.

He scientifically examines cause and effect but he does so with the
help of catechisms mass-produced by official tragedians for tragedians:

(*Despacio*) ¡Cielos! Si mi aflicción me dará treguas
para observar con ánimo tranquilo
cuán graves son las causas, cuán difícil
es el remedio de mi actual peligro?
¿Al Bravo Rey Don Sancho no he jurado
defender a Tarifa y su castillo?
. . .
Soy en el mando de esta fortaleza
sucesor del Maestre Don Rodrigo,
Prometí sostenerla...
¿Lo prometí?... Pues a cumplirlo.
. . .
¿No me expondrá mi hazaña generosa
a un arrepentimiento bien tardío?
¿Arrepentirme yo? ¿De qué?...

repeating himself in different words when ideas fail him:

augustia igual, tormento semejante.

and when it is necessary to assert his nobility more forcibly he unblushingly reverts to the most hackneyed strains of Corneille:

Primero fui buen español que padre.

On the whole it is the music which determines the development of
the conflict not the conflict the music. Guzmán leans on the music of
the interludes because his own ideology cannot support him or itself.
His process of thinking is determined from without. Perhaps he is at

his best at a devotional moment when, in a prayer for superhuman grace to supply what is lacking in his human weakness, he draws on the common experience of a sense of helplessness:

> ¿Queréis clemente una segura senda
> mostrarme en tan obscuro laberinto?
>
> . . .
>
> Disipad las tinieblas de mi mente.
> Soy hombre, y débil, pero en vos confío.

but we have heard almost the same words before in Moratín's *Hormesinda*[27] and Cadalso's *Sancho García*,[28] where the speakers' ears were still tuned to sounds of the Golden Age.

More interesting than Iriarte's potentially good moments, however, is one of his failures. At the climax, lured by the same corpse-candle that Jovellanos pursued at the end of *El delincuente honrado*, he followed the more intimately harrowing possibilities of his tragedy, searching for human and homely qualities within a heroic state of mind in order to show what a struggle between heroic decision, and the private pain it involves, really means in human terms and how a man's painful reasoning makes his heroism intelligent. Though Iriarte partly resolved Guzmán's struggle between private pain and public duty by pointing, not unskilfully, to the highest Christian example and source of grace:

> ¿haré mucho
> si por su ley un hijo sacrifico?
> Por ella se ha de dar la propia vida
> doy la que a mí se debe, que es lo mismo.

a solution was perhaps of less artistic and intellectual importance to him than the processes of the research, which he was not dramatically qualified to undertake, into the commonplaces of pain. When, after heroically throwing a knife to the Moors below that they may slay his son, Guzmán wonders how he will later be able to face the boy's

27. *Hormesinda* . . . en vano fuerte
         me intento hacer. Soy débil mujer flaca
         . . . Dios eterno, . . .
         Dadme en este conflicto fortaleza . . . (Act V.)

28.   *Alek* O Ser Supremo, cuya inmensa ciencia,
         demuestra de los hombres la demencia
         desnuda nuestros flacos corazones
         del cúmulo horroroso de pasiones . . . (Act III.)

mother, he is seeking to humanize heroic pain without otherwise establishing himself as a human individual. Assailed by morbid curiosity to see the end for himself, he leans over the wall, and from his scholar-hero's point of relative sublimity he swings down to a ridiculous 'humanity' on a string of broken syllables.

> *Con acento y ademanes de desmayo:*
> Y que . . . (La voz . . . me falta)—¡O Patria mia!
> Cedo . . . al dolor . . . mas no a tus enemigos.

This does not improve the play, but even as a failure it demonstrates how, in a relatively classical setting, a deep distress might potentially humanize the soul of idea-less heroics.

The musical pattern is conceived on a more elaborate scale than Rousseau's for Guzmán is meant to arouse more complex emotions than the two-dimensional Pygmalion. In all consciousness Iriarte appears to have tried to develop the genre in this direction, especially in passages suggestive of dramatically related light and shade. At least one major pause heightens the importance of the trumpet and bugle blasts it separates. They occur, insistently repeated, near the end, when the speaker is tense with waiting,[29] and remind us of the external dramatic effects which Iriarte would have known in Jovellanos's problem play[30] *El delincuente honrado* where, in a paralysed silence of fear, the bell tolling the hour of execution was the only tongue to speak. In contrast, Guzmán's final movements up and down the steps, that figure so much in opera, to the wall-edge, immediately before and after his glimpse of events outside, call for continuous music which settles eventually into a dirge-like wail of flutes, a treble sympathy for the death of a young boy.[31] The effect in general is therefore more pretentious than in Rousseau's fantasy. It shows that in limited ways Iriarte was capable of melodramatic suggestion and could keep his external effects under control. The play was a theatre success. And melodrama in Spain turned from idylls to take the path of national heroics. From a dramatic impression it became a drama.

Samaniego's parody of *Guzmán* is contained in a 'letter' professedly

29. The trumpet sounds twice, at intervals, then 'Después de un rato de silencio, suena un clarín tan cercano que se conozca le tocan dentro del castillo, precediendo a esta llamada un redoble de atabales.'

30. See pp. 404 ff. below.   31. See note 2, page 569.

from an uncle to a nephew and itself ridiculing the reverence shown by the Iriarte brothers, notably Tomás, for their famous Uncle Juan. In this fiction-framework and in the short Preface which mocks Iriarte's interpretation of his historical subject matter and his shilly-shallying hero,[32] he is more consistently ingenious than in the main body of the text. His parody takes the form of regular, gloss-like additions to Iriarte's lines calculated to produce bathos at every turn of the original argument. Since many of Iriarte's lines themselves contain the seeds of bathos the task of the parodist was made easy. Nevertheless, most of Samaniego's interpolations are, for a man of his intellect, incredibly puerile. In the following example, which shows his additions in italics, it may be seen that he was likely to do less harm to Iriarte than to himself:

> En el tropel confuso de encontrados
> afectos y de ideas con que lidio,
> *todos en mi mollera aposentados*
> *y en roerme los cascos tan activos*
> *que ya empiezo a dudar si mi cabeza*
> *es algún queso de ratones nido,*
> en las arduas y tristes circunstancias
> que más y más estrechan mi conflicto
> *y me tienen lo mismo que un gazapo*
> *entre el hurón y el cazador metido . . .*

Yet, however infantile in wit, Samaniego was mature enough in judgement and correctly underlined all the major weaknesses of this particular *Guzmán* and of the whole melologic tendency. On the subject of ideas he made much of the artificiality of Guzmán's problem of decision. To present a real problem a dramatic personage must first have real character. Otherwise his difficulties will slip out of focus and his reason and his emotion, which might convincingly have been at variance on certain issues, will pursue each other round a critical decision taken by the dramatist for the sake of taking action. Iriarte had not distinguished between mental problems and clashes of feelings, as Samaniego observed. Emotional decisions are more popularly appreciated in literature than mental problems and permit much saving in thought. Samaniego noted that an honourable military governor, like

32. See note 3, page 569.

Guzmán, could not logically be presented with a problem of choosing between the safety of his son and the safety of the city. That would be an unprofessional problem not even within the understanding of the humblest soldier. The only convincing problem in the circumstances was how best for the governor to deal with his human distress over the inevitable loss of his son. The only choice before him was between taking this loss well or badly. Iriarte, Samaniego realized, had missed the human and dramatic point. He had made an untenable problem and he had turned an act of anguished bravado, the unnecessary throwing of the knife, into a critical act of decision.

On style, the parodist, who was always acute, is also occasionally amusing. If Guzmán was improbable in his states of mind he was more improbable in his forms of expressing them. Samaniego glossed the effeminate reactions of the great leader like this:

> esta parte del muro . . .
> sírvame ya de solitario asilo,
> donde alivio me den mis reflexiones;
> *y aunque sean ajenas de mí mismo*
> *nadie oírmelas puedo: mas si acaso*
> *algún soldado escucha mis suspiros,*
> *al sentirlos, creerá sin duda alguna*
> *que son de una mujer no de un caudillo.*

Guzmán's sentimental, but more natural memories of his son as a child, inspired by and themselves inspiring other books of sensibility, were also obvious subjects for caricature; so was Iriarte's rhetorical padding which Samaniego exposed by means of absurdly extended similes in the 'classical' style. The straining problem strained word-values. Only a little extra pressure was needed from the parodist to distort them altogether:

> Por no ser desleal, seré verdugo:
> ¿y de quién? ¿De algún bárbaro enemigo?
> ¿De algún perverso delincuente? Dime
> ¿de quién, padre inhumano, de quién? Dilo.
> *Dilo, dilo ¿de quién? ¿Y de quién, dime:*
> dime, dime, de quién? De mi chiquillo . . .

The detailed directions for variations on the musical mood or the speech-tone which Iriarte could not manage to relate to a live system of thought or feeling is heartlessly satirized in this inconsequence:

Allegro, porque se me antoja; pero el Sr. Guzmán volverá a reflexionar con igual lentitud sin hacer caso del aire que llevare la orquesta, que podrá tocar si quisiere con instrumentos de tripa, esto es, de cuerdas de intestinos.
. . .
Dejando el tono de aflicción y ternura, se recobra y prosigue con serenidad como si tal cosa no hubiera pasado. . . .

While Iriarte's instructions on vocal pitch delivered him, Samaniego knew, into the power of actors whose idea of increasing tension was to shout oftener and more loudly than usual:

Con resolución y entereza, aumentando por grados la fuerza de la voz.
Aumentando más y más la voz . . .
Aumentando la voz todo cuanto permitan sus pulmones . . .

As irony would have it, the fastidious Iriarte was welcomed to the Príncipe by no less tousled a spokesman than Luciano Francisco Comella, who, only the previous year, had been the subject of great misgiving in an *Informe* from the Literary Censor.[33] That Comella's *Introducción* for the performance of *Guzmán el Bueno*[34] should have been required as an advance assurance to spectators speaks not only of the place which he already occupied in popular esteem and therefore of the sureness of his popular touch, but of the continuing dependence of all tragic performances on prefatory coaxing. Though the *Guzmán* might be expected to make a popular appeal through its music, it was a relatively new venture of the distrusted tragic class. The points strategically made in this *Introducción* therefore obviated difficulties which the company, from its experience, could foresee.

Most important was the apparently casual announcement inserted into the argument of the *Introducción*, which, as usual, takes the form of a discussion among the players in their own persons, that a comic piece would also be performed on the same day. So that the sting was taken out of this tragedy before it ever appeared:

33. See p. 480 below.
34. *Introducción para la escena heroica trágica intitulada 'El Guzmán' Por L. F. Comella.* There is a manuscript, licensed for 1791, in the Biblioteca Municipal, Madrid.

> ... que al festejo
> ayude con lo jocoso
> a hacer plausible lo serio.

The context into which so vital a piece of information is set is a discussion among the players about forthcoming programmes, during which a question innocently put by one of them as to whether any nation can boast of finer model characters for drama than the heroes of Spain, brings the sad reply that according to foreign-minded nationals—'semi extranjeros'—no Spanish playwright is capable of doing her heroes literary justice.[35] At which juncture comes Comella's opportunity to assure spectators that here at last is the national drama for which, albeit unknowingly, they have been waiting: a drama as traditional in theme and sentiment as it was modern in technique.

It was just as well for Iriarte's sensibilities that Comella's *Introducción* was tidied up before setting out to welcome the scholar in public. A censor had had the slapdash 'semi extranjeros' changed decorously to 'los preciados de viajeros', and had removed certain vulgarities.[36] It would appear that nobody had seriously related a statement jocularly expressed by the characters of the *Introducción* about their general aim of staging works which would bring in money for very little effort with this new genre in particular. Melodrama fitted their bill better than Comella, Iriarte, or the Censor realized. But irony was not yet content. For the result of this ill-matched, though successful association was not, as poetic justice demanded, the establishment of the Censor's good boy, Iriarte, as the leader of melodramatic fashion, but his immediate displacement by the disfavoured scribbler who had 'introduced' him. Within a few months Comella began to prepare his own melodramatic career, and the course of melodrama in Spain sympathetically changed to his dictates.

Comella's one-act *Doña Inés de Castro*, licensed in 1791, very shortly after Iriarte's *Guzmán*, is called an '*escena trágico-lírica*' to suit the Censor's principles, Santos Díez González having objected to Comella's description of 'diálogo' applied to a scene largely composed of monologue. It is, then, like Iriarte's *Guzmán*, a tragic recital on a subject of national history, and the two characters involved, alternate speakers, rather than a dialogue team, are there to represent intensively selected

35. See note 4, page 569.   36. See note 5, page 569.

thoughts and feelings, in reduced time and space, at a crisis of frustration. The Censor's reaction was to snort with disgust and to advise his colleagues to have the play rejected, not because of its exclusive aims and the general form, which he approved, but because he felt that historical monologues, specializing in famous moments of frustration, called for a more dignified interpreter than Comella. The tacit comparison with Iriarte heavily loaded his pronouncement.

> . . . Y siendo la acción capaz de mover, por sí misma, el terror y la compasión, que son las pasiones propias de la tragedia, se halla en este escrito destituida de una expresión noble, patética, sublime, y de todas las demás cualidades, que requiere la materia. El estilo es menos que mediano, muchas veces toca en bajo, y aun arrastra por el suelo; y choca continuamente la impropiedad del lenguaje. Cuando semejantes dramas pudieran admitirse en el teatro, sería por su singular mérito, y relevantes cualidades, que fuesen capaces de llamar la atención, y que por esto les hiciesen dignos de alguna singularidad . . . pero careciendo de todo esto, me parece que no debieran admitirse, por honor del mismo teatro, y de los revisores que examinan las piezas.[37]

Indeed there was little dignity in *Doña Inés de Castro*. Even when such unintentionally comic effects as these were cut or altered:

> *Pedro* ¿Clavas en mí los ojos? ¿Después lloras?
> ¿Y das, mirando al cielo, un gran suspiro?

and the worst of Comella's diction corrected, the tone was still nearer to the ridiculous than to the sublime. The climax reads like burlesque:

> *Pedro* ¡O Inés muere, o yo muero, Santos Cielos!
> O los dos hemos muerto a un tiempo mismo.

One wonders if Comella and other melodramatists remembered Jerónimo Bermúdez's *Nise lastimosa*, an unsteady tragedy reprinted in 1772 in vol. vi of the *Parnaso español*, and containing soliloquy-material very suitable for melodialogues and *unipersonales*.[38]

If Iriarte may be said to have established a national *melólogo puro*

37. *Doña Inés de Castro*, MS. B. Mun. Censura for 3 September 1791.
38. Compare:
> *Don Pedro* . . . esta alma tuya que tengo dada,
> *(solo)* aunque esta tierra gozas, si te gozas
> sin mí, que yo sin ti viviendo muero . . .
> (*Nise lastimosa*, Act I.)

Comella was already departing from it. He did not try to exteriorize a process of thinking or feeling but told a dramatic story. His composition imitates Iriarte's changing musical moods; but one is too well aware that they change to suit the audience rather than the character. The setting is Metastasian:

> El teatro representa un jardín magnífico con asientos, fuentes etc. El foro, galería con entrada al palacio de Dª Inés, con dos ramales de escalera para subir, y un descanso antes del piso de la galería: a cado lado del teatro habrá una puerta con verjas de hierro transitable. Después de un ritornelo brillante se descubre el teatro, y aparece Dª. Inés en la galería buscando a D. Pedro, quien un poco antes habrá bajado para salir por la puerta, midiendo el tiempo, de modo que cuando D. Pedro salga, Dª. Inés se asome. Interin esta acción muda, tocará la orquesta un armonioso piano.

The posturing is no longer insinuatingly reflective, as in Iriarte, but active, storied, dramatic. The letter-trick in the pantomime described below is pure cloak-and-sword. Such busy 'running hither and thither', such delirium, such emotional *extremos*, even more dangerous to give into an actress's hands than to place on her lips, were parodied as confirmed characteristics of the new genre only two years later:[39]

> Se queda Don Pedro fuera de sí por unos instantes. Doña Inés hace aquellos extremos regulares de la situación, y al volver en sí el Príncipe deja caer la carta, que Dª. Inés cogerá con disimulo, y después que está asegurada de que ha vuelto el Príncipe, se irá a un lado a leerla; y al verlo él correrá precipitado a quitársela. Todos estos afectos y sentimientos serán expresados por la música.

At the end Inés dies in Pedro's arms and the curtain falls on a lament to music while he passionately embraces her corpse.

Comella was aware, nevertheless, that the music, particularly in softer moments, should express thought. But, being even at a greater loss than Iriarte to define those thoughts to himself, he put his heroine into an exhausted sleep from which she might emit a few obvious clues to her feeling in the form of disconnected exclamations, which, as Comella had already learnt, could tide him over her periods of mental insufficiency. Thereafter he left the burden of her thinking to the composer, merely suggesting that 'the music should suggest her ideas':

39. See *Perico el de los palotes*. It is discussed on pp. 381 ff. below.

. . . Música que tenga relación con el sueño a que está entregada Da. Inés, la que a pocos instantes dirá estos dos versos que la música dejará percibir.

      Inés No me matéis . . . Traidores . . . de mi vida,
          no hagáis a la perfidia sacrificio.

Sigue por otros instantes manifestando su inquietud, y la música manifestará sus ideas. Vuelve Da. Inés, y dice despavorida:

      Imágenes funestas, sombras tristes . . .
      no conturbéis mi pecho; mas ¡qué miro!
      ¿dónde estoy? Mis jardines no son éstos . . .
      éstos son, éstos son, que yo deliro.

Despite the Censor's advice, *Doña Inés de Castro* reached the stage where it was played at intervals during the nineties. Santos Díez González had been able to find nothing morally wrong with it and in view of the theatres' need of new material for its frequent changes of programme he could do no more than register his disapproval. After this woeful exercise in melodramatic tone, Comella's 'lyrical tragedies' mercifully improved.[40]

By one of nature's ironies, which do not spare literary history, it sometimes happens that a writer whose serious output is itself an unconscious parody will attempt to improve on nature's sense of humour by writing formal parodies as well. This is exemplified in Rodríguez de Arellano, almost any of whose works was obviously intended by nature to be a grotesque warning against excess. It is further remarkable that his formal parody of melodrama, *El Domingo*, is by far the best play he ever wrote[41] and apparently gave him a taste for melodrama proper. His own serious melodramas seem to have learnt from parody where most effectively to dispose bathos.[42] Arellano, however, adapted himself to stage fashion. If the theatres appreciated parody of any strange new species, he was ready to supply it. If melodrama during the nineties took firmer hold of public imagination than might have been anticipated, he evidently was ready to supply that kind of drama

40. For examples of other melodramas on national themes see Spell, op. cit., pp. 125–6.
41. There is a manuscript copy in the Biblioteca Municipal, licensed for 1791. A printed edition is dated Madrid, 1810. See also Coe, op. cit., p. 73.
42. Melodramas by Arellano are *El negro y la blanca*, licensed in 1797, and *La noche de Troya*, licensed in the same year. Manuscript copies of both are in the Biblioteca Municipal, Madrid.

also. One must not take his principles over-seriously. The pity is that the sense of amusement he shows in *El Domingo* did not inform some of his later work.

If one is obliged to study Spanish melodrama, Arellano's *El Domingo* which portrays the brooding species at the height of the first phase as a musical monologue, will make a painless introduction. For *El Domingo* is not only a pleasantly amusing sketch, but an accurate one, and shows how, by 1791, the 'melologue' had already achieved distinctive form. It must start with a carefully arranged tableau. In this instance the stage directions, anticipating early photography, fussily place the figure in a stiff, insinuating stillness. There is an underground room whose sub-terranean aspect may, or may not, be related to a new vogue for dun-geons, crypts, caverns, and other appurtenances of picturesque gloom; but it would certainly seem to bear some relation to the closed room, with its simple table and water-jug, where the hero paced to music in *Hannibal*.[43] Arellano's room has a small window at one side; a small table, supporting an empty wine-bag is symmetrically placed at the other. Our centre-piece Domingo, the coachman, sits between them on a bench, deep in thoughts which will continue to occupy him while the orchestra plays the prelude.

It is just as well that Arellano described the *sainete* as a burlesque,[44] otherwise an audience of the later nineties might have taken this Domingo seriously, so faithful is his reasoning to the logic of melo-dramatic 'thought'. Even the descents into bathos hardly surpass the unintentionally comic effects of the serious melodramas of the age. His self-analytical passage from one mental phase to another follows the course originally laid down for all enlightened dramatists by the analytical characters of Richardson under the influence of popular philosophism which was the eighteenth-century equivalent of the popular psychology of today. Let us observe the sequence of Dom-ingo's reasoning. It will serve as a key to the mentality behind the melodramatic experiment.

When the sympathetic music expectantly pauses, Domingo's first instinct is mentally to investigate his surroundings, for only little by

43. See note 6, page 570.
44. See the full title of the printed edition of 1810: *El Domingo, Escena sola, monólogo, soliloquio, lamentación, declamación, o llámese como quisiere, que a su autor le importa poco el nombre*. It is further described within as *El Domingo. Escena ridícula-uni-cocheril*.

little is the audience to be brought to the crisis of his emotional trouble. The century had learnt cautiously to approach a mental or emotional difficulty from all angles. From place, then, he dazedly passes to the idea of time which is helpfully illustrated at this point by the chirruping of a few common sparrows understudying the poetic lark. Now, slowly, that the full force of the situation may be thoroughly impressed on the public, also, incidentally, that the melodramatist may make his scanty ideas stretch as far as possible, Domingo's waking consciousness unsteadily seizes on the wine-bag pointedly awaiting interpretation, and, in awestruck reverence before this 'dulce prenda',[45] like Don Quijote before the wine-jars from Toboso, and also like one of Are-llano's tragic heroes at his unsteadiest,[46] he is moved to vocative anguish.

Now comes the mood sacred to melodrama, the dallying mood of memory inspired by the vocal silence of a symbol, and pricked into activity by the spurs of interrogation. Who was the tyrant of that dark yesterday who locked up Domingo with an empty wine-bag? This question being artistically answered, the spectators, prompted by energetic music and his restless pacing of the stage, are invited to consider the righteousness of Domingo's anger and of his desire for vengeance. They follow him through slightly softer moods of memory, with a slightly gentler accompaniment, learning more of the history of his plight, his past revelries and his present desolation, only gradually and indirectly, for the melodramatic experiment bravely strove to break the tradition of direct narration. After which tenderly informative retrospection and a sensible eighteenth-century determination to be reasonable even in distress,[47] Domingo turns creatively to the future to

45. Amable bota, prenda de mi vida,
. . .
dulce consoladora de mis males,
. . .
¡Ay dulce bota, cuando Dios quería!

46. See *Marco Antonio y Cleopatra*, produced in 1793, where Antony finds Cleopatra's crown and royal cloak, and cries, with an unfortunate variation on a classic theme:
¡Ay dulces prendas por mi mal halladas,
dulces y alegres, cuando en otro tiempo
os ilustró mi esposa!

47. Poco a poco, pesar; pena, despacio;   treguas con la razón, y meditemos
unos breves momentos haga el juicio   antes de resolver un desatino.

make the imaginative plans that melodrama projects ironically into contrast with the constrictive present. That solid feature of the lyric scene, that *prenda*, the wine-bag, becomes the artistic drag on his flight. Drawn inexorably back by it to the present, when the play is halfway through, Domingo is inspired to recognize that wine-bag as his own, with what emotion, what memories, what conjectures, what final despair and what variations on the musical theme, the reader may imagine for himself.

If one is tempted to wonder at this stage how the author, having brought his hero, slowly, but steadily, to realize the true state of affairs —in blunt words, that without hope of escape, he has been locked up by his master in company with an empty bottle for being drunk and disorderly—can make a tragedy out of a not very tragic situation, one's knowledge of melodrama is not as extensive as Arellano's. Tragedy at its most poignant is self-made. Domingo therefore has no difficulty in making it as he goes, like a spider spinning its thread out of nothing. Repetition, always effective, without being mentally exacting, intensifies the emotional stress. 'Suppose' goes on the fertile intellect spinning its self-producing tragedy, though carefully observing the reconstructive stages of conscientious eighteenth-century logic, 'suppose the wine-bag had been left full'. Would it have stayed full? Would it not have found worthy burial in 'the living cask of my belly'? So vivid are these imaginative circumstances as Domingo compares emptiness and fullness that he grows fractious. Did all the trouble he took surreptitiously to fill that wine-bag produce no better result than inglorious emptiness? Then vindication for this deflating outrage becomes a matter of principle. It behoves him on first thoughts, while the music remains passively meditative, to consider a more temperate future where the dishonour done to wine-bags would be avoided by abstention. But no, the doubt obtrudes, as in all melodrama, just as the climax seems about to have passed; no, he will never be able to face the dishonourable ridicule that a decision to reform would provoke. The worthier, the only honourable way out is to take his own life: 'morir es necesario'. So decide the typical protagonists of this philosophical genre. After which decision, it is only a step, easily taken with the aid of courageous music, to the next stage of fixing upon the instrument, and of setting about dying, by inches, that the process may receive as full a psychological significance as possible. There is generally a dagger, sword, cup of poison, or other serviceable tool left handily awaiting this moment. Neither Domingo nor the audience has noticed so far that a full wine-bag has been negligently left under the table. Had it been visible before, it would, in any case, have spoilt the symmetry. But now it comes in useful to provide Domingo with the idea of drinking himself to death. And, as this sweet death steals hotly through his senses, the fatal symptoms, which announced the end of his colleagues from the two parts of *Manolo, El héroe de la manzana*, and other famous tragedies, which he doubtless remembers, now announce his own: the trembling of limbs, the sight confused by a rocking world, the cold-hot sweat, the gasps, the failing voice!

> Parece que se cae este edificio,
> . . .
> las tiemblas se me piernan;
> . . . Ya estoy de sudor frío
> o caliente cubierto . . .
> . . . ya es hora . . . sí, ya muero. . . .
> A Dios señores . . . que . . . se acabó el vino.

'He falls,' insist the directions, 'and so does the curtain.' He falls, a bourgeois hero, of a bourgeois age. He falls in amiable mockery while Spain non-committally sits playing for time.

Meanwhile another playwright, who from his initials would appear to be the popular Moncín, wrote a *Fin de Fiesta* entitled *El asturiano aburrido* which was performed in 1793[48] and into which was inserted a melodramatic monologue apparently by José Concha.[49] The Asturian of the fiction is a tiresome guest of whom his unwilling hostess is determined to rid herself by making him the butt of all the jests, and the caricatured victim of all the 'Italian' machines, in a *comedia de magia* then being prepared for her other guests' entertainment. While this joke of the evening is being arranged with a company of Italian players, the lady's young son, Periquito, entertains the company in a *unipersonal*, with intervals of music, called *El joven Pedro de Guzmán*, that is, a new

48. See *El asturiano aburrido, Fin de Fiesta*, by L. A. J. M. It is recommended for licence in 1793 in a manuscript existing in the Biblioteca Municipal, Madrid.
49. Subirá gives the author of the monologue as J. Concha. His name did not appear in 1793 but was given when the monologue was published twelve years later. See Subirá, op. cit., pp. 288 ff.

version of the *Guzmán*-episode, taken from the standpoint of Guzmán's son.

The Censor on this occasion was not unimpressed. Evidently Iriarte's version had predisposed him to favour the whole subject, and he had been thinking his own thoughts on effective presentation. Ignoring the alternating precocity and ingenuousness of the unlikely 'niño', he concentrated his attention on the crisis which occurs when the boy, captive in the Moorish camp outside the walls of the besieged city, triumphs over his hopes that his father may yield to affection, and symbolically calls on the Christians to supply the knife, the sacrificial implement of his own death. The Censor, greatly interested, like all his contemporaries, in practical effects, thought that if the knife were flung over the wall, as originally prescribed, without a visible thrower, the effect would be 'cold' and undramatic. Perhaps his instinct was surer than his reason, for the incident must surely look like nothing so much as a feat of *comedia de magia*. At all events he wanted the knife to be thrown by Guzmán's father from a point on the city wall where he would be dramatically visible. The Censor probably had in mind a triangular tableau, with Guzmán senior at the top, the Moors at one end of the base and the child-victim, striking an attitude of solitary pathos, at the other. But the change he suggested was mainly in the interests of stage realism:

> . . . hallo que se debe prevenir a la compañía cómica que en la parte del monólogo en que va puesta esta señal * hagan más de lo que previene la acotación del poeta, para que la representación sea más verisímil y teatral; y será que cuando se haya de arrojar el puñal por el padre del niño Guzmán aparezcan gentes en el muro con bandera parlamentaria, y precediendo ciertas demonstraciones insinuantes y proprias del paso en moros y cristianos, arroje el puñal el padre del niño Guzmán retirándose al puesto de la muralla con los suyos, y concluyéndose la escena toda a vista de los espectadores: pues si se arroja (como previene la acotación) el puñal por encima de la muralla, sin que se vea quien le arroja, es un hecho frío, improprio, y nada teatral: lo que pueden remediar del modo que digo, por ser muy fácil respecto de que no es menester añadir versos, ni gente, pues sobra con la que hay. Por lo demás no hallo reparo en que se permita representar.

The monologue itself was meant to suggest the urgent development of the boy's own decision in that divided state of mind which the epoch knew to be the most dramatic scene of conflict. What the author actually did, however, was to present a mere series of emotional moods, broken, rather than linked, by as many moods of music. Bewilderment, frantic rebellion, depressed submission, reflection, mental rehabilitation, temporary doubt and vacillation, final victory over self, do not, as a collection, constitute a dramatic conflict, or psychologically explain a decision, unless severally and collectively they are integrated into personality. But in that these moods and their music at least symbolize a process of thought they represent modern dramatic planning. Moreover, Concha, if it were he, had a smattering of modern learning and tried to shade in the moods of young Guzmán with depth-strokes. This is especially notable in the stage of reflection.

The first movement, previously outlined by the orchestra, begins with Guzmán's agonized self-questioning and the rhetorical presentation of his plight to the audience, this being the method hallowed by tragic tradition. It continues with a newer feature—a determined appeal to the parental hearts of spectators. The diction, however, haunts the old scenes of Arandan rhetoric and ever hovers on the brink of bathos:

> *Niño* ¿Qué es esto, corazón? ¿Cómo me oprimes?
> ¿Cómo así con anuncios tan funestos
> me predices un golpe lamentable
> en donde se consuman mis alientos?
>
> . . .
>
> En el primer albor de mi mañana,
> en la primera aurora, en el extremo
> de dejar la puericia, así amenazas
> el fin, ya, de mis días?
>
> . . .
>
> ¡Ah madre de mi alma! ¡Ah padre mío!
> Qué poco que miráis por este Pedro . . .

The next movements show him first exhausting himself in rebellion against the thought that a nation's honour should depend on him, and then telling himself, with would-be pathos, that it is beyond the power of his tender age to assume the nobility promised by the noble blood in his veins. In the fourth movement he begins to quote from philosophical phrase-books of the day. Wondering why life should have designed such torture for him, snatching him from his 'mother's lap' and bringing grief upon his house, he wishes, rather deistically, that, instead of being born he could have remained a part of the 'Sovereign mind'. Whereupon, confirmed in the quiet mood by thoughtful music, he enters the Movement of Reason, beginning—and as historical observers we must not smile—with a naïvely mature pronouncement allying him with the philosophers of enlightenment:

> Pero aunque cortas luces me acompañan
> quiero reflexionar.

This is the stage at which he weighs the pros and cons, reasons about the motive for his capture, and comes to the reluctant conclusion that the honour of Christians depends upon his willingness to die. For a moment, reason having convinced him, he is bold:

> Soy Guzmán.

But, prompted by more thoughtful music again, he remembers his mother, and experiences the mood of Doubt. Fortunately, being so philosophically inclined and a reader or importer of Shakespeare, he can now see beyond present disaster and remember, in other words, that the valiant only taste of death but once, at an instant

> que, aprovechado bien, inmortaliza
> el honor de los héroes más excelsos.

after which reflection, turning to the practical idealism within his grasp, he calls towards the Christian ramparts for the symbolic knife.

The knife falls to music; and it must be said that the common humanity of the good little boy permits him, for the moment, to be taken aback. But this music, now breaking out of its interludes to accompany him continuously throughout the rest of his trial, is set in a tone which does not allow him to yield, and he goes off to die in the wings in a fine burst of sentimental rhetoric fit to break our hearts:

> . . . Infeliz Pedro
> que sin tu padre y madre entre crueles
> hoy vas a perecer a un golpe fiero!
> Madre del alma, padre generoso,
> mi sangre sacrifico al nombre vuestro . . .
> Y a la memoria, al mundo y a los hombres
> dejo de mi familia el nombre eterno.

As might be expected, the performance of the child *melólogo El joven Pedro de Guzmán* in 1793[50] at once suggested a parody, and *Perico de los palotes* appeared in the same year, its child protagonist soliloquizing outside the schoolroom door while he waits for the master's threatened vengeance to descend on him.[51] The mimicking overture begins with the now traditional *forte* diminishing gradually to a speech-point of *piano*. The atmosphere is supplied by schoolboys monotonously chanting within, and Perico passes in turn from the sobbing posture and the thought-posture to the posture of resolution:

'Perico estará sentado con los puños cerrados, puestos en los ojos sollozando; se levantará; pensará un poco; después irá hacia la puerta, y dando tres golpes, dirá con la mayor aflicción . . .'

all of which emotions, say the directions, in the words of the melodramatists who put the onus of thought on the composer—all of which will have been expressed by the music.

Perico caricatures the obvious absurdities of the child-hero apparently without malice. He emphasizes Guzmán's self-conscious reasoning to pathetic music:

Música brillante en que se pasea con la mayor bizarría y de pronto se para rascándose la cabeza.

> Mas ¡caramba!
> que el impulso del brazo del maestro
> es terrible . . .
> ¿a quién acudirás en tanto apuro,
> Perico? Discurrirlo será bueno.

Música patética, ya se queda discursivo.

He echoes the unchildish rhetoric:

> ¿Para esto vine al mundo? ¡Dura estrella!
> ¿Para esto . . .?
> ¿Para esto . . .?
> ¿Para esto una gallega me dio el pecho?

passing with a jolt, as the above shows, to nursery reminiscences. Going one better than Guzmán who arrives, in his own words, straight

50. See p. 377 above.
51. *Perico de los palotes* or *Perico el de los palotes*, like *El joven Pedro de Guzmán* formed part of a set of short pieces though it was complete in itself. There is an undated edition in the British Museum. Normally, it appeared as part of *La función casera* of Comella, and Subirá takes it to be the work of this author. See Subira, *El compositor Iriarte*, p. 335.

'from his mother's lap', Perico thinks pitifully of his infancy with his wet nurse. Delirious fear and anguish fashionably distort his vision, and, like the nightmare that came to the troubled sleeping of Comella's Doña Inés de Castro, they intensify the atmosphere with fever. For the last phase, his phase of philosophic resignation, when master and boys come to bear him off to his punishment, he speaks throughout, like all good heroes of his kind, to continuous music.

Comella, after his melodramatic excursion in *Doña Inés de Castro*, walked a little more prudently in this genre. But it was still difficult for a literary critic to take him seriously, and although his tragi-lyrical *Asdrúbal* of 1793 was reviewed approvingly by the *Memorial literario*[52] which perhaps had learnt by then to pass relative as well as absolute judgment, it made the Censor resignedly amused. On moral grounds, if a suicide were to be presented at all, thought Santos Díez González,[53] who was not squeamish on the subject, it ought not to be presented as an act of laudable heroism, and a hero surely ought not to seem so savage. On literary grounds the Censor protested that words or phrases like 'ludibrio', 'penurias', 'densitud', 'cien veces huye y ciento retrocede', are 'hardly conducive to the enrichment of our language and the preservation of its purity . . .'. On historical grounds he objected to certain anachronisms and inaccuracies; on grounds of common sense to the unlikely blasphemy of the iconoclastic Asdrúbal:

> Con justicia la piedad de los Númenes detesto;
> su clemencia abomino.

The Censor could afford to be easy on moral scores, for he was comfortably aware that spectators, far from sympathizing with stage suicides, heartily laughed at them.[54] His chief concern in allowing the play to be performed was that critics, especially the sharp-tongued *Memorial literario*, expressly named, might take his passive permission for active approval. He therefore placed it on record that he would allow this bad but morally innocuous tragedy to pass because there was nothing better to take its place.[55]

52. See *Memorial literario*, January 1794.
53. There is a manuscript with *censuras* for 1793 in the Biblioteca Municipal.
54. '. . . suicidio, el que pudiera ser tratado con indulgencia, a vista de que ya los espectadores se ríen, en lugar de llorar estos suicidios, a que están acostumbrados sus ojos en el teatro', *Censura*.   55. See note 7, page 570.

Already Comella was shaping melodrama to his rampageous ideals. So far the music lavishly accompanying every change of attitude and sentiment in melodrama had made some pretence, nevertheless, of symbolizing thought. Now it is also given the practical function of producing 'effects': of swelling out the noise of battle, for instance, or of 'imitating the blows of the battering ram' while temples crash and walls collapse. No wonder the Censor was apprehensive of the comments of the *Memorial literario*.

Fortunately for this functionary's peace of mind Comella's *Los amantes desgraciados*, of the same year,[56] described as an 'escena trágico-lírica' and later known as *Los amantes de Teruel*, was quieter and nearer the Rousseauesque tradition. The scene staged in a 'richly furnished chamber' on the heroine's wedding-day reduces its seat of action to the bride's distracted heart; and the musical moods, vigorous, tender, melancholy, and languid, succeed each other decorously as she thinks of her former lover. The theme of the lovers of Teruel had always made a strong appeal to Spaniards. As it dealt neither in breakable bridges nor fireable walls it did not disconcert literary critics. The *Memorial literario* on this occasion had little to complain of and chiefly confined itself to noting how far this play, with its dialogue and pauses for music, had travelled from the original conception of melodrama.[57]

No account of a popular or popularized genre of the late eighteenth century is representative without mention of Gaspar Zavala y Zamora who, with Rodríguez de Arellano and Valladares y Sotomayor, made up the famous, or as intellectuals would have it, the infamous, triumvirate of the Playwrights of the People. Zavala y Zamora was evidently less interested in melodrama than Comella, but he made a contribution to the genre with *El amor dichoso*,[58] a play in two acts for several characters. Being a dramatist of some originality, he chose a different kind of subject matter from that of the Spanish *melólogos* so far presented. *El amor dichoso* is a pastoral composition imitating the moods of the melodrama in vogue but avoiding the grandiose and the intense. The

56. *Los amantes desgraciados. Escena trágico-lírica*, MS. The *censura* is for 1793. An edition with the title *Los amantes de Teruel* was printed in Valencia in 1817. A melodrama on a related theme *La casta amante de Teruel, Da. Isabel de Segura* appears in the collected works of Nipho. See *Colección de los mejores papeles poéticos . . .*, Madrid, 1805, vol. ii.

57. See *Memorial literario*, September 1793.

58. See note 8, page 570.

author touched tragedy only to turn it into joy. He introduced a *gracioso*.

For his pastoral theme Zavala borrowed the atmosphere of eclogue and gathered verbal nosegays from illustrious poets of nature:

> Adiós montes: adiós floridos prados,
> dulces y gratos para mí algún día . . . (Act I)

The pastoral 'set' is equipped with upland meadows, sheep, brooks, trees, well, and bridge. Accomplished shepherdesses are to be seen rustically making cottage-cheese, filling pitchers with milk—presumably of ewes—arranging flowers artistically in little baskets, and decorating lambs with ribbons. Their shepherd partners are not far away. The music gives prominence to the flute. Eclogue languor induces, not perhaps eclogue reasoning, but certainly eclogue melancholy:

> *Cae traspasado de dolor en el poyo de piedra: música triste, con la cual, va poco a poco volviendo de su abatimiento, en cuya situación, dice con languidez:*
> ¿A otro su mano? ¿A otro?
> *suspendiéndose arrebatado, mientras tocan dos compases de música fuerte.* (Act I)

This melodrama, which tells of a poor young man and his Belisa whose family, wealthy farmers, consider him beneath her and will not consent to the match, permits of much poetic writing on trees, some incidental comedy, the presumed death of the swain—with a mock funeral—procession to doleful music—and, at last, the happy discovery both that the poor young man is alive, and that he is the son of a gentleman. The tone, then, departs from that concentration of distress which gave other forms of melodrama their experimental value.

More faithful to the newly established school of melodrama which sought to express abstract tragedy of mind and soul, was Comella's one-act *La Andrómaca* appearing also about this time[59] and probably inspired, through a Spanish version, by a portion of Apostolo Zeno's *Andromaca*.[60] It described itself proudly as a 'tragic melodrama' and included among its principal features the orthodox posturing to music and the recitals which, whether involving one character or several,

59. There is an undated manuscript in the Biblioteca Municipal, Madrid. The drama was being played in the theatres for instance in June 1794.
60. See pp. 117 ff. above.

gave a broad impression of monologue both because the speakers were not always talking to each other but exercising themselves in tragic utterance, and because the predominating effect was of the protagonist's introspection. The Comellan details are shoddy, but the play cannot be dismissed merely as a popular travesty of the intentions of his betters. That would be to simplify very complex impulses of the dramatic times. The Comellas who, with their sharp sense of the theatre, selected unerringly from prevailing atmospheres the urges which their century struggled to assert, were often nearer to the nerve-centre of eighteenth-century reason and often pointed the way more surely to modern dramatic naturalness than the inhibited playwriting academicians. It is true that they had bad taste, which, in literature, is a mortal sin. But, historically, they were among the most realistic exponents of their epoch's tortured mentality.

It is the preoccupation of the practising dramatists with melodrama that solves for us the social riddle behind its oddities. The Comellas wrote it because they knew what would interest a mixed collection of stupid and intelligent spectators of their day. The dull-witted would find enough variety of sound or sight in it to keep themselves amused. The intelligent would find satisfaction for their progressive thought and feeling in a 'close-up' of human or particular, as opposed to super-human or universal, frustration, and might employ their detective instinct—as active in the eighteenth century as in the twentieth, and for the same scientific reason—to check practically, by the gestures, postures, revealing silences, and pointed music, the complexity of human experience which the protagonist only half explained in words. Melodrama might have been a show for the epoch's eyes and ears. But, in its rudimentary way, it was also a mental exercise in close analysis and co-ordination as well as a histrionic training school in controlled expression. Also, in times when actors had not yet learnt to work as a team, when, as we have seen, the companies were beginning to assume that tragic acting for full-length drama was the preserve of specialists yet to materialize, the insinuating, apparently unpretentious melo-drama had an important formative influence on individual actors whose resources in pathos were otherwise limited. Alarms sounding through the public's spiritual consciousness were represented increasingly, in the *drame* or melodrama, in the temporary misfortunes of the first, or the final catastrophes of the second, as a concentrated agony of lifelike distress. But the nagging sense of tragedy came less commonly from conscious preoccupation with ultimate realities than from a shapeless fear of fear, and for ordinary purposes the need for the expression of this was met and satisfied by tense human disasters placed at an abstract remove by music.

The tragedy of *La Andrómaca* lies in the incidental circumstances rather than in the result, for eventually Andrómaca's child is saved and in gratitude she responds to Pirro's generosity by promising to admit his love. There are several characters. Sometimes the alternate monologues give place to dramatic exchanges of talk. But established melodramatic features are heavily marked. The stage is prepared with the arresting decorations copied from Italian productions of opera, but these are adapted to the close atmosphere of melodramatic implication. The lengthy directions prescribe an unchanging night-view of a wood outside Troy with ruined walls and anchored Greek ships in the background. At the front of the stage stands the tomb of Héctor with Andrómaca weeping on its steps. This scene at first may appear a little overcrowded. But attention is to be focused on the heroine as she postures in the light of the sacred fire, dumbly acting for some time before she begins to speak. Now she is to weep; now, turning to the ships, to cast glances of hatred, which would need considerable rehearsing if the audience were to maintain its gravity; now she is to fix her eyes, with extreme tenderness, on the ruins; and so on. It is only when the music has 'expressed all her feelings' that the recital begins. The actress has a chance to insinuate herself into the audience's favour before she opens her lips, which in tragedy is convenient.

Into these studied surroundings enters Pirro whose first words are as descriptively studied as his setting:

> *Pirro* Sólo el sagrado fuego de la pira
> que alumbra de Héctor el sepulcro frío,
> en tan lóbrega noche comunica
> alguna escasa luz a estos recintos.
> La oscuridad me impide que ver pueda
> de Andrómaca mi bien el dulce hechizo.
> He venido a estas horas a encontrarla
> para manifestarla mi cariño.

A child is at hand to be shown his father's ashes and to stimulate his mother to louder frustration. But it should be noted that one of her spasms of impassioned resentment is followed by a silence, express directions being given that no music is to be played. Moreover Andrómaca is instructed during this interval to seem to return to realities and to weigh up her situation; after which pause for thought she is to continue in a tone subdued by awareness of her circumstances. There, then, thrown into rather absurd relief are the exercises in expression which the Riccobonis had said must give point to speech. Five-act tragedy had usually been a bad training ground. Too much was said to too little purpose. Here there was time and space to practise.

> *Andrómaca* Y si a herir cansado desfalleces
> Andrómaca sabrá prestarte brío.
> *Pausa sin música en que reconoce su deplorable situación, y después que vuelve en sí, dice en tono débil:*
> ¿Dónde está Héctor? ¿Dónde están los griegos?
> Mas ¡ay! que sólo veo mi martirio
> y las tristes memorias . . .

The declamation is not, on the whole, worse than that of tragedy proper. Comella still conceived of tragedy in terms of high-flown rhetoric, descriptive or exclamatory. But, remembering his experience at the discouraging hands of Santos Díez González, he was now watching his grammar more carefully, and his taste had improved. He had not altogether failed to notice that the most effective scenes of his model were ones of sober reasoning. These he had tried to reproduce in arguments, for example, between Pirro and Ulises about Astianacte's potential danger to the State; or between Pirro and Andrómaca on the subject of the child whose safety his mother was unwilling to trust to a Greek. The moments of dramatic tension are promising, as, for instance, when Andrómaca, questioned as to the boy's whereabouts, cannot forbear to glance towards the tomb where he is hidden:

> *Ulises* ¿Por qué? Andrómaca, miras el sepulcro?
> ¿A qué viene el temor, muerto tu hijo?
> *Andrómaca* El temor se ha hecho en mí naturaleza.

So that although the melodramatic features of *La Andrómaca* are prominent, they are largely devices of atmospheric pathos subordinated to

ordinary dramatic ends, and the play bears something of the relationship to ordinary play-production of that day that the modern radio
drama bears to the modern drama of the theatre.

About the same time as Comella produced *La Andrómaca*, Fermín del
Rey gave the stage another version of the Trojan tragedy in *Policena*.[61]
In melodrama, as in tragedy, model subjects became the heads of thematic families. Cyclic drama, like serial stories, evidently gave spectators a happy sense of continuity and intimacy.

Apart from its value as a period piece, this drama has the distinction
of carrying one of the *censuras* in which Santos Díez González, irritated
by the unintelligence in literary matters of his ecclesiastical colleagues,
spoke out in the cause of stage liberty. The occasion finds him vigorously defending the rights of the stage hero to commit suicide, in the
proper circumstances, if he so desires and so long as he does not set
himself up as a heroic model. An Inquisitor Ordinary, looking for
danger where no danger was, had objected on religious grounds to
Policena's suicide, and, with a muddled sense of fitness, had demanded
that she fall dead from 'passion'.[62] This the Literary Censor could not
in common sense allow to pass unchallenged. He was a vigorous advocate, let it be remembered, of verisimilitude, and he could not agree
that it was in the least verisimilitudinous either that a pagan lady should
be guided by Christian principles, or that she should die so conveniently
from mere passion. Besides, goes on her advocate, tackling the Inquisitor on his own ground, is it morally worse to kill oneself with a
material weapon than to kill oneself with the weapon of an evil passion?

La pasión que expresa la pieza es *coraje, rabia, despecho.* Y digo; es acaso
menos *injusta,* y *criminosa* la muerte provenida de coraje, despecho, y rabia?
. . . Si no me engaño, es común opinión de los teólogos que las acciones
exteriores, o la exterioridad de las acciones, no añade cualidad esencial, que
aumente su malicia intrínseca. Con que si en el citado Decreto no se halla
reparo en que se permita representar una muerte rabiosa, y desesperada,
tampoco yo le hallo en que se permita el suicidio. . . . Este es mi parecer,
salvo el respeto que profeso a los decretos del Juzgado Eclesiástico. . . .

The Literary Censor lost his case. But the *censura* is an excellent example

61. See *Policena. Escena trágica,* MS. with a *censura* for 24 January 1794. Fermín del
Rey is also the author of the melodrama *Areo, Rey de Armenia,* played in 1797.
62. '. . . cayendo muerta la nominada Policena sin herirse, sino poseída de la pasión
que expresa en la pieza, y de ningún modo se represente el criminoso, e injusto suicidio.'

of eighteenth-century sanity in properly informed quarters and is worthy of a better object than the melodramatic lady, Policena.

This melólogo too is obviously influenced by Italian opera. A 'grand staircase' in the temple suggests the imposing action of a Metastasian *Demofoonte*[63] or *Achille in Sciro*.[64] In emulation of operatic vastness Fermín del Rey arranges garlanded priestesses about the burning pyre and places captive Trojan women as foils to the central figure of Policena who, bewildered in her festive robes, dumbly wonders during the opening movement *allegro* what strange movement is afoot. The grand staircase tensely rises to the back of the stage for the entrance of the chief priestess who will enlighten her.

One can anticipate that in circumstances like these the conflict within Policena's own mind will not be very intelligent. Her self-questioning about her present appearance, her memories of the fall of Troy, and— this to tears and lugubrious music—of the savagery, in particular of Pirro, her desire—to crashing chords—to bathe her hands in her enemies' blood, her present sense of fear, make less interesting contributions to the cause of reason than those of the elder and younger Guzmán. Fermín del Rey, like other popular adapters of High Tragedy, was carried away by an indiscriminating fondness for decorative effects for which poor Policena with her anger, fear and depression is only an excuse. So at the climax, when the chief priestess sweeps down the tensely stretching staircase, and when, by a process of chanting and *aria* she conveys to Policena the information that she is to marry Pirro there and then, or die, Policena, posing dramatically in relief against the grand background of flaring power and menace, has little time to develop the vital human doubts which, melodramatically, ought to be dividing her mind. She does, however, mention them, if only quickly to dispose of them:

> ¿A quién confiaré mi fatal suerte?
> ¿A quién dudo? A mí misma. Sí; yo puedo
> enmendar mi destino.

She also observes, after loud music, the melodramatic pause. And it is when this interval of self-communing is over that she drives herself,

---

63. See 'Atrio del Tèmpio d'Apollo, magnifica, ma breve scala . . .' (Act II, ix.)
64. 'Aspetto esteriore di magnifico Tèmplo dedicato a Baco, donde si descende per due spaziose scale divise in diversi piani . . .' (Act I.)

offending the Inquisitor and stimulating the Corrector's sympathy the while, to the passionate decision of committing suicide. Her last broken words, it may be worth noting, are designed to make the 'realistic' appeal frequently attempted by a 'higher' type of tragedy that the parodists had been realistically mimicking for decades:

> Voy . . . digna de mi . . . estirpe a vuestro seno,
> no me lloréis . . . troyanas . . . envidiadme,
> e imitad mi furor . . . ¡oh Dioses! Muero . . .
> no víctima de Aquiles . . . sacrificio . . .
> del terror . . . de la rabia . . . y del despecho.

Comella again appears on the melodramatic scene in 1796 with his *Hércules y Deyanira*,[65] a composition belonging to the same class as *Asdrúbal*, notable chiefly for the violent action of the principals in throwing themselves into the flames on a stage half-obscured in smoke, and for the scenic machines that work to music showing Olympus with its gods and the hero and heroine now apparently happy and cured of their burns.

Two pieces of 1797 also follow this growing practice of taking from melodrama what is useful for purposes of dramatic effect and avoiding the closely reasoned process of an individual's decision. Diego Casabuena's *Ifigenia en Táuride*,[66] though called a 'melodrama trágico' is really an ordinary tragedy in two acts, with musical interludes and bouts of miming for popular variety. All the main characters of the story 'in Tauris' are present. The priestesses are also there. The very confidante is waiting to catch the fainting Ifigenia in her arms, and Pilades arrives in the nick of time to prevent the major catastrophe. Here too is illustrated the new tendency to cast diction in loftier poetic terms, so that the music becomes in effect not rationally progressive but decoratively statuesque.

Perhaps the most ambitious feature is a sacrificial hymn to Diana during a tense dialogue between Orestes and Ifigenia. But that is an old conception of music in drama. There is descriptive talk of dreams and visions, half classical, half reminiscent of the international grave-digging that had been furthered by *Hamlet* and may even have been noticed by the author of *Noches lúgubres*. Nevertheless, Ifigenia was not meant to

65. See *Hércules y Deyanira. Melodrama trágico*, MS. B. Mun. The *censura* is for 1796.
66. See *Ifigenia en Táuride. Melodrama trágico*, MS. B. Mun. Licensed for 1797.

be above or below rational processes of thinking. Directions on the subject though vague are voluble. The interpretative action, it will be observed in the following direction for an interlude, is left, wisely no doubt, to the actress. But a specific request is made for a musical agitation of wind instruments denoting urgent cogitation:

En este intermedio tocará la orquesta una música que denote el estado de reflexión y de sobresalto en que Ifigenia se encuentra. De reflexión discurriendo sobre los medios más oportunos para salvar a Orestes; y de sobresalto sobre la incertidumbre de la fuga de Pilades, esperando con ansia el momento de la vuelta del esclavo que le condujo, a darle la gustosa noticia de haber huido. Todo lo cual se expresará por medio de una sinfonía en que tengan la mayor parte los instrumentos de boca.

The *censura* for Rodríguez de Arellano's one-act *Armida y Reynaldo*[67] of the same year provides another example of the Literary Censor's professional sense of justice. The drama commended itself no more to his artistic esteem than to that of posterity, but he tartly objected to the maltreatment of the playwright's lines by an ecclesiastical censor who, after suppressing certain phrases, had substituted words which destroy the metre, and who had disapproved of concepts which none but an over-literal mind could possibly take amiss. Again Santos Díez González carried the argument on to his colleague's own ground of orthodox logic. But though he clearly could have vanquished him in theory he seems not to have gained his point in fact:

... he notado versos corregidos por uno de los censores que me preceden, los cuales dejan de ser versos por habérseles añadido palabras, que además de ser impropias, les hacen redundantes en sílabas: y particularmente he advertido que al folio sexto vto donde decía. . . .

... quita el amor del mundo Ubaldo mío . . .

añade el censor la palabra 'infinito', que sobre destruir el verso, me parece hace que resulte una proposición errónea teológicamente, pues el amor de Dios, aunque es infinito en sí mismo, no lo es respecto de las criaturas, que de su naturaleza limitadas, son incapaces de ser objeto del amor infinito de Dios: y así soy de parecer, que no se siga esa corrección mal entendida, según mi dictamen, especialmente cuando el poeta se explica en términos que no dejan razón de dudar sobre la inteligencia del amor mutuo de las criaturas todas del universo: amor que otros filósofos han llamado 'armonía', por lo

67. See *Armida y Reynaldo. Primera Parte*, MS. B. Mun. Licensed on 30 January 1797.

391

que llegaron a decir, que esta concordancia y correspondencia universal en las cosas, es un cierto tono que Dios las dio en el momento de su creación: y ése es el sentido en que claramente se explica el autor de esta composición.

Armida y Reynaldo, a piece for several characters, taken, it is stated, from Tasso,[68] is not altogether unpoetic, though it includes decadent dialogue of this nature:

> *Armida* Dulcísimo embeleso . . .
> *Reynaldo* Dueño hermoso . . .
> *Armida* Ídolo de mi alma . . .
> *Reynaldo* Amable hechizo . . .

and some maudlin effusions which very properly have been cut for acting purposes.[69] But the chief impression is of spectacle and sensation accentuated by music. Even in the short space of one act a storm rages, fire and flames make lurid illumination, and a chariot of fire ascends towards the flies. But studied posturing at quieter moments is not neglected. For in the musical introduction to the scene, which represents a wood on the coast, Reynaldo is instructed to lie sleeping, while Armida, attractively garlanded and carrying flowers, is told to stand looking at him: a useful exercise in histrionic repose.

Social preoccupations which had provided five-act tragedy with some of its more convincing conflicts did not go very conveniently to music. Yet so alive was this sphere of mental experience by comparison with that of problems dead and gone that it could occasionally influence even the unlikely world of melodrama. The indefatigable Rodríguez de Arellano attempted to assert this influence in 1797 in the two-act *El negro y la blanca*, though it meant reducing music and mime to subordinate positions. The play, in the *Zaïre* and *Soliman II* tradition revolves round the theme of Oriental highmindedness and racial equality, and proclaims its propaganda of enlightenment through the noble and sensitive African potentate, Gondar, who refuses to permit human sacrifice, or the selling of slaves, and who, on discovering that his beloved Dutch Clarisa remains faithful to her white love, magnanimously frees her:

> *Gondar* . . . soy rey de mí mismo: las virtudes
> no están tan desterradas de los negros
> como el vulgo ignorante lo examina:

68. See *Gerusalemme conquistata*.   69. See note 9, page 570.

tú partirás, y yo a morir me quedo.

. . .

Sólo te pido que de mí te acuerdes
alguna vez, que al pundonor modesto
no se puede oponer una memoria,
de un cariño tan puro, y tan atento.

. . .

. . . aprovechemos
esos tristes momentos desgraciados,
estos crueles trágicos momentos
en disponer tu ausencia, y mi sepulcro,
donde sólo podré encontrar sosiego. (Act I)

In this version the jealous white lover turns out to be a blackguard,
and it is nice to know that the loyal Dutch lady, after being pushed into
the sea by him and rescued by noble Gondar, decides to give her hand to
the latter. Even so, one could wish that she had chosen different words
to accompany the gift:

> *Clarisa* Alza a mis brazos, virtuoso negro,
> que ya de todas mis amantes ansias
> serás el blanco. (Act II)

Music occurs at appropriate intervals and special emphasis is given to
Oriental decoration. Since Arellano was not interested in Unities, even
in melodrama, the scene variously depicts a sea coast with moving ships
and a bustle of embarkation, a prison, and a Metastasian temple with
'two splendid staircases' where priests, boys, and black attendants are
gracefully disposed. The melodrama ends with a startling dance of
blacks and whites.[70]

By 1798 the Literary Censor was probably very tired of melodramas,
then at the height of their popularity. He objected testily to Comella's
Séneca y Paulina of that year,[71] not only because of the author's still
lamentable grammar, but because, he declared, the subject was so im-
proper as to be unfit for public presentation. Perhaps at a different time
and in relation to a better dramatist, the Censor, accustomed as he must

---

70. Other melodramas by Arellano are: *Himeneo*, licensed for 1799; *La noche de Troya*,
licensed for 1797; *Temístocles*, called a melodrama, though it is translated from Metastasio's opera, licensed in 1800.
71. See *Séneca y Paulina. Drama trágico*, MS. B. Mun. It is licensed for June 1798.

have been to the refined improprieties of the Ancients, might not have objected. The tone of the *censura* implies that his relations with the Comellas of his day were becoming strained to breaking point. Again only the fact that the unbusinesslike players had cut him short of time and wanted to produce the drama the very next day made him willing, he said, to pass it at all. Even then he demanded alterations before it was released. One wonders if the exasperating players managed to put in an extra rehearsal:

> . . . hallo que sobre la impropiedad del lenguaje, y bajeza de pensamientos, contiene una acción atroz, e indigna de ponerse a los ojos del pueblo . . . No todas las acciones verdaderas son dignas de los espectáculos. Además de eso hay una solicitación impura de parte de un soberano, y ésa en público. Sin embargo esta función está estudiada y destinada para manaña: El Sr. Juez Protector en vista de todo, resolverá lo que tuviese por conveniente, en virtud de este apuro, y . . . aprobada la pieza por la Vicaria Eclesiástica, y el Teólogo Censor que antecede.

Most of the offending parts in the Censor's manuscript have been covered with the revised version which is pasted so firmly over them that they can not be deciphered. Readable offences seem less morally objectionable than politically inexpedient. Probably the Censor's attitude had been affected by recent scandals at Court. The Comellas, as will transpire later, were for ever putting his political discretion to the test.[72]

> *Séneca* [pero contempla
> antes de verlo con maduro juicio,
> que aquéllos que se acogen a la sombra
> del frondoso laurel del poderío
> pocas veces se libran de las iras
> del formidable rayo del destino.]

> *Nerón* [Entre ellas lucirás como la luna
> luce entre las estrellas. Sí, bien mío,
> y cuando de mi amor acompañada
> salieres a ostentar el poderío
> los vivas de una plebe alborotada
> llenarán de lisonja tus oídos.]

72. Other melodramas by Comella are: *El Idomeneo* of 1792; *El negro sensible*, licensed for 1798; and *Sofonisba*, licensed for 1795.

By the end of the century the melodramatic system had divided into two streams. One followed the original course of the solo recital as marked out by Iriarte.[73] The other branched from it to form broader emotional situations requiring several characters, with one predominating, and developed, as a tributary, an ordinary short drama with generous adornment of mime and music.[74] In the original melodrama mime and music were, or were meant to be, mental adjuncts. In derivatives they were physical decorations. Over two decades most popular playwrights attempted both monologue and full-scale melodialogue.

But obviously the life of a close, closed monologue was limited. To be original it demanded more than mediocre ability from author and actor. For development it was dependent on interior ideology in which playwrights were at their weakest. It was hardly a drama in its own right. Its function in the self-corrective civilizations of Europe was to rehearse the presentation of detached states of mind in order that they might later be re-incorporated in full-length drama to deepen and mature it. The other varieties of melodrama did not have this function. They were more concerned with the development of scenic production and were naturally the dramas most prone to sensationalism. Yet all melodramas, however humble, helped to translate tragedy and pathos from impersonal into human terms. The exaggerated sensibility and over-studied posturing that gave us the modern use of the word 'melodrama' merely marked an early stage in the growth of a self-conscious psychological drama that we call modern.

Other features now commonly associated with the name 'melodrama' —the lugubrious settings and supernatural horrors popularized in the rest of Europe by Pixérécourt and others—are scarcely to be found in Spain before the Peninsular War, and afterwards characterize pieces which are not melodramatic in the musical sense. The usual example

73. Further examples are: *Anselmo, o el curioso impertinente, escena cómico-trágica unipersonal . . . intervalos de música*, by J. J. Isurve, 1791 (Coe, 17); *Hero y Leandro. Monólogo lírico*, by León Pujaz, based on Florian, Madrid, 1793; *Bernardo del Carpio en el Castillo de Luna. Soliloquio trágico con música en sus intervalos*, by Jorge Mira y Percebal, Orihuela, 1794.
74. Further examples are: *Areo, Rey de Armenia*, melodrama by Fermín del Rey, played in 1797; *El amante estatua. Pieza de representación, y música*, by D. J. A. P. y S. (Porcel y Salablanca?), n.d., MS. B. Nac.; *Diálogo trágico titulado La Raquel . . . Sacado de la historia, y adornado con intervalos de música*, by 'Un aficionado' (Madrid), n.d.

given of the Spanish play of horrors, Quintana's *El Duque de Viseo* of 1801, is so mild a version of Lewis's *The Castle Spectre* as to be almost unrecognizable. Its apologetic dream-skeletons are not nearly so sensational as the Spanish phantoms of the Golden Age. Its sole relation with melodrama is in its tragic posturing and gesture. Melodrama continued to be written for another decade or more,[75] but the Spaniard has never taken kindly to morbid horrors, and the later melodramas are variations on those of the nineties save in so far as they tend to develop into full-length plays and to assimilate the more acceptable foreign novelties of presentation like storms, wild landscapes, and Gothic ruins. An example is the anonymous *El valle del torrente*[76] of 1817, a year of many melodramas after the French,[77] in which the scene, picturesquely set with some of these details is 'in the neighbourhood of Lourdes' where Victorino, 'dumb', like the dumb, gesticulating Francisque of Pixérécourt's *Coelina*, of 1800, goes through an emotional pantomime perhaps more detailed than we have witnessed hitherto:

Victorino se queda inmóvil de sorpresa; y en seguida manifiesta hallarse agitado de horribles convulsiones . . . Permanece en la misma posición, el cuerpo inclinado hacia adelante, los ojos centelleantes, la boca entreabierta, y moviendo los labios con frecuencia.

Also the play shows that a new generation had learnt from studied arrangements of posture and action against meaning backgrounds to experiment in the liberating mysteries of atmospheric violence:

Durante este último diálogo, Reimbó se dirige a la capilla, y se oculta entre sus ruinas . . . Victorino sube a ella, y se le ve atravesar por las ruinas y arrodillarse delante de un altarcito, que estará en la misma punta del peñasco. Valentín y Julia se arrodillan también en la escena, y en este instante sale Reimbó . . . y acercándose por detrás de Victorino, le da una puñalada, le precipita en el torrente, y huye con precipitación . . . La tempestad que habrá ido creciendo gradualmente, llega en este punto a su mayor fuerza . . .

But the full story of that form of expression belongs to another era.

75. See, for example: *El Idomeneo*, by Eugenio de Tapia, played in 1799; *Celina o el mudo incógnito*, from Pixérécourt, in 1803; *El enredo provechoso* in 1805; *Tipo-Saib o la toma de Seringapatán*, from the French by Enciso Castrillón, in 1806; etc., etc.
76. *El valle del torrente, o El huérfano y el asesino. Melodrama en 3 actos*, Valencia, 1817.
77. For example: *Los cuervos acusadores*; *La condesa Genoveva*; *El viejo en la montaña*. For French and German influences on Spanish melodramas see Spell, op. cit., 124 ff.

Approach to Low Tragedy

He, like all authors, a conforming race!
Writes to the taste, and genius of the place;
. . .
He forms a model of a virtuous sort,
And gives you more of moral than of sport;
He rather aims to draw the melting sigh,
Or steal the pitying tear from Beauty's eye;
To touch the strings that humanize our kind,
Man's sweetest strain, the music of the mind.[1]

SINCE the loud spokesmen of religious and moral welfare had placed the European stage in the position of having to justify its utility in word and deed, the instructive element tended to be overstressed. Because it was not always easy to take a practical moral lesson from Greco-Gallic tragedies which many thought more barbarous than elevating, the friends of stage and morality, looking for a serious drama on more immediate and obvious utility, found it, as they thought, in the new French and English dramas dealing with the distresses of commoners, or humanized gentry, which we know by the various names of *Drame*, Domestic or Urban Drama, Drama of Sensibility, Sentimental Drama, Lachrymose Drama . . . and which here are classed for convenience under the general name of Low Tragedy. The master-models of High Tragedy had illustrated how unusual, high-placed personalities might have been expected to think and behave. The eighteenth century was willing to accept their authority and to believe that characters of High Tragedy, the noblest form of drama, must be drawn from the upper classes where every act is so magnified by publicity that it becomes, to all appearances, fatefully irrevocable. But the mind of a

1. Prologue to Edward Moore's *The Foundling*, London, 1748.

lonely Orestes or a subtle Néron, or, if neo-classical tolerance admitted irregular parallels, of a hypnotic Celestina or intellectual Hamlet, was an individual mind, disconcertingly above the average. And the scientific preparation of the age which studied the working of provable realities, which tested and checked for itself, and which drew its conclusions from the weight of majorities, disposed it to distrust the unusual.

Jovellanos, a man of the new light, with a sense of responsibility towards the common citizen, thought that the stage should help to form his civic virtues and that these virtues might be demonstrated, constructively and clearly, in the persons of, for example, 'honourable, incorruptible magistrates', faithful and constant friends, 'magnanimous princes',[2] like, he might have supposed, the much admired Frederick of Prussia. Forner dangerously stretched a similar ideal to the point of suggesting that the stage could supplement ordinary methods of instruction; for instance, by illustrating to the public a government's policy.[3] But the 'government' he had in mind just then must have been an idealized, Rousseauesque projection of reality, purified from the ulterior motives of ordinary political propaganda. Moreover, Forner, on this occasion, was speaking expediently in support of a petition to re-open a provincial theatre which the Audiencia condemned. In any case this satirist was too Spanish to believe everything that was said about a foreign paragon like the drame. Once, indeed, mimicking the solemnity with which the age regarded the 'utility' of such drama, he had satirically sketched an 'instructive' plot taken from the essential facts of agriculture. It presented characters usefully employed in digging, ploughing, manuring, sowing, reaping, and, in the last act, their work done, over-eating round the pot. A feminine variation depicted women engaged in spinning, cooking, ironing, and, since the new technique was to teach pleasantly, singing to the rhythm of the broom, while their menfolk knowledgeably discussed the newspaper. The long speeches of such plays, he sneered, might be reserved for specific instruction in single domestic crafts:

2. *Memoria para el arreglo de la policía de los espectáculos y diversiones públicas, y sobre su origen en España.* B.A.E. xlvi, pp. 480 ff., see p. 496.

3. *Consultas sobre que debían representarse comedias en la ciudad del Puerto de Sta. María, sin embargo de haberse opuesto a ello la Real Audiencia y el Acuerdo,* 1795. See Cot. *Licitud* ..., pp. 270-1.

¡Y cuánto más crecería la instrucción y el deleite, si los autores vertiesen largos discursos sobre el modo de cortar con gracia unos calzones, de dorar un pollo, de cuidar de una casa, o de varear los alcornoques?[4]

However, the literal critic, clinging to the tangibilities of what he understood to be Aristotelian precepts, still conceived of 'instruction' in an exclusively pedagogic sense and looked to Low Tragedy to illustrate, on a private, middle-class scale, and by pathetic process rather than by ultimate catastrophe, what classical tragedy, with its terrifying finality of doom, illustrated at the highest level.

Broadly, Low Tragedy was expected to show the fall from their bourgeois pedestals of wicked or misguided tyrants in commerce, the professions, and other accessible departments of life. It was also expected to arrange for the vindication of their demonstrably honest, industrious, and resigned victims; for victims who rebelled, or answered or fought back, seemed, before 1789, to be lacking in moral perfection and in loyalty to the ideal State which might liberally consult and favour its creators, the intellectuals, but which to anyone else must be a dictatorship. That this pedagogic idea of instruction could not bring out the best in dramatists many supporters of the new genre knew as well as the perverse Forner. But the principle of Low Tragedy was a progressive dramatic ideal precisely in so far as it recognized the tragic potentialities of the commonplace. In ordinary life, which the man of reason then chose to dissect, tragedy may be experienced partially or temporarily. It may not mercifully kill, but lingeringly frustrate. It may not swoop and crash, but fitfully writhe in tendencies of character.

Despite the moralists, there is usually an unbiased, a case-book mentality behind the best Low Tragedy. There is a desire to tap the sources and examine the processes of normal human motives and tragic effects. There is an impersonal curiosity, important primarily for itself, but one which made use of prevailing social conditions for the application of its activity: a curiosity accompanied by, though nearly always confused with, the desire for specific moral or social reforms. The apparently bourgeois interests in these dramas, which were not only those of the bourgeoisie, the social propaganda and colouring, the middle-

4. See *Carta dirigida a un vecino de Cádiz sobre otra del L.J.A.C., un literato sevillano con el título de 'La loa restituida a su primitivo ser'*, by 'Rosauro de Safo' (Forner). It is published in Cot. *Licitud . . .*, pp. 277 ff.

57809

class backgrounds, the idealized sensibilities, were channels of expression rather than sources of inspiration. In the long run they were almost irrelevant. To see them proportionately we should take less notice of middle-class accidentals used for the epoch's applied dramatic thought, and more of its reason for using them. It knew that the common man, as a mentality, belonged not to one, but to all classes. But he was useful in his middle-class dress, partly because the middle class was a good point for plotting an average, partly because the middle-class mind was the one most disposed by circumstances to lend itself to the cause of State-directed utility advocated by philosophers, partly because the middle-class mind was both the most available for scientific experiment in real life and the most comprehensible to the majority of authors. Therefore middle-class man in this sense was often put forward to demonstrate how the average human mind functions under given circumstances and stresses. The restless fear of the age might lead it towards possibilities, exceptions, and details as yet unaccounted for, but these were sought in accessible persons readily understood. The commonplace object of experiment is explained not only by a political and economic accident, but by the fact that the commonplace is the most acceptable reality to aristocrat and commoner. Eighteenth-century interest was ultimately in man as man, not just in man as a member of the middle class. The 'sweetest strain' to the thinkers and writers of the epoch was, theoretically and impartially, the 'music of the mind'. Nevertheless, it was natural, for an age which thought itself democratic, to look for the middle mind in the middle class, and—in the industrial circumstances—to turn the common man into an object of social sentimentality and political propaganda.

Unfortunately, the ideal of instruction and the accessibly human themes through which it expressed itself in drama lacked subtlety and discrimination. Humanitarianism was a cult which led straight to stage ranting and to a sentimentally simplified contrast of weal and woe; to an excess of 'melting sighs' and 'pitying tears'. Enterprising playwrights, however, clung to the more solid features in the dissolving scene. It needed only a guiding hint from intellectual quarters—dropped during an argument in a coffee-house, for instance—to reveal to them that in their characters' urban misfortunes lay a criticism of prevailing social conditions: the neglect of public responsibilities by leaders of society;

inequalities before the law; the extortions of the rich; unfair standards of pay or reward; antiquated methods of education; irregularities in all public services; the subjection of women; and so on. The most intelligent playwrights, instructed through abstracts, avoided thereby the worst of the sentimental or propagandist influences, and, openly or covertly, according to the latitude allowed them in their particular corners of Europe, turned the plot into a thesis, introducing spokesmen for various points of view on such subjects as justice, the conduct of commerce, parental discipline, and other themes brought out in those days for rationalistic consideration. The more fundamental and debatable the matter, the more dramatic was the conflict likely to be and the nearer to thesis drama of modern times.

A self-conscious English and French interest in the 'music of the mind' was conveyed to Spain at its dramatic purest, which does not necessarily mean at its most inspired, in a translation by Luzán of Nivelle de la Chaussée. Evidence showed that the individual intuition of Spanish scholars of the fifties sometimes outstripped their corporate principles, and that, contrariwise, their free awareness of the peculiar meaning of the age was commonly blunted by a scrupulosity, inherited from their French advisers, over the interpretation of formulated ethics and aesthetics. Within the Academia del Buen Gusto, so busily engaged in erecting self-confines, it was not only Montiano who responded to calls from beyond the limits of definition, but also the lawgiver, Luzán. Montiano, in a vague and general way, had been receptive to the idea of a new literary and histrionic realism capable of revolutionizing tragedy, and, however inadequately, he had tried to demonstrate the naturalness of speech which must be its outward expression. Luzán, in 1751, when he translated Nivelle de la Chaussée's *Le Préjugé à la Mode* as *La razón contra la moda*,[5] was working along parallel, urban lines to demonstrate the kind of theme-medium through which to exteriorize a realistic pressure of thought.

This drama, translated with eager faithfulness, is steeped in those preoccupations of the day which originated in self-doubt. The solution of plot may be artificially engineered. But, as in the novels of Richardson

5. See *La razón contra la moda*, Madrid, 1751. It is dedicated to the Marquesa de Sarria, the patron of the Academia del Buen Gusto, and the Dedication is signed 'El Peregrino', Luzán's name in the Academia.

with their incidental posturing and unnatural conclusions, the strongest impression received is of an intensive self-questioning, largely based on the writer's own observation or personal experience; of the human pursuit of human motives through a labyrinth, constructed by book-logic, of mental situations and relationships; of tragedy in relativeness.

In a Preface to the edition of 1751 which mentions by the way that he had judged it best to substitute Spanish names and metres for the French, Luzán re-introduced the two preoccupations which had haunted his *Poética* and all the theorizing of his day. Is the drama useful? Is it verisimilitudinous? The first, which had evolved in opposition to an earlier preoccupation with stage validity, is brought in perhaps formally and mechanically, though the lawgiver was doubtless affected too by his active ideal of a modern drama with realistic values.[6] At all events, as well as in the moral ending of La Chaussée's drama, where all poetic dues are awarded and the principals avoid ultimate tragedy, he found utility with verisimilitude in the incidental working out of the theme. It was not just the obvious conflict of 'reason' and 'fashion' that impressed him in this play of manners. Its central argument against the unfashionableness of remaining in love with one's wife he certainly thought a 'useful' subject for moral meditation, especially in sophisticated France. But the unnecessary situation in which La Chausée's married protagonists find themselves, each in love with the other, each torturing himself or herself with the fear that their love is making a social partnership intolerable, each fearing, for the partner's sake, to show his love, yet each undermined in confidence by the false indifference of the other—this social situation, acceptable as it might be to the tortuous mentality of Frenchmen, whose social living conditions were complex, could only seem abnormal to the more simply living Spaniards. Which fact may explain why the translation did not reach public theatres. Luzán himself, fresh from his first-hand study of Parisian customs, and realizing that the play had practical point in French society, must have been less impressed with the moral than the method. La Chaussée chose a subject of domestic manners because that was a natural thing just then

6. 'No parezca extraño que yo mencione utilidad cuando hablo de una comedia: las buenas deben aprovechar deleitando; y si sus autores se contentan con el solo deleite, desde luego deben tenerse por malas en una República bien ordenada; y por pésimas, si mezclando al deleite algún género de veneno, volviesen en estrago de las costumbres lo que se inventó y se destinó para su corrección.'

for a French dramatist to do. But behind the writer's mannered theme is his urge to demonstrate the ways in which mind moves and to try to draw mentally realistic conclusions from observed processes. Luzán, as a true son of his age, was clearly fascinated by La Chaussée's realistic process of reasoning. He particularly noticed the characterization, which attempts complexity, and the interweaving of social and personal motives.

The Frenchman, it will be remembered, makes Sophie a temporary victim of fashionable conjugal indifference in that, seeing the results of this fashion in her relatives and friends, she herself has become afraid to marry. But the subtlety of the problem is in its incidentals: for example, in the argument in Act I between Argant and his niece, Sophie, as to whether Constance, his married daughter, is really happy or not; in the refinements of self-torture in Act II when D'Urval, Constance's husband, grows aware that, embarrassing as it may be, he loves his wife yet fears that if Constance should guess his secret she will grow too possessive; in his worries of Act III about whether Constance, used to neglect, may not have lost her love for him and be unable to respond to his overtures even if he can bring himself to make them; in his bewilderment over the meaning of her outward serenity, and his embarrassment over choosing a means of broaching the subject of his love to her; in his preoccupations in Act IV over her possible infidelity; in his mental sufferings during Act V when he receives proofs of her innocence; in his proud, silent shame.

Doubts, fears, self-distrust, watchfulness over the motives of motive —these are the natural marks of the age. In La Chaussée only artifice could bring the supersensitive pair to ideal felicity and satisfactorily separate false values from true. Since La Chaussée has no dramatic dynamics, Luzán was unlikely to learn from him how to be a good playwright. But, even more realistically than Montiano, he was here exercising himself in ideological ways and means. The endless intricacies of domestic mentality, as exhaustively traced in the novels of Richardson, and followed, selectively, by his French imitators, were the natural preserves of an epoch which wanted to explain itself to itself and to check its own reactions scientifically.

The tragic element in Low Tragedy, which *Le Préjugé à la Mode* dimly foreshadows, operated indirectly and temporarily. Most domestic tragedies of the later decades are brought by artifice to a happy conclusion. But, until the last moment of such plays the atmosphere tends to be one of distress unrelieved, even in the most 'popular' examples, by comic touches. They are, in their way, therefore, genuine tragedies. They assume that tragedy in ordinary affairs may be present in means as well as in ends, in temporary misfortune as well as in final cataclysm; though it took a much more spiritually balanced generation of playwrights, a hundred years away, to appreciate the idea that the most subtle tragedy of all lies neither in incidental misery nor final disaster, but in situations patched up to a happy conclusion that carry within themselves, deposited for the future, the nervous strain of past experience.

So it was towards a new emphasis of tragedy that the eighteenth century uncertainly travelled: a tragedy having less to do with sword and poison-cup, with historic battle, siege or fire, and more to do with common stress and strain. This conception of tragedy was not original; for small, common, and private tension was always implied by the old masters even when they dealt specifically in tragedies on the largest scale. What was relatively new in Urban tragedy was the presentation of common and private stress in dramatic isolation, in its detachment from heroic context.

But neither Luzán himself nor his colleagues of the Academy of Good Taste were more than passively aware of the artistic rationalism moving over their remote horizon. Creative Low Tragedy in Spain was the product of a later decade in which all the necessary conditions for its composition and its acceptability in public theatres coincided. Like rationalized High Tragedy, with which it has certain features in common, it was the product of Arandan atmosphere, and it fully manifested itself in 1774, inevitably in a theatre of the Sitios, in Jovellanos's *El delincuente honrado* which Lord Holland, even from his foreign standpoint, could appreciate as 'a drama of great merit',[7] and which showed how a contemporary problem, burning naturally within the mind of the times, could bring drama artistically up to date.

By 1774 in France and England most of the experiments in modern

7. See *Further Memoires of the Whig Party. 1807-21*, London, 1905, p. 368. The play was first published under the pseudonym of Don Toribio Suárez de Langreo. The Biblioteca Nacional has two early editions: Madrid, 1787 (at present missing) and Madrid, 1793. An undated edition of Barcelona was later published under Jovellanos's name.

dramatic thinking, talking, and acting, had been tried out. The ideology of Encyclopaedists had combined with Shakespearian influences to change the conception of Tragedy. The French bookishness of a La Chaussée had been loaded with the English dynamite of Lillo's *London Merchant* and Moore's *Gamester* which supplied the lifelike tensions, the powerful downrightness of style and diction derived from the Elizabethans. And although French translations of the sixties and seventies —Saurin's *Beverlei*, or Mercier's *Jenneval*—suppressed or veiled the naked force in English dramatic power, French playwrights usually knew the originals and had assimilated their native atmosphere, often in London playhouses, so that their own way of thinking was no less influenced by what they rejected than by what they voluntarily received. Diderot, his mind informed by English complexities of characterization and the English art of the theatre, had produced *Le Fils Naturel* and *Le Père de Famille* with their attempted construction of realistically disturbed states of mind and their urgent directions to the actor on studied nervousness. An edition of Fenouillot de Falbaire's *L'Honnête Criminel* had appeared in 1767 helping to strengthen international interest in the pathos of passive, domestic sacrifice and the irony of misdirected blame. Within the last three years Mercier had produced his most influential examples of domestic pathos in *L'Indigent*, *Le Déserteur*, and, in 1774, the thesis-drama *Le Juge*[8] with which *El delincuente honrado* has so much in common.

With his fellow Arandans Jovellanos belonged to the international society of *ilustrados* in which these dramas were conceived. His success is due to the fact that he breathed the authentic atmosphere of rationalism in its making, and, unlike the 'Comellas' who later developed the new ideas that *El delincuente honrado* represented, he was independent of translation and hearsay. Not that Spanish translations or adaptations of the *drames* were lacking, though in the seventies they were fewer and their influence less popularly active than in the eighties. Voltaire's *L'Ecossaise* and Moore's *The Foundling* had been translated for the Sitios in the early seventies.[9] But if the general foreign atmosphere, if even individual influences entered liberally into the composition of *El delincuente honrado*, Jovellanos did not confine himself to particularized borrowing. Just as Huerta, who, under the direct influence of *Zaïre*

8. See note 1, page 570.   9. See p. 142 above.

produced something vastly different from *Zaïre*, so Jovellanos, whose liberal dramatic education owes much, directly, or indirectly, to Lillo and Moore, Sedaine, Diderot, and Mercier, produced his 'drama of great merit' with individuality.

As became a modern, liberally minded artist and a serious man with heavy public responsibilities in legal and political spheres, Jovellanos shared his epoch's love of problem-theses. Johnsonian clubs and Ferney house-parties liked to set themselves practical problems for social debates which certainly encouraged dispute as a purely intellectual exercise, but which were at least conceived as instruments of knowledge and shapers of mental honesty. Jovellanos who, as a Criminal Judge, or Minister of State, was in close touch with the practical problems of his times, evidently read, spoke and argued with as much constructiveness as receptivity, and in the prose of *El delincuente honrado* he was better situated for thesis-thought than in his metre-bound tragedy, *Pelayo*. His man-made problem, presented after decades of experimental strainings, by scholar-dramatists, in transcendent problems of an unreal past, reads most refreshingly. Borrowing the general conception and technique of Low Tragedy from his foreign contemporaries, he nevertheless chose a subject which interested him professionally and personally. This was the clash of legal and human responsibilities involved in the system of duelling—a matter also of topical interest just then in Spain. Laws against duelling had recently been revised, and the social problem of frustrated honour produced by the State's sweeping condemnation of all individual vengeance by killing was, in its eighteenth-century context, as real to the autor of *El delincuente honrado* as to the author of *Le Philosophe sans le savoir*.

Hardly less progressive than its thesis is the dramatic style of *El delincuente honrado*. Its intensity, its hint of power even, is due both to the playwright's own imagination, within the dramatic tradition of Spain, and to those new disciplines which provide the effective crises in *Raquel*. The nervous concentration of urgency in limited time and place,[10] and a suggestion of the inevitability of explosion were due to sensitive application of the classical Rules. But Jovellanos also set an excellent example, followed unfortunately by few intensive tragedians

10. The action takes place within the precincts of the Castle of Segovia, and the time represents some twenty-four hours.

at that period, of occasionally relieving the cumulative effect of tension by comic punctures, not large or hearty enough to release all the air, yet natural enough to give necessary respite from the threat of suffocation. These humorous moments in the Age of Reason had been prompted by England. But Jovellanos, once made aware of their value in modern circumstances, could manufacture his own comedy from traditional materials in Spain.

The most unfortunate feature of the drama from the artistic stand-point was its use of external instruments of tension, which, though not untastefully employed by Jovellanos, were gleefully adopted by sen-sationalists to produce domestic equivalents of the battlement-scaling and bridge-firing that arrested the development of High Tragedy. It was natural that Jovellanos should use them. They had equivalents in melodrama and expressed the desire to bring inner thoughts and motives to outward life. It was inevitable that they should be exaggerated, even by the moderate Jovellanos. But in Spain he was so far ahead of his own generation in Low Tragedy that his contemporaries, assimilating too easily the external sensations of this drama, never caught up with his inner and most essential intention.

The play illustrates Forner's remarks on the right kind of imitation, which he thought should concern itself more with the universal quali-ties of good taste in a model than with a particular theme, form or style:

> Los preceptos de las artes son universales, les aplicaciones pueden ser infinitas. Si para escribir yo una historia, en lugar de imitar la destreza de la aplicación que se percibe en una historia ajena, me pongo a contrahacer el giro, orden o constitución que dio a su obra aquel arífice, ¿qué otra cosa seré sino un esclavo de la ajena invención, sujeto a caer en sus defectos o des-cuidos? . . . Abandonar, pues, esta observación, y ocuparse en trasladar la forma exterior de los escritos extranjeros, es querer formar el carácter de todo un país . . .[11]

The *Memorial literario*, referring to a revival of *El delincuente honrado* in 1793, immediately thought of *Le Déserteur* which had been performed in 1789 in translation[12] from Mercier's original of 1770. In this, an army officer, having discovered his long-lost son in the person of a

11. *Exequias de la lengua castellana*, C.I.A.P., pp. 73-4.
12. See *Memorial literario*, December 1793, and p. 456 below.

deserter, is in the position of having to sentence him to death; and, from Mercier, Jovellanos seems to have borrowed part of this idea, together with the atmospheric alternation of insistent sounds and silences and the heroine's unnerving hysteria, for the crisis of his last act. Mercier's Judge, in *Le Juge* of 1774, a drama also producing a long-lost relation, has many qualities in common with Jovellanos's idealized Don Justo, who was the product of the Spaniard's bookish study, as the more human Corregidor, Don Simón, was a product of his everyday experience. Jovellanos would know Sedaine's *Le Philosophe sans le savoir*, with its criticism of the code of honour, and with its duel, which, though seeming sublimely reasonable to the hero-participant, left his family to bear the brunt of the suffering.[13] Don Simón expresses the same idea in Spanish when he protests:

Estos muchachos quieren disculparse con el honor, sin advertir que por conservarle atropellan todas sus obligaciones. (Act IV, vi)

And it is significant of the intellectual trend of thought in Spain that the year of the appearance of *El delincuente honrado* was the year of the composition by Cándido María de Trigueros of the Real Academia de Buenas Letras de Sevilla, of the 'comedia lastimosa' *Los ilustres salteadores:*[14] a largely undistinguished drama which, however, in dealing with rival factions in Spain during the War of Succession, and with their ideals of honour and duty, inserts a realistic tirade against the animal savagery inevitably stimulated by civil wars of ideals:

¡Qué negro furor, qué desesperación engendras, cruel guerra civil, sanguinario espíritu de partido . . .! ¡Ah! que no puede ser justo un partido que alimenta tanta desesperación, tanto furor, tanta crueldad . . . ¿Por qué, Gran Dios, me has destinado un esposo tan duro, y tan inflexible? No es él duro, no es inflexible, no es cruel, yo le conozco, humano y tierno es; esta furiosa guerra, esta guerra civil le ha hecho cruel, hombre es Benet, la discordia le ha convertido en fiera . . . ya somos más fieras que las fieras con que vivimos . . . (Act IV).

The *pundonor*, private and public, that prime motivator of stage conflicts, was at long last coming up for unemotional inspection and might

13. See J. Sarrailh, 'À Propos du *Delincuente honrado* de Jovellanos' in *Mélanges d'Études Portugaises offerts à M. Georges Le Gentil* [Lisbon, 1949].
14. The original manuscript is in the Biblioteca Nacional.

easily be descredited as immoral, illogical, unenlightened, and anti-social. The dramatic problem was what to put in its place, which problem Trigueros, whose proud anti-Bourbon outlaw is conveniently left with his honour intact when Felipe's opponent retires from the fray, cowardly evades.

Jovellanos might adopt foreign theses and the latest methods of scenic interpretation, but the much debated question of the duel which he thoughtfully chose as his theme was transferred to a Spanish context and discussed from a Spanish angle at a time when any theme concerning legal procedure in his country where the working of the law was expensive, unequal, and slow,[15] would be sure to arouse strong feeling. The same native instinct informed the best features of his dramatic style. When he wrote *El delincuente honrado* he was watching his foreign contemporaries, but he was also conscious of his native inheritance, and in his Preface to an edition of 1787 he makes proud mention of the geniuses of the Golden Age. This explains why *El delincuente honrado* towers above all the Low Tragedy produced by Spain in the last three decades of the century, and why, despite its relative sobriety, it was acceptable, in the original or adapted forms, from the day of its first performance.[16]

One suspects, indeed, that Jovellanos was guided more by his intuition than by the logic which he bandied with his French translator in 1777.[17] The latter, assuming after his Gallic fashion that the Spaniard, whom he admired, had pre-arranged every quality in the dramatic characters according to the rigid chart of Gallic theory, had asked for elucidation on the complex Don Simón, Corregidor of Segovia, a man clearly meant, he thought, to be professionally just, humanly compassionate, and of a certain nobility of soul, yet a man who did not always behave justly, compassionately or nobly in the drama and must therefore be to the French mind an inconsistent character, a dramatic freak. But probably just what puzzled the Frenchman was not, as Jovellanos, in his reply, seemed to think, that Don Simón, described in Act III by

15. See Desdevises du Dézert (G), 'Les Institutions de L'Espagne au xviiie siècle' in *Rev. Hisp.*, vol. lxx, 1927.
16. See the author's 'Advertencia' to the 1787 edition reproduced in B.A.E. xlvi. His claim is substantiated by published theatre lists. See Bibliography and Coe, p. 62.
17. This was the Abbé de Valchrétien. The correspondence is reproduced in B.A.E., *El delincuente honrado* was played in French at Cádiz where there was a French colony. See Sarrailh, *L'Espagne Éclairée* . . . , p. 330.

Don Justo, Alcalde de Casa y Corte, as the 'good-hearted man with unsound principles',[18] should present an instance of his muddled good nature in one scene, conflicting with his professional scruples in another. It was rather, perhaps, that, in the tradition of the famous *Alcalde*, he could be flippant when a Frenchman, though not an Englishman, would expect consistent sensibility, and, more especially, that his erratic reasoning about the situation should momentarily come as near the truth as the more logical reasoning of his consistent colleague Don Justo. Despite *comedia*-conventions, Spain could appreciate the dramatic force of a realistically two-plane mentality.

In Jovellanos's instinctive view of this situation the two officials of the Law, professionally juxtaposed, are not so much contrasted as fitfully complementary, just as two men of the same profession and with different temperaments would be when similarly placed in real life. Jovellanos himself, already experienced in Criminal Law, was in a position to know what members of the profession were really like, and how the interpretation of the Law half depended on and was half independent of each man's individuality. Besides, to a Spaniard guided by the dramatic instinct of his race, a character with more than one side to his nature did not call for explanation. He was tacitly conceded a right to stage existence. The best characters of Spanish drama had been allowed at their best moments to develop individuality on the human initiative which their creators unconsciously transferred to them. Certainly Jovellanos produced his most life-like effects when his characters individualistically tried to wrest from him his control over the dramatic partnership he had established with them. Therefore his attempts to justify certain 'irregularities' of character to his fastidious translator are unconvincing and read like an afterthought. The most notable fact about these magistrates is that, when faced with a problem, they both, for the best part of the first four acts, behave like normal, serious men of a world of lifelike responsibilities, applying their common sense to a solution. Moreover, Jovellanos was more advanced than his translator in having come to view the Unity of character, even in theory, as something distinct from fixity. The Rule is not, he reminds him, that the character should 'never change, but that he should not behave out of character'. At the same time it says much for his intuition that its

18. Don Justo's words are: 'tiene muy buen corazón, pero muy malos principios'.

fruits will bear rational analysis by translators, reviewers,[19] and spectators. Intuition carried him to an artistic level beyond the range of the mere intellectual.

As for the reasoning and cross-reasoning engaging the characters' minds in the stage course of their problems, one is struck by their desire to explore several points of view, and their freedom from easy dogmatism; as if they, like all their contemporaries in real life, had been trained to a restless distrust of appearances. Don Justo and Don Simón, much as the Frenchman feared for their literary integrity, might have argued intelligently at, let us say, the Turk's Head or the Cheshire Cheese where the company was usually too open-minded to be exhaustively consistent. Generally there is also an Anglo-Spanish realism in the humanitarian attitude of these characters that avoids the excesses of the over-consistent humanitarianism of France, because, perhaps, a humanitarian outlook in Spain and England had been taken more for granted, and, though political revolutions might be needed to right abuses, a revolution to assert the dignity of man as a human individual was scarcely necessary. In Spain the poor, the erring, were often treated unfairly or tyranically, but they have never, by tacit social snobbery, been despised or ignored. For which reason the need to enforce the principle of social *Fraternité* was never ideologically understood in the Peninsula. Imitations of French thesis-*drames* in the eighties could not be incorporated into the Spanish pattern of understanding as they stood. They were popularly acceptable mainly because of their external sensations.

But the problems and principles debated in *El delincuente honrado* are Spanish; so are the private attitudes of the two professional men: of Don Justo, sent by the government to Segovia to re-open an old case of duelling, and Don Simón, Corregidor of that city and the criminal's father-in-law. To a nation with as strong a respect for the written Law as England the regulations against duelling, though not observed in practice, might seem theoretically reasonable. If the Law claimed that the killer in a duel of honour, even if he had been the wronged or provoked party, was guilty of murder, the English, on the whole, might be

19. The *Memorial literario* of December 1793, after renewed performances of the play, eagerly took up the discussion of Don Simón's character, agreeing with the author against his French translator.

theoretically prepared to modify their conception of personal honour to conform with State reason. France debated the subject with some heat.[20] But the philosophy of enlightened world citizenship tended increasingly to discredit codes of private vengeance in France and England and to relegate then to an age of muddled thinking, especially after the pronouncements of Rousseau. It will be remembered how his broken hearted Julie bestirred herself to compose for her lover a miniature thesis on the subject of honour 'qui ne craint pas le vice, mais le reproche'.[21] It will be remembered too how the young Boswell, worrying about his honour one September night of 1764 after he had allowed a Frenchman to call him a scoundrel and get away with the insult, had philosophized himself out of his shame, and, in his elaborate way, had arranged a mutual *amende honorable*, in words, before witnesses.[22] Beverley in *The Gamester* states the attitude of the Age of Reason, when, left, in Act IV, to meditate on his own misguided behaviour, he reflects that man's boasted 'honour' is only another name for 'pride'. A character in Sedaine's *Le Philosophe sans le savoir* elaborates on the same misuse of the *pundonor* :

> Préjugé funeste! abus cruel du point d'honneur, tu ne pouvais avoir pris naissance que dans les temps les plus barbares; tu ne pouvais subsister qu'au milieu d'une nation vaine et pleine d'elle-même, qu'au milieu d'un peuple dont chaque particulier compte sa personne pour tout, et sa patrie et sa famille pour rien. (Act III, ix)

The more inflammable Spaniards, however, with little individual or collective regard for the written Law, were harder to convince that 'honour' could spell merely 'empty pride', and the death penalty insisted upon by Fernando VI for both participants, provoker and provoked, in a duel was too drastic to be understood. In matters of *pundonor*, especially those not readily definable, Spaniards always tended to be extreme, and to believe, as in their hearts they still believe, that compromise in the most important, which, for them, does not necessarily

---

20. See Sarrailh, *L'Espagne Éclairée* . . . , pp. 538 ff.
21. *La Nouvelle Héloise*, Part I, Letters lvii ff. Compare examples of honour-thesis given by Sarrailh in 'À Propos du *Delincuente honrado* de Jovellanos' (ed. cit.), a work which I was only able to obtain after this chapter was written. M. Sarrailh deals with the possibility of several French influences on the Spanish theme, all of them, however, of the most general nature. Possible dramatic sources are as mentioned above.
22. See *Boswell on the Grand Tour*, ed. F. A. Pottle, London, 1953.

include political, spheres was, and is, hypocrisy. If the individual, then, sincerely put his individual honour above the State's collective need of public order, and if, so far, the Law had, specifically or tacitly, sanctioned his active guardianship of his own honour, the new law punishing the aggrieved party with death looked unjust even to the level-headed Don Justo of this play, even to its legally minded author whose superscription to his work runs, in the words of Act I, scene v, 'Es cosa muy terrible castigar con la muerte una acción que se tiene por honrada'. Nor was a change of outlook effected quickly. In 1787 the *Correo de los ciegos* . . . is still much exercised about the right and wrong conceptions of honour.[23] A lecture to the Academy of Jurisprudence of Barcelona delivered late in 1788 and reported by the *Memorial literario* in the new year[24] protests that the general public is still incapable of regarding the duel of honour objectively, and tries to suggest methods of undermining popular resistance to the laws against duelling, for instance by educating the young to appreciate the absurdity of personal vengeance:

Ellos no llegan a comprender el poderso recurso que halla el hombre de honor insultado, en su honor mismo, y en la satisfacción que le presta su interior inculpable; enteramente persuadidos que sola la venganza es el tribunal a que puede apelar en este lance, y que sólo la sangre de su contrario puede lavar las manchas que su honor padece. Ésta es la piedra angular de los duelistas y del duelo, y éste es el que ha de servir de objeto a este discurso, en el que haré ver con la brevedad posible, primero su *origen y progresos*; seguidamente lo contrario que es a la religión, a la razón, y a todos los deberes más sagrados; y en fin las penas que contra él han fulminado todas las legislaciones, añadiendo algunas advertencias que pueden servir para desterrar las ideas que fomentan su uso.

This topical question with its two warmly opposed points of view was therefore natural material for dramatic debate. At last responsible characters had one interesting subject to talk about with contemporary feeling. It is all very well, argues Don Justo, for this law to operate where affronted men, by temperament and circumstance, can afford to parade civic philosophies before their unprejudiced neighbours; but where climate, education, customs, national temperament, and legal tradition have placed the defence of the individual's honour in his own

23. *Correo de los ciegos* . . . , 18 April 1787.   24. See note 2, page 571.

hands, the affronted man who does not defend himself is a social out-
cast, and the law against duelling, as it stands, is consequently unrealistic:

> . . . en un país donde el más honrado es el menos sufrido, y el más valiente
> el que tiene más osadía; en un país, en fin, donde a la cordura se llama
> cobardía, y a la moderación falta de espíritu, ¿será justa la ley que priva de la
> vida a un desdichado sólo porque piensa como sus iguales; una ley que sólo
> podrán cumplir los muy virtuosos o los muy cobardes? . . . hoy pensamos,
> poco más o menos, como los godos, y sin embargo, castigamos los duelos
> con penas capitales. (Act IV, vi)

It is all very well, reasons Don Simón, on two occasions, more in-
coherently and selecting a different, though equally realistic angle of the
problem, it is all very well for the youths of Spain to dabble in French
philosophy, but when it comes to a matter of honour they will use their
'philosophy' to rationalize the righteousness of the duel and then to
rationalize the inculpability of the survivor. On the first occasion his
son-in-law angrily protests:

> ¿Sabéis que quien no admite un desafío es al instante tenido por cobarde?
> Si es un hombre ilustre, un caballero, un militar, ¿de qué le servirá acudir
> a la justicia? La nota que le impuso la opinión pública ¿podrá borrarla una
> sentencia? Yo bien sé que el honor es una quimera, pero sé también que sin
> él no puede subsistir una monarquía; que es el alma de la sociedad; que
> distingue las condiciones y las clases; que es principio de mil virtudes polí-
> ticas. . . .

and Don Simón is derisive:

> ¡Bueno, muy bueno! Discursos a la moda y opinioncitas de ayer acá;
> déjalos correr, y que se maten los hombres como pulgas. (Act I, v)

On the other occasion Don Simón has just heard that Torcuato's friend,
Anselmo, has been arrested for complicity in the duel case now being
re-investigated, and he works off his irritation on his daughter:

> . . . Que vaya, que vaya ahora a defenderle tu marido con sus filosofías.
> ¿Qué, no hay más que andarse matando los hombres por frioleras, y luego
> disculparlos con opiniones galanas? Todos estos modernos gritan: la razón, la
> humanidad, la naturaleza. Bueno andará el mundo cuando se haga caso de
> estas cosas. (Act II, ix)

Further material for heartfelt discussion, brought this time by
Torcuato when he hears that his friend has been arrested, concerns the

use of torture to extract confessions from witnesses.[25] The modern case against torture had been put impressively for Spain by another Northerner, Feijoo.[26] Jovellanos held the same civilized ideas. Very properly he touched more lightly on this subject than on the main thesis of his play. But incidental discussion, in minor scenes, of topics on which modern Spaniards could feel strongly gave the play ideological density. Torcuato's speech rang the more urgently and realistically for the fact that Jovellanos had considered the subject of torture as a specialist in Law,[27] and that he was deliberately calling attention to professional and popular debates in which Spain, like the rest of the Continent was engaged.[28] In such ways the characters are supplied with something intelligent to think or talk about in the process and in the intervals of making fateful decisions.

Like many Liberals of his day, Jovellanos saw that new legislation which might be intrinsically good, could be bad in effect if the national mind were not prepared for it; and his own conflicts in the matter brought the mental conflicts of his drama more satisfyingly to life. Here, however, he was not dramatizing a straight clash between advanced thinkers and reactionaries, but a many sided conflict, typical of times of transition, when one idea may exist plurally, in different stages of absorption, and when no given man is quite sure what he and his opinions represent. For this reason, and because incidental talk on the subject of duelling is used in genuinely incidental places to make the characters' mental life more real, the play is full of ideological promise.

Since the personal views of the Judges cannot free them from the fulfilment of their duty as instruments of the Law, the dramatic conflict may be said to be twofold. On one hand is the conflict within the profession—that is, not between the two Judges—for even Don Simón, though he may hope aloud for a loophole in the Law when his own family becomes involved, and see Don Justo raising his somewhat

25. 'Si se obstina en callar sufrirá todo el rigor de la ley . . . Y tal vez la tortura . . . (*Horrorizado*) ¡La tortura! . . . ¡Oh nombre odioso! . . . ¿Es posible que en un siglo en que se respeta la humanidad y en que la filosofía derrama su luz por todas partes, se escuchen aún entre nosotros los gritos de la inocencia oprimida?' (Act II, xiv.)

26. See *Teatro crítico* . . . , *passim*.

27. Sarrailh calls attention to Jovellanos's publications on torture: *Informe sobre la abolición de la prueba del tormento*, and *El interrogatorio de los reos*, during his period of office in the criminal courts at Sevilla during 1768–78. See *L'Espagne Éclairée* . . . , p. 538.

28. See note 3, page 571.

priggish eyebrows,[29] submits to the Law's decisions—but between the Law as it is and as ideally and ironically it might be. On the other, is the more specific conflict between Don Justo's love for Torcuato, the criminal, newly discovered to be his son, and his duty. Fortunately the second conflict is chiefly confined to the last and weakest act.

In the first four we have, for the most part, an excellent representation of a peaceful family shaken out of its normal habits into a situation of cross-tensions by a piece of catastrophic news. As is common in family crises, suppressions and half suppressions are exercised in different degrees towards different members of the household out of a mistaken kindness, and much of the very convincing suspense of the early scenes is due to this homely fact. Into Torcuato's peaceful domestic life drops the news that the Government is re-opening investigations into the death of the Marqués de Montilla, his wife's first husband, who, un-known to all but Torcuato's friend, Anselmo, and a servant bribed to disappear, had fought Torcuato, the aggrieved party, in a duel and had been killed by him. Hearing now that this servant has been arrested, and knowing that nothing can prevent the truth coming out and his own eventual arrest and execution, Torcuato believes that he can best mini-mize his family's suffering by fleeing before the worst happens under the pretext of a business journey to Madrid. It is in the high-pitched tension of this urgent secrecy that the early acts are set. At first Tor-cuato tells neither Laura, his wife, nor Don Simón, his father-in-law. Much of his nervous strength is therefore dramatically sapped by the effort to appear normal, and the scenes concerned successfully underline the dramatic value of his strained state of mind. There is the dialogue between Don Simón and Torcuato, quoted above, on the subject of duels and occasioned by the news that Don Justo is coming to re-open the Montilla case, in which Torcuato argues heatedly in his concealed self-interest that since a man's honour is the basis of political virtue it behoves the Law to protect it, and in which Don Simón affectionately rallies him on his mixed ideology. There is the brief scene of trans-ferred irritation between Torcuato and his grimly comic servant who has mentioned to members of the household that Torcuato is closeted with Anselmo when he has been told to say that his master is out, and whose misdemeanour provokes the anger of suppressed anxiety:

29. See note 4, page 571.

Torcuato (*inquieto*). ¡Cómo! Pues ¿no te previne . . .?
Felipe. Vos no me previnisteis que callase.
Torcuato (*con severidad*). Anda a ver si hay algún retorno de Madrid, y ajústale para después de mediodía. ¿Entiendes?
Felipe. Muy bien Señor—¡Qué mal humor tiene!

There is the scene with his friend, Anselmo, whom he has secretly sent for, and who, first thinking that Torcuato's troubles are domestic, treats the urgent summons with jocularity, complains about being dragged out of bed so early, starts to give him some domestic advice, and at last allowing himself to be told the facts, enters into Torcuato's mood and needs. There is the scene with Don Simón at the end of Act I when Torcuato is publicly told the news he already knows privately, that the servant-witness has been arrested, and when the repetition is unconsciously rubbed into his sick, suppressed fear by the typically good humoured Simón:

> *Simón*. (*Se va y vuelve*) ¡Ah! ¿sabes que han preso a Juanillo? . . . ¡Don Justo adelanta terriblemente en la causa! . . . él es activo como un diablo (*Yéndose*) Sí, como un diablo . . . !Fuego!

In Act II comes the scene of Torcuato's uncomfortable discussion with the housewifely Laura on his needs for the 'business' journey, of her own private worries over the suddenness of this strange journey for which he wants to take an unconscionable amount of underclothing; of her small ironic cares over the dinner which he and his servant must take before they go; and of the frustration experienced by Torcuato in his efforts to depart quickly and quietly, reminiscent perhaps of those experienced by Dorval in his efforts to leave Clairville's house in *Le Fils Naturel*. This pressure of time is a feature very deliberately and ironically insisted upon. In Act II, in fateful circumstances on one plane, the characters are waiting for the trivial announcement, on another, that dinner is served. The interval is nervously crowded with domestic details: Simón's chatter and teasing on the undue solemnity being paid to Torcuato's short absence; a summons to the Corregidor to deal with a 'perpetual litigant,' and Torcuato's comment, with lively sympathy, that perhaps on the result depends the subsistence of the poor wretch's family;[30] the arrival of the coach which is instructed to wait till after

30. A rather similar passage occurs in *Le Juge*.

dinner and about which Felipe continues to fuss throughout the act; Laura's demand, when they are free from Simón's presence, to be taken into her husband's confidence; Torcuato's breakdown into the truth, Laura's terror, and the arrival of Don Justo with the news that Anselmo has been arrested for bribing the servant in the Montilla case; the shocked garrulousness of Don Simón on his return; Don Justo's awareness of Laura's distress; Torcuato's decision to confess publicly. It is upon all these tense emotions that the servant does at length arrive to announce the serving of the soup, Don Simón then emphasizing the abnormal by the relief with which he flippantly clutches at the normal:

> *Juan.* (*En el fondo*) Señores, la sopa está en la mesa.
> *Don Simón.* ¡Santa palabra! Vamos, vamos a comerla antes que se enfríe; que lo demás lo descubrirá el tiempo.

In Act III, after Don Simón has humanized one good incidental scene with his views, as a father-in-law, on Torcuato's career, and another with his complaints to the distraught Laura that between her tears and Torcuato's sudden decision not to undertake the urgent journey, he is at a loss to understand his own household, he and Don Justo are at last acquainted with the news that Torcuato has given himself up. Now Don Simón's reactions are psychologically much more interesting than those of Don Justo who is, as far as he knows, an impartial observer, objectively impressed with the nobility of character of Anselmo and Torcuato, and very dubious about the ultimate justice of indiscriminating punishment in affairs of honour. Don Simón, a more robust and complex version of Sedaine's Pater Familias in *Le Philosophe sans le savoir*, is at first seized by a sense of outrage, as might be any responsible head of a family on hearing of the criminal irresponsibility of one of its members; and, however disconcerting this sudden harshness of an affectionate character might be to translators, he gives a most lifelike representation of anger and disappointment produced, not by anger or sudden hatred, but by nervous shock. His unsympathetic attitude, which drives his daughter to the understanding comfort of Don Justo, is the same as was his attitude against Anselmo when he had heard of his complicity, and on that occasion, to Don Justo's observation that the young man did not look like a criminal, he had bitterly replied that in his experience the worst criminals could look like saints.

Don Simón, in fact, is a lifelike man of unimaginative impulse: an ordinary man, who depends on precepts which he has not co-ordinated for himself because he has not engaged in comparative observation; an obstinate and easily ruffled man, because life does not conform to principles taken out of their context; a good-hearted man, suffering from disconnected emotions; a professional man, who tries to hide these in bluffness; a man of great dramatic potentialities, because his character, by the very force of its sincerity, is conducive to ironic and realistic misunderstandings. Here he is angry in proportion to the degree of shock he has experienced. This state of mind, however, is temporary. His half apologetic change of tone when his daughter swears that if her husband dies she will die too is sufficient explanation of his general bewilderment:

Simón. (*más aplacado*) ¡Laura! ¡Laura! . . . Yo no sé lo que me pasa¡ tantas cosas como han sucedido en sólo un día me tienen sin cabeza.

As an extra psychological refinement, he then reverts to a half-stunned fit of retrospection, natural to any man of common sense:

Simón. pero, señores, lo que yo no puedo comprender, es por qué este hombre nos calló su situación. Al fin, si me lo hubiera dicho, yo no soy ningún roble . . . Pero haber callado . . . haberse casado . . .

So far the characters have been relatively natural. Perhaps Torcuato becomes bookish when he theatrically tells Laura that the man whom all are seeking, the man who killed her husband, is himself. But young men often do become melodramatic under emotional stress. It is a sign of the youthful aggressiveness of their importance to themselves and psychologically justifies the exhibitionism of nineteenth century emotionalists. In response, perhaps women too, though their own species of exhibitionism is usually reserved for less tragic cases, may sometimes self-consciously 'sink into a chair' and utter the equivalent of 'Oh, cielo!' Moreover, Laura, acting the part of the afflicted wife, drives her thoughts fairly realistically, if a little stiffly, backwards to worry over his lack of trust in her, and forwards to his peril and his cruelty to her in refusing to flee and abandon his friend. Even her cry to the unsympathetic Simón in Act III that she will die with her husband rings in the circumstances like natural hysteria. But after Act III, and with the exception of the professional discussions in Act IV between the two Judges, and of a refreshing visit of Simón to the prison in the tower, pestered, he says, by Laura, and brandishing in his unhappy embarrassment his most tactless heartiness:

Simón. (a Torcuato) ¡Muy buena la hemos hecho, Torcuato! ¡mira en qué estado nos has puesto!

the play, artistically, may be said to decline.

In Act IV the martyr-hero, mindful of his French contemporaries, is already posturing in chains. Under the influence of that acute sensibility idealized in fiction by the indelicate epoch, he covers his face with shame at the very word 'illegitimate' which, he at last brings himself to confess, had provoked him to fight, and which is now unexpectedly to proclaim him Don Justo's son, with his *pundonor* ironically martyred in the Judge's service. Most regrettably, however, it was Act V which remained longest in stage-memory. Doubtless this would be the act most zestfully performed by the cultured young amateurs when the drama was played in its author's honour in 1797 and earned his dubious private comment 'bastante bien'.[31] Jovellanos in this act had gone in foreign pursuit of a sensibility which, despite the French translator's decision to modify its more extreme manifestations, was the sensibility of Diderot set off by some of the atmospheric effects borrowed by France from England. The whole act, strangely dissociated in tone from the others, would have served as the text of pure melodrama. Even in Act I Torcuato had frenchily defended to Anselmo his right to shed tears, on the grounds that they are signs of a right sensibility.[32] In prison, complete with chains, and dressed for execution, he is the object of the tears of the rapidly deteriorating and consistently sensitive Don Justo. Unable, for the weight of his fetters, to reach his new father's feet and ask his blessing, he stands pathetically calling 'Father' to which appeal Justo is too deeply moved to reply. As in melodrama, as in Le Déserteur, sound is even more important than decoration, and the striking of the fateful hour—French travellers may have experienced its force in performances of Macbeth—heralds a lugubrious procession of the officers of Justice who bear the prisoner away to dismal military

31. See *Diarios*, ed. cit., vol. ii, p. 395.
32. *Torcuato:* Si las lágrimas son efecto de la sensibilidad del corazón, ¡ desdichado de aquél que no es capaz de derramarlas! (Act I, iii.)

music. After Torcuato's exit, a confused shouting outside is followed by a fearsome 'melancholy silence'. Don Justo and Laura wait in a pantomimic sensibility, of restraint and hysteria respectively,[33] for the decisive sound of the death-bell, which then tolls naggingly for several minutes, reminding us of the insistent knocking in *Le Philosophe sans le savoir*, and the execution bell in *The London Merchant*. The news of a last-minute reprieve after the emotions provoked by the death-knell (rung mistakenly), is a cheap anti-climax, and one is grateful for Don Simón's breezy:

> Buen susto nos has dado, hijo; Dios te lo perdone.

Jovellanos's potentialities were so good that one is unfairly surprised at his melodramatic exhibitionism which was a defect of his times: at the tears, shrieks, and shocks of Act V; even at the mild melodramatic restraint of the more controlled characters who dispose themselves quietly with heads in hands or occasionally fling themselves dumbly into chairs. His sense of humour, though it flashes back occasionally in Don Simón, disappears altogether during Anselmo's account of how, when he finally reached the King, the royal eyes had filled with tears of pity, just as it disappeared in the account of how the guards had wept like babies[34] when Torcuato gave himself up to save his friend. But the whole Court was reported, by a narrating character, to have wept at the sight of Barnwell before the Judge in *The London Merchant*; and that ill-fated youth, half choked by his 'tears and interrupting sobs', had confessed 'without accusing or once reflecting on Millwood, the shameless, author of his ruin' (Act V, i). Sensibility was a two-edged weapon. *The London Merchant* had much to answer for.

Evidence that Jovellanos's problem-play as performed in the Sitios was too advanced for the times is first apparent in the verse adaptations made for public theatres. One, a five-act version of 1777, seemingly by Valladares y Sotomayor, and entitled *¿Cuál más obligación es, la de padre o la de juez?*[35] follows Jovellanos's theme and dialogue, but in jaunty

---

33. See, for example, *Laura corre como furiosa; su padre manifiesta también mucho dolor, y la sigue sin hablar . . . [Laura] cae al suelo . . . levantándose con furor . . . vuelve a caer en los brazos de su padre . . .* (Act V, v.)

34. '. . . hasta los centinelas, viendo su generosidad, lloraban como unas criaturas.' (Act III, vi.)

35. There is a manuscript version in the Biblioteca Municipal, Madrid licensed for 1777.

popular metre blights the possibilities of his influence. By a change of emphasis from thought to plot the drama, like a modern 'book of the film', loses its link with literature. The density of incidental reasoning, tension and characterization disappears. Incidental debate, including the argument on Law, is cut down to the requirements of the drama's 'story' value. The result is an unlikely tale of action and sensibility enlivened by intervals of male and female clowning, for into this did the tense humour of *El delincuente honrado* degenerate.

It was a woeful anti-climax. Where Jovellanos had so carefully excluded from Don Justo's professional mind any possibility, any means of tampering with the Law; where he had projected the major conflict abstractly as between absolute and relative aspects of the Law; where he had made the clash of professional and private feelings an incidental, emotional effect of Don Justo's unquestioning death-judgement to which he took for granted that he must resign himself, Valladares shifted the accent to the Judge's melodramatic anguish of deciding what was his duty. With the death-warrant in his hands, this Don Álvaro—the names are changed—raves like a Guzmán el Bueno, who also, as a Governor, should have known that he had no choice, in his professional capacity, but to hold the fortress for his country and leave his son to die. Here is the kind of unreal doubt which often figured in parody:

> *Don Álvaro* Pues muera mi hijo:—no muera,
> que es una crueldad no oída
> jamás! Este cruel proceso
> en pedazos se divida.
> Pero mal Juez ¿qué haces? . . . (Act III)

Jovellanos's Don Justo, instead of affecting to decide a problem in fact decided for him by Law, had taken the more practical course of telling Anselmo in his Appeal to the King to mention that he, Justo, was in the abnormal position of having to sentence his own son. And when the King's eyes filled with tears it might well have been because he could imagine, not the terrible strength of mind required by the Judge to make his 'decision', but the fact that the machine of Law can mechanically forge undreamed-of ironics. Indeed it is in asking us sentimentally to admire such free, personal 'decisions' which no soldier, no public man is free to refrain from making, that Low Tragedy loses its universal opportunities.

Nor did Valladares realize the harm he was doing to the development of dramatic thought by reverting to irresponsible patterns of speech in this vein:

> *Rita* ¡Dulce esposo!
> *Pablo* ¡Amigo amado!
> *Camilo* ¡Amo mío!
> *Simón* ¡Amable hijo!
> *Álvaro* ¡Qué espectáculo tan triste!
> ... (Act II)

or in this:

> *Álvaro* Adiós en fin.
> *Jacinto* Adiós, padre.
> *Álvaro* Y en tal mal
> *Jacinto* Y en tal tragedia
> *Álvaro* Iluminadme, Dios mío.
> *Jacinto* Dios mío, dadme paciencia. (Act II)

Apparently he did not grasp the atmospheric significance of the tolling bell, the best, because the most restrained dramatic feature of Jovellanos's last act, for he omitted it, and instead concentrated on the exhibitionist shrieking and swooning. To him the highlights of the play were not the thesis-arguments, but the sensational death-sentence passed by a father on his son, and the emotional disclosures of their relationships—the features that Spain, in company with all Europe, was popularizing as instruments of 'sensibility'. The censors raised no objection to Valladares's version. One, Fray Pedro Fernández, was pleased to find the play 'instructive', the description on which censors of Low Tragedy based its claims to life. Another five-act arrangement in verse, called *El delincuente honrado*, made by González de la Cruz[36] manages also to give the drama's problematic and instructive qualities a puerile finish diverting attention from its modern potentialities.

Thesis-dramas of the eighties and nineties, written by artists greatly inferior to Jovellanos, were normally less concentrated, and for practical reasons, both of popularity with the public and deference to increasingly suspicious censors, introduced their theses inconspicuously

36. We have seen a manuscript of 1800.

by secondary stage entrances. However, the idea that a man's conception of honour might be egoistic rather than moral was very suggestive to the rationalistic times. In drama it is echoed again in Ramón de la Cruz's *El divorcio feliz* a play drawn from Marmontel's tale 'L'Heureux Divorce', meant originally, perhaps, for private performance, for when it reached the censor in 1782 it arrived with the self-corrections of the author, who knew to a nicety what the censor would or would not, could or could not, approve. The title was changed for propriety to *Cuanto destruye un capricho y vale una reflexión. La Matilde.*[37] Also Cruz judiciously changed the cynical speech of Don Quintín which, from the misconceptions of *pundonor*, passed on to question other traditions criticism of which the Church and Government could not afford to publicize. So

> ¡El honor no es otra cosa
> que un adorno, una decencia!
> El matrimonio una pura
> formalidad: y la oferta
> de fidelidad, obsequio
> entre los que lo celebran;
> de suerte que en la substancia
> todo es una friolera.

becomes the milder:

> ¿Sabéis lo que es el honor?
> Es una gran friolera,
> para mí y otros muchos
> que son de mi propia escuela.

In the anonymous *El Premio de la constancia o el matrimonio feliz*, of 1793, a comic labourer touches on the subject of honour with meaning jocularity:

> *Roque* ¿Qué es la honra en muchas gentes
> del siglo que hoy conocemos
> tan ilustrado? Un adorno
> como el collar de los perros.
> ¿De qué sirve? De maldita
> la cosa: estarse muriendo
> de hambre, y siempre boca abajo
> en la cocina el puchero. . . .

37. MS., B. Mun. The *Censura* is dated 1782.

But a more typical example of the new way in which old honour was used is its sentimentalization, with death-drum, and screaming heroine, by Bernardo María de Calzada in *La subordinación militar*[38] a play ultimately of German origin[39] licensed in 1785. It makes pathetic use of the court martial of one Walton who, pricked in his honour, has drawn against a superior, because, we are made to feel, that action, being the lesser of the two evils of insult accepted or insult revenged, was regrettably unavoidable. Accordingly the position in which he has landed himself calls less for objective reasoning about principles than of heavily emotional sympathy for misfortune. The play is an example of how easily emphasis could be shifted by the popular mind for which Calzada exclusively catered.[40]

38. MS., B. Mun.   39. See note 5, page 571.   40. See note 6, page 571.

12

Theme Shifts

Low Tragedy presented in an ethical light, agreeable in principle to censors and critics, convenient to authors and actors, was treated from the first with the prejudiced respect reserved for a vehicle of social improvement. The scale of remuneration drawn up in 1807 for various classes of drama, does not, it is true, allot the highest royalties to writers of this genre, their portion being 5 per cent for their lifetime of the box-office takings,[1] as compared with 8 per cent to writers of original tragedy and comedy and 3 per cent to translators. But by then Spanish critics were saying what Goldsmith had said in 1773: that this kind of drama was easy to write.[2] By then it was also assumed that if domestic pieces were not precisely 'translated', they were, as *The Critic* delicately put it, 'taken' from the French.[3] So that 5 per cent, representing a stage between genuine originality and translation, must have seemed a fair estimate of their experimental worth. There is a way of translating, said the *Correo* in 1790, when foreign sensibility was at its height, 'which leaves foreigners and nationals unable to decide to which of them the work really belongs'.[4] This method of borrowing, if direct translation was to be financially penalized, was obviously convenient, and would explain the chronic reluctance of dramatists to admit that their compositions were not exactly 'new and original', their tendency to use disguising titles, and even, by a change of title, to revive works already performed. The *Memorial literario* protested in the May of 1787,

1. See note 1, page 572.   2. See note 2, page 572.
3. '*Sneer* . . . that's a genteel comedy, not a translation—only taken from the French: it is written in a style which they have lately tried to run down; the true sentimental, and nothing ridiculous in it from the beginning to the end.' (Act I, i.)
4. *Correo de Madrid; o de los Ciegos*, 9 January 1790. See Letter from 'Don Yo' describing the visit of Buen Gusto to Parnassus.

426

when an old play on the Guzmán-el-Bueno theme was 'sold as new' under a different title,[5] and on this subject too a censor expressed himself forcibly in 1778, when he recognized *La viuda sutil*, received as new by his guileless colleagues, as only another title for *Las cuatro naciones*, itself not original.[6] It was, in fact, a translation of Goldoni's *La Vedova scaltra*, a verse arrangement probably by Valladares of his own prose translation *Las cuatro naciones o viuda sutil* which Santos Díez González had passed as such a few months earlier,[7] with the rider, however, that he considered prose a dubious medium for comedy.

The best European exponents of Low Tragedy had had the sense to realize that the moral teaching, demanded by literary welfare workers, does not itself make drama, and that virtue consistently resigned to adversity is poor theatre. Like Jovellanos some of the most successful writers transferred dramatic interest to the thesis which the martyr-protagonist merely helped to illustrate, and a relatively good dramatist such as Moore, Mercier, or Jovellanos, took the opportunity to develop minor characters which, being freer to express their incidental humanity, are usually more interesting than the martyrs. Some daring spirits took a hint from Richardson, whose 'artless' tales of 'private woe'— Lillo's description of Low Tragedy[8]—are only 'artless' to the uninitiated. For he had rediscovered for his times that an infallible way of making 'good love' both popularly and intellectually interesting was to give detailed examples of what good lovers should avoid and of the depths of vice from which they could ascend to virtue. When Mercier's fop, De Lys, says to the provocatively virtuous Charlotte in *L'Indigent*: 'L'example de Paméla est un peu fort', he might have been excused for remembering that English innocent not only as the personification of goodness, but as the foil for a zestfully detailed study of man's frailty. Indeed the French writers of *drame* never dared to present the rake in the full realism of his English personality, never dared, or cared, to

5. The reference is to the play *Más pesa el rey que la sangre* 'sold' under the new title of *El vasallo más leal y grande Guzmán el Bueno*.

6. See note 3, page 572.

7. His *censura* is dated 23 April 1788. See also, for instance, the complaints of the *Memorial literario* of December 1793, that the play *Tener celos de sí mismo*, parading as 'new', is really a play of the previous century.

8. ' Forgive us then, if we attempt to show,
   In artless strains, a tale of private woe,
   A London 'prentice ruined is our theme . . .'
   (Prologue to *The London Merchant*.)

427

place the heroine's mind in the necessity of resolving her own ambiguities of thinking and desiring. The French playwrights, nearly all indebted to Richardson, albeit a little scandalized at his exhaustiveness, found it more seemly to provide their Pamelas and their libertine heroes with artificial codes of feeling and behaviour, so that the lady could always be trusted to have a right mind in all things, and the rake at a fixed moment could be relied on to reform for ever. Consequently the theme of the contemporary hero-rake, reformed by the virtue of a contemporary working-girl, lost so much humanity as it went about the continent that by the time it crossed the Spanish frontier it had become a wan wraith of its hearty English self.

French inventiveness was unaccustomed to functioning in realistic inconsistencies of character. Instead it now worked busily in the field of humanitarian logic, and, inflamed by the political and social feelings of the times, enlisted in the causes of social welfare and political liberty. If poverty is depicted, it is often set in a poorly camouflaged thesis on the neglect of the poor, the mismanaged relationship of wealth and labour, the tyranny of rank. If the play involves the responsibilities of public men, it raises questions of injustice and corruption, often, of course, by a heavy parade of the opposite virtues. The Spanish version of this drama of social morals will emerge later.

In the typical French *drame*, then, characters did not throw off their incidental thoughts incidentally in the English style which assumes that the spectator is recognizing clues and is following them up for himself. They arranged them neatly in pointed major speeches. Virtue was not usually mixed with vice in one person. The squalor and sordidness of poverty became, by an academic remove, the material of argument. The rugged downrightness of English dramatic speech, which should not have startled honest Spanish ears, was decorously smoothed, losing in this refining process even more of its vitality than of its crudeness; and almost invariably a prose original, if translated through French into the directness of Spanish prose, was then popularized in traditional verse-patterns which twisted social ideologies into hackneyed figures of speech.

Since the epoch's attention had focused on social problems, the dramatic theme assumed more intrinsic importance than in any other period with the possible exception of our own. Drama, regular or irregular, had meant a broad harmony of thought and dialogue, the theme serving chiefly as an agent of practical organization. To the receptive world of letters in the past a striking topical theme in an outstanding author's work might have roused interest for itself. But, when another poet had been constrained to 'take' it, he had usually done so less for its theme and plot-value than because the theme or plot, by its originality, had thrown ideas, characters, situations, or verbal ingenuities, into artistic relief arresting enough to inspire the creation of parallels. In the eighteenth century, however, the theme was not merely a way of organizing dramatic urges coherently. It was not, as in the past, artistically independent of the social conditions that had suggested it. It was itself the chief dramatic quality of a play: a means become an end. It could not interpret the spirit of the age. It could only reflect and exemplify. Original and artistic thought-content of Low Tragedies was negligible. In some ways they resemble the documentary plays of modern broadcasting. To some extent they are charts of public opinion. They seem to exist primarily to tell a cautionary social tale. Yet they had their literary justification in that they demonstrated at least one manner in which dramatic subject matter could be modernized; and so their illustration of states and levels of contemporary social consciousness were more important for the interior development of drama than mere themes usually are.

Each influential dramatization of a French or English social idea became the leader of an international group of dramas differing from each other mainly in emphasis. Normally the group-leader propagated certain of the peculiarities of detail created by the original dramatist which had first made his play a stage success, and these tended to be reproduced by all the members of the group, giving to that group an identity distinguishing it from other groups using the same theme or from independent dramas based on the same or a similar social idea. From the presence or absence of such incidental details it is generally possible, therefore, to determine whether the theme of any given play belonged to any one of the international theme-groups, or whether it was derived from the social ideas of the times independently.

The Spaniard first became aware of these theme-families when travelling on the Grand Tour by coach or by book, and Arandans admitted them to the theatres of the Sitios where their influence, if not dominant, was permeating. They began to infiltrate into public theatres during the later seventies but were not fully active until the eighties and nineties, by which time popular dramatists had learnt to adapt them to conservative national taste. Nevertheless, when they did reach the public they came with their identification marks still about them, which fact helps us to determine how much of a so-called 'new' drama of the social kind in Spain is an independent reflection of that country's own social awareness, and how much had been passively absorbed from foreign sources. Many popular Spanish playwrights took in their themes passively from the nearest theme-family. But others borrowed themes to apply them to Spanish social conditions and showed that Spain herself was sharing in European changes of outlook.

The main European theme-families, derived from England and France, crossed and recrossed the Channel and influenced each other constantly. Lillo's *London Merchant*, or *The History of George Barnwell* of 1731, not exactly new to England in its domestic atmosphere, was new in emphasis. Its practical philosophy, its commercial principles very fully discussed by Thorowgood and Trueman over their account-books at the beginning of Act III, as if on the level of a thesis:

> *Thorowgood* . . . I would not have you only learn the method of merchand-ise . . . merely as a means of getting wealth. 'Twill be well worth your pains to study it as a science. See how it is founded in reason, and the nature of things; how it has promoted humanity, as it has opened and yet keeps up an intercourse between nations. . . .
>
> *Trueman* . . . I have observed those countries, where trade is promoted and encouraged, do not make discoveries to destroy, but to improve mankind by love and friendship . . . etc.

presented themselves as tokens of the new enlightenment. Its accessible, and therefore analysable, interests and conception of responsibilities, its sense of the importance and dignity of the commonplace, coincided with and dramatically illustrated changing standards of values. However, there was still Elizabethan virility in the pathos of *The London Merchant*. Foreigners felt its power; and it became father of an international family of dramas about honest trade, commercial catastrophes, misunderstood apprentices, self-sacrificing friends—like Jovellanos's Torcuato and Anselmo—thoughtful interviews in prison and, in the shadow of the gallows, farewell-scenes with tolling bell and tears.

Mercier, when recasting it in a Paris background as *Jenneval, ou le Barnevelt Français* in 1769,[9] recognized this power and declared that the problem before him was how to preserve it without offence to French sensibilities. He liked, he said, the farewell-scene between the apprentice friends.[10] The incidental friendship of the youths was a novelty to a French playwright. Lillo had learnt to develop it from Shakespearian tradition. But Mercier did not quite know how to use it and Jenneval's French friend, when faced with the need to recognize his defects, becomes self-righteous. Mercier also used, with transparent earnestness, the drama's business-ethics, though he rearranged them somewhat, as he reorganized the vices and virtues of the unconventional characters the better to apportion their poetic dues. He did not care, however, to accompany his apprentice to the very gallows, where a French audience, he thought, would have no tears to spare for murderers.[11] So Jenneval is halted before a crime takes place.

In Spain, though the private woes of sensitive apprentices in trading houses became common from about 1780 onwards, and though the ideal of the dignity of trade and manual labour, proclaimed by Carlos III and much ventilated in the press,[12] had acquired the force of propaganda, the closest version we have found to Mercier and Lillo is Zavala y Zamora's *El Triunfo del amor y la amistad, Jenwal y Faustina*, played in 1804.[13] This retains the prose, but, probably for a Spanish reason, to occupy us later, rejects the philosophies of commerce—the thesis for which the prose was needed—and makes a livelier distribution of incident among three acts instead of five. Mercier, not to say Lillo, might have failed to recognize a Jenwal, now living in Bristol, and moving, nevertheless, in circumstances smacking of Castilian cloak and sword. So that perhaps Zavala y Zamora had some justification in calling the piece taken from the French, 'original'. Moreover, while he disregarded or judiciously avoided the important matter of the ethics of trade—indeed, like most of his countrymen he may simply have found that subject unpalatable—he appears to have learnt, perhaps from *Le Préjugé à la Mode* or its imitations, that his characters should have

9. See L. S. Mercier, *Jenneval ou le Barnevelt Français. Drame*, Paris, 1769. Like the English play it is written in five acts and in prose.
10. See Preface to *Jenneval* . . ., ed. cit.   11. Ibid.
12. See, for example, *Correo de los ciegos* . . ., 4 August 1787.
13. A manuscript in the Biblioteca Nacional has a licence for 1804.

minds of their own with which to puzzle and to doubt. His best scene is an interview between the strong-minded heroine and her father, in which the lady, secure in the knowledge that she has Spanish precedents, spiritedly opposes her father's idea of a suitor for her, and cannot understand, she says, why he should abuse her duty of obedience:

> . . . cómo pueda extenderse [his right to obedience] hasta recibir de su mano nuestra desgracia eterna. Si las leyes sostienen este ilimitado derecho en los padres, o son injustas, o no es el matrimonio como todos le definen. (Act I, iv)

She has even thought sufficiently along practical eighteenth-century lines to ask her father to put himself in her place and consider what would be the result of marrying in hatred:

> Yo aborrezco a Vangrey; supongo que no tengo motivos para ello: que sus cualidades sean apreciables: que puedan hacerme venturosa: ¿quién me asegura que he de vencer esta aversión, cuando me vea unida a él? (Act I, iv)

Small wonder that, when she goes away to cry, her father puts her obstinacy down to her reading:

> Son insufribles estas mocosas, en llegando a leer cuatro novelas. (Act I, v)

But the major emphasis is now on the love conflict and Jenwal's magnanimity. The trading background is mere decoration. Weaknesses of character that ruined the original Barnwell's life and career are no longer available to throw into contrasting relief the thesis-justification of trade as a public repository of moral and social responsibility. Zavala's drama is a travesty of *The London Merchant*. It moves jauntily and ends happily. Apart from the independent character of the well-read Faustina, possibly only one other feature is of interest. The hint of humour in Lillo's adventuress, Millwood, and in Lucy, her maid, which had become more decorous in Mercier, revives gustily in Zavala y Zamora's servant, Enriqueta: for instance, when her mistress begins to come round after a swoon:

> *Faustina* Jenwal cruel . . .
> *Enriqueta* ¡Qué Jenwal, ni qué cuerno! Levantaos. . . . (Act II, ii)

or in her bustling embarrassment in Act III when, having sold her possessions to help her master in his misfortunes, she refuses to discuss her sacrifice:

Faustina ¿Qué has hecho?
Enriqueta Traer luces, que estaba ya harto oscura esta pieza.

With such modifications the story of poor apprentices in love with wealthy merchants' daughters, of the hazards of commerce, with bankruptcy, imprisonment, and opportunities for displays of business-integrity and magnanimity, repeated itself in different shapes and affected more 'original' experiments. A much earlier Spanish version, though farther from Lillo's is Manuel de Ascargota's *Las ceguedades del vicio y peligros del rigor. El joven Carlos*, of 1776, arranged in five acts in verse, from the prose of Mercier, and substituting Spanish for English local colour. Valladares's *Los perfectos comerciantes* of 1782 and his *El fabricante de paños, o el comerciante inglés* of 1783, a verse impression of Falbaire's prose adaptation of Lillo, *Le Fabricant de Londres*,[14] are much farther from the original. *Los perfectos comerciantes*, a childish romance about commercial hazards among friends, villains, a ne'er-do-well, and a cultured young lady who reads *La Espectadora*,[15] can discriminate between passion and reason, and eventually marries the reformed black sheep, nevertheless is alive to the importance of the commercial ethics of *The London Merchant*. Valladares cannot develop these in dramatic debate but he blurts them out through the mouth of the merchant Don Lorenzo who refuses to sell the honour of his trade by calculated bankruptcy.

Lorenzo . . . eso sería
perdernos más. ¡Cuántas casas
llegaron a su exterminio
por esos tratos, que agravian
la conciencia, y el honor!
. . . .
El que quiebra por desgracia,
es digno de compasión;
mas quebrar con depravada

14. See Fenouillet de Falbaire de Quingey (C.G.), *Le Fabricant de Londres. Drame en cinq actes et en prose*, Paris, 1771. It was played in the same year. Valladares's version is closer in wording to Falbaire's than to a Spanish prose translation of Falbaire entitled *El comerciante inglés* of which we have seen an anonymous and undated edition of Barcelona.
15. See note 4, page 572.

433

intención, es un delito
capital, y el que lo causa
acreedor ha más castigo
que un salteador; pues quebranta
la ley del comercio; y burla
a las ajenas confianzas.
Patricio ¡Qué honradez! Ah, si así todos
los comerciantes pensaran,
¡qué feliz fuera el comercio!

El fabricante de paños o el comerciante inglés, with its office in London,
and a moonlight view in Act IV of the Thames at Westminster Bridge,
inserts into this business world another favourite foreign theme of
milords and illegitimate daughters, and presents the realistic scenes of
domestic misfortune typical of Fielding's *Amelia*. Outstanding is the
scene of the arrival of the bailiffs, when the cloth-merchant's workmen,
dressed in their aprons, walk pictorially across the stage as in a melodramatic frieze, denoting by their bowed heads and hanging arms the
helplessness of the broken firm.[16] A precocious child, common to
many sources, drives home the pathos in what is meant to be ingenuous
irony.

The prose ethics of trade therefore provided drama with another
realistic topic of conversation. Even José de Concha's *El buen criado*[17]
whose theme has rather more in common with Molière's *L'Avare* than
with *The London Merchant* hints at the commercial problem of whether
or not it is good business to economize. An anonymous *El comerciante
de Burdeos*,[18] clearly from another French adaptation of *The London
Merchant*, debates on the motion that it is degrading for a gentlewoman
to marry into commerce, and contains speeches emphasizing the worth
of commerce to the State, the public benefactions of the merchant class
and its economic superiority over the aristocracy in keeping wealth in
circulation. This stress is not quite the same as that made by the English
Thorowgood whose preoccupations were with trade as a science and
as a field of practical honour and uprightness. But trade is deliberately
invested with intellectual and gentlemanly dignity; while the practical

16. See note 5, page 572.
17. It is called a 'Pieza seria moral'. We have seen a manuscript copy of 1775. B. Nac.
18. There is an undated manuscript in the Biblioteca Nacional.

necessity experienced by the age of admitting into the society of 'gentlemen' the rich trader to whom wealth had given power, with the ideological problems of adjustment that this entailed,[19] is echoed in speeches like the following:

Dupuis. Yo me admiro que un hombre como el. . . . Baron, a quien no se le puede negar el talento pueda (?) encapricharse en una preocupación gótica de que el comercio es un estado vil. . . . Los días de la ignorancia y de la barbaridad ya han pasado.

For variety, a French shift of emphasis produced a group of dramas in which the furniture and talk of trade were reduced to a minimum and the emotional repercussions of financial hazards were extended to a perilous maximum. In these, the interest usually lies in the magnanimity of two merchant colleagues each of whom in turn comes to the rescue of his friend's business reputation by sacrificing his own fortune and honour. An obvious example is Beaumarchais's *Les Deux Amis ou Le Négociant de Lyon* which followed hard on the heels of *Jenneval* in 1770 and appeared in Spain, retaining its prose form, in a version by Domingo Botti called *Los dos amigos o sea el negociante de León*.[20]

The natural trend of French comedy in the thirties was also conducive to the establishment of domestic sensibility and the questioning of traditions. Destouches, La Chaussée, Voltaire, had been using bourgeois settings or characters and had transferred to slightly more serious drama, neither pure comedy nor tragedy, the violent revelations of identity—friends turning out to be related, fathers unexpectedly revealing themselves to long lost children, and so on—which received new values in situations of drastic domestic poverty or other prosaic misfortunes.[21] The old French obsession with the theme of a contested marriage-arrangement now often expressed itself sensationally in scenes of privation and imprisonment, and of emotional repentances or farewells that *The London Merchant* had made famous. The elaboration of the theme of domestic penury at its most exaggerated, its most French, appears in Mercier's *L'Indigent* of 1772, which begot innumerable Spanish children.

19. Compare *Sarrailh*, op. cit., pp. 236–7.
20. We have seen an undated edition of Barcelona.
21. See, for instance, Destouches's *Le Glorieux* (1732), La Chausée's *La Fausse Antipathie* (1733) or *Mélanide* (1741), and Voltaire's *L'Enfant Prodigue* (1736).

By the middle of the century Samuel Richardson and Henry Fielding had supplied the continent with its model, middle-class heroines, and a number of reformable rakes: Pamela, the well-read servant whose virtue was rather strong meat, Clarissa, a county flower dragged through the gutter as a victim of her parents' insensibility and her lover's passion; the more erring but more practical Amelia, visiting debtors' prisons, busily reforming her attractive rake of a husband and tending her needy children; the tortuous 'Mr. B.', the naughty Lovelace; the irresponsible Booth. We meet some of them in, for example, La Chaussée's *Paméla* in 1743; and if Spaniards preferred more colour and less domesticity they had an alternative version in the next decade in Goldoni's popular *Pamela* which became even more colourful in the opera, *La Buona figliuola*[22]—translated by, it has been suggested, Ramón de la Cruz, in 1765[23]—and helped to spread the fashion for the good mothers, good sons, good fathers, and good servants who are scattered sentimentally across the title-pages of so many English, French, Italian, and Spanish dramas and short stories.

Interest in the servant-mentality, at least as illustrated by that of so pretty and sensitive a maiden as Pamela, is one which the century could not let alone. Well behind the dramatic scenes a preoccupation with the equality of all men and a curiosity in the working of all types of minds was vigorously developing. But the novelist or playwright usually captured a mere sentimentalization of the political theory and produced a nauseating series of interviews between master and servant, masterfulness and proud servility, bland authority and gruff devotion, petty tyranny and dignified resistance, misunderstanding distrust and undeserved victimization—all calculated to achieve the exquisite embarrassments by which these authors liked to think they were depicting the subtleties of human sensibility. Pamela, brought before her hard master in dutifulness and distress made a fascinating model. Her letters became great source-books of stage directions:

He put on a stern and majestic air; and he can look very majestic when he pleases. 'Well, perverse Pamela, ungrateful runaway,' said he, for my first

22. See *Cecchina, ossia la Buona figliuola*, played in Venice in 1755. The libretto was composed by Goldoni who based it on his own *Pamela fanciulla*. There is a second part to the last entitled *Pamela maritata* (Sevilla, 1764, etc.). For Spanish translations see P. P. Rogers, *Goldoni in Spain*, Oberlin, Ohio, 1940.
23. See Cot. *R.X.*, pp. 69 ff.

salutation: 'You do well, don't you, to give me all this trouble and vexation?' I could not speak; but throwing myself on the floor, hid my face and was ready to die with grief and apprehension. He said, 'Well may you hide your face! Well may you be ashamed to see me, vile forward one as you are!' I sobbed, and wept, but could not speak. And he let me lie, and went to the door. . . .

In the eighties a close Spanish translation of Goldoni's *Pamela* appeared in two Parts in verse,[24] presenting in spite of picturesque modifications, the modest, self-questioning heroine of old, still shocked and ashamed, but still in love for all that with Milord Bonfil who is a softened edition of 'Mr. B.'. As was usual in plays of the Pamela-cycle, the Andrews, her rustic family, emerged from the semi-obscurity of their Richardsonian existence and came into the full limelight to radiate rustic worth and set good examples as rustic philosophers. On the other hand, Pamela's good old Scots father after Goldoni, turned out to be Count Auspingh in political exile, which naturally distracted Spanish and Italian attention from peasant values,[25] the philosophical equalizations of estate, and the social criticisms that had readily occurred to Pamela's mother in La Chaussée when she heard that her daughter was to marry into the gentry:

> Prends l'esprit de ton rang, et non pas la licence. (Act V, vii)

But it was in La Chaussée that the cynical La Jewks most conveniently summarized for playwrights the good girl's typical activities:

> Triste, dormant fort peu, ne mangeant presque rien,
> Pleurant comme une sotte, écrivant comme quatre,
> Et vous traitant toujours de cruel ravisseur. (Act I, i)

In making his translations, or recasts, the Spanish playwright took note of these qualities and missed neither La Jewks's potentialities for comic irony, nor the flippancy of this French Don Juan. The result evidently proved very actable, for the *Memorial literario*, reporting the Spanish

---

24. *La bella inglesa Pamela en el estado de Soltera, escrita en prosa italiana por el abogado Goldoni, y puesta en verso castellano: Iª Parte*, and *La bella inglesa Pamela en el estado de casada.* . . . The first part was announced in the press in 1784 and both parts in 1787. See Coe, *Catálogo* . . ., p. 27. There are also editions of Valencia and Madrid, 1796. The translator is anonymous.

25. See, for example, the Pamela-type *La Faustina*, translated and arranged from P. Napoli-Signorelli's *La Faustina* . . ., by Fermín del Rey and played in 1786. An edition of Signorelli's play had been published in Parma (in 1778) and there were other editions.

---

production of 1784, noted how each player entered into the character he represented—a feat not to be taken for granted—and said that the five days' performances had been successful.[26]

A translation of part of the original novel, in novel form, appeared in an experimental volume in 1794[27] cautiously 'accommodated' to Spanish customs, and with the promise of more volumes if the first should prove successful.[28] A gullible reviewer of the *Memorial literario* believed, apparently in all sincerity, that Richardson's aim had been to reform the depraved ways of English life, and that in *Pamela* he had merely edited a collection of real letters[29]—a popular idea at one time, no doubt, even in depraved England, but one which must have worn thin there and in most of Europe by 1794. This enterprising year, however, also saw a Spanish translation in novel form of the original *Clarissa* though this time confessedly through the French.[30] Fielding's *Amelia* followed in 1795.[31]

Another theme-group, distantly related to the Pamela-Clarissa group, centres on a poor young couple quietly bringing up their children in the rustic virtues, until one fine day an aristocratic parent of husband, or wife, discovers their retreat and, in a scene of melting tenderness, either forgives them for their elopement years before, or is forgiven by them for the parental tyranny which drove them into the wilds. Here they have learnt the lessons of pure goodness and wisdom from the local children of nature and acquired a Rousseauesque sensibility that also finds an outlet in a Spanish novel of 1793 called *El alcázar de la sensibilidad o los matrimonios felices. Anécdota de Jacinta y Estuardo.*[32] Baculard d'Arnaud's novel *Fanni, ou la nouvelle Paméla, histoire anglaise*, its English adaptation *Fanny, or the Happy Repentance*,

26. See *Memorial literario*, February 1784.
27. *Pamela Andrews, o la virtud recompensada, por Tomás Richardson [sic]: traducida al castellano y acomodada a nuestras costumbres por el traductor*, vol. i, Madrid, 1794. It is advertised in the August issue of the *Memorial literario*. The translator is anonymous.
28. Four volumes were advertised in the November issue of the *Memorial literario* of the same year.
29. See *Memorial literario*, August 1794.
30. *Clara Harlowe. Novela traducida del inglés al francés por Mr. le Tourneur siguiendo en todo la traducción original revista por su autor Richardson, y del francés al castellano por D. José Marcos Gutiérrez*, Madrid, 1794, 2 vols.
31. *Historia de Amalia Booth, escrita en inglés por el famoso Fielding, traducida al castellano por D.R.A.D.Q.*, Madrid, 1795, vol. i.
32. It appears under the writer's initials: D. J. L. T. y A.

from the French of M. d'Arnaud, published in 1767, and Marsollier's play *Richard et Sara*[33] are conspicuous members of this large family.

Heroines finding themselves in abnormal plights of moral ambiguity had an influential precedent, less tantalizing than Pamela or Clarissa, in Beaumarchais's Eugénie of the play of that name, in which the lady, who knows how to make the most of her embarrassment, learns that her supposed marriage is not legal. Spain witnessed her tortured reactions in Ramón de la Cruz's translation, *Eugenia*, made in 1772. Another fruitful source of theatrical embarrassments was Lessing's *Minna von Barnhelm* which supplied, for instance, *Los amantes generosos*, indirectly derived through the French,[34] and various other dramas with virtuous heroines exposed to ambiguities in public inns. Domestic troubles in wayside inns where opposed parties could conveniently meet by accident, were increased under the influence of Armand's *Le Cri de la Nature*, of 1769, translated as *El grito de la naturaleza*, probably by Valladares, and performed in 1784.[35] Stage-inns were not new. But in the interests of sentimentality they achieved international revival.

Amelia was adopted, apparently by Comella,[36] and probably through a French intermediary, in *El amor conyugal o La Amelia*, a play of excessive sensibility and nearer in this respect to *Pamela* or *Clarissa* than to *Amelia*. This Gallicized lady follows her husband, in man's dress, to the wars in Philadelphia, rescues him from the battlefield, and sucks poison from his wound, only to have him swooning to music through three acts and raving of having infected her. In the end it is he who unnecessarily dies on the spot, out of pure refinement of distress; and a very subtle death-performance he puts on:

33. See B. J. Marsollier des Vivetières: *Richard et Sara*. We have seen an edition of Geneva and Paris, 1772.

34. See D. G. F. R., *Los amantes generosos* 'compuesto en francés sobre un modelo alemán' by Rochon de Chabannes, Madrid, 1801. *Teatro nuevo español* (vol. iv). The French play is *Les Amants Généreux*, played in 1774.

35. The play exists in a manuscript in the Biblioteca Municipal, Madrid, licensed for 1784, and is attributed to Valladares. See also, for example, *El hallazgo venturoso y verdadera condesa* anonymously translated from the *Vera condesina* of Francesco Cerlone and played in 1788.

36. There is a manuscript copy, undated and without the author's name, in the Biblioteca Municipal. Comella is given as the author of a play of this title by the *Memorial literario* for November 1794, where the play referred to seems to coincide in its details with the anonymous drama we have seen in the Biblioteca Municipal.

Amelia se queda como aturdida, las lágrimas se le retiran sin quedarle más acción que para levantar de rato en rato los ojos al cielo, fijarlos en los de Carlos, e ir a ver si respira, y el sentimiento no le deja ejecutarlo. Carlos hace un gran extremo para alzar la cabeza con los ojos maribundos . . .

while Amelia, always the practical one, is left to make the arrangements for shipping home the corpse and her own poisoned self, prepare a double tomb in 'Hammersmith', and arrange with her father, when at last she has time for it, to die in his arms.

Edward Moore, who helped to popularize the Pamela-theme in *The Foundling* of 1748[37] which resembles it but which produces the heroine's gentle ancestry that Italy and Spain, through the Italian, preferred, which accentuates the characters' tendencies to reason analytically, or indulge in hearty rakishness of this kind:

> *Young Belmont* [replying to a suggestion that he should marry Fidelia]. And hang myself in her garters next morning, to give her virtues the reward of widowhood. Faith, I must read *Pamela* twice over first. (Act I)

and which was translated by Mme Riccoboni in 1769,[38] set a more virile fashion afoot in *The Gamester* in 1753. Since Beverley, the hero of this last play, is already married, the heroine's personal allurements are less important than those of a Pamela or a Clarissa, and her own and the hero's maturer personalities benefit accordingly. As in *The London Merchant* the realistically tragic ending after the English tradition was usually too 'strong' for foreign taste. The prison-scene where Beverley slowly dies, a suicide racked by torturing poison, taken, it transpires, with an ironic lack of necessity, was modified from version to version. But the general idea, the moral details of his loose living and repentance, the mental details of his self knowledge, some of the characters—for example, his maturely drawn wife, who was to have much influence among the more vigorous of her sex now that wives were coming to the fore—his false and true friends, some of the situations and sentiments, and the tense prison-scene, with or without the final tragedy, were very stimulating. Saurin's *Beverley*[39] of 1767, despite its overtransparent moral philosophy and chastened diction, is a close imitation. But one of *Saurin's* most unforgivable additions is Beverley's six-

37. See note 6, page 572.   38. See *Oeuvres complètes*, Paris, 1818, vol. v.
39. See also Diderot's translation and that of Bruté de Loirelle. Gaiffe, op. cit., pp. 53–4.

year-old child, Tomi, who in those times of dislodged sentiments and disorientated values lisped on the lowest level of pathos, being, though not an orphan, of the new type of dramatic infant that caused an English pamphlet satirically to conceive of a poignant tragedy introducing the whole Foundling Hospital.[40] Tomi, however, was a sturdy philosopher and preacher. A related infant type ridiculed in Moratín's *Comedia nueva*, where he insistently cried for bread at inopportune moments, we still, unfortunately, have to meet. The Tomis, whether preaching or starving, were fatally easy to imitate.

Beverley, which exaggerates the original tragedy by presenting the overwrought gambler in such a state of self-despair that he toys with the idea of killing Tomi to free him from hereditary misery, is accommodatingly supplied, on the other hand, with a spare last act, ending happily, for the kind of audience which preferred its pathos that way, and causing the obnoxious Tomi to interrupt his father as the poison-cup is at his lips. The anonymous Spanish translator in *El Beberley o el jugador inglés* which reduces the five acts to three, enterprisingly takes the tragic alternative, but, not knowing that Tomi is an interpolation, pays him much attention, for indeed in the French he is painfully conspicuous. This versified drama advertised in 1779 as a *comedia 'nueva'* did not offer itself as 'original', but, according to a note on the title-page of the licensed manuscript, it was played with the alternative title of *Estragos que causa el juego. El Beberley* 'so that it should not sound English'.[41] As Spain was going to war with England in 1779, the true nationality of the *Gamester* would not perhaps be popular. The Censor himself objected to a passage of 'bad doctrine' in Act I, not, it would seem, however, because of any English or French enlightened thinking, but because the Spanish imitation expressed itself too heatedly on the subject of love, being offensive, therefore, to the moralists who had objected to stage licentiousness.[42]

Though courageously choosing the tragic ending, this drama is an

40. Boswell, *London Journal*, ed. cit., p. 172 n. 3: 'We would suggest to Mr. Malloch the useful hint of introducing in some of his future productions the whole Foundling Hospital, which, with a well-painted scene of the edifice itself, would certainly call for the warmest tears of pity and the bitterest emotions of distress. . . .' (From *Critical Strictures on the New Tragedy of 'Elvira'* . . ., by Boswell in collaboration.)
41. '. . . porque no sonara cosa de Inglaterra.'
42. The passage is partly blocked out with paper pasted over the original verses but the general sense can be gauged from what remains.

even greater travesty of *The Gamester* and *Beverley* than is *Jenwal* of *The London Merchant* and *Jenneval*. It adds unimaginatively to the length of unimportant French speeches. For example, the nervy English:

> *Mrs. Beverley* Now, methinks, the lodgings begin to look with another face. . . . (Act I, i)

becomes a typically enumerative passage in French:

> *Mme Beverley* Ce salon que j'ai vu si richement orné,
> ses meubles, ses tableaux, ses glaces, sa dorure. (Act I, i)

and loses in garrulous Spanish verse all its remaining force:

> No era yo más venturosa
> que hoy soy, cuando estaban estas
> paredes, bien adornadas
> de ricos paños de seda,
> de pinturas, y cristales;
> pues si bien se considera:
> estos muebles que echas menos
> aborrecerlos debieras
> como invenciones del lujo,
> contra la naturaleza. (Act I)

Young Tomi, given a Gallic inch of licence, now takes a Spanish yard and turns impertinent:

> *Tomi* [to Beberley] ¿Qué le ha hecho vd. a mi madre
> que salió de aquí llorando?
> *Laureta* Calla, Tomi.
> *Beberley* Déjale
> hablar.
> *Tomi* Me das un enfado
> cuando sin razón me riñes
> que no puedo tolerarlo.
> Si en presencia de mi padre
> prorrumpiese yo algo malo
> su merced me reñirá,
> pero tú no.

Such were the dangers of a Rousseauesque education. Nor does the poison-scene improve under Spanish auspices, least of all when the

442

suicide reflects that his poison is the kind commonly used for exterminating vermin. Nevertheless, Beverley projected a strong dramatic personality and was the father of many loose-living French and Spanish characters who moralized on the badness of their own examples and the evils of society while—interrupted or not—they lifted poison-cup to lip. Another Spanish version of the *Gamester*, but showing influences of several international themes, is Manuel Fermín de Laviano's *La buena casada* of 1781,[43] in which the worthiest of wives has to contend with a gaming husband, resist the advances of a marquis, and attend to her baby in its stage-cradle. This infant seems to have been even less conducive to pathos than six-year-old Tomi, for, according to reports, the audience found it irresistibly comic.[44] Also of the style of the *Gamester* and perhaps borrowing from *The London Merchant* is Zavala y Zamora's *El bueno y el mal amigo*.[45] Sometimes the English-born sinner lent characteristics to other types of gamesters derived, not from the English play, but from more conventional dramas like Regnard's *Le Joueur*. An example of this phenomenon may be seen in *El delirio, o las consecuencias de un vicio* translated from St. Cyr by Dionisio Solís.[46]

Meanwhile, in France of the sixties, a whole cycle of edifying domestic matter was released with the publication of the collected tales of Marmontel as *Contes Moraux* examples of which had already become known separately. Though perhaps more useful as source-books for comedy,[47] they also made suggestions to writers of *drames*. They could provide semi-psychological studies popularizing the epoch's interest in the machinery of mind and behaviour. However slight, they normally indicate a potential thesis, for Marmontel was interested incidentally in problems of cause and effect though he subordinated these to a conventional organization of moral dues. The 'Bad' Mother[48] in her blind exclusive affection—which not uncommon trait gave the tale reality—idolizes one child at the expense of the rest,

43. There is a manuscript in the Biblioteca Municipal licensed for 1781.
44. See *Memorial literario*, September 1784.   45. It was performed in 1793.
46. It seems to have appeared first in 1802 and is a play with music. We have seen an edition of Valencia, 1816.
47. See Clarence D. Brenner, *Dramatizations of French Stories in the Eighteenth Century*, University of California Press, Berkeley and Los Angeles, 1947. Other important tales considered by the author as source-books of comedy are collections of Voltaire and La Fontaine.
48. See the tale, *La Mauvaise Mère* in the 3-vol. edition of La Haye, 1765–6, vol. i.

and some point is given to the resulting characters of the children. A 'Good' Mother,[49] clearly a reader of *Emile*, devotes all her energy, at the sacrifice of her own pleasure—a more revolutionary idea in the days of cheap nursemaids than it is nowadays—to the education of her little Emilie, and pilots her sensitively and persuasively through the reefs of impressionable adolescence. There is a fairly Good Father of a dissipated youth who may have been one of the prototypes of a fairly good father of the dissipated youth in Comella's *El poltrón o el indolente*.[50] A model young lady, with a Pamelan disposition to philosophize, comes from the same tale.[51] There is a good friend, imported originally from England where he was given to soliloquies and sacrifices and to pouring the cool waters of philosophical analysis over inflamed situations. He is borrowed for a self-conscious play by Ramón de la Cruz[52] in which this master so far forgot himself among foreign sentiments as to pen these vapid lines:

> *Nelson* . . . O respetable
> dulce amistad, yo te ofrezco
> conservarte sin mancilla
> en el más oculto seno
> de mi corazón.

and to blush, for a crazy moment, at the spectacle of a Europe in its uncivilized complexity as compared with the civilized simplicity of continents nearer to nature:

> *Corali* ¡Ah bárbaros europeos!
> Si el oprimir los más puros
> y sencillos sentimientos
> de naturaleza: si
> burlar el más vivo afecto,
> y desmentir las pasiones
> por los humanos respetos
> son vuestras costumbres, a ellas
> y a vosotros os detesto.

This must have been the kind of sentiment that brought the original *Contes* to the attention of the Inquisition in 1782.[53] There is a self-styled philosopher bleakly persisting in a misanthropic existence,[54] a

49. *La Bonne Mère*, op. cit., vol. i.
50. It is licensed for July 1792.
51. *L'Ecole des Pères*, op. cit., vol. ii.
52. See note 7, page 573.
53. See Sarrailh, op. cit., p. 296.
54. *Le Philosophe soi-disant*, op. cit., vol. i.

type which went back to Molière and forward to Kotzebue, and established Spanish connections, of which the most important for our purpose will be through the German, at each stage of development.

More directly influential—still in a thematic sense—is Marmontel's Oriental Soliman II of the tale of that name[55] which is related to the semi-historical story of a Christian slave-sultaness dramatized by Cervantes in *La gran sultana*. Marmontel's Soliman was to be well known on the French and English stage, though in varying guises, and sometimes was confused with the enlightened monarchs of an Orient according to Voltaire.[56] A provocative opening remark to this tale, so typical of a generation satiated by the old heroics, 'C'est un plaisir de voir les graves historiens se creuser la tête pour trouver de grandes causes aux grandes événements', is almost a challenge, and raised Peninsular response from Comella's Frederick II of Prussia who modestly tried to impress upon his stage-subjects that he too was made of flesh and blood. Stage-kings were to be famous for their little rather than for their big human motives. They were to be seen, like children to a mother's understanding, in their unprepossessing discomfiture. But that historic moment had not yet arrived.

Soliman II, who took himself more lightly than his precedent, the magnanimous Orosmane of *Zaïre*, and who went flashily into Rodríguez de Arellano's *Solimán II*[57]—a drama in 'insufferable verse' said the *Memorial literario* and without verisimilitude, characterization, manners, or morals[58]—remained nevertheless the complete gentleman. He was remembered for that fact; but also for his decorative background, his beautiful slave-girls who could sing or dance, for the lovely Roxelane who spiritedly told him what she thought of him, and for his remark on the way to the mosque for his wedding:

Est-il possible qu'un petit nez retroussé renverse los lois d'un Empire?

These were light-hearted features and were generally 'taken' in the spirit in which they were intended. At the same time the tale is not devoid of psychological subtlety and revives the French interest for analysing erotic passion, an exercise which any Spaniard was more

55. *Soliman II*, op. cit., vol. i.
56. See pp. 236 ff., above.
57. It seems to have been played first in 1793.
58. See Coe, p. 210.

445

willing to learn from *Solimán II*, or its new dramatic derivatives,[59] than from the French classics.

Zavala y Zamora's *Los desgraciados felices por Acmet el Magnánimo*, licensed in 1792, belongs to this dramatic family of noble heathen potentates betrothed or wedded to willing Christian slaves. It takes up the story where Marmontel's leaves off, and, along with the contemporary furniture of statues, fountains, and pyramids, supplies a burning mosque. But the characters' views are not, on the whole, as contemporary as the furniture. The speakers subscribe, in seventeenth-century words to the Divine Right of Kings[60]—which was prudent of them in 1792—and in spare moments they soliloquize unprovocatively on, for instance, the famous conception of sleep as the image of death. They move in a breathless atmosphere of cloak-and-sword and have less time for social thinking than the characters of *Zaïre*.[61]

Other French collections translated in the last decades provided further sources of dramatic material. An example is *Las veladas de la quinta*, twelve tales from the French of the Countess de Genlis,[62] including *El calderero, o el mutuo agradecimiento*, *El Czar Iwan*, *Snelgrave, o el poder de un beneficio, Pamela, o la adopción feliz*, which duly appeared later on the stage. A Spanish reviewer found these tales more 'moral', he said with satisfaction, than the majority of modern novels.[63] It must be remembered, however, that most reviewers erred on the side of prudishness and it must not be assumed that the Spanish Press was in the habit of issuing anything more indelicate than the slightly frivolous *Solimán II*.

The epoch's dispassionate researches into mental behaviour brought it in due course to the consideration of the peculiarities of the minds of women and the potentialities of the feminine mentality for developing along enlightened lines. Therefore, various old problems concerning women's rights and education began to present themselves from a new angle. The Spanish woman has always been a powerful force behind the scenes; and in the consciousness of her power has seldom wanted,

---

59. See, for instance, C. S. Favart's *Soliman II ou Les Sultanes*, played in 1776 and printed in Paris the same year.

60. See note 8, page 573.

61. Another play belonging to this cycle is Comella's *La buena esposa*, played in 1786.

62. This will be *Les Veillées du Château* published in several volumes in 1784.

63. See *Correo de . . . Madrid*, for 24 May 1788.

or needed, to assert it bookishly. But there were intellectuals in the Age of Reason, who, having read Locke, or *Pamela* on Locke, or *La Nouvelle Héloïse* on both, or having met some of the famous French and English hostesses of the day in their drawing rooms, studies, and laboratories, were ready to ventilate the grievances of the Spanish woman and to extend her sphere of influence. Early in the century Feijoo had pronounced energetically against the views that woman is essentially inferior to man, and he had lectured his public on her intellectual potentialities: 'su aptitud para todo género de ciencias, y conocimientos sublimes'.[64] The majority of the enlightened, however, needed more time to get used to the idea that woman could or should contribute to learning. For her own part, the Spanish woman, excusably enough, did not seem to hanker after the kind of education which made Pamela and Julie notorious. Nor did she appear to envy the French, English, and Italian women in real life who were making less pedantic reputations as hostesses in intellectual society. Her complaints were based chiefly on human grounds. Her most outstanding grievance was that her parents, like French parents, had the power, moral if not always legal, to force their daughter into a marriage against her will or to prevent her from marrying a man of her own choice. This, a long accepted evil, had been perennially exploited in drama. The Golden Age regarded it emotionally and dramatic values had been found in the contrast of the heroine's helplessness with her parents' authority, or in a comic clash of filial and parental ingenuity. But now the subject which had paid so many plot-dividends in the past was debated with fresh energy by moral and social reformers anxious to translate theory into practice, and was the livelier in their minds because legislation of 1766, and later years,[65] had endeavoured to strengthen parental authority as a means of preserving society from new disintegrating influences. So that this, making common cause with other problems of women, entered the thesis drama where self-sacrificing friends, reasoned renunciations, and the latest forms of exhibitionism, gave it a contemporary poignancy.

The traditional view of those who feared to tamper with the sacred

64. See *Teatro crítico . . .*, vol. i, 'Discurso', xvi.
65. See, for example, R. Altamira, *Historia de España*, Barcelona, 1913–14, vol. iv, pp. 133 ff.

dignity of womanliness—for that is how, by conviction, or for their greater comfort or convenience, men had regarded the limitation on women's movements—tended to produce pure comedy in which the ideal of women's emancipation and education rubbed satiric shoulders with *petimetrismo*. Here the versatile Comella, always in the forefront of fashion, took up the theme, again winning himself commendation, this time in *El abuelo y la nieta*, a 'play with music' performed in 1792.[66] It is warmly welcomed by the Censor, Pedro Centeno, for ridiculing the more extreme ideas of Rousseau—in the speech of the heroine's grandfather, for example, on the subject of acclimatizing the body to all atmospheres:

> Igualmente mande al aya
> que en verano, y en invierno,
> fuese a la hora que se fuese
> saliese a la huerta en cuerpo,
> sin resguardarla del sol,
> ni del rigor de los hielos. (Act I)

or of teaching this little child of nature to appreciate peasant values even if that meant her descending to peasant-levels. Comella may have been drawing on foreign sources. But the Censor, in referring to the play's 'models':

... verso fluido y corriente, argumento ... oportuno, y tiene tanto más de verisímil, cuanto es sobradamente común, y visibles a cada paso sus modelos. ...

was probably thinking more broadly of Iriarte's famous satire on female education, *La señorita mal criada*, performed in 1791, a play on so similar a subject that, as the *Memorial literario* remarked, *El abuelo y la nieta* could scarcely fail to coincide in some incidents 'unless it was, in fact, that Comella had deliberately copied Iriarte'.[67]

Other popular playwrights also found it a useful comic theme at least for *sainetes* or incidental scenes. Zavala y Zamora had his inevitable say on the subject in *El día de Campo* of 1793.[68] Later, the problem of the forced marriage was capably dealt with in comedy by Leandro Moratín whose *El sí de las niñas* has serious undertones. Certain advanced

66. See note 9, page 573.   67. *Memorial literario*, September 1793.
68. MS. B. Mun. The *censura* is for July 1793.

authors, looking to Mercier rather than to Molière, had already brought the questions of women's rights and grievances into full-scale problem dramas. For instance, a Spanish *Franval y Emilia* of 1785 is a prose drama recast from an Italian recast of Mercier's *Les Tombeaux de Vérone*[69] and retains most notably from the original the serious strictures on a parent's readiness to sacrifice his daughter to his selfish *pundonor*.

This domestic theme, however, was politically safe and socially dignified. In Spain, where the heroine was traditionally spirited, it evidently seemed proper even to the careful muse of the Literary Censor, Santos Díez González himself. He is credited by Moratín with a *Casamiento por fuerza* under which title there exists a manuscript of 1795 with curiously tense *censuras*.[70] Mariana, the heroine of this play, has been forced by her father into marrying a rich but excessively foolish Don Cosme, and, after a wild, despairing effort to end her married misery by taking her own life, she resigns herself to the Christian principles which forbid her to do so. The play therefore ends with a patched-up solution, notably modern, because instead of foretelling happiness for the couple ever after, it merely outlines the possibility of reasonable comfort so long as both are disposed to be tolerant, and it leaves the girl with her battle of self-discipline still in process. The moral was meant for her father. Other censors, however, to whom Santos Díez González, if he really were the author, may have sent his script anonymously, seem to have assumed that the moral lay in Mariana's acceptance, even in extreme circumstances, of her father's right to dispose of her. They objected to the title, evidently because it would appear to criticize parental authority, and to the references to suicide and her state of 'slavery'. We may remember that the Literary Censor was no enemy to stage suicides so long as they were not committed by Christians, and apparently he saw no reason why suicide, desired, but renounced on Christian grounds, should raise objections. It was natural, therefore, that when he came to write his own official *censura* for the drama he should show annoyance at his colleagues' obtuseness. With what might well be personal indignation he poured scorn on the

69. See *Vencen el rigor de un padre osadía y sumisión. O sea Franval y Emilia.* We have seen an undated edition of Barcelona. It was tortuously 'taken' from *Dorvil* of Francesco Albergati Capacelli who recast it from Mercier.

70. See the manuscript in the Biblioteca Municipal, Madrid.

censors' amended title—*El novio prudente*—which brings the foolish husband on to the side of parental rightness, and, as he said, destroys the whole point of the drama:

Su objeto (of the play) es hacer ver que la indiscreción y violencia de los padres en obligar a los hijos a tomar estado contra su voluntad, cuando ésta procede arreglada a razón, y justicia, es exponerlos a un precipicio. . . . Es menester no haber leído la comedia, o entenderla al revés para creer que un novio tan necio y malicioso y tan imprudente por su genial estupidez se llame *El novio prudente*.

Eventually the play was passed on his terms—perhaps he revealed his identity—and over the censors' corrections are firmly pasted copies of the original speeches.

The play in a quiet way is good, too tasteful to admit propaganda, but sufficiently conscious of social realities to underline the married woman's dilemma where her wishes have not been consulted, and to insert other mild, incidental hints, for example in this speech on the need for disinterestedness in making ecclesiastical preferments, in Act I:

> *Carlos* Las canongías, Señor,
> no se logran por empeños,
> el mérito solamente
> pone al sabio en candelero
> donde alumbre, y gocen todos
> el resplandor de su ejemplo.
> Al pretendiente, tan sólo
> le toca hacer manifiesto
> su mérito; y nunca debe
> echar mano de otros medios.

It also responds to the operatic atmosphere of the times—Santos Díez González was not unsympathetic to dramatic music[71]—by making room for a song; so that when the maid-servants fold their linen in Act I they do it, as in a Goldoni-*libretto*, rhythmically to music.

Earlier, in his heroic *El sitio de Calés* of 1790 Comella had already stated the general principle of women's natural rights through his Margarita, who, at one point, talks like a potential suffragette:

71. See *Instituciones poéticas* [Madrid, 1793], p. 141.

Siendo los seres iguales
que existen en nuestros cuerpos,
¿por qué causa han de gozar
los hombres más privilegios
que las mujeres? (Act I)

And although it is true that the privilege she claims on this occasion is the heroic right to die with the men in battle, and although her logic is blurred by emotion, she shares with several Comellan heroines the distinction of recognizing social anomalies relating to women, and of asking pertinent social questions.

The Censor appears to have been deeply interested in the subject of this drama. The growing idea of improving the education of women and the revolutionary change in moral and social values that this entailed was a pleasing challenge to the enlightened. He had previously commended even Comella for elaborating on the theme in *El matrimonio por razón de estado*, played to celebrate the Queen's birthday in 1792. The irony of his remarks on the unfortunate results of State marriages, was not, one must assume, intentional:

. . . se representan las malas resultas de los casamientos que se hacen, no por voluntad sincera, sino por otras miras ajenas de la cristiandad de un contrato, que ha de elevarse a sacramento. . . .[72]

Sensibility as a cult sprang from the methodical mind of France and was logic carried to excess. It had become imperative to re-open the study of the nature of man, though the epoch, Rousseau included, conceived of 'nature' and 'naturalness' as something much more moral, principled, and disciplined than we do, and in the spirit of the Encyclopedia expected man to function according to definable impulses. But it was not enough, the keener spirits felt, merely to catalogue the outward acts and sayings of the ordinary 'human being'. He must be surprised, somehow, into betraying his undeclared motives and emotions. Moralists being in the ascendant, current theories assumed that intelligent persons should be able to deduce the ulterior meaning of man's complex self-expression to the last degree of its moral implication. The observer's reason was supposed to subtilize his perceptions, his perceptiveness to give to his moral receptivity that sublime *finesse* which was the eighteenth-century ideal of superior feeling.

72. See Censura for 8 December 1792.

Aspects of man's naturalness were therefore the dramatist's subjects of demonstration. But to reproduce selected naturalness in a delicately natural way was not as easy as it looked. Talma, an advocate of English dramatic methods, had vigorously discussed that fact in his *Réflexions* ...[73] 'Plus le pinceau devait être naturel', said Mercier in his Preface to *Jenneval*, 'plus il demandait a être manié avec art'. And Santos Díez González, asserting, in 1789, that actors objected to tragedy on the ground that it required too much 'naturalidad', went on to say as a corollary that tragedy required 'too much art and knowledge for the expression of the affections'.[74] French playwrights, after the first tests, usually had the honesty, an attractive quality of the period, to admit their inadequacy. As we have seen, it led them to study a foreign art of the theatre, to decide that a declamatory style was not invariably the best style even for High Tragedy. Now it led them to experiment in close domestic interiors.

This is the ideological context of Diderot's *Le Fils Naturel* of 1757, which tried to supply the inhibited Dorval with a delicately adjusted system of feeling and then make it work in suggestive indirectness. This too is the explanation of Diderot's elaborate stage directions which are intended to produce the effect, not merely of sensibility, but of sensibility naturally interpreted. Europe was much impressed: for it is always easier to appreciate the symptoms of one's own age when they have been exteriorized in formulae. Spain, which had paid little heed to Montiano when he pleaded for human naturalness in High Tragedy, when he saw the vague shadows of the future, was now ready to study the art of expressing naturalness artificially, with the male starts and head-clasping and the female swoons and hysterics believed to be illustrative of intense domestic feeling. Not that playwrights in this respect were departing altogether from real life. It is true that women do not, and assuredly did not, need, even when tightly laced, to faint and shriek in moments of distress. But as a matter of exhibitionism or judicious policy they often did; some of them still do. Since woman, veiled by the mysteries of her semi-retirement, was considered the more sensitive being, the fashionable man, the artist, the gullible intellectual, the young dilettante found it logical to believe that delicacy of feeling was most naturally expressed in some of the affectations that

73. Ed. cit.　　　74. *Informe*, ed. cit., p. 203.

women, for their own good reasons, saw fit to parade. The sensitive hero, then, behaved as the playwright saw certain sensitive young men behaving, and as he believed that a man of highly trained perception ought ideally to behave.

The historical importance of *Le Fils Naturel* lies largely in its stage directions. The instructions for producing a studied, nervous intensity are manifestations of the now self-conscious desire to suggest feelings too deep and delicate for words. 'We speak too much in our dramas',[75] said the author; though he had allowed for plenty of discussion in his own play, for example, on heredity, man's instinct for order, the forming of children's character by parents, and so on; moreover he had rightly allowed time for characters engaged in discussion to convince or fail to convince one another, and for attitudes of mind to form themselves gradually. But to compensate for his characters' full-length arguments when reason drove them to argue, he had filled the emotional scenes, particularly those between friends remodelled from *The London Merchant*, with stammerings and awkward silences, with wild words repeated in different tones, with agitated pacings up and down, and with sensitive weeping:

Clairville . . . se jette dans le sein de son ami. Il y reste un moment en silence. Dorval verse quelques larmes sur lui, et Clairville dit . . . d'une voix basse et sanglottante. . . . (Act II)

or:

Clairville regardant Dorval avec ces yeux, Dorval ne peut les soutenir. Il détourne la tête, et se couvre le visage avec les mains. . . . (Act III)

Further, it may be remembered to what greater pantomimic lengths Diderot was prepared to go when, waxing ever more enthusiastic in the third 'Entretien' on the *Fils Naturel*, he imagined it as a potential tragedy with Dorval falling, in slow motion, on his sword, and those who discover him 'crying out, weeping, falling silent and crying out again'. These were the influential novelties which accompanied the victim of illegitimacy on his European rounds and kept the theme-family intact.

Le Fils Naturel was translated and published in 1787, unfortunately in

75. See *Entretiens sur 'Le Fils Naturel'*, ii.

verse, by Bernardo María de Calzada.[76] Apart from abridgements for practical convenience, or a few judicious cuts and modifications: for example the substitution of the harmless word 'capricho' for the provocative 'fanatisme' in Constance's

'Je connais les maux que le fanatisme a causés. . . .'[77]

or the omission of references to unenlightened times when the 'monster' barbarously advanced with sword in hand invoking the name of God,[78] the original is conscientiously followed even to the inclusion of the long, unSpanish scene of exhaustive argument in Act IV. So that although the translation lost the prose-intensity in its prosaic metre it demonstrated the essentials of Diderot's experiment.

His *Père de Famille*, as baldly translated by Villarroel,[79] possibly suffers more, for the author of *La Religieuse* paused here deliberately to condemn what he, though not Spaniards, considered the barbarity of monasticism; and Cécile's suggestion in Act II that she should go into a convent provoked talk about 'living tombs', 'prisons', and the pathetic sighs of innocents immured in silence. A note attached to the translation explains that some passages have been suppressed in order to shorten the play, and others 'for more serious reasons'.[80] These last, as one would expect, include the strictures of Cécile's father on monastic 'uselessness'. Instead, the Spanish Père de Famille limits himself to criticizing the unwisdom of entering a convent without a vocation: the only argument indeed that would be reasonable to a Spanish audience.

Much more surprisingly the translation ignored the melodramatic repetition of the Father's half-crazed 'Rends-moi mon fils . . . rends-moi mon fils', as the boy, following Diderot's careful directions reluctantly moves away from him in Act IV. Probably the explanation was that the translator needed to abbreviate. But he was strangely unperceptive not to notice the dramatic force of the repeated *cri de coeur*. External effects tended to grow in translation rather than to diminish.

Another French play of those years to make a European impression

76. *El hijo natural, o pruebas de la virtud. Comedia en prosa de Diderot. Puesta en verso por . . .*, Madrid, 1787. Diderot's discourses are not included.

77. Act IV.   78. Ibid.

79. *El padre de familias*, by L. M. de Villarroel, Madrid, 1785. There is a copy in the Biblioteca Nacional.

80. 'Se han suprimido algunos pasajas, así por abreviar la comedia, como por otras razones más serias, que se pueden ver en el original.'

was Voltaire's sentimental *L'Ecossaise* of 1760, translated, into prose, by Tomás de Iriarte for the Sitios, and into octosyllabic verse by, apparently, Ramón de la Cruz.[81] It is true that Voltaire's exiled Scot, 'Monrose' disappoints our expectations of Highland vitality, but there is a hearty English merchant who, trying to force the distressed heroine to accept his financial help, is shocked to hear that she has misinterpreted his motives:

> Rassurez-vous, mademoiselle, je ne vous aime point de tout.

and who supplies the shy Northern bluffness which was then becoming a fashionable foil to the *finesse* of the man of sensibility. In translation neither all of these features nor all the incidental reflections on life and letters were pruned away. Iriarte, in Arandan times and in Sitios precincts, was able to translate with all the greater freedom for the fact that Voltaire was then thought to be merely the editor of the play. But even in the revised verse edition published for a wider public the original sentiments, which in any case were fairly harmless, did not greatly suffer. Perhaps the most notable change is the substitution in Act I for a direct attack on State policy:

> *Un autre.* Je me soucie bien d'une pièce nouvelle. Les affaires publiques me désespèrent; toutes les denrées sont à bon marché; on nage dans une abondance pernicieuse. . . .
>
> *Frélon.* . . . L'auteur est un sot, et ses protecteurs aussi; les affaires publiques n'ont jamais été plus mauvaises; tout renchérit; L'Etat est anéanti. . . .

of a more harmless and generalized piece of human grumbling:

> Lo que más cuenta me tiene
> es que los víveres vayan
> caros; porque es perniciosa
> en el día la abundancia. . . .
>
> . . .
>
> *Freydon* El autor es un idiota,
> y un salvaje quien le alaba.
> Los negocios no han estado
> en disposición tan mala
> jamás. Todo se encarece
> y en siglos no se abarata. . . .

81. See Cot. *R.X.*, p. 107. We have seen an anonymous, undated, verse edition of Barcelona which appears to correspond to Cotarelo's description.

English themes had been heavily watered down by the tears of Gallic sensibility before they reached the Pyrenees, but the theses of Louis Sebastien Mercier, himself greatly influenced by English ideas, took a vigorous form of propaganda, so topical, so realistic, and, in the humiliated Peninsula of the time of Carlos IV, so expressive of Spaniards' discontent, that it powerfully informed the minds of popular playwrights even, as will be seen later, where these were not free to reproduce their liberal-tainted ideas directly. Among the most openly imitated of Mercier's plays was the relatively innocuous *Le Déserteur* of 1771, with its sentimental theme of the deserter tried by his own father and recognized by him at an emotional point in the drama; with the atmospherics of alternating drum-beating and silence, and the lightly rakish jocularity of the deserter's friend, Valcourt.

Even this effusion of picturesque pathos, however, was not lacking in incidental criticisms against the conduct of public affairs; for example in this speech:

Eh bien! que pouvons-nous y faire, mon cher M. Hoctau? Depuis qu'une furie militaire agite les nations, que les souverains se sont un jeu de la guerre, tous les peuples tour à tour, attaquent et se défendent. La marche de ces armées ne se règle point d'après nos avis. Payons en silence, voilà notre lot; heureux si par ce moyen nous échappons aux horreurs qui nous environment. (Act I, i)

which a Spanish translator[82] turned into language that discreetly left the 'sovereigns' secure in their dignity and authority:

> Señor mío, a los vasallos
> de honor, prudencia y talento,
> sólo les toca callar,
> y pagar; el movimiento
> y marcha de los soldados,
> no se hace al arbitrio nuestro,
> si no al de los soberanos,
> que son absolutos dueños.

Needless to say, much of Mercier's genuine force of argument is dissipated elsewhere into wordiness. One gathers, on the other hand,

82. *El Desertor . . . escrita en francés por M. Mercier. Traducida . . . por D. . . .*, Madrid, 1793. This would appear to be an edition of Olavide's translation advertised by the *Memorial literario* on its performance at the Cruz in 1789. See the number for May 1789.

that the drama's military flourishes made a notable impression and that it was performed with a great show of what the *Memorial literario*, who called it the 'first military play in the modern style', described as 'comparsas de soldadescas, tambores, pífanos etc.'.[83]

Branching out of this theme are tense soldierly dramas of all sorts with killing or insubordination for honour's sake, with embarrassing court martials, sensational death-sentences delivered by a parent obliged to judge his son, or a son obliged to sentence his father; with last messages and prolonged farewells, lugubrious scenes at the scaffold, friendly sacrifices, wifely hysterics, and last-minute reprieves. The group is marked by its dramatization of embarrassment which, maudlin as it looks to us, was meant to suggest the refinement of sensibility that the age attributed to the mentally cultivated. One such example in the anonymous *Los cuatro días tristes del Sargento Grinedal* which, with some variation of contributing circumstances, makes much of the prison-scene, the sentence and the reprieve, was so reasonable and sober that the Literary Censor—ironically enough, for he does not seem to have recognized a French or Franco-German origin despite the drama's gallicisms, later noted by the *Memorial literario*[84]—could describe it as worthy, on the whole, of the cultured stage.[85]

L'Indigent, which appeared in 1772, was much more outspoken than *Le Déserteur*, and its strong criticism of the idle rich and the arrogance and selfishness of the powerful could scarcely be given free circulation in later times in Spain when María Luisa had made herself notorious for her love of luxury and Godoy for his arrogant ambition. Even under the liberal Carlos III certain of the arguments, on passing into Spanish in 1782,[86] softened their propagandist tone by the use of slightly different wording, and Mercier's De Lys was converted from a general social menace into a particular villain. In acting copies some risky sentiments are marked to be omitted: for instance in Act I this free variation on Mercier's theme that the undeserving rich are wasting the substance of the deserving poor:

83. Op. cit.   84. See *Memorial literario*, September 1789.
85. See note 10, page 573.
86. See the anonymous *La pobreza con virtud nunca queda sin premio. La costurera*, MS. B. Mun. It has a licence for 1782. It is probably the same as the play advertised by the *Memorial literario* in September 1786, as translated by Francisco Flores Gallo, with the slightly different title *La pobreza con virtud al fin encuentra su premio. La costurera*.

Mas no es mucho; pues se ve
por repetida experiencia,
que no se sabe apreciar
aquello que poco cuesta;
y caudales adquiridos
sin la preciosa molestia
del propio sudor, no pueden
tener jamás subsistencia.

At the same time Simón, the poor worker, who has been moralizing with comparative intention on the virtue of working by the sweat of the brow, destroys this idea of the dignity of work by the wistfulness with which he remembers that the accomplishment of embroidering, now earning him his living, had been acquired for recreation in the happier days when his family could live a life of ease. For the honest Spanish, and indeed, French or English ideal, was not so much equality of work as equality of leisure. In strange contrast to the cynical denouements of modern domestic dramas, the average solution to the problems of the hero-worker was to find him unexpectedly a rich, or at least noble parent, and let him thankfully turn his back on sordid manual labour. The French Revolution was still some years distant and the problem of reforming mankind still seemed an exclusively moral one.

Unhappily this meant, in the irresponsible dramatic context of eighteenth-century Spain, that as *L'Indigent* turned into Spanish it lost its thesis value and so its opportunity for experimenting in ideas, and shifted all the emphasis to obvious features of sentimentality: the intensive miseries of the loving brother and sister, as, cold, and starving, they work all night at their craft; their inability to sell their wares; the tyranny of their heartless landlord, who, seeing that they can not pay for their lodging, lets it to a rich man for his dogs; their purchase with their last earnings of a cloak for their old father who shivers in a debtors' prison; their resistance to the rich man's attempts on the girl's virtue. The climax when 'brother' and 'sister' are found to be unrelated, and the girl an heiress, and the denouement when the rich young rake flings himself penitently into the arms of his uncle, formerly the shivering prisoner, were naturally destined to bring out the worst in all who touched this theme.

The translator also entered wholeheartedly into the new French language of silence and gesture. While the 'sister' takes her over-earned rest at the beginning of Act I and her 'brother' goes on with her work, music and clapping resound ironically from the regions where the rich young man is expensively enjoying himself. But there are startling reversions to the senseless jauntiness of the Bazo-ridden sixties, especially in such chorus-effects as this:

> *Simón* Adiós.
> *Jacinta* Adiós.
> *Los dos* Y él permita
> dar luz a nuestras tinieblas. (Act I)

In fact at one point in Act IV 'father', 'brother', and 'sister' can even bring themselves to speak in trio.

The gay dog, De Lys, becomes less intelligent in Spanish. The telling details in argument which make debate sound lifelike turn casually into summarized generalities. Mercier's leisurely movement, giving time for the natural development of incidental ideas, is speeded up. It might seem as if nothing progressive were left. But it must be remembered that health lay in the domestic drama's passiveness. So far Spanish domestic drama was unoriginal. But it was the only form of drama into which modern ideology could be poured. Its emptiness was more valuable than the traditional fullness of High Tragedy. That social debate and new public ideals or problems could go well into Spanish when used by an intelligent artist was already proved by *El delincuente honrado*.

Mercier's *Le Juge* does not seem to have been translated directly during the century. But its quiet reasoning, its revolutionary propaganda on the equal rights of man, and—more regrettably—the 'five or six' children of the last act and the violent revelation of identity, had their effects indirectly. What no popular playwright was yet able to dramatize, however, perhaps because spectators would not let him, was an impression of the natural pace of thinking and reasoning. Even today, only select audiences have the patience to let dramatic characters develop their thoughts at natural intervals. The average audience did not, and does not, want the trouble of relating for itself what was said in one scene with what may be deduced in another in order to find its own answer. And popular authors could not live by catering for minorities.

In 1789, when repentant rakes and hypersensitive working girls, lisping innocents, and a few bluff men of common sense had been rubbing enlightened shoulders in ambiguous English and French circumstances for several decades, Kotzebue produced a composite impression of the ideas they represented in *Menschenhass und Reue*. Literary Germans were to have an effect on Spain's nineteenth-century Romantic movement. But the languorous aspect of a *Werther*-theme, for instance, would never make much appeal in any form of Spanish literature, and in the eighteenth century a suicidal hero of a Christian age would neither have appealed to the public nor would have been approved by the Censors.[87] For the time being it was the third-rate and even subliterary German authors who crossed the Pyrenees, and of their number Kotzebue was undoubtedly the most presentable. The triumph of his *Menschenhass und Reue* is largely explained by the fact that he was able to enhance the favourite features of Low Tragedy, as he knew it, with picturesque details of landscape, technical tricks of atmosphere, and new refinements in histrionics. In fact he did for bourgeois drama, albeit a little more thoughtfully, what opera had done for High Tragedy.

Here we have a grand landscape showing a castle in the distance, and, in the foreground, the hut of the brooding misanthrop—not a little reminiscent of the cottage of the boorish Rousseau at the Hermitage in the Park of La Chevrette. Within the castle is a sensitive, accomplished lady, befriended by the owners and shrouded in genealogical mystery, loving country solitude as fashion required, rising early to see the oxen yoked, in a scene that looks like the morning sequel to Gray's *Elegy*, and playing Mozart sonatas. There are violent revelations of identity, and reconciliations brought about by infants crying piteously 'Mother . . . father . . . dear mother . . . dear father . . .'. But there is also a narrated dog whose fidelity is insisted upon with Northern *tremolo*. Further, there is an idiot, more promising than the dog and probably 'taken' from the witless society in Shakespeare, chasing his butterflies while others sob and storm, gibbering to himself, ineffectually shouting and shouting, we are told, when the Count falls into the water off-stage, and shouting again by association of ideas when he recounts this incident. Less Shakespearian or Rousseauesque are the Chinese bridge, the ruins,

87. There is a dramatic version, *El Verter, o El abate seductor*, of Valencia, 1817, in which the suicide has disappeared.

460

and such other furniture as we come upon in the statue-strewn, cave-studded, and wilderness-fringed gardens of the times, from Walpole's Strawberry Hill or 'Aspasia's' pleasure grounds, to the 'savage place' of Kubla Khan.

But seemingly most impressive of all to contemporaries was the big confession-scene when the accomplished playerof Mozart lifts the veil from her mysterious past to disclose to her friend and benefactor at the castle her sin of abandoning her husband and children to follow a lover, and the story of her haunting repentance. It is noteworthy that her friend, if shocked, is sympathetic, for her generation, brought up, vicariously, with redeemable scamps like Lovelace, whom she mentions in all naturalness, and ambiguous adventuresses like Amelia, was interested in mixtures of virtue and vice and liked to appear intelligent enough to keep an open mind. Significant too is the fact that, while incidental morals are not too self-righteously insisted upon, final dues are distributed strictly according to moral convention; and that, after another big scene of repentance and farewell between the sinner and her newly discovered husband, the misanthrop, a grand reconciliation is eventually stage-managed by the children. Grand-scale repentance had a double value. It gave moral justification to the dramatic use of a multitude of interesting sins, and, in consequence, it put dramatic life into virtue, which the century hitherto had reduced to a state of such flabby imbecility that no artistic purpose could be served by it. Besides, most audiences of this affectedly genteel and decorous century were unaffectedly glad to be shocked.

As in *Le Fils Naturel*, the dramatic effect of the scene of repentance depended wholly on movement and posture, especially at the moments of most exquisite embarrassment—for example when Kotzebue's inhibited husband and wife, meeting after their long separation, in fear and suspicion, seem ironically to be shaping this opportunity for reunion into a preface for a final parting:

Beider Hände liegen in einander, beider Blicke begegnen sich wehmüthig. Sie stammeln noch ein Lebewohl! und trennen sich, aber indem sie gehen wollen, stösst Eulalia auf dem kleinen Wilhelm, und Meinau auf Malchen.

This drama was translated in 1800, with certain modifications, chiefly made for the purpose of shortening the discursive scenes, by Dionisio

461

Solís who reduced the five acts to three and turned the prose into verse.[88] He was deeply impressed, he said in a Preface, with the pathos of Kotzebue and considered that it was admirably conveyed in Spanish by the tones and attitudes of the actors Pinto and Rita Luna. What he did not say was that he knew the pathos of Kotzebue through the French of Mme Molé, with whose aid he had so transformed this drama that, as the *Memorial literario* complained,[89] the German author might hardly recognize it as his own work.[90] The part of the misanthropic Baron seemed to Solís particularly subtle and complex. And although a modern critic would scarcely agree with him on this point, the part would certainly call for much of the artificially 'natural' movement and posture that the period found enthralling.

Solís revised the witlessness of Peters—a much more promising character than the Baron—because, he said, the part seemed ridiculous; but he appreciated the idea of introducing scenes of humorous relief, and turned Peters accordingly into a *gracioso*. He followed the potential complexities of character in the gruff, kind-hearted Baron who was in the popular German tradition of gruff, kind-hearted characters[91] perhaps derived from England. He cut down some of the effusions on the joys of country life, possibly because he did not feel those joys himself, or had not read that he ought to. He omitted the references to Mozart and Lovelace, doubtless for similar reasons. But he played up the 'big' scenes and was happy to tell us how heartily Spanish audiences had wept —if not quite so heartily, it must be added, as they laughed when the play was parodied some months later by Miñano in *El gusto del día*.[92]

Low Tragedy like High Tragedy took some of its trappings from Shakespeare. Lugubrious graveyards made fashionable in the rest of the continent by productions of *Hamlet*, were not popular with Spaniards who did not, and do not, care for concentrated horror. But characters of assorted virtues and vices stimulated the Spaniard's imagination. Interest in the philosophical soliloquy was attaining the proportions of

88. See *Misantropía y arrepentimiento. Arreglado a nuestro teatro*, Madrid, 1800.
89. See *Memorial literario*, October 1801.
90. See note 11, page 573.
91. See Bruford, op. cit., on J. C. Brandes's *Der Graf von Olsbach*. This play was translated, in prose, as *El Conde de Olsback*, by A. García Arrieta, according to Moratín, and published in 1802. See Coe, p. 51.
92. See pp. 505 ff. below.

a cult and was acquiring some of the mannerisms which the comprehensive *Critic* had satirized in England:

Puff. Now, sir, your soliloquy—but speak more to the pit, if you please—the soliloquy always to the pit, that's a rule. (Act III, i)

Foreign importations, figuring on the majority of Spain's playbills between 1800 and 1808, were further characterized by metereological atmospherics of English origin; landscapes of Ossian; garden decorations of French and English mansions; sophisticated castle-interiors from Italian opera; and lectures on education, civics, morals, and, sometimes, religious toleration, from Voltaire and Rousseau. Assiduous importers were, for example, Féliz Enciso Castrillón whose *Los dos ayos*—to mention one of perhaps a hundred of his pieces—was taken from Fabre d'Eglantine and played in 1802; Francisco del Plano, whose *La orgullosa*, from Destouches, was played in 1801; and José María Carnerero whose *La novicia o la víctima del claustro* of 1810 was taken from Monvel. There is an anonymous *Pablo y Virginia* of 1800. There are fantasies from Kotzebue and Pixérécourt, and innumerable versions of other foreign favourites. Some playwrights, like Dionisio Solís, translator of *Romeo and Juliet* and Alfieri's *Orestes*, showed a taste even determinedly eclectic. But in one way or another, nearly all playwrights of those years depended directly or indirectly on foreign subject matter.[93]

Threading a casual way through all the solemn theme-groups went an irresponsible English story which, in the innocence of its play, touched the epoch's sociological consciousness and influenced all forms of dramatic thinking.

It originated, for practical eighteenth-century purposes, in a merry little composition of 1737, by Robert Dodsley, jauntily called *The King and the Miller of Mansfield* and based on an old ballad.[94] The potential force of a disarming, playful style, when the subject it lightly touches happens accidentally to coincide with an epoch's serious thinking, can be enormous. Debate in a straightforward thesis drama may become exhausting. It may sap the audience's energy of interest. But sauciness takes men unawares and finds them at their most vulnerable. This play-let is a trifle; but it helped to encourage, may even have started, the

93. See Cot. *Máiquez, passim.*
94. This ancient ballad is included in the Percy *Reliques.*

fashion for a genre quite unlike itself—that is, the cumbersome but important eighteenth-century military thesis drama, in which Comella at the other end of Europe and of the century did his worst and best.

The most notable feature of the English comedy is the exposure of a king,[95] incognito, to the careless criticism of a frank peasant. And while kings in the old, heroic sense were growing unfashionable, kings exposed to embarrassments, or brought, if only momentarily and wishfully, to the human level of commoners, were sure of interested acceptance. Doubtless an ordinary sense of irony has kept folk-tales of kings in circulation in all countries. All countries must have been able to supply their local stories of the almost inevitable embarrassments suffered by escaping royalty in times of civil war. There were folk-kings who let cakes burn and were scolded for it by shrewish housewives. There were kings or princes who hid in oak-trees; who were smuggled out of political difficulties in the disguise of serving maids; who, like Henri IV of France were the centre of stories of magnanimity; or who, like Pedro el Justiciero, or Juan II of Castile, went reprehensibly gadding and revelling by night as commoners and heard in their junketings, so the stories go, many an unpalatable home-truth.

The idea, then, was not English only. Many an author who borrowed the popular *King and the Miller of Mansfield* or its French version, *Partie de Chasse de Henri IV*, of 1766, could supply additional details from his own country's folk tales. Nevertheless the English playlet, with its sequel, *Sir John Cockle at Court*, had certain favourite features which kept re-appearing abroad, often with verbal echoes of the English. Conspicuous among these features is the casual, optimistic tone, holding no hint of sentimentality or even of sensibility. That was subject to change. Others are the characters: the diffident, receptive king lost in the chase and unrecognized by the poaching peasants; the jolly miller, with his democratic views which tickled the political susceptibilities of France, and with his startling downrightness; the miller's son, in love with a girl who has been seduced by a lord; and the miller's homely womenfolk. Incidental reflections and some ironic repartee were often 'taken' wholesale; for instance, the king's prose soliloquy on kingship in Sherwood Forest:

95. In the ballad of the *Reliques* it is Henry II, and the action takes place in Sherwood Forest.

I am lost, quite lost indeed. Of what advantage is it now to be a king? Night shows me no respect: I cannot see better, nor walk so well, as another man. What is a king? Is he not wiser than another man? Not without his counsellors I plainly find . . . Well, in losing the monarch, I have found the man.

the miller's comment on court life, used here, the tone suggests, with no ulterior motive:

King. I am not used to lie, honest man.
Miller. What, do you live at Court, and not lie! That's a likely story indeed.

his refusal to become familiar with people 'before I know whether they deserve it or not'; his views on manners:

Miller. Now I think the more compliments the less manners.
King. I think so too. Compliments in discourse, I believe, are like ceremonies in religion; the one has destroyed all true piety, and the other all sincerity and plain-dealing.

his proud refusal to accept money; or, more particularly, his rebuke to the king for addressing him familiarly in the second person:

Miller. Prithee don't thee and thou me . . .
King. Sir, I beg your pardon.

which Mercier borrowed in the second act of *L'Indigent*. The final scene when the king's men arrive and his identity is revealed, to the miller's confusion, though not to his discredit in the eyes of the king who dubs him knight and rights the wrongs he has heard about, was the normal climax in all derivatives. But it is the subsidiary incidents, which also crossed the Channel and the Pyrenees, that preserve the identity of the original in its imitations. The scene where, the king ignored, the miller's family hangs on the words of the son of the house who has recently returned from London and satirically describes the life at court; the popular scene in which the women tell ghost stories and so frighten themselves that they are afraid to answer the door, proclaim Dodsley's influence in many a folk king-tale of the day where all other 'miller' features are transformed. The songs, like 'How happy a state does the miller possess', tended to be increased in imitations, many versions becoming more truly classifiable as comic opera.

In the English play everything is subordinated to the humour, and the jovial miller has little in common with his democratic descendants. The same is true of the sequel, *Sir John Cockle at Court*, the humour of which is naturally based on the successes of the first part and becomes more self-conscious.

The King and the Miller of Mansfield, Gaiffe tells us, was included in a volume of English pieces published in France in 1756.[96] In 1762 it was used by Sedaine in the semi-operatic *Le Roi et le Fermier* which was privately performed for the entertainment of a learned Basque society about 1772,[97] and it was converted by Charles Collé into *La Partie de Chasse de Henri IV* published in 1766. Of these the nearer to Dodsley's, despite its French setting, is the second, for Sedaine, who keeps the English setting, assumes the miller's death, concentrates on the love-story of the miller's son Richard, and adds a picturesque storm-scene. It was in the preface to this play that Collé declared his intention of showing the 'hero in undress',[98] an idea which accounted for more bad drama in France and Spain than he could have imagined. That he should find it necessary not only to apologize for substituting 'familiar' for 'heroic' language, but to instruct the actors to avoid a declamatory style, is also noteworthy. Actors of the sixties did not take the familiar rendering of familiar words as a matter of course.

Collé used Dodsley's play, with all its popular details, as a complex incident in a French historical context: the scenes with the frank, bluff miller, including the one in which the king is forbidden to use the second person singular; the victimized peasant-girl, now rather Pamelan in her virtue; the 'ghost'-scene; the songs; the king's monologue. But Collé has the king mildly flirting with the daughter of the house, and that feature on the journey across the Pyrenees became permanently added to the story, together with other details of the French historical tale into which Dodsley's play was transplanted. Moreover, there is a strong tendency in Collé for the gay irony of the original to deteriorate into sentimentality, and for the most popular features to become ex-aggerated. It was naturally in their Gallic form that such features crossed the frontier into Spain.

The Peninsula had its own folk-equivalents of the King-and-the-

96. F. Gaiffe, *Le Drame en France au XVIIIᵉ Siècle*, Paris, 1910, p. 52.
97. See Sarrailh, op. cit., p. 230, 1.
98. See '*Avertissement*' to *La Partie de Chasse* . . . , ed. cit., p. vii.

Miller, or Alfred-and-the-cakes episodes. The eighteenth century re-membered a native version, for example, in Matos Fragoso's *El sabio en su retiro y villano en su rincón. Juan Labrador* where the hunting king is Alfonso el Sabio, 'menos cazador que amante', and given to semi-philosophical speeches deprecating his title of 'wise'. The Spanish play has much in common with the English ballad and drama, and France probably knew all three. Indeed the *Memorial literario* of 1803 quotes Batteux as saying that *Consini y Enrique IV*, which came from *La Partie de Chasse . . .*, was derived from *El sabio en su retiro*.[99] The French liked the amorous attributes of this 'sabio'-king. Perhaps they also liked the aggressive individualism of the gruff peasant-protagonist who is a heavier edition of the Mayor of Zalamea:

> Que yo también, si se mira,
> soy sabio en mi retiro,
> soy rey de aquesta alquería . . . (Act I)

Maybe his praise of natural solitude suited their modern mind:

> ¡Amada soledad mía!
> Sólo tu silencio adoro,
> sólo tu quietud me alivia . . . (Act I)

But if the original English and Spanish king-plays and ballads crossed each other's paths in France they are, in their own countries, parallel rather than related. The ideas are similar, the situations and most of the sentiment different. The point at which they most nearly approach each other is where the English miller rebukes the King for his familiar form of address and where the Spanish farmer rebukes Alfonso for deferring to him at table:

> *Juan Labrador* Excusada
> es aquesa ceremonia,
> por no decir ignorancia,
> mandarme sentar a mí;
> vos estáis en mi posada,
> os toca el obedecerme
> sin que repliquéis palabra;
> sentaos vos, porque yo solo
> puedo mandar en mi casa. (Act II)

99. See Coe: *Catálogo . . .*, p. 50.

However, when Ramón de la Cruz wrote *La molinera espantada* he was drawing, through *La Partie de Chasse . . .*, on the English and *Le Roi et le Fermier*. The proof is in the mill-milieu and the ghost-episode, taken in conjunction with some of the characteristic episodes of plain-spokenness always attached to the folk-king versions. Cruz's play is a kind of sequel to *The King and the Miller of Mansfield*, and was not, apparently, derived directly from the English, for, as in Sedaine, who does not use the ghost-scene, the Miller is dead, and the ghost-scene with the alarming knocking at the door, which Collé had popularized, becomes the central action, though the ghost is supposedly that of the miller himself. Cruz was too imaginative not to make the story his own. In converting his ironical sources into a taut *sainete* he was in his element and—doubtless unknowingly—he came much nearer to the irresponsible spirit of the original than either Sedaine or Collé.

But other Spaniards took the English, French, or Hispano-Gallic model more seriously. It lent itself to the self-righteousness, to the political and social tendencies in contemporary thinking; and that is its main connection with the *drame*. In Spain its influence was indirect and dispersed rather than · immediately derived, but it was no less significant for that fact.

Rodríguez de Arellano's *Consini y Enrique IV*[100] shifts the accent to the love-interest, and in this and in his effusions on nature draws nearer to *El sabio en su retiro*. The peasant family concerned is not a miller's family, but there is a significant, if passing, reference to a miller at the end of Act I. Arellano clearly was affected by the matter of the European theme-cycle but illustrated his own tale with details from Matos Fragoso: for example, in the episode of seating-etiquette. Two very eighteenth-century features are touched upon. One is the King's meditation on his human weaknesses:

'Soy cobarde en ciertos casos' (Act II)

and his moments of sensibility, for instance when thinking of his subjects:

Ah, no conocen el tierno
corazón con que los amo. (Act II)

The other is the march-past of the guards at the end—a link with the

100. The manuscript in the Biblioteca Municipal is undated.

military play, the opera, and the melodrama.[101] Also there is something about the descriptions of night and the storm-scene with thunder, lightning, wind, and, 'if possible', rain, that suggests acquaintance with famous blasted heaths. This brooding talk is not very Spanish:

> Llega digo otra vez, noche,
> el negro manto despliega
> que crímenes apadrina.

The ghostly 'Gothic' themes which pleasurably pricked the scalps of English and French audiences, and whose unspeakable mysteries inspired the melodrama of Pixérécourt, had first issued as novels from the scarifying imaginations of Horace Walpole, Mrs. Radcliffe, Mathew Lewis, and their German imitators. But neither in novel nor dramatic form did they make themselves at home in Spain where horror for horror's sake is not usually acceptable. There are a few mild scenes in family pantheons—in González del Castillo's *Una pasión imprudente ocasiona muchos daños*,[102] for example, where the heroine, emulating Juliet, is conveyed in a drugged, death-like sleep to a subterranean vault. There are translations and adaptations of Pixérécourt himself, mostly after the end of the century.[103] There are Hamlet-inspired soliloquies fit for the graveside, but not, outside Cadalso's *Noches lúgubres*, usually delivered there. They have been heard in High Tragedy. There is fantasy of sorts in the well-known *Duque de Viseo* of Quintana, a milk-and-water edition of Lewis's *Castle Spectre*. Quintana's Enrique is allowed to dream of his murdered sister-in-law who, being transformed into a fetid skeleton, proceeds to kiss him, while tombs are rent asunder and their occupants come forth shouting 'fratricide'. But there is no genuine apparition as in *The Castle Spectre*. It might not have appealed to the censors who were chary of untheological phantoms. The dream itself is not so wild as the English dream of dancing skeletons, vivid and terrible enough to inspire, it may be, the author of *El estudiante de Salamanca*:

The tombs were rent asunder; bands of fierce spectres rushed around me in frantic dance; furiously they gnashed their teeth while they gazed upon me ... (Act IV, ii)

101. See note 12, page 573.
102. See *Obras completas*, Madrid 1914.
103. See, for example, the melodramas *Las minas de Polonia* of 1805, *El perro de Montargis* of 1816. Other examples will be found in Coe, op. cit., *passim*.

Quintana was hardly the man to let himself go to this extent and when he had tamed the bristling ghosts, cleared some of the atmosphere, suppressed much of the medieval colour, and omitted the English tragic humour, *El Duque de Viseo* did not look remarkably 'Gothic'. Ghostliness did not seem verisimilitudinous to a country lacking the draping mists of Lewis's Conway Castle. The European craze for the Gothic is present to any notable extent before 1808 only in decoration for melodrama, and even there it does not usually extend to more than a castle glowering on the backcloth.

❧ 13 ❧

Drama of Domestic Thesis

B Y the late eighties and the nineties the dramatic themes and theses of Europe which had entered Spain in translation were inspiring popular Spanish dramatists to launch into 'enlightenment' on their own account. These writers were to be seen at work in three special fields of activity: the Domestic, the Military, and the reconstructed Heroic dramas, all of which were affected by the thesis-trend of Low Tragedy in general and all of which were technically organized to accord with the new cult of 'naturalness'. A verisimilitude of modern reasoning and behaving, the gauge by which the worth of High Tragedy had come to be measured, was an even more obvious criterion for evaluating the tragedies of ordinary men, since here the critics could judge from common experience, and during the last two decades they increasingly censured the misunderstanding and mismanagement by authors of human causes and effects. Typical of them is the shrewd *Memorial literario*, now objecting that a dramatist's 'good' man should change his nature and become bad overnight, and that his 'good' and 'prudent' man should give credulous attention to the first unsubstantiated slander he hears against those he loves;[1] or now, as a matter of practical fact, protesting at the unlikelihood, in given circumstances, of sensational death by starvation[2] which had become the favourite means of producing stage pathos. This standard of verisimilitude is a mere extension of the coded verisimilitude of the *Poéticas*, just as, in many respects, 'regular' Low Tragedy is a broadening of aristocratic disaster. Lifelike ways and means were studied by both classes of tragedians. But the distinguishing feature of Low Tragedy was not just the inclusion of commoners and their interests, but

1. See the review of *El marido de su hija*, October 1786.
2. See the review of *La víctima del amor conyugal. Sibila, Reina de Jerusalén*, May, 1787.

empiric insistence that aristocrat and commoner should differ in thought, feeling, and speech, only where they differed in real life. Even Domestic Tragedy might use aristocrats, but it treated them on a human level, and burst the neo-classical fiction of their idealistically stereotyped form of tragic existence and of their social inviolability. It freed the commoner. But perhaps its more important function was to release the nobleman from such unnatural bondage.

Literary Arandans and their protectors had been too highly placed either publicly to sponsor unexpurgated 'enlightenment' or to believe it expedient food for mass thought. They were selective. There was a difference between airing odd theories, inspired broadly by the Savoyard Vicar, and specifically by *Zaïre*, on the psychology of education, the meaning of honour, or other fascinating subjects, in the privacy of the Sitios Theatres, or at the Fonda de San Sebastián, where the company would regard them neither more nor less dispassionately than was intended, and presenting them in the playhouses of Madrid or of that other flourishing theatrical centre of the time, Cádiz. There was a difference between reviewing modern theories in a journal—the Spanish press between 1786 and 1790 was full of Lockian and Rousseauesque theories of education[3] and proclaiming them one-sidedly from the stage. Even in their relative seclusion the Arandans had preferred to leave the responsibility for new social ideas to French originals, and, with the notable exception of Jovellanos, restricted themselves, so far as ideas were concerned, to translation and cautious adaptation. Timidity of this kind which increased towards 1789, may be better understood today than it would have been some decades ago. The twentieth century now knows that it has not yet proved the moral, social, or spiritual advisability of releasing revolutionary ideas to the unmeditative masses while these ideas are still in the process of formation and still only half understood even by the thinkers who have evolved them. The experience of history shows that unless new ideas are released in a predigested form they can be taken for the opposite to what was originally intended. The fact that the French public was carrying intellectual logic to unintellectual extremes alarmed authorities in 1789 not only in Spain, but in England; and the revolutionary excesses in Spain of the later nineteenth century were in their turn the effects of ideological indigestion.

3. See, for example, the *Correo de los ciegos* . . . for those years.

The intellectuals, then, were relatively discriminating, as intellectuals, left to themselves, tend to be. But by the eighties and nineties, the most dangerous political periods, the popular playwrights had become aware that, bland heroics having had their day, the acceptability of serious drama depended on how far its ideology could be modernized. Hence their active interest in the social themes from beyond the Pyrenees. In some ways it may seem strange that ideas, present in and for the most part comprehensible to all European society of the eighteenth century, should depend so urgently in the theatres on foreign plots and themes. But the Spanish playwright of the times, no philosopher and not much of an artist, did not appreciate new ideas unless they were presented and illustrated through the 'story' medium of some dramatist or novelist who had already made his reputation. He was still unsure of the technique required to make ordinary situations about ordinary people as interesting as aristocratic heroics. One telling feature of the experimental stage of his own technique and that of his foreign masters, was, for example, the loose, episodic structure of the plot allowing for the insertion of disconnected scraps of philosophy, social criticisms, or even politics, and for sodden padding of tears, hysteria, renunciations, repentance—scenes and other obvious forms of 'modern' sensibility. Another was the character who stood a little detachedly from the plot, to advise, philosophize, dispense justice, act as a moral example, and engage the rest in rational debate whenever they were emotionally free to give him their attention. Thought and feeling were still, for the most part, inexpertly separated. But the love-scene lost its gallant irresponsibility and often disappeared. The principals were usually husband and wife already, and their love was bound up with parental or social responsibilities. Humour, where it existed, lost its gaiety and grew meaning, watchful, and grim. Popular playwrights, like their modern equivalents, seized on the illustrative details of foreign themes or theses. Their enterprise, greater than that of the intellectuals, for with no public responsibilities to consider they were undiscriminating and had nothing to lose by daring, lay in their efforts, not only to adapt and elaborate on the French originals, but to produce national parallels illustrating the same ideas with local emphasis.

Nevertheless, if new principles of thought took longer to assimilate than their illustrative novelties of plot or staging, it must be remembered that the form which shapes itself to a new need is the first sign of the new need plainly to manifest itself. Cándido María Trigueros might talk vaguely on the subject of Reason in philosophical verse:

> Tú, Razón que me alumbras, enciende hoy bien tu tea:
> descúbrete cual eres; todo mortal te vea;
> y sea yo eco sólo de tus demonstraciones;
> mas eco, que destierre locas supersticiones.[4]

But these ideals could not be applied in drama until the playwright had assimilated their implications. He therefore experimented in forms as channels of expressing his ideological urges. His *Cándida, o la hija sobrina*, a prose *comedia lastimosa* of 1774, direfully writhing in problems of identity like a domesticated *Oedipus*, borrows the exterior gesturing and posturing of *Le Fils Naturel*, and, in search of all the mysteries of rational feeling, bids its raving hero, Amato, rave in studiously varied tones.[5] When Valladares recast *El delincuente honrado* in 1777 and wrote a Spanish version of the *London Merchant* in 1783, he had not really absorbed their judicial and commercial thought-content, and had seen in new art little beyond a new scenic style of emotionalism guaranteed, like all new forms of emotionalism, to succeed with the masses. Even to the end of the century, as Domínguez Ortiz has recently observed, the Spanish trader looked for no greater dignity in his trade than that it might eventually provide him with sufficient wealth to retire from it and to make his children leisured persons.[6] No amount of propaganda on the subject could convince the individual Spaniard that it was more honourable for a man of means to work or even passively to retain business interests than to be idle. Response to the most purposeful thesis plays shows that unless a playwright were dealing with ideas hallowed by national tradition he usually misplaced his thought-emphasis and unintentionally commended himself to the public on secondary considerations.

The best example of this is to be seen in Trigueros's blatantly documentary comedy *Los menestrales*, winner of a competition organized by the Municipality of Madrid in 1784 to celebrate the birth of royal twins. Its theme exemplifies the Real Cédula of 1783 which

---

4. See *El poeta filósofo* . . . , Sevilla, 1778.
5. There is a manuscript dated 1774 in the Biblioteca Nacional.
6. See *La sociedad española en el siglo XVIII*, Madrid, 1955, p. 186.

recognized the eligibility of craftsmen for municipal office and for patents of nobility so long as they did not abandon their professions to live at leisure. This was a difficult subject to present to a country which had no conception of a powerful merchant class capable of becoming a ruling element and therefore potentially equal in importance to the aristocracy. Indeed, Trigueros, whom we already know as an artist of considerable culture and a certain ability, was not subtle enough to make contact with his hearers' natural ambitions as human beings and so to transcend their futile preoccupations with empty rank and pride. The play is prefaced by a shameless opportunist statement from him on the subject of royal condescension and vassal-gratitude:

Para que el teatro sea bueno y digno de aprecio, es necesario que sea conforme a su institución, que es lo mismo que ser arreglado a la sabia intención de los Augustos Soberanos que le protejen . . . Los rezagos de la legislación feudal, de la nobleza gótica, y del orgullo arábigo-escolástico, han dejado un buen número de preocupaciones que oponen terca resistencia a los sabios esmeros del gobierno, y de la ilustración de un siglo filosófico que en despecho de los actuales ignorantes será algún día la época que más honre al género humano.[7]

an old approach which itself is proof that Trigueros was not the man for the undertaking to make spectators think enough to develop their over-simplified political ideas. They were evidently ready to enjoy the theme and to laugh at Trigueros's farcical portrayal of social wrong-mindedness. But it would not appear from the report on performances in *El Memorial literario* that they had necessarily grasped the point that they were being told to honour manual work for its own sake.[8] They were used to dramatizations of human frailties exaggerated to the point of comedy and did not take them too seriously. *Los menestrales*, despite its urgent didacticism,[9] was merely another example of farce. The *Memorial's* correspondent shows, for his part, that he had taken up the point somewhat incorrectly by quoting what seemed to him a parallel social lesson in Lope's *Tellos de Meneses* where Tello *père* reprehends his

7. *Los menestrales*, for performance in the Príncipe on 16 July 1784. It is preceded by an allegorical Loa on the birth of the twins by Ramón de la Cruz. The author's Preface has no pagination.
8. See note 1, page 574.   9. See note 2, page 574.

son for the elegant clothes he has donned for his visit to the capital.[10]
For Tello's mind was informed by a late Renaissance philosophy which
assumed a mixture of natural determinism and religious resignation,
whereas eighteenth-century philosophy—though Trigueros was not
fully aware of this—was immediately provoked by industrial and scientific necessity and looked forward to a self-determinism which would be
assisted by the State and would stress the superiority of all forms of
labour over voluntary idleness. Trigueros, not knowing where and
how to concentrate his missionary energy, had turned what ought to
have been a thesis drama into a cautionary comedy. The purport of *Los
menestrales*, which amused audiences with an abundance of incidental
song and banter, was not vivid or realistic enough to affect them once
they had regained the street or to inspire intelligently other playwrights
on the look-out for new material.

Valladares, in 1784, appeared to be trying, and failing, both to iden-
tify himself with the kind of Caroline enlightenment which had served
Trigueros's civic turn, and to dramatize the popular foreign sensibility
with which the middle classes had come to be credited on the stage: two
preoccupations producing the effect on this occasion of cancelling each
other out. For his *Vinatero de Madrid* of that year was a hispanization of
the outward signs he had seen of ideas holding no practical meaning for
him. The poor, virtuous wine-seller of the play, a *madrileño*, was
presented realistically in a miserably furnished room among his wine-
skins, and his horizon, physically and mentally, was limited by the linen
which his daughter had washed for a Marquis, the Milor of the case, and
had strung all too pointedly on a line across the stage. Despite the
bourgeois furniture, and undoubtedly because of the maudlin distractions
of the washing, Valladares managed to miss the realistic sensibility for
which the bourgeois scene originated. Our laundress had been promised
marriage by the Marquis before he had taken advantage of her station.
Later he had developed qualms and scruples about marrying beneath
him. Her father 'defensor de mi honor', had marched off for justice to
the mayor. Thereafter, in scenes of duelling and of other manly acts of

10. See Part I, Act I, especially the words:
    Tello ¡Ay Tello! la perdición
    de las Repúblicas causa
    el querer hacer los hombres
    de sus estados mudanza.

positive nobility, the foreign suggestiveness evaporated, as it often did when a Spaniard mistook foreign sensibility for his own captious sentiment of honour. Moreover the bourgeois atmosphere of wine and washing was fully dispelled by the discovery that the wine-seller was of noble birth; so that any objection to the marriage of his daughter and her Milor was automatically removed. Nevertheless, before things had come to this pass, the trader made some attempt to turn his situation into philosophy. Not that he saw any nobility, or any universal or transcendental value, in trade as trade, like Thorowgood of *The London Merchant*. He could not, in fact, conceive of philosophy beyond variations on the safe theme of Christian resignation to one's unfortunate circumstances. But at least he knew that he ought to philosophize. Which awareness, rather than the content or style of his meditations, was what ultimately mattered for dramatic development. At some point —preferably under the emotional stimulus of frustration—the most responsible character of domestic drama was expected to some degree to think. In the nineties there would be more original subjects to think about. Until then the habit of arranging places for reflection and selecting characters to occupy them had a value at least formative.

Again, the models for this aspect of drama were foreign; though Jovellanos must have inspired Valladares as well. But the wine-seller's experiment in thought must be accepted for its habit-forming value. Intrinsically it does not impress:

> *Juan Pérez* [vinatero]
> Mira, cuando cuesta el pan
> más sudor, luego al comerlo
> es más delicado, más
> dulce, y hace más provecho.
> Cada uno tiene su cruz.
> ¿Sabes por qué son de hierro
> unas, y las otras de oro?
> Porque se llevan con menos
> o más tolerancia. . . .
>
> . . .
>
> ¿De qué sirve la nobleza
> sin buenos procedimientos?
> Si a la virtud no conoce,
> y la persigue, es lo mismo

477

que un sol eclipsado, pues
pierde así su lucimiento.
Y ¿quién le ha dicho al Marqués
que tan bueno ser no puedo
como él? . . .

Nor did the characters of the play succeed in becoming the natural people of ordinary society that the new artistic ideal demanded. At least one critic expressed the epoch's sensitiveness to verisimilitude of situation and behaviour by declaring that the supposedly commonplace action and characters were untrue to life.[11]

When the most notorious of the popular playwrights, Luciano Francisco Comella, felt the urge to advance into the modern stream, he sensibly applied for a grant from the Corregidor[12] to procure foreign models, expressing his readiness to improve what he knew to be his low standard by an intensive study of them. These foreign models were not, of course, text-books of aesthetics and philosophy, but French domestic plays with an international reputation beside which Comella's own dramas are less despicable than might at first be supposed. By 1789 he had already experimented with a new kind of military play in his Prussian trilogy, *Federico II*, discussed more fully in the next chapter, where martial colour came constructively to the relief of domestic tearfulness. He knew already the famous example of modern sensibility in the poverty-stricken *L'Indigent*, as translated in the early eighties, and, with variations, which usually meant elaborations, he had worked it up as a scene of the first act of *Federico II* . . . Part I.

This takes place in a poor cottage where, in the theatrical lamplight, Cristina and Carlota, from utter weariness, have fallen asleep over their work, doubtless in emulation of Charlotte of *L'Indigent alias* Jacinta of *La pobreza con virtud*. . . .[13] And that we may appreciate the inhabitants' living conditions to the full, we are brought back to the same house in the merciless light of day to observe the lack of comforts and to hear the children crying for bread. Other characters in other plays are exposed to similar miseries. A Cecilia, made popular in Comella's light-hearted

11. See 'Los cirujanos del teatro en crítica a la comedia del *Vinatero de Madrid*', Madrid, 1785. It is reviewed in the *Memorial literario* for August 1785.
12. See Carlos Cambronero, 'Comella. Su vida y sus obras' in *Revista contemporánea*, 1896, vols. 102–4, where the application is reproduced.
13. See pp. 457 above.

play of that name,[14] is starving in a sequel, *Cecilia viuda*, of 1787, and with the sensational charity of her kind bestows her last crust on a beggar. There is an introspective air about this sequel, due to the fact that it was written for private performance by the household of the Marqueses de Mortara, with Comella himself in the part of the Platonic Don Fernando opposite the Marchioness's Cecilia. In such circumstances it must have seemed slightly tactless of this author to attempt to define Fernando's innocent relations with the lady, to insist on the possibility of pure friendship between two persons of different sexes, and to criticize those who, judging solely by prejudice, or appearances, impute impure motives to the pure. These ideas of intellectual friendships are typical of the epoch. But to some extent Comella was imaginatively thinking himself into the part, as is evident from the fact that he found the sentiments easy to develop. Some people tend to self-dramatizations in real life, usually in scenes outside their own experience yet within idealized projections and extensions—happy or tragic—of their own and their friends' circumstances. Comella, the internal evidence of all his plays suggests, was one of these: a misunderstood child enjoying the mental picture of repentant friends weeping over his deathbed. Like the child's, too, his dramatic fancies probably went unsuspected by his friends for what they really were. He also made use of his role in this play to comment on natural goodness and political injustice—exteriorizations of a different kind:

> *Fernando* ¡O, cómo a las almas grandes
> las humildes avergüenzan!
> Éstas su piedad prodigan
> movidas de la clemencia,
> y muchas de aquéllas sólo
> por halagar su soberbia. . . .

One wonders how the aristocratic audience received such ponderous preaching which, possibly only for reasons of brevity, was cut out when the play was produced in public. But the spectators on this social occasion may have been less discriminating than a public audience and would doubtless be more concerned with how their player-friends

---

14. *La Cecilia* is licensed for June 1786. It is a musical play ultimately inspired it would appear by Nicola Piccinni's opera *Cecchina* based on Goldoni's *Pamela*. See p. 436 above.

looked and recited than with what the recitations meant. When Comella told the Corregidor that his plays had won the esteem of intellectuals[15] he was probably thinking of these fashionable audiences whose manners the intelligentzia itself frequently accepted as intelligence; and it cannot be repeated too often that the popular dramatists appealed to all sections of society except an exclusive scholarly minority. While Comella's *Federico II* might be treated with scorn by the artistic or learned few, it was produced not merely for groundlings, but, for instance, was later played before Fernando VII with the great Máiquez in the part of Federico.[16]

But much of Comella's output written before he entered on his intensive study of foreign models often merely reproduces odd situations he had seen translated, without taking advantage of the ideological opportunities which those situations suggested to foreigners. So the two-part *Cecilia*, taken from the Italian, his *Jacoba*, set in London, his *Federico II*, Parts I and II, his *Pueblo feliz, Luis XIV*—plays which in his application for help he mentions as having already received the applause of a large public, and of certain intellectuals—are written more in traditional than in foreign style. The seigniorial tyrants look like emaciated reproductions of the old Spanish lordlings. Louis XIV—though not Frederick II—presides in heroic convention; the action, with its urgency of plotting and duelling and its ironical errors, is basically cloak-and-sword with perhaps a tendency towards a meaning tone in the dialogue which is not quite so traditional. The pastoral scenes and the incidental music of the *Cecilias* recall the atmosphere of the lighter Italian opera as does also the attention paid to scenery and posture. Santos Díez González, in his memorandum on Comella's application for a grant does not agree that on the strength of these plays Comella should be encouraged.[17] The noble sentiments of Kings Frederick and Louis he found as cheap and undignified as any serious modern critic would find them; while the best he could say of the Cecilias and Jacobas was that they were merely less defective than other

---

15. See Cambronero, loc. cit.   16. See Cot. *Máiquez*, p. 377.

17. '. . . pues se sabe que no ha seguido carrera de estudios, ni se halla instruido en la crítica y lógica que le muestre el camino de hacer juicio cabal de las cosas . . . Es un ingenio abandonado a sí mismo, y sin los auxilios del arte; y esto se prueba con la errada opinión de que necesita dramas extranjeros que le sirvan de norma. . . .' See Cambronero, op. cit., p. 581.

popular characters he could name. History, especially contemporary history, he said, made unsuitable dramatic material. For the mind of this censor, like the minds of his intellectual contemporaries, was alive to the incongruities and lack of mental realism in popular adaptations of Spanish and foreign history. He thought it proper to demand a better cultural equipment in a potential recipient of public grants than Comella was able to supply, and it was here, comfortably astride his hobby-horse, that he made the aforementioned demands that the playwright be properly educated in moral philosophy, social history, classical literature, and general aesthetics.[18]

Once he had energetically delivered himself of his strong opinions, the Literary Censor was wont, like the good Spaniard he was, to turn to his victim with a more human concern. At this relaxed moment he suggested, therefore, that Comella, unworthy as he was, should be granted the favour he asked, not because it was reasonable, not that on any account Comella was to regard it as a reward for his performance to date, but that other dramatists might be encouraged to write in the knowledge that the State was not indifferent to their progress.[19] Wherefore Comella—and by extension his compeers—received at least a backhanded stimulus to be modern.

By 1789 Zavala y Zamora had also dabbled in the novelties of starvation-scenes and let loose a number of rakish Milores to test the virtue of Anglo-Gallic heroines, though as yet he was even less conscious than Comella that he was trafficking in democratic innuendo. Zavala, who had launched his heroic *Carlos XII, Rey de Suecia* in 1786, and who had kept, and was always to keep nearer to the Spanish heroic conception of drama than Comella, was content with multiplying sensational incidents. His dramas are notable chiefly for their complexity of plot. Oddly enough this brought him into less trouble with censors than his rival. Santos Díez González was repelled not merely by Comella's inferior grammar, but by the fact that the untutored dramatist misused his foreign ideology in Spanish practice. Zavala's not

18. See p. 59 above.
19. 'No obstante lo dicho, acaso podrá ser útil para animar a los ingenios el gratificar a alguno, y así pudiera hacerlo V.S. en este caso; pero de modo que no se califique ni suene como premio, pues las obras de D. Luciano no han llegado al punto de merecer tanta distinción, ni su ingenio está dotado de las cualidades que se requieren para hacer progresos *en obras dignas y de verdadera estimación*.' Cambronero, Op. cit., pp. 581–2.

uninteresting, and perhaps rather more grammatical plays of adventure were generally easier to assess, and his typical Spanish vitality prevented the sentimentalism in which he indulged now and again from going to extremes. He never drained the foreign cup to its dregs. Yet if for that reason his plots came to less artistic harm than Comella's his thinking came to no positive good.

His *La Justina*, licensed in July 1788, is set in Paris. It is a sentimental play about the sufferings of a wife who has been abandoned by her husband for another woman and who is reduced to the dire poverty that enables Zavala to insert the popular European scene of children asking for the bread their mother cannot give them. Like French *drames* it was a 'regular' play, approved as such by Santos Díez González who went so far as to defend it against the objection of the Ecclesiastical Censor that it expressed undesirable feelings—these, for example:

> *Barón de Lain* ¡Qué disparate!
> ¿Cuándo un abrazo ha ofendido
> el racato de una niña?
> Vaya, no hubiera creído
> en el talento de usted
> semejante desvarío.

which the Literary Censor, a supporter of proper literary rights, claimed to be admirably in keeping with the speaker's vicious character, demonstrably vicious.[20] We know that the Literary Censor's patience was often tried as much by the unliterary minds of his fellow Censors as it was by those of the playwrights, and it will be recalled that on several occasions—for instance when he objected that the ecclesiastical alterations did not scan—he had expressed himself strongly on his colleagues' lack of imagination.[21] At the same time the perverse Clarissan tendencies of this Justina to yield humanly, despite her better feelings, to the attractions of her tormentor, were too much even for Santos Díez González. He could not allow the human factor to threaten the unity of model virtue. One of her most complex English moods he simplified to a fine fury of harmless Spanish *pundonor*. The gentleman

20. 'Puede seguir lo tachado en estos versos, por ser propio y consiguiente al carácter que se atribuye a esta persona: y de lo contrario ¿cómo pudieran pintarse los caracteres de los viciosos que hacen el contraste de la virtud, para que ésta brille en su oposición?' See the *Censura* of 1788. The manuscript bearing it is in the Biblioteca Municipal.

21. See p. 391 above.

has been threatening to kill himself in frustrated love of her and she takes the weapon from him:

> Justina [*abrázale*]: El cariño
> y tu persuasión triunfaron
> de mi altivez, de mi mismo
> respeto, y de cuanto tiene
> más incontrastable y digno
> el honor y la virtud.

which now becomes instead:

> Justina Morirás al fiero golpe
> de aquel terrible cuchillo
> que mi corazón traspasa,
> y da muerte a mi albedrío.
> El ciego amor te introdujo
> en mi pecho. ¡qué mal hizo!
> pues es forzoso arrojarte
> del lugar que has merecido,
> para que aunque amor lo sienta,
> entre a ocuparle mi primo.

Richardsonian features are also suppressed in an anonymous *La criada más sagaz* of 1787,[22] a free Spanish adaptation 'from the Italian', presumably of Goldoni[23] who in *Pamela fanciulla* had been one of the first to appreciate the dramatic qualities of Pamela's interior strife and the stage potentialities of a society in which women are the mental equals of men. The Rosa of the adaptation, a high-born servant, solving her master's professional law-cases for him, is unconvincing, but it seems a pity that the Literary Censor, who, ironically enough, only passed *La criada más sagaz* because he was anxious not to discourage the playwright's efforts,[24] should have felt obliged to disapprove of the only ways then open to originality.

22. See note 3, page 574.
23. We have seen a manuscript copy in the Biblioteca Municipal with a licence for 1787. See also Coe, *Catálogo*, p. 55.
24. 'No obstante estos, y otros defectos, que omito por no ser prolijo, soy de parecer (salvo meliore) que se conceda la licencia, para representarse, menos lo rayado; pues es justo no desanimar los ingenios; antes bien es menester fomentarlos; y más, que los mismos yerros suelen ser causa (si se notan de buena fe) para no caer en otros iguales, después de advertidos.' *Censura*, August 1787.

Zavala's *Las víctimas del amor, Ana y Sindham*, which was to have been performed in the December of 1788 and was held up on account of the King's illness, is taken, he says, from an English novel, presumably *Pamela*, perhaps through one of its many stage-versions in English, French, or Italian, or from adaptations of d'Arnaud's Pamelan *Fanni*.[25] There is an Italian air about the scene where Pamela, a ten-year-old maid of the mountains is brought in to sing for Milor. But some of the trials of the original Pamela, or Clarissa—for the playwright seems to have assimilated a general Richardsonian impression—are transferred here to her lady mother, Milor's daughter, secretly married to Sindham, Milor's servant, and who, Clarissa-like, dies, disinherited and starving, a stagey death in an aura of forgiving and forgiveness. The *Memorial literario* devoted some space to pointing out the drama's conspicuous improbabilities.[26] But the most significant element borrowed by Zavala is the incidental posturing: kneeling in petition or in repentance, the waving of anguished arms, the prolonging of tearful farewells. Perhaps his most progressive feature is his conception of sentimental repentance, for Cecilia, the cause of all the trouble, admits her fault in time to let Ana die with a martyr's reputation. The extended scenes of repentance figuring in foreign dramas were already suggesting new possibilities to Spain and eventually would encourage playwrights to combine virtue and vice in one person. Even Ana is not entirely blameless in marrying, however legally, someone of inferior rank against her father's wishes. The Censor, in fact, approves her death on this score, considering it a useful lesson to the young.

Evidently Zavala y Zamora was not so unperceptive that he failed to notice Richardson's scientific interest in complexity of character even though it had been modified by the Englishman's French and Italian intermediaries; for in a Preface, chiefly notable for its scrupulosity, he particularly mentioned that he had tried to demonstrate character of varied kinds, sustained through varied circumstances. Yet he did not really understand 'character' to be more than juxtaposed characteristics of juxtaposed persons, and for the critics' benefit, he discussed his modern tactics in the safe terms of standard *Poéticas*, fussily claiming extenuating reasons for slight deviations from the Unities, and disingenuously requesting his public to decide for itself whether the drama

25. See pp. 438 ff. above.   26. See *Mem. lit.*, May 1789.

should be considered true tragedy or not.[27] The Literary Censor, who could seldom resist an argument over dramatic principles, took him up on this question of what a drama, dealing with commoners, but involving a tragic action, illustrious in itself, should be called. Observing that Zavala's model had not, in fact, been called a tragedy abroad, he commented, with some satisfaction, on the ambiguity of prevailing foreign aesthetics which permitted indeterminate genres, pointing out that this 'confusion' was at least as remarkable as the 'confusion' so readily imputed by foreigners to aesthetic thinking in the national tradition of Spain. Here the Censor's comparison of Spanish and French inconsistencies did not mean, naturally, that he was urging the return to, on the one hand, and the adoption of, on the other, the strict classical criterion which he personally reverenced; nor did it mean that here his chief concern was to defend the Spanish *comedia* for which he had a Spaniard's affection. It meant that he was unconsciously reflecting the epoch's new standard of values by which any dogma might become suspect. Low Tragedy presented a modern philosophy indivisibly social and aesthetic. Once its complex ideology and its technique could emerge from adolescent awkwardness and assert themselves in literary terms, serious drama would receive a fresh lease of life and enter a stage of development unforeseen, as the Censor knew, by the *Poéticas*. So he was not averse to Zavala's *Víctimas del amor*, which commended itself to him as a modern version of the *Amantes de Teruel*, and passing over a few mild irregularities, permissible, to a Spanish mentality, he confined himself to improving passages where the author's verse was trite or wordy.[28] Zavala's professed concern in the Preface about literary disciplines probably commended him as teachable. Comella, the Censor despaired of.

Zavala's *La hidalguía de una inglesa. María Jacoba*,[29] however, brought the Censor into opposition with him on the subject of unequal marriages. The Spaniard, even today, is repelled by the thought of marriage between persons socially unequal. To him also the idea that a son could ignore his father's wishes for his concerns still seems a threat to society, an encouragement to youth to develop its most irresponsible qualities

27. See 'Advertencias al lector' prefacing the undated edition in the Biblioteca Municipal.
28. See note 4, page 574.
29. A manuscript copy of this in the Biblioteca Municipal has a *Censura* for 1790.

and especially its self-centredness. Jovellanos, in 1796, asked to make peace between a parent of his acquaintance and the eldest son who had married for his own interests instead of for his father's, believed it just to leave the boy 'abandoned to his father's righteous displeasure'[30] and, mindful, perhaps, of the State's efforts to bolster parental authority and politic class distinctions,[31] woodenly claimed that it would be wrong for anyone 'to uphold such examples of filial disobedience'.[32] So when the Rosvik of this play complains of his father's tyranny and blind prejudice in objecting to an unequal match for him, and when he swears to his lady-love that neither his religion nor his honour will allow him to break his vows to her, the Censor coldly observes in the margin that a hero should speak of his father with moderation, and that there are famous theologians and lawyers to deny that either religion or honour oblige Rosvik to keep a vow which he has had no right to make. Moreover, after objecting, with justification, to the swashbuckling Judge of the play who, at a suggestion that appeal should be made to the King, was unprofessional enough to declaim in decadent heroics:

> Yo solo soy el Rey
> en Bristol.

and after objecting to a description of Rosvik by the meddlesome Jacoba—who, he said, had no right to come into the plot at all—because she ends on a didactic note of political *égalité*:

> *Jacoba* . . . merecía
> por sus virtuosos hechos
> ser modelo de los hombres,
> que no hay más que una justicia
> para grandes y pequeños.

the Censor, in his summing up of the case, declares that the maligned father of the play who tried to prevent his son from marrying outside his station was merely acting as any sensible father would act in those circumstances:

30. *Diarios*, ed. cit., vol. ii, p. 222.
31. See p. 447 above, and A. Domínguez Ortiz, *La sociedad española en el siglo XVIII*, ed. cit., p. 54, which refers to the Pragmática of 1775.
32. *Diarios*, loc. cit.

Pues el viejo no hizo más, que lo mismo que haría otro cualquiera buen padre: que es procurar separar a su hijo de un casamiento desigual, y conformarse gustoso en siendo igual.[33]

Meanwhile, Comella's foreign models were having a strong ideological effect upon him, for in the 'nineties, while never losing sight of the preference of the Spanish public for novelties of action, he accentuated his incidental philosophizing, indulged more openly in social criticism, and looked to his own country for practical illustrations of the foreign ideas which he had absorbed, over-selectively, in the field of foreign drama. The indigent Comella, a man of some talent, as Santos Díez González admitted, but of little breeding; a dramatic artisan, protected, insufficiently, by the local gentry; a self-made scribbler beneath the notice of the intellectuals; a person of enterprise, not completely unsuccessful yet frustrated in his need of material and social advancement; a popular favourite, just outside the social and literary pale: this Comella provided in himself the right soil for the experimental bedding-out of social unease. By 1790, after the many rebuffs of the Censor who rightly refused to favour Comella's popular successes with his literary blessing, the unfortunate playwright, with so many claims to sympathy, had accumulated sufficient grievances to help him to assimilate the sociological ideas from abroad. Consequently so far as drama is concerned, it is Comella and his kind who most vividly illustrate for us the eighteenth-century ideas in their process of adjustment. Jovellanos on honour and integrity, for example, was bookish. Comella, a victim of social inequalities could bring his views to the understanding masses with a more realistic force of grievance. And since, like the masses for whom he wrote, he had few artistic inhibitions and knew no professional restraint but what was imposed on him from without, he often revealed with startling frankness the mood of the Spanish middle classes of which he was a member, and thrust into startling prominence the dramatic value of a realistic thesis.

In 1790, in his translation of the Italian *I falsi galantuomini*[34] as *El Duque de Borgoña. Los falsos hombres de bien*, Comella entered the critical

33. *Censura.*
34. P. P. Rogers in *Goldoni in Spain* ascribes this play to G. B. Viassolo who wrote under the pseudonym of Camillo Federici. See Rogers, p. 79.

mood of the original with zest. The spatter of corrections on the censored version is evidence of his indiscretions. An argument in Act I on the meaning of the word *honradez* and its conventional interpretations renewed one of the favourite topics of that century which was finding incongruities in many professions of faith and codes of behaviour, and which, in the natural course of reasoning and readjustment was transferring merit from passive or inherited values to acquired and active ones. But the fuller meaning of shifting values, the full context of these re-shapings of opinions, modifications of ideals, and readjustments of balance is normally grasped only by the mind of the philosopher. The Comellas and audiences saw it in the form of simplified signs and slogans, in moral and political particularism. A jaundiced review of the Spanish code of honour, either in its aspect of social and personal self-respect, or in that of professional integrity, could too easily turn into a criticism of the way of life of the gentleman, who, in 1790, was a link more important than ever with political tradition, and of the honesty of public servants on whom the stability of the State depended. In this play aspersions are cast on the parading of the name of integrity: that is, the whole idea of honourable behaviour in its shift from individual to civic tension is viewed in the perspective of special discontents:

> *Conde* Veréis como la honradez
> todos tienen en los labios . . .
> Y así, yo no quiero nombre
> que se aproprian los malvados,
> quiero ser hombre de bien
> tan solamente, y no honrado. (Act I)

Doubts are expressed that a man can be judged simply by his external actions:

> *Duque* ¿Con que aun de mí vos dudáis?
> *Conde* Y no debéis extrañarlo,
> porque por vuestras acciones
> no sé si sois bueno o malo. (Act I)

or that he can even know himself. Social disillusionment is insisted upon; so is the ultimate equality of rich and poor and the inevitability of the rebellion of the poor against their tormentors:

... si a los pobres
ningunos remedios bastan
a sus males.

Duque Algún día
destruirán vuestras entrañas
hombre insensible.

All this in 1790 was hardly judicious, and where Comella was too faithful to the original or too warm in his translation, as in these instances, the Censor underlined his arguments or substituted harmless lines for provocative passages: for instance, the suggestion, dear to the century, but, it was thought by the moralists, liable to confuse the public mind, that apparent goodness or badness is not necessarily to be judged at face value. It would not do just then, the Censor realized, for the spirit of doubt to be ennobled into a popular philosophy even if he participated in social doubts himself. Comella, however, was usefully learning when and where to put contemporary thoughts into contemporary mind-machines.

The Censor, when Comella's *El buen labrador* came to him for examination in the August of 1791, observed that it presented a theme with which the name of the author was now becoming associated: that is, the harmful effects on the tenantry of the gentry's empty pride and idleness. At this subject in general Santos Díez González did not appear to be shocked. Like most thoughtful Spaniards he probably agreed with its criticism of the landed gentry, and since the play was couched sufficiently in traditional Spanish terms of peasant-rights and landlord-tyranny, and in this case did not touch too meaningly on too many modern topicalities, he raised little objection to it, merely finding that it might have been better written, and requiring the alteration of a few of the speeches.[35] Social criticism is most pointed in a speech of Act I objecting that the lower orders are ever expected to be at the gentry's beck and call, which passage, whether for its ideology or its length, was cut at least for acting purposes:

35. 'que (aunque por distinto medio) demuestra en substancia el mismo objeto, que su autor ha propuesto en otras, de alabar la aplicación, y vituperar la desidia, y vanidad que por preocupación siguen algunos hidalgos en perjuicio suyo, y de los pueblos en que viven. Los pensamientos, y razones no tienen todo aquel nervio de que es capaz la materia: y los caracteres de las personas están destituidos de los colores más vivos. ...'

Pretonila Ellos quieren que los mozos
los hablen con el sombrero
en la mano . . .
que los hagan los recados,
y que reciban en premio
de su mano una paliza,
si no lo hacen con esmero. . . . (Act I)

Act III contains some heavily emphasized hints to the State on the duties of the rich. These too are cut in the actors' scripts:

Benito . . . que las cargas que interesan
al estado, es necesario
que ayuden a sostenerlas
los ricos, porque el estado
por sí no basta a atenderlas.

Casual criticisms on similar subjects are dropped here and there in the rest of this play, and in many other dramas written near this time by other authors: for instance in *El parricida inocente*, by José Calvo de Barrionuevo,[36] who attacks the manufacture of silk luxury-articles for the rich, and suggests, with a somewhat muddled knowledge of economics, that it would be better to divert money from luxury-trades to the provision, for example, of free schools where girls might be trained in more useful womanly crafts and in moral virtues for the greater edification of the rich:

¡Qué acerba
penalidad introduce
en el alma la miseria!
¡Qué horrores, qué confusiones,
causa! y con qué indiferencia
la miran los poderosos!
pues como carecen de ella
nada les aflige, nada
les obliga a socorrerla.

or in the semi-heroic, semi-historical drama, *La escocesa Lambrun*, of Comella, played in 1793:

36. It was presented to the censors and banned, though not on these social grounds, in 1786. See Introduction, p. 27.

Enrique ¡Que habiendo en el mundo
de esta clase de miserias,
. sin haberlas socorrido,
se eche a dormir la opulencia!

or in military plays discussed in the next chapter.

In such domestic dramas Comella and other popular playwrights were clumsily practising the new techniques by which themes and characters must acquire their modern reality. We may say that they were giving expression to the local and common effects of the world thought-shift. In this respect Comella was probably at his most intensive and came into most violent collision with the Censor in *El duque y la duquesa* belonging to the same danger year of 1791 when any social criticism smelt of propaganda and when even mild propaganda might have upset a nation's political balance. This drama will therefore serve for a more extensive analysis of Comella's new technique.

It treats of the domestic affairs of a Duke and Duchess into whose household enters a Marchioness with whom the Duke, despite himself, falls in love. But the peculiarly modern aspect is the attempted presentation in the Anglo-French manner of a private atmosphere of discomfort and distrust, and the mixture of failings and virtues in the Duke who struggles unequally against a great obsession and whose modern wife brings him back to conjugal happiness by a sympathetic yet calculating process of reason. Here, then, in emphasis, the theme made the gentry's problems less heroic and more realistic than the Censor thought was wise. Not that he denied such problems could exist. His attitude was that the general public, with whom the moralists were concerned, would not be edified by penetrating to the more defective corners of the gentry's domestic affairs. He knew, in fact, that the times might make such exposures politically dangerous. So that to a certain extent one can appreciate his point of view, while regretting that the dramatist's freedom objectively to analyse the weakness of noble characters should have had to be sacrificed.

No debe ser el teatro la escuela de personajes tan altos, cuando en él se ven representar sus debilidades, fríamente contrastadas.[37]

On the other hand, the simple substitution of the title *La razón todo lo*

37. *Censura* of August 1791.

491

vence for the provocative *El duque y la duquesa* obviated nearly all the difficulty. In the corrected version Don Tomás struggles with complicated obsessions for Doña Juana in the political safety of the well-to-do middle class, and is saved by the complicated reasoning-power of his very modern wife.

Some victory, therefore, was gained for technique. As for the rest of the drama, reminiscences of several of the favourite European themes contribute to domestic tension and incidental philosophy. There is a touch of a gallicized *King and the Miller of Mansfield*, or, as it may be, a modernized *Sabio en su retiro* in the outlook of the peasant Isidoro who, arriving with a basket of strawberries for the Duke, whom he calls simply his 'friend', talks to himself of the great houses where feeling is subordinated to etiquette, where there is no sincerity . . . and has the last phrase cut for his pains. He is most like the miller-*sabio* in his refusal to wait on the Duke's convenience:

> *Isidoro* . . . aborrezco
> estas casas. Llega un hombre
> a visitar a sus dueños
> sin ningún fin, y le ponen
> mil reparos para verlos. (Act I)

But he goes just too far for the Censor, and we have an example here of how a playwright could be hampered, not so much in his choice of theme or thesis, as in his realistic development of its details. When Isidoro, having been told that the Duke, to whom he wishes to offer a gift of strawberries, is out, and the Duchess engaged, begins to criticize the inaccessibility of the gentry and becomes warm and detailed in his resentment at their reception of less deserving people:

> *Isidoro* Y llega un mono con fines
> que no sé, ni saber quiero
> y sin que nadie lo estorbe,
> se zampa a lo más interno
> de la casa, aunque la dueña
> se esté peinando, o vistiendo (Act I)

his free speech is cut, as it is also in other places where he comes too close to realities. Perhaps this talk was cheap and injudicious. But Comella was learning how to dramatize contemporary sentiments and his experiments were important both for themselves and for their suggestiveness to his literary superiors.

Isidoro, one of the principal characters, illustrates enlightenment by being able to dictate moral principles to his social betters, and bestow his advice and have it humbly accepted as if he were a mixture of a miller-*sabio* and a peasant character from Mercier. It is he who, on hearing that the Duke has contributed heavily to the new hospital, condescendingly remarks that that is how he likes to see the gentry's interest employed. To him, despite his touchiness and rudeness, which Comella could not raise above absurdity, the Duke confides some of his private problems; and Isidoro makes up a quarrel with his lord on hearing that the Duke has democratically set his own servants to work for two hours a day on a new road that he is constructing for the benefit of the peasants. On this occasion Isidoro also takes it upon himself to pay a dubious compliment, which sounds like something between heavy sarcasm and elephantine wishfulness, to the reigning monarch and his much criticized ministers:

> *Isidoro* Sin duda las ha aprendido
> de nuestros amables Reyes,
> y sus próvidos ministros,
> que cuanto juzgan que pueda
> redundar en beneficio
> del pueblo, tanto establecen,
> o prestan su patrocinio. (Act III)

On this occasion the Censor was hardly in a position to question the face-value of the socially directive sentiments.

It is also Isidoro who, treading on firmer ground, treats the Duke's eighteenth-century yearnings for the simpler life of manual workers as rhetorical, saying plainly that while he has heard many of the Duke's class talking in the same strain, he has never known one of them to put such desires into practice. To the house of this peasant philosopher the Duke in his misery goes to rest, to soliloquize on the claims of reason over passion, to let himself be guided by Isidoro's moral principles and to agree to abide by his marriage ties. Isidoro is meant to be a strong character, half humorous, half severe, and possessing the unspoilt wisdom and moral purity which the century, in face of all experience to the contrary, tried to believe was the natural inheritance of all men.

The humour, unfortunately could be conveyed by Comella only as a form of gruff touchiness which sounds merely petty. But the social awareness of Isidoro and the Duke is very significant. Their interest and co-operation in schemes of social development is in itself an attempt to sketch from contemporary models, and one must be ready to excuse the bald propaganda of, for instance, the songs of the Duke's democratic fruit-pickers:

> *Duo* El trabajo dirigido
> al bien común del estado,
> debe ser más fomentado
> que cualquiera otra labor.
> *Coro* Fomentada la aplicación
> es el alma de la nación. (Act III)

Still more significant, however, is the fact that schemes and principles are discussed and debated at all, and that, before the drama breaks up into the final litter of explanations, the Duke's mental and emotional life is reviewed on the several human planes that modern interests require.

The successful management of this complicated human stratum of thinking and feeling was an artistic ideal which the century had in mind but in drama could not yet achieve. First it was necessary for the semi-private thinking of people sensitively attuned to the new spirit of curiosity to seep fully and easily through the pages of the Diaries, Journals, and Autobiographies which were the psychological triumphs of the epoch, and eventually influenced Spain even though Spaniards did not very notably contribute to them. Comella himself was too unsteady to organize all his borrowed ideas successfully. But the attempted density of *El duque y la duquesa* is historically valuable. The high placed man is given—however crudely—responsibilities of various kinds with which to occupy his mind. The plot and action, while not irregular, allows for light and shade—for the light relief of peasant songs or Isidoro's 'humour', and for the shadow of tensions made complex by cross-interests and self-analyses. The basic idea of the play, so reminiscent of La Chaussée, that the rich couple can afford to be mutually indifferent, touches a real problem arising from the greater freedom, independence and education of well-to-do women who, in France and England depended less than formerly on their husbands and homes.

494

If bored or neglected at home they were often capable of occupying their minds or feelings elsewhere. Their education often dictated to them other means of winning back a straying husband than coquetry, hysterics or resignation. So the dialogue attempts to record the shades of tone in the tense evasions of the educated wife and obsessed husband, to underline the evidence of suppressions and hesitations, to catch the tones of self-conviction in the making, or—as in a scene where the Duke gives confused orders to his servant—the nervous movements of a state of agitation.

Another scene of interest in the deliberate manufacture of tension occurs at Isidoro's house where the peasant has shut up his noble friend to prevent him from straying after his ignoble desire. Like Diderot's Père de Famille who repeated in various forms and terms of distress 'Give me back my son', the Duke keeps repeating in his agitation: 'Abrid la puerta, amigo', looking straight up in experiment from his own ridiculous level to the perfection of Ibsen's 'Give me the sun' at the terrible end of *Ghosts*. The mental maturity at which Comella aimed naturally evaded him in practice, not only because of his own inadequacy, but because the tricks of plot—the juggling with portraits and the listening at the arras—which are permanently acceptable in comedy—were too physical for the mental level on which this serious drama was planned.

Of the other domestic plays which Comella wrote in the 'nineties *Los amores del Conde de Cominges*,[38] a sedentary drama, in Marmontel's tradition, about a family mystery in which a tyrannical father thwarts the love affairs of the hero, is nearer to circumstantial comedy than to the moralistic *drame*. The Censor approved of its regularity. *El ayo de su hijo*,[39] which had been returned to him for correction in 1798 belongs to a similar category and is of present interest only, perhaps, for the fashionable brusqueness in certain characters, or the self-conscious cult of sensibility forced, for example, upon Josefa, together with an equally self-conscious parade of interest in the whole meaning of man and the everyday world:

38. There is a manuscript copy in the Biblioteca Municipal with a *censura* dated 1796. The play is the 'First Part' of a suite the rest of which we have not found.

39. In the *censura* in the manuscript copy in the Biblioteca Municipal, dated June, 1798, the censor states that the play had been examined in the previous February and had been returned to the author for revision.

Nicolás Hé aquí los hombres de bien
a quienes por sus rarezas
llama el mundo estrafalarios,
porque a fondo no penetra
los corazones humanos.
Sus palabras, sus ofertas,
sus acciones, su carácter
todo, todo me interesa . . . (Act I)

But by this time Comella was keeping censors busy with an offshoot of the domestic drama in which his social propaganda developed a stronger form.

The Comellas, then, had boldly innocent ways of getting modern social problems through the stage door. If, after the diplomatic Spanish manner, the monarch was praised publicly for social virtues he did not possess, the unenviable censor could scarcely object. A brazen, though anonymous, example of this is found in a drama for the King's birthday in 1793, called *El triunfo de la Filosofía*.[40] It is a wishful eulogy, allegorically dressed, of Carlos's virtues and wisdom. Included in the personnel, however, is a schoolmistressy character called Philosophy—a better name would have been Moral Reason—who takes upon herself the duty of dealing with, as the author delicately describes them, the only remaining enemies of Carlos's enlightenment, namely, Ocio, Vanidad, Lujo, and Molicie. Carlos IV himself, it transpires, wants progress, wants everybody to work and to be rewarded for work; but his 're-maining' allegorical enemies are undermining his valiant efforts. Ocio, a transparent person, declares that he can still rely on the co-operation of the powerful who take their ease while the labourer toils in vain; and when Molicie regrets that the powerful have been known to help the poor and set up academies, fraternities, and other useful institutions, Ocio cynically informs her that, like the ignorant creature she is, she judges by appearances and does not search for the deeds behind the pious words of the great:

. . . Ah, si observas
la conducta interior de muchos hombres
que levantan la voz en todas esas

40. *El triunfo de la Filosofía. Drama para el día 4 de noviembre de '93. En celebridad de los días de nuestro católico monarca.* The manuscript bears a *censura* dated October 1793.

juntas, y que declaman con las frases
más altas, y patéticas, apenas
la causa se ventila del honesto
ciudadano, verás que no concuerdan
sus obras con las voces proferidas
para iludir al fin las gentes necias.
Todo es propio interés, todo en sus casas
reposo. La inacción, y la indolencia
sellan siempre el carácter de estos falsos
protectores del hombre.

Lujo too is gleefully outspoken on the subject of the rich, the great, and the elegant:

Yo tengo de mi parte al poderoso.
Los nobles me protejen. Las bellezas
me buscan y distinguen. Los activos
negociantes me extienden, y fomentan.
Por el contrario el desvalido solo,
la turba de sofistas, la severa
ridiculez, con otros entes raros
tu singular apoyo son.

and although Philosophy wins with the help of the gods and an earthquake, and although the performance ends ceremoniously with a chorus of praise to the King of Spain, he has, one feels, been weighed in the balance and courteously found wanting.

In greater or lesser degree other popular dramatists of the nineties began to insert modern sentiments into traditional forms of drama hardly calculated to hold them. Some, like Zavala y Zamora, began to appreciate the possibilities of complex character, or of heroic character streaked with human failings. Some, like Comella and Valladares, overheard in the distance the manifestations of the rights of the common man. Certainly they must have lent as much attention to their foreign models as to each other's successes, for although most enterprising speeches of the domestic dramas of Comella and Valladares were removed before the plays appeared upon the stage, yet the social propaganda of their colleagues and imitators was always expounded in the same terms as theirs and was as promptly suppressed. All developed a talent for drawing social complaint from unlikely persons.

For example, Fermín del Rey's *La fiel pastorcita*[41] is a play as lyrical in image and activity as this dramatist knew how to make it. The shepherds, said the Censor, were so discreet in their poetic simplicity, that they were not like shepherds at all. He was right. Irene prattling lyrically about her little white lamb; Robert, the tyrant, forcing her to choose between killing someone she loves and marrying himself, are exaggerations of well tried themes. But a certain philosophical mood, not born of universal contemplation on the hills but of close scientific analysis, comes over certain of the characters at intervals. Rosmiro, the old shepherd, indulges it lengthily in Act II on the subject of knowledge, driving his thoughts along with the help of rhetorical question:

> La ambición de saber nace
> con el hombre, y se acrecienta
> con el saber . . .
> . . . ¿Pero qué hombre
> en sí mismo estudia y piensa?

Other characters turn at times to contemporary social problems as in this sarcastic speech, for example:

> Quien poderoso ha nacido
> siempre tiene razón; . . . (Act III)

and are duly silenced.

Fermín del Rey was accordingly more careful when he presented another domestic drama in *La viuda generosa* two years later. The censors found little to object to in it. He would seem to have taken the general idea from Faciolle's one-act, prose *La Veuve Généreuse*[42] and expanded it into three acts. But Faciolle's play is a comedy, innocent of the socialistic point which Fermín del Rey gave to *La viuda generosa*. Moreover, the French heroine who benefits from the widow's generosity is known as an indigent gentlewoman from the beginning and is not, like her Spanish equivalent, earning her living as a servant. The Spanish maidservant, Isabel, beloved of her master's son, seems distantly related to Pamela, and with her rustic father appears in an affecting scene at the end of Act II where she postures in kneeling position before her master on leaving his service to beg his forgiveness for being

41. *La fiel pastorcita, y tirano del castillo.* The manuscript has a *censura* for 20 September 1790.
42. See C. A. Faciolle, *La Veuve Généreuse*, Paris, 1788.

the object of his son's love. She is not concerned, however, in 'obscene' titillations, the relief of the drama being more clownish than rakish, and she ultimately solves the problem of mixed marriage, genuinely immoral to the social mind of Spain, by proving to be of gentle birth. It is true that the author could not leave social propaganda alone. Both on the question of freedom of choice in marriage, and on the dignity of labour he has his cautious say—for example on labour:

> *Esteban* Para trabajar nacimos
> y para cobrar de nuestro
> sudor el precio debido.
> ¿Cuán inútil es la vida
> si los hombres la invertimos
> en ociosidades! De este
> origen nacen los vicios. (Act III)

But the moderation of the generous widow, who eventually stands down to let the serving maid, once her gentle birth is disclosed, wed the hero, supported also the dignity of the leisured classes. Doña Brígida knows how to speak with that gentlewomanly condescension capable of surviving even the French Revolution:

> Una criada . . .
> me avergüenzo de decirlo,
> trátese a esas pobres gentes
> con agasajo, y cariño
> porque son nuestros hermanos,
> mas sea sin abatirnos.

Accordingly the play appeared, unmutilated. On the other hand the anonymous *La mujer firme*[43] of the following year, 1793, drove the Literary Censor into the political open. On the surface it is a harmless, if somewhat foolish, drama in the pastoral tradition of Goldoni's *Il filosofo di Campagna*, Marmontel's tale *La Bergère des Alpes*, and the imitative Fermín del Rey's *La fiel pastorcita*. In a lyrical setting of meadows and sheep live the secretly high-born heroine, her supposed uncle, a farmer, her rustic lover, and an unattached lady who runs a poetic Academy for the edification of the peasants. The idyllic atmosphere of this community is shattered, first by the refusal of the girl's

43. The play should not be confused with *Lo cierto por lo dudoso o la mujer firme*, of Vicente Rodríguez de Arellano, which is a recast of Lope de Vega's *(Dejar) lo cierto por lo dudoso*.

'uncle', who waits instructions from her own family, to let her marry a rustic; by the not ineffective quarrels, half tense and half humorous, between her 'uncle' and her sweetheart's offended father who cannot see why one peasant should not be socially good enough for another; and by the arrival of the girl's aristocratic brother who for a time also opposes the match.[44] It was, however, because he was of a philosophical temperament and yielded to his sister's wishes that he brought the fuming Censor into the open. One would think that sometimes the playwrights deliberately tempted this poor functionary. By 1793 they must have known, like Ramón de la Cruz in his self-corrected *La Matilde*, precisely what they might say and what they might not, and perhaps Santos Díez González's impatience with them on many occasions, and what sometimes looks like his unfairness, was due to this perpetual baiting.

Two vital points were stressed here in the *censuras*.[45] In the first place, the Church, in its literary innocence, had taken the author at his face value and judged the charitable sentiments of the play according to Christian lights. There was nothing wrong from the standpoint of the Evangelists either with marriage between those of different stations, or with sentiments about the equality of all men before God. The Ecclesiastical Censor, going so far as to describe the matrimonial intentions of the high-born girl and the peasant boy as 'justísimas', confined himself in other respects to altering only a few provocative words like 'robar'. But we may remember from other examples that the Ecclesiastical Censors, over-rushed, and frequently ignorant of literary contexts, tended to judge by words alone. For instance, Santos Díez González irritably protested here that a censor, in suppressing the obscene word 'robar', had serenely allowed the whole passage expressing the idea of the *rapto*, together with the scene in which it occurs, to stand. The question is of interest, then, as a matter of method and principles in

44. See p. 498 above. A Comellan play with a similar background, though without propensities to propaganda, is *El dichoso arrepentimiento*, based on Baculard d'Arnaud's novel, *Fanni, ou, La nouvelle Paméla, histoire anglaise*. The edition we have seen of this last is undated. Marsollier's *Richard et Sara*, played in 1790, also has theme connections.

45. There are two *censuras* by Santos Díez González dated 27 September and 28 September respectively. The first in date is written on a loose sheet and was perhaps sent privately. It says the same in effect as the second but in more detail. It is also the one containing the protests at the findings of the Ecclesiastical Censor, which probably explains why it was not written on the manuscript itself.

censorship. One gathers from the rest of the *censura* on this occasion that the sensibilities of the Literary Censor had been hurt by a suggestion that, in finding fault with the corrections of the Church in the past, he was himself too lax. In this report he was therefore determined to convince the Juez Ecclesiástico that, far from being lax, he was aware of dangers which the Ecclesiastical Censors passed over.[46]

The other point was more serious still and brought the Literary Censor to the illuminating necessity of defining his own principles. Taken in the international context of contemporary events and predisposing literature, the mixed marriage in general, and a certain speech in particular, suggested ideas less related to Christian principles than to irresponsible propaganda. The speech of the aristocratic brother on yielding to his sister's wishes reads thus:

> Yo en todo caso prefiero
> las virtudes a la cuna.
> De semejantes sujetos
> siendo honrados hace Dios
> tal vez varones excelsos,
> porque ensalza a los humildes,
> como abate a los soberbios.
> Laureano tiene unas prendas,
> según dicen, que venero,
> mi hermana ha favorecido
> su amor con sus sentimientos
> yo no soy algún tirano.

Happily for his intellectual honesty the Censor tried to explain his apparent obscurantism in wanting this speech suppressed, and one must admit that he came out of his ordeal not ignobly. It is only one step in thought to approve the superficial advantages of easy-going enlightenment. It takes two steps to reach the possibilities of delusion. So his objection was to the dangers of loose talk and loose thought. It is all too easy, said he, to pick out statements, true in themselves, like, 'La virtud se ha de preferir al nacimiento' or 'La nobleza es menos que la humanidad, si carece de virtudes', etc., and then to bandy them about in any circumstances convenient to the speaker, and to use them as war-cries

---

46. See note 5, page 575.

in seditious contexts; the dangerous fact is that no cause, however misguided, will define itself in terms manifestly unethical, but will present its motives as a popular aspect of truth.[47]

From this standpoint the popular dramatists with their unassimilated, unintegrated propaganda are indeed examples of dangerous foolishness. In modern Europe such writers would not everywhere be suppressed but they would be regarded in all countries as politically biased, at times even deliberately subversive. Their barely concealed criticism of the reigning monarch and his ministers could scarcely be tolerated even now. Many a play, suppressed for political reasons in eighteenth-century England, was far less outspoken than some of the Comellan dramas, especially those criticizing monarchs and governments that will appear in the next chapter. For the times, Santos Díez González was reasonable and intelligent. For the times, the popular playwrights who found all their new material in contemporary social problems were erring gracelessly in the right direction. Reason was on the side of both and the eventual value of the situation consisted in the fact that neither side completely won over the other. The best domestic drama of a later day is real and vital in so far as it is based on that very divergence of scruples and principles; on the fact that two opposite points of view can be individually and compositely reasonable; on the technical experience that strong feeling on any subject is most expressive when it is restrained, yet that restraint itself must be self-expressive.

Additional evidence of the social preoccupations of the times may be found, for instance, in Francisco Durán's *La industria madrileña, y el Fabricante de Olot, o los efectos de la aplicación*, played at the Príncipe in 1790,[48] which reflects the contemporary efforts of enlightened authorities to develop Spain's industry by adopting foreign methods and machines to which the general public, through nationalism, distrust, or conservatism, was often opposed. The misunderstood heroine, disguised as a man, had enterprisingly learnt to copy foreign cotton goods,

47. '. . . Proposiciones al parecer verdaderas; pero que si no se fijan, y declaran, muy falsas, y subversivas de la distinción de clases . . . Proposiciones, que deben explicarse, para que cada cosa quede en el lugar que corresponde. Ningún sistema sedicioso se propaga con proposiciones abiertamente falsas; siempre lleva de bastidores proposiciones aparentemente verdaderas, . . .', *Censura*, 27 September 1793.

48. The anonymous satire *La comedia, y los dos candiles* . . . of 1790 (see Bibliography), jeers at this author's borrowings from *El pueblo feliz* of 1789, discussed below.

and the serge manufacturer with whom she lodged, to the greater complication of the plot, had been awarded the Cross of Carlos III for his high example of industry. So it was artless of the *Memorial literario* to assume that the noisy failure of this exemplary drama was due merely to some uncircumspect episodes such as Madrid must have seen on the stage before. More likely it was due to the tedious maxims on industry and commerce disposed opportunely through the drama, and to the all too patent preaching against prejudice, peninsularism, and laziness.[49] Since similar disturbances had occurred in 1789 at performances of Comella's *El pueblo feliz*, another 'documentary' play in which a welfare-working Corregidor founds a Patriotic Society and odiously offers prizes to work-girls to encourage a higher output, the fault would appear to have been the authors' lack of subtlety.

A less blatant example is the anonymous *El premio de la constancia o el matrimonio feliz*[50] of 1793, a play about Badajoz where, in Act I, a gentleman, in reduced circumstances, is working as a bricklayer on a house realistically in process of structure, and attempting not very successfully to think in soliloquy. These pauses for 'thought' certainly coincide, as the Censor approvingly observed, with suitable rests in the action. But the thoughts themselves unfortunately fail this hero all too soon. He is left floundering in words alone:

> *Genaro* Ea corazón respira
> pues ya es bien entres a cuentas
> contigo mismo; no es tiempo
> que un solo momento pierdas
> sin hacer . . . pero es ocioso
> exhalar al aire quejas
> inútilmente. ¿Qué juicio,
> qué concepto es bien que deba
> formar de este acaso cielos?

to subside eventually into exclamation. Moreover, the author, even at this late day, could not free himself from the resounding verbal climaxes of seventeenth-century fame; also, when he compared the 'natural' differences of rich men and poor men with the preordained differences in species of birds and beasts, and flowers, the Censor irritably took

49. See note 6, page 575.   50. See p. 24 above.

him up on a point of natural logic[51] reminding him that birds, beasts, and flowers are not ordained to be rich or poor.

Mor de Fuentes looking back in 1800 on the rise and development of the domestic drama, which he characterized as 'tearful' as opposed to tragic or comic, expressed the attitude of many critics by pronouncing neither for, nor against it. He passively assumed, and the assumption is its justification, that it had a right to exist as representing some aspect of nature, as revealing the truth, which had enchanted the eighteenth century, that the vicissitudes of commoners are as tragic as those of aristocrats. His somewhat muddled Preface to *La mujer varonil* of 1800 accepts the *genre* as a regrettable necessity, for he was a Classical traditionalist and saw it as episodic emotionalism contrasting unfavourably with the composite forethought of Racine. One concrete suggestion of his, however, if it had been taken to heart, might have gone far to counteract the mesmeric influence of the posturing *Fils Naturel*. His Classical mind disliked the exhibitionism of the new sensibility. So he himself, he says, tried to be simple and restrained and to preserve a sense of construction. Thus we revert to the instinct of Montiano who frustratedly sought a more real 'nature' without the emotional ostentation which was the only means of impressing its importance upon a changing mentality. The 'pathetic sinkings' as Sterne called them to Eliza, the tears, the depression, the hysterics of the sensitive 'soul in the street' are the results of eighteenth-century logic carried farther than theoretic logic should go. They were cultivated for the purpose of presenting the 'soul in the street' realistically. But logic in writing so often defeats itself by a lack of artistry, of the intuitive anticipation of factors which only come into existence in the process of creation: the qualities, in fact, of artistic or intellectual genius. The close, moist atmosphere of nearly all the dramas we have been considering was enervating to a classicist, whose conception of tragedy was drastic but tonic, and also to the Spanish traditionalist who has always disliked effeminacy. To weep and wail intensively in this distressing strain does not, psychologically speaking, impress upon an audience the force of pain and woe which by itself soon begins to sound artificial. Excessive tears made

51. Santos Díez González writes, 'Los pobres y los ricos son desemejantes en lo civil, pero no en lo natural; y así no viene bien la comparación de *brutos, aves, y plantas*', *Censura*.

impossible demands on the dramatist's technique. Tears prevented the actors from learning to be natural. As Tweedledee intelligently put it to the weeping Alice, 'You won't make yourself a bit realer by crying'.

Nevertheless the newness and yet the universal obviousness of domestic tears made them far more acceptable than the aristocratic tears of High Tragedy. It is significant that they provoked few parodies, presumably because the drama of everyday problems seemed for the time being, and despite its outward artificiality, too real to laugh at. The only notable parody comes uncompromisingly into the category of satire and takes itself as seriously as the domestic tragedies themselves. This is Andrés Miñano's irritable outburst in 1802, entitled *El gusto del día*.[52] It was directed against the drama of intensified sensibility which, since the appearance of Kotzebue's *Menschenhass und Reue* in 1789 had given new meaning to the stage tears of Europe and a renewed lease of life to the sentimentalists, for his dramatic muse had dared to linger over moral ambiguities naughtily learnt from Richardson. Even *El Rutzvanscadt* is, by comparison with Miñano's parody, a work of good natured tolerance. Miñano was a man with a singleminded mission, and, like most men with missions, could not allow himself to be wholeheartedly amused by the object of reform. His was not the unquenchably human intellect of the writer of *Joseph Andrews* who had ridiculed the earlier phases of the sentimental *genre*, and who, despite venomous thrusts irrelevantly dealt at certain living persons, soon allowed his story to absorb him. Nor had Miñano the casualness of the typical Spanish parodist who, after the national style, helped to create a disarming atmosphere more powerful, because more permeating, than didacticism. But *El gusto del día* is capable of amusing and is considerably more ingenious than *La comedia nueva* with which it has didactic affinities. It is a parody half descriptive, half active. The central character, an impressionable married lady, Doña Dorotea, an inveterate theatre-goer, is liable to come under the spell of any sensational novelty and to dramatize her own life in the light of what she has seen on the stage. A creature equally lacking in realism, for the same reason, is the Marquis of Bombonera who is to be married to Doña Dorotea's

52. *El gusto del día* was published in Madrid in 1802 and also in Valencia in the same year. There is a manuscript copy in the Biblioteca Municipal. It was attributed to Miñano by Moratín (*Catálogo* . . ., ed. cit.). It is composed of two acts and is in prose.

daughter on the very day of the production of *Misantropía y arrepentimiento*, the newly made Spanish version of Kotzebue's sentimental masterpiece.[53] The sensible men of the play are Dorotea's husband, Don Ruperto, and his friend of the ominous name of Don Alfonso del Moral, who is another edition of Moratín's Don Pedro, though, since both are common characters in the world's history of satire, he is not necessarily an imitation.[54]

Much of the play consists of arguments for and against ambiguous sensibility and of criticism of dramatic theses derived from dilettante—excursions into Newton, Descartes and the rest. These arguments are punctuated by lectures from Don Alfonso, who is a broader-minded man than Moratín's Don Pedro, having, moreover, the judgment to perceive that the low standard of drama in the playhouses is not the result of failure to copy foreign models but a feature of the age no less typical of France than of Spain. Incidentally he has an aversion to the Unities[55] and in some respects might have been an admirable person to enter into argument with Don Pedro whom Moratín had allowed too readily to have the last word. Miñano is more subtle than Moratín in these satirical lessons in Bad Taste. There is a pleasing character, better than any of *La comedia nueva*, in Doña Jacinta, daughter of the lady of sensibility, who at a poignant moment in the production of the great *Misantropía* . . . , when by rights she should have been sobbing her womanly heart out with the rest of the audience, had suddenly been overcome by her sense of humour and moved irresistibly to smile. That smile, which had affronted Bombonera, whose Pathetic principles were rigidly Gallo-Germanic, and who declared in outrage that he would follow the example of a gentleman reported by the Paris press to have broken off an engagement with a rich beauty solely because she was amused by a representation of pathos,[56] had endeared her to Don Alfonso. It certainly endears her to the modern reader and is one of the happiest touches in eighteenth-century satire.

Direct parody is introduced at the climax in Act II following the visit to the theatre. Overcome by emotion, by the heat of the theatre,

---

53. This translation or adaptation was made by Dionisio Solís and was published in Madrid in 1800. It successfully brings out and emphasizes all the worst features of Kotzebue and generally manages to suppress his best ones.

54. *La comedia nueva* was played in 1792.

55. See note 7, page 575.   56. See note 8, page 575.

by the press, and, says the indelicate servant who brings the news, by the smell, Doña Dorotea is brought home in a faint. Now ensues an entertaining scene in which the comedy takes on an earthy tang reminding us of moments in Cruz. Doña Dorotea's fainting fit, so much in keeping, she knows, with the behaviour of sensitive spectators of Kotzebue in Paris, prefaces her passage from humdrum respectability to the studied unconventionality of the heroines of Kotzebue, and from spectator she turns player. For she will have it, in her deranged condition, and much to the bewilderment of all but Don Alfonso, that, after the fashion of the latest phase of sensibility, she is a sinning woman. Therefore she proceeds to act out the great repentance scene, catching sentiment and sin from the infectious *Misantropía.* . . . Her husband, ignorant of the origins of her moral disease, begins to play in earnest the outraged spouse. Only the presence of mind of Don Alfonso, a practical and well-informed person, saves the embarrassing situation:

Don Alfonso. Sosiéguese vm. amigo, y reflexione que su mujer está desempeñando perfectamente el papel de Arrepentimiento; vm. no va haciendo muy mal el del misántropo; concluidas que sean estas escenas, entraremos el marqués y yo a representar también los de reconciliadores de dos tiernos esposos.

He even has the dramatic grace not to point the moral. Perhaps he is preoccupied with Jacinta with whom he has fallen in love because of the report that she smiled. The reconciled husband, however, makes up for the lover's distraction by pointing the moral himself with direct application to his potential grandchildren, making a worse job of it than Alfonso would have done.[57] But Jacinta, who smiled in the wrong place, is a lovable personification of Spain's passive sense of proportion. Like the Spanish *graciosos*, like all the company of the Manolos, she was there to prove that throughout the chaos of experiment ran Peninsular reservations.[58]

57. *Don Ruperto.* [no] . . . han de seguir otras máximas que las que dicta la razón y el buen juicio, ni asistir jamás a otras comedias que aquéllas que hagan reír honestamente, ridiculizando los vicios y extravagancias de los hombres para conducirles por este medio a su enmienda.

58. See note 9, page 576.

❦ 14 ❦

Military Thesis-Drama

W HEN, in 1789, the *Memorial literario* described Mercier's *Déserteur* as the 'first modern military drama to be played in Spain in military style'[1] it was referring specifically to the trooping and marching of stage soldiers, the beating of stage drums, and the other military effects 'off' and 'on' which Jovellanos had cautiously adapted in *El delincuente honrado* to increase dramatic tension, and which had begun to filter into popular heroic dramas like Valladares's *El Emperador Alberto I y la Adelina*, or *Saber premiar la inocencia y castigar la traición* in the early eighties.[2] This sensational feature was partly the result of the epoch's admiration for the new military science of Prussia, the spectacular smartness of Prussian military exercises, the new formations required in musket warfare which Spain, like other nations, was busily rehearsing,[3] the glamour of a soldier-monarch, a leader in uniform, publicly active, whom Spain, prone to hero-worship, would have liked to possess again, and of a smart, imposing army.[4] Partly it was a natural evolution of the scenic trooping and display in grand Italian opera and its Spanish imitations where military escorts add visual grandeur to the staircase-scenes and accompany the exaltation of the campaigning hero with martial instruments. A play obviously exemplifying this last tendency is Valladares's *Exceder en heroísmo la mujer al héroe mismo. La Emilia*, a rhetorical, happy tragedy set in ancient Rome and so enlivened with music and military trooping, that, of eighty-six plays he had written

---

1. See p. 456 above.
2. The first was played in 1781, the second in 1782, see p. 577, n. 7 below.
3. See Fernando Díaz Plaja, *La vida española en el siglo XVIII*, pp. 70 ff.
4. On the Spanish army, see Desdevises du Dézert (G), op. cit.

to date it had become, the popular author said, the most applauded.[5] Melodrama also was wont to borrow martial effects.

But although soldiers and soldierly exercises are conspicuous and essential features of the genre which in Spain may be called the 'military thesis drama', it is the thesis, now at a royal instead of at a commoners' level, rather than the militarism of this type that makes it historically notable. In France, England, and Germany the play about military heroes is often indistinguishable from ordinary heroic drama; Mercier's *Destruction de la Ligue* is an example of the modernization of an old heroic ideal. It might also merge into the foreign domestic drama where, as in Engel's *Der dankbare Sohn*,[6] soldiers are involved in domestic affairs and the monarch-hero is worshipped in his absence; or where, in camp-settings, misunderstood young captains might be tried at court-martials while their wives scream hysterically in the background and their more sternly controlled comrades wretchedly beat their drums of death. In Spain, however, the new military element could not easily be absorbed into the national heroic genre which was still extremely popular, and which, with its tradition of complex, virile action, was not suitable either for concentrated sensibility or mere marching up and down. In Spain the military thesis-play, new in most of its features, remained distinct, therefore, from heroic drama. Although it was close to domestic drama in several respects, it developed differently from that type also.

This curious play, of great historical importance, placed in the centre of its military setting, not a captain, military judge, or disguised grandee, but an idealized foreign monarch who episodically dispensed the enlightened laws of a Utopian Dictatorship, ignoring the code of honour of Spain's heroic tradition, and adopting the criterion of practical reason according to which the judgements of the codes of chivalry tended to be reversed and values adjusted to the human circumstances of individuals. The presiding monarch was surrounded by the misunderstood and the misunderstanding whose private affairs spasmodically entered the drama's secondary action; and one of his chief functions was to stimulate social discussion for the purpose of directing it into a thesis. Eighteenth-century travel, famous letters, travel-books, and diaries, were drawing attention away from home experience and

5. See note 1, page 576.   6. It was published in 1771.

suggesting fresh, possibly superior, ways of life. The reason why this epoch projected an ideal foreign governor on to the screen of its imagination was because it was preoccupied with the idea of an enlightened State administered by unprecedented intelligence. The reason why this governor was a dictator-monarch, resplendent in uniform, surrounded by military paraphernalia, and addicted to state processions—sometimes with horses, if the squeamish censor were not looking[7]—was because the military personality of the philosopher-monarch, Frederick the Great of Prussia, had become a sensational legend which reached its climax with his death in 1786 when the press of Europe broke into such a frenzy of anecdote as kept dramatists supplied with material for a decade. Frederick the Great was not, naturally, the only hero of military drama. In response to popular interest the *Correo de los ciegos de Madrid* published, between 1786 and 1790, a whole series of popular Lives of Great Monarchs, including Charles XII of Sweden,[8] Peter the Great of Russia,[9] Ivan IV of Russia,[10] the Empress Maria Teresa of Austria,[11] Stanislaus I of Poland,[12] and Gustavus Adolphus of Sweden,[13] and so provided one of the most accessible sources of additional dramatic material. All of these monarchs appeared, in one guise or another, in the Spanish theatres of the last two decades. But it was Frederick the Great who established the modern precedent, and it was merely for the sake of variety that playwrights passed on to other personalities famous enough to be of topical interest, but remote enough in place to preserve an illusion of omniscience and to be credited with the same or similar exploits and adventures. As a reviewer noted in 1786, the playwrights' tendency was to draw, with small concern for history, on an international pool of figures and incidents.[14]

7. For example, Santos Díez González, in a *censura* of Comella's *Los hijos de Nadasti,* objects to the horses in the play and demands that they be removed: '. . . Se puede permitir su representación, omitiendo lo rayado, y el sacar al teatro caballos, ni jinetes que confundan con su ridículo aparato en lugar tan estrecho. . . .' It is dated 1795, and is typical of his efforts to combat the whole fashion.

8. See *Correo de los ciegos de Madrid,* 5 January 1787.

9. Op. cit., 12–16 January 1787.   10. Op. cit., 9 March 1787.

11. Op. cit., 18 November 1789.   12. Op. cit., 28 July 1790.

13. Op. cit., 28 August 1790.

14. See *Memorial literario* of March 1787. '. . . en la mayor parte de ella se hallan aventuras muy comunes en los poetas dramáticos de estos tiempos, que aplican unos mismos lances a diferentes personas y reinos. . . .' The play under review is *Perderlo todo en un día por un ciego y loco amor; y falso Czar de Moscovia,* then being performed at the Príncipe.

Mercier, the democrat, spoke realistically rather than cynically when, in the Preface to the *Destruction de la Ligue*, he approved of what Gaiffe has since called 'the cult of great men':[15]

Il est toujours bon à une nation d'établir un fantôme qu'elle pare de toutes les vertus qu'elle voudrait inspirer à ses monarques.

Such is the explanation of the 'phantom' literature about Henri IV and of plays like Madame Bernard's *Le Petit Chemin de Potsdam, ou Quelques Anecdotes de la Vie de Frédéric II.*[16] Mercier's principle is understandable enough for an age which both believed in perfection through reason and refused to be blinded by all fleshly appearances of perfection so far presented. Precisely because of this half idealistic, half realistic attitude, the cult of great men involved the recognition of imperfections, or, at least, of contrasts and complications of character that left those great men—usually kings, until 1789—open to criticism and analysis. But the great must be painted for the popular imagination in picturesque detail, and, as in the King-and-the-Miller cycle, the 'phantom' tales are spiced with whimsical words of wisdom and acts of readily assimilated irony. Moreover, the eighteenth century was less interested in the heroic battle than in the little private details of a militant monarch that brought him within the emotional reach of Everyman.

This relative phantom of the ideal, with a public head for just government and scientific tolerance, was also provided with a private heart and even private nerves, for the age was interested, not in man mechanical but in man human, and disposed to reason about its hero's larger public attributes from the standpoint of his small private motives and idiosyncracies. It was an age willing to shift its judgements and alter its principles to agree with the latest evidence and in this way it may be said to offer its special contribution to public thought. The pliant hero had no fixed universal qualities. He was a circumstantial hero whose everyday life lay open to inspection that his great occasions might be in human focus, his small intimate interests and characteristics finding the proper human level implied by Marmontel when he said sardonically in his introductory remarks to *Soliman II*:

15. See F. Gaiffe, *Le Drame en France au XVIIIᵉ siècle*, Paris, 1910, p. 226.

16. There is an edition of Paris (1793). A similar example is C. A. Chambelland de Besançon's *La fin de la Ligue ou Henri-Quatre à la bataille de Fontaine-Française* of which we have seen an edition of 1800; and there are many others.

C'est un plaisir de voir les graves historiens se creuser la tête pour trouver de grandes causes aux grandes événements.[17]

To investigate human and private motive beneath public behaviour is a magnificent ideal for a dramatic genius but a snare for the second-rate. Where the popular playwright dealt in royal greatness he made his Dictator-King an exhibitionist; where in littleness, undignified; where in tenderness, effeminate; where in individuality, eccentric; where in nervous tension, childish; where in play, a fool. But it is the century's ideal behind this impossible monarch that matters historically. The 'phantom' is an undeveloped reality of social thought.

On the academic and literary levels the supposedly paradoxical Frederick II, for those who did not have too much to do with him, acted well enough as a phantom-example of enlightenment. The presence at his Court of great French exiles who enjoyed his tolerant hospitality, at least until his protection became too exacting, bathed him in reflected glory. Famous men in famous English coffee-houses had discussed him with lively interest. Tomás de Iriarte had corresponded with him, and incidentally in the *Mercurio histórico y político*, which he took over in the still liberal days of 1772,[18] he had published articles on some of the least known of European countries—Russia, Poland, Sweden—countries which in emulation of Prussia, were to provide the European imagination with supplementary phantoms. Forner in his *Exequias de la lengua castellana* admired this Frederick's humanity. Also in Arandan days, the Literary Censor, Ignacio López de Ayala,[19] translated one of many foreign histories of the reign of this 'hero of our Age'[20] explaining in the Preface that he did so for its enlightening instruction on military and political matters. We should note that though this version includes no personal anecdotes, and so nothing of the intimate material of the drama of sensibility, it gives a general impression of Frederick's humanity contrasted with the severity of his discipline and his busy military activity. Also it contains details of

17. See *Contes Moraux*, ed. cit., vol. i, p. 31.
18. See Cot. *Iriarte* . . . , p. 105.
19. Ayala was Literary Censor until 1789 when he was succeeded by Santos Díez González.
20. See *Historia de Federico el Grande, actual rey de Prusia, sacada de diferentes Memorias, . . . con los planes de las principales batallas, y con sus más útiles ordenanzas de gobierno civil, militar, y político*, Madrid, 1768.

wall-storming, bridge-burning, and battle-planning which fired dramatic imaginations. The more picturesque of the personal stories of the hero, with anecdotes of his eccentric generosity or discipline, appeared, for instance, in French in 1777,[21] or in Spanish in Damián Cerdabar's *Pasajes escogidos de la vida privada de Federico II, Rey de Prusia, con algunas observaciones sobre el estado militar de su reino: sacadas de un anónimo francés* of 1787, which explains that Frederick II 'established the military discipline which the whole world has tried to imitate'.[22] Other works stressed the King's epigrammatic wisdom.[23]

When the anecdotal interest in the Hero of the Age was heightened by his death in 1786, Spanish dramatists could have helped themselves from any one of a dozen sources of supply. On 20 October, 1787, the *Correo de los ciegos* praised and summarized a biography translated from the Count J. A. Hippolyte de Guibert who dealt with the Prussian's politics, philosophy, and military science.[24] A more influential French work was *Vie de Frédéric II, Roi de Prusse* by Thiébault de Laveaux,[25] published in 1788, which used a book of German anecdotes—*Anekdoten und Karakterzüge aus dem Leben Friedrich des Zweiten*[26]—and insisted that it was not a 'history' but a 'Life' of Frederick II, and that its author's aim had been to collect all the most interesting details published about the great man. This colourful Life was doubtless the one reviewed enthusiastically in the *Espíritu de los mejores diarios que se publican en Europa* on 20 October 1788. It certainly contains most of the favourite anecdotes retailed by European playwrights. Among them are stories of the imperturbable Frederick talking comfortably to his generals while bullets tear the branches of the trees behind him and make his officers jump; the hair-raising story of the disobedient Captain writing to his lady-love in forbidden candlelight and disturbed by Frederick who was making a private tour of inspection and who dictated, for a

21. See the anonymous *Observations sur la Constitution . . . des armées de S.M. Prussienne, avec quelques Anecdotes de la Vie privée de ce Monarque*, Berlin, 1777.
22. '. . . estableció la disciplina, que todo el mundo ha querido con esfuerzo imitar, y el maravilloso mecanismo que tan fuertemente liga todas sus partes', op. cit., p. 2.
23. See, for example, *Pensamientos escogidos, de las máximas filosóficas de Federico II, actual Rey de Prusia entresacados del espíritu de los monarcas filósofos, y puestos en castellano por D. Jaime Villa-lópez*, Madrid, 1785. It is reviewed in the *Memorial literario*, November 1785.
24. See note 2, page 576.
25. It was published in Strasbourg and Paris during 1788-9, in 7 volumes.
26. The work is anonymous and was published in Berlin in 12 parts between 1787-9.

postscript to the letter, 'Tomorrow I shall perish on the scaffold'; a contrasting story of Frederick's affection for a Captain who had killed a brother officer in a duel but who was allowed to escape from prison while the King turned a blind eye; the story of the valet who, while trying to poison the King, was told jocularly 'You look as if you want to poison me' and who, after his breakdown into confession, was forgiven; stories of erring officers; stories of starving families 'punished' with pensions or promotions; stories of peasants and the King in disguise; King-and-miller stories confused in origin and development. Equally accessible and more suggestive was Madame Bernard's one-act play, *Le Petit Chemin de Potsdam ou Quelques anecdotes de la vie de Frédéric II*[27] in the first scene of which Frederick's officers relate sentimental anecdotes about their master. The main action deals with his lodging in disguise in the house of a poor widow and her precocious child who charms the guest by his loyalty and devotion to his mother, and with the revelation that the lady, now in the hands of the bailiff, is the widow of one of Frederick's bravest officers and has fallen on evil days through no fault of her own. Moreover, the popularity of *Le Petit Chemin . . .* may well have set the feminine, the maternal, tone found commonly in the anecdotal dramas and may have helped to put into the minds of dramatized leaders of men the things that motherly women fondly hoped to find in their originals. These and many more tales playing on the human contrasts in the fierce, philosophical King and stressing bitter-sweet embarrassments with a feminine appreciation of 'scenes', were sentimentalized by the popular playwrights, filled out with social propaganda, and sometimes—at their best—worked into social thesis-dramas.

The way in which the Frederick-matter served the modern interests of French and Spanish playwrights may be seen at its simplest—that is, nearest its origin—in dramatizations of the sleeping-page incident, one of the best known, because one of the most sentimental, of all the anecdotes. It told how, on ringing for his page and getting no reply, Frederick went to investigate, and found him asleep with the end of a letter protruding from his pocket. Having no scruples about reading other people's correspondence—and what would have been the history of drama if such scruples had ever mounted the stage?—he read how

27. See p. 511 above.

the page's mother was indebted to the boy for sending part of his small wages to alleviate her distress. Greatly touched, the whimsical Frederick put back the letter with some money which later the boy pulled out in his fear and confusion while he was excusing himself to his master for having slept at his post. The anecdote, after allowing Frederick for awhile to amuse himself in a fatherly way at the boy's nervous expense, ends in a parade of the Frederickan motherliness then regarded as an attribute of the finest kingly disposition.

On using this incident, Comella's German compeer, J. J. Engel, heightened the scene of confusion as a popular playwright would; inserted complications to elaborate the plot; and prolonged the note of sentiment. Engel, whom Robertson, in the two-and-a-half lines which his sense of proportion allows him for this little scribbler, describes as a 'popular philosopher of homely ethics', published his one-act drama, *Der Edelknabe* in 1774. The Leipzig edition of this year paraded an emotional frontispiece showing the Prince looking down with tenderest compassion on an over-innocent Page asleep in a chair. Which paternal compassion is the sentiment dominating the drama. An English translator including the play with other Engel pieces in an improving anthology for children, *The Juvenile Dramatist*,[28] could even describe them as 'a Selection of plays from the most celebrated German writers upon education' and could say that:

... It is a well known fact that German literature is now very deservedly in high estimation in the British Empire, and the works of such men as Felix Weisse and Engel, which now make their first appearance in this country, need but the bare mention of their names, to entitle them to public approbation.[29]

We must force outselves to realize, however difficult the exercise may be, that the Frederick-matter in which Frederick himself was sometimes merely The Prince—the popular eighteenth-century equivalent of a phantom-Cortegiano, or Héroe—and other military and domestic effusions were taken by the masses seriously, and that the intellectuals, if despising Engels and Comellas, believed in the serious principles behind their experiments and themselves produced dramas not readily distinguishable from theirs. Engel's adults leave us cold. But

28. This is an anonymous collection published in Hamburg in 1801 in three volumes.
29. See the translator's 'Preface' directed to 'The Public', vol. i.

the speech and behaviour of his children are not always unconvincing.

A French translation was made by Friedel with the title *Le Page*,[30] and there is an anonymous and undated Spanish *El paje*.[31] The Engel-matter subjects the Page to a greater test than he undergoes in straight-forward anecdotes by making the Prince provide him with money to be used as he likes, and by suggesting to the child's acquisitive imagination the new watch which he needs to fulfil his duties more punctually. It also brings his mother to court and makes her the centre of zestfully piteous scenes of explanation, embarrassment, and gratitude. It gives the Page an Ensign brother who is as selfish as the infant Page is self-sacrificing, as well as a guardian-uncle, a Captain, who is ashamed of his sister's poverty.

Indirect as is the Spanish translation through French, so it would appear from the use of words like madama, the little boy himself still seems his natural age. The detail about his being sent to find a watch with directions as to left and right positions, and his inability to dis-tinguish, is, as far as it goes, touchingly amusing:

Príncipe. ¿. . . Sabes distinguir la mano derecha de la izquierda?

Paje. La derecha y la izquierda, Señor (*reflexionando y mirando atentamente sus manos*).

Príncipe. (*poniéndole la mano en el hombro*) Anda, amiguito mío; acaso sabes distinguirlas como el bien y el mal . . . ¡Que no pudieras conservar perpetua-mente esta dichosa inexperiencia!

Directions for the child's movements are generally natural too, another restrained example being the critical look which he is directed to cast at the author of a book on education who is also Director of the College to which the Prince decides to send his Page:

> *Príncipe* ¿Querrás irte con él?
>
> *Paje* (*depués de mirar un momento al Director*)
> Sí, Señor.

One hopes that the author-Director was not Rousseau, for the Page is a more natural child of nature than Emile and far more likable. But the moral rests on the bounties and paternal interests of the 'Prince' whose heart is open to the smallest of his subjects and whose human qualities—

30. See Gaiffe, p. 69, n. 4.

31. We have seen an undated manuscript in the Biblioteca Municipal, Madrid.

though he reminds the boy that he can be as severe as he is kind—the playwrights for purposes of popular appeal knew how to enhance.

Other versions of the Sleeping Page were sometimes more sophisticated. Dezèdes's *Auguste et Théodore* in 1789[32] made the Page much older and gave him a colleague-friend. It also supplied him with a sister conveniently staying, with her mother, within reach of court, at the Inn of the Four Nations—reminiscent of Goldoni—and so able to fall in love with the colleague-friend. The boy in this version is involved in suspicions for having the money in his pocket, before he is cleared by the 'Prince'; the action is enlivened by songs; and the fashionable gruff humour of Northern fame is inserted into the grumbling landlord of the inn.

This French version disclaimed any relationship with Engel, probably in all sincerity, for the Page-anecdote and its characteristic details could have been obtained from several source-books. But the protest, in support of its independence of Engel's drama, that this 'Prince' is not even called Frederick[33] convinced nobody, least of all the Spanish translator, Rodríguez de Arellano who called his play *Augusto y Teodoro o los pajes de Federico II*[34] and translated some of the final words:

> . . . Ah! le bon Roi! le Grand Roi! le bon Roi:

as:

> Viva el Gran Federico. . . .

The songs are omitted in the Spanish version which otherwise keeps close to the French and takes a special interest in small details, making Frederick wipe his eyes for very tenderness at one point, and at another referring to this life-size hero as obliged to work all night and, unnecessarily, one would think, sleep in his boots.

Whatever the real Frederick may or may not have been like, and whatever the social influence he may or may not have exerted, this was the confused and sentimentalized 'Phantom' which the sociology of the period required and to which playwrights tried to give contemporary expression. By extension other monarchs—Maria Teresa of Austria, Charles XII King of Sweden, Peter the Great of Russia, etc.—also had

32. See *Auguste et Théodore, ou les deux pages*, by N. Dezèdes and [the] B[aron] D[e] M[antauffel] which was first played in Paris in March 1789 and published in Paris the same year.

33. See 'Avertissement', ed. cit.   34. It was played in 1802.

sensational stage doubles, but they were known more for their activity than for their receptivity and served rather the interests of the contemporary heroic drama whose qualities will be discussed later.

Comella's *Federico II, Rey de Prusia* was dispatched by the Censors on 30 December of the ominous year for sovereigns of 1788. The first Part of what was to be the notorious three-part suite did not at first occasion much misgiving. There is a self-conscious Frederick with a dramatic flair for behaving unexpectedly. There is a sensitive officer, Enrique, dismissed from the King's service for alleged correspondence with the enemy. There is a scheming villain, Manfeld, who has denounced Enrique unjustly. There is the typically eighteenth-century friend of the hero, a Captain, who believes in Enrique's innocence, and who, in the sub-imaginative way of the times, is the son of Enrique's worst enemy. There is a crucial scene in Manfeld's tent where Enrique, who has gone there with murderous designs, is found by the Captain and smuggled out by him when the raging owner returns. There is then a scene in which the Captain is imprisoned for refusing to reveal his friend's identity even to the King. There are pathetic scenes at dusk and, for variety, also at dawn, in Enrique's humble home where children cry for bread and the atmosphere of depression is punctuated now and again by hysterics. There is a scene in which, on reading that a reward is offered for information about libellous writings against the King, Enrique falsely confesses to the deed in order to obtain the money for his family. There are scenes of state: a series of royal audiences, to bring out the individuality of the King's judgement and method and the contrasts in his character. There are unhumorous scenes of humour between Frederick and his blunt servant Quintus to give light relief, or, as Comella may have seen it, a grim irony, to the central pathos.

All this time, Frederick, pointedly determined, as the embodiment of Justice, that every accused man shall have fair play, has been exercising his famous receptivity over Enrique's case. Seeking first-hand evidence, he has been stealthily moving behind the scenes, sometimes conspicuous by his very absence, or he has been passing erratically in and out of the plot to the discomfort of his subjects and the inconvenience of the dramatic organizer. When his ex-officer is brought to trial the King is in possession of the truth, which he has been tortuously and craftily sifting from lies throughout the drama; so that the climax, with the evidence against the self-convicted Enrique at its blackest, sees the hero restored to favour and his enemy disgraced.

The attempt to suggest the presence of personality by implying that the chief character of the background and foreground prepares for his startling activity in the latter sphere by his disciplined receptivity in the former, is the bravest feature of the Comellan experiment; for personality was the one quality that could raise modern drama above mere social propaganda. But Comella's difficulty consisted not so much in transferring the famous personality from history and legend to a pedestal in drama, as in maintaining it there with decorum for the length of three acts. To support him under this strain the dramatist was obliged to call in exterior aids. The idea of impressing a political personality upon an audience by presenting it at intervals in scenes of military display has occurred to greater minds than his, not in literature alone. Moreover, in reality and in legend, Frederick II supplied his own military effects. Prussian military training-methods with scientifically inspired manœuvres and drill-formations, the outward signs of a new, terrifying efficiency, were feared, admired, and discussed[35] by the whole of Europe to the point of an obsession which Comella reflects. The consistently active monarch was more at his ease in the battles of heroic drama. Frederick II, passively presiding over a faultless mechanism of military drill, was a new conception of power in reserve and threat in repose. But it is a pity that Prussian parading coincided in Comella's imagination with parading in Italian opera. The military display, the martial music, too often turned the reasoned walking of the more thoughtful characters into operatic prance and strut. A typical direction is the following:

Espaciosa llanura con vista del castillo de Spandau: sale en formación el cuerpo de tropas que pudiere; da vuelta por el teatro, y se forma, quedando las banderas en medio. Saldern va delante, y Mollendorf detrás con las espadas desnudas: Saldern manda las evoluciones necesarias. (Act III)

The eager persistence of this stylized parading in Part II, especially from Act II onwards, would itself suggest an obsession more than fictional. It should be thought of in the terms of a modern equivalent:

35. Typical of this interest and discussion in non-dramatic fields is, for instance, the *Correo*'s long article of 5 August 1789, on the recent French book on military technique by Puiségur. The reviewer eagerly comments on the technique of Frederick II and is obviously fascinated with the details of the new methods of training and discipline.

for instance, the popular obsession, reflected in plays or in films set in airports, atomic stations, or hospitals, with the mechanics of these institutions, the dramatized noises of which, the occupational uniforms, movements, or atmosphere of urgency, the professional danger, the clash of technical interests, prepare the mind of reader or onlooker with realistic tensions well within his topical imagination. In Parts II and III there is a certain amount of sectional fighting that has almost the value, in the playwright's view, of a scientific demonstration of military methods. Consequently it does not compete with the full-scale battle elaborately conceived, for other dramatic purposes, by Zavala y Zamora:

... Después de haber pasado la columna viene la gran guardia; delante de ella vendrá el Sargento; en el centro, etc. . . . (Part II, Act II.)
... Atacan las tropas de Federico a una parte de las tropas que tienen cercado a Quintus, las que abren paso y se salva Quintus, uniéndose con las del Rey, que a su tiempo irán desfilando en retirada, presentando la bayoneta siempre al enemigo. . . . (II, Act II.)
... Vanse las tropas del Rey formadas . . . etc. . . . (II, Act II.)

Comella's *María Teresa de Austria en Landaw*, boasting many elaborate scenes of parade, contains one scene largely devoted to elementary drilling:

... A un tiempo todos los reluctas hacen el ejercicio, unos al compás de la caja, y otros sin ella, según lo adelantados que están. . . .

> *Capitan Roht* Uno, dos; uno, dos; uno,
> dos: alargue vd. el paso
> algo más, uno, dos: uno,
> dos. Extienda vd. ese brazo
> de esta suerte; esta cabeza
> derecha. . . (Act I)

A grand march-past, with its special figures, is reserved for the last act:

El General Kenvenhuller mandará poner sobre las armas en la plaza de Landaw; todas las tropas que puedan formarse en ella. . . . Los cuerpos han de formar el círculo de la plaza, con el orden regular, al compás de la música. . . . Las tropas se abirán en dos filas por donde pasan los Reyes. . . . Después que han dado vuelta se colocan en el centro de la Plaza . . . formando un círculo vistoso que la rodee toda. (Act III)

When Comella approached details of Frederick's private life, dearer to the century even than his soldierly exhibitionism, Santos Díez González, who was not unimpressed when he read the play and stated that it contained potentially interesting situations,[36] refused to pass certain speeches the familiarity of which made the King undignified. Specially offensive to him were parts of Frederick's first, self-conscious speech which the Censor called inopportune, unworthy of a great and wise monarch, and smacking of subversive doctrine. The original speech is interesting to examine for several reasons. It begins with three blunt lines which the Censor allowed to pass, for, although they deal with the monarch's prosaic boots, Santos Díez González, himself a realist, was disposed to accept a judicious amount of Royalty in naturalness. Besides, Frederick's boots had an aura of anecdotal sanctity:

> *Federico* Ya estoy vestido: ahora bien,
> las botas ponerme es fuerza.
> Aquí están, ¡o pesia a tal!

It was when Frederick proceeded to turn the act of putting on his own boots into reflections on the fact that kings, like ordinary men, were born with hands to tend to their own needs, or into other related meditations, that the Censor felt that this Prussian was going too far, that indeed he was verging on what Santos Díez González later described as 'Quaker cynicism'.[37]

Además de no ser oportuno este monólogo aquí me parece ajeno de un rey sabio y grande pues contiene una doctrina que huele a la soberbia cínica y desprecio de las costumbres y usos que prudentemente se adoptan en la sociedad civil y mantienen el orden y policía de ella.[38]

Even though these royal indiscretions were pasted over with inoffensive substitutes, some critics still looked dubiously at the drama's success when it was played to crowded houses from 19 June to 5 July.[39] It is notable, however, that, like Santos Díez González, sober journals took the drama seriously even if they found fault with details. It was new in idea. It dealt with an idolized personality. Its 'interesting situations'

36. '. . . y constando de situaciones que interesaran en el teatro, de costumbres, y algunas otras cualidades que podrán contribuir al gusto de los espectadores. . . .' *Censura*.
37. See the 'Informe' of Santos Díez González on Comella's dramatic attainments, ed. cit., p. 579. 'También hice reformar el carácter de Federico, pues era de un filósofo cínico, o de un cuákero, que son los cínicos de estos tiempos en la substancia.'
38. *Censura*, op. cit.   39. See Coe, *Catálogo*, p. 96.

were modern in conception. The sentiment was up-to-date. Its detail was contemporary if not always strictly accurate.[40] The severe *Memorial literario* of June 1789, unbending so far as to speak of the 'beauties' of this work,[41] took it seriously enough to be concerned about its many soliloquies and noted 'some carelessness' of diction. The *Diario* of July, in view of the drama's success, was even worried about its possible effect on the real Frederick's reputation. Argument turned, in a modern manner, on whether his personality did or did not suffer from Comella's familiar language. Rightly the *Diario* decided that the Comellan Frederick looked bedraggled:

La mucha fama del nombre que lleva (en el título) ha hecho que concurran atropelladamente a verla los apasionados en la representación; . . . pero cuánto rebajarían de su preocupado entusiasmo aquéllos principalmente que creyesen ver alguna cosa tan extraordinaria como lo era el Rey de Prusia.[42]

and gave as evidence the fact that instead of using noble language, befitting his dignity, he made inane pronouncements, and that all characters spoke as if they came from the 'lowest of the low'. The *Memorial literario's* 'some carelessness' is a truer criticism, and the *Diario's* general impression is more accurate than its detailed reasoning. For 'lowest of the low' does not really mean here that the characters speak as if they were illiterates from the slums, but that they do not observe the conventions of characters in traditional literary drama. Comella's reputation in part has suffered undeservedly for this reason. Nowadays, kings have a right to appear in drama as they privately are. They do not normally commit provincial faults of pronunciation. They speak kings' English, or Spanish. But they may use ordinary words; and few are shocked if on informal occasions they resort sometimes to slang. The aesthetic difference between a good twentieth-century drama of the private lives of kings, and Comella's *Federico II* is in the sensitive way in which the good modern playwright selects his colloquialisms. The reason why Federico II looked bedraggled was not, as the *Diario* assumed, because he said ordinary things in ordinary words, but because Comella did not see that one ordinary phrase might be artistic

40. The *Diario* of 31 July 1789, protests that Comella's use of the dagger in the cause of outraged honour is unPrussian and accordingly inverisimilitudinous.

41. 'A vuelta de las bellezas de esta obra se encubrían algunos lunares defectuosos; . . .'

42. *Diario*, 31 July 1789.

and another—perhaps because of associated ideas—might not. His modern instinct to bring his monarchs down to earth was justifiable, and that is why the critics of Part I at least took the drama relatively seriously. But the technique of selectiveness on the level of ordinary conversation was not yet developed. Critics, huddled round traditional criteria, were rightly suspicious. Moratín in *La comedia nueva* was pedantically scornful of the Comellas. González del Castillo, parodying Comella's inanities in a *sainete*, was amused.[43] Neither, understandably enough, was aware of the historical importance of Comella's experiment.

The moralists had tried to convert the stage into a pulpit. And, so far, didactic tragedies had been conspicuous for their dullness. But the realistic morals of Frederick II are irreproachable without being invariably tedious. By the 'beauties' of the work the critics chiefly meant its morals: the Prussian's personal sense of responsibility, his translation into practical human detail of his ideal of transcendent justice. The underlying thesis which this urgent drama tries to prove is that a monarch as father of his people and example to his children, ought to be able to take a first-hand interest in his subjects, and that the method for reaching judicial decisions on everyday problems is intelligently to weigh the evidence on both sides. The examples, trivial and elaborate, brought forward to illustrate this argument are often incongruous to the point of grotesqueness. But the character had more realistic meaning for the Spanish public, who had been unable to make a personal hero out of Carlos III and had no hope of being able to admire the weak-kneed Carlos IV, than had all the excessive heroisms of ancient Christians or Numantians. The ideal of equality before the Law and the social dignity of all men was palpitatingly actual, even if Spain had not yet defined the lines along which she wished to see it realized. Well might the critics talk, in this sense, of 'beauties'. It was Comella's illustrations which eventually disconcerted them. The Phantom-King must be compassionate; but when, even with anecdotal sanction, he refuses to let Manfeld find him a shelter from the sun as they sit down to rest in the fierce heat, he sounds merely fussy; when, in order to keep public money free for public expenses he talks about cutting down his own little luxuries, he sounds naïve; when, sharing his soldiers' bad bread,

43. See note 3, page 576.

he says that if generals ate the common soldiers' rations they might know how badly the army is fed, his tone sounds less fond than foolish. It was for such reasons, as well as for colloquial turns of phrase, that critics feared a loss of dignity in the character of Europe's hero. At the same time he is not less mature than the 'great' heroes of Spanish neo-classical drama who are not men at all, but only a bundle of qualities of which some, like 'Honour', are of very dubious Christian value. His little acts of kindness, eccentricity, or self-revelation, showed later dramatists where to seek relief from rant and how to fill space between major activities.

But the comparative seriousness with which the critics viewed this drama was dispersed by its sequels. Encouraged by success, the author naturally stressed the novel details which had strained artistic principles already. While the general public continued to applaud the sentimentally illuminated Frederick, literary critics grew nauseated. The *Memorial literario*, which had found 'beauties' in Part I, spoke disgustedly in 1790 of the excessive military parading in Part II. But in some ways Part II, or *Federico II en el campo de Torgau*, [44] is retrogressive in more traditional qualities. The plot incorporates the love-story of the man whom Frederick condemned to death for writing to his sweetheart by forbidden candle-light, and who, in this version, after being captured by the enemy, in mistake for Frederick, and after performing signal services for his country, is pardoned. Here not only does the dramatist play inartistically on the external qualities which brought him success in Part I, but he introduces some love-scenes in the Golden Age tradition, though, it is true, they are not given much emphasis. Also Frederick, for all his modern belief in calling a spade a spade is sufficiently affected by the old *comedia*-atmosphere at times to indulge in archaic flourishes like these:

> *Federico* . . . os llamo sólo
> para deciros que sepa
> vuestro valor que mañana
> apenas la aurora bella
> conduzca al día he resuelto
> vencer, o morir. (Act I)

44. It was played in 1789.

Nevertheless Comella continued to labour heavily in more modern directions. He was at great pains to depict his hero as thoughtful: an attribute firmly underlined in the opening scene when Quintus notices that he seems preoccupied; and this is substantiated by his expressed worries later over the critical military situation, the numbers of his own men, the strength of the enemy, and like problems, before his decisive encounter with the Danes. The traditional hero sometimes gave these matters perfunctory attention, but he was usually confident even in danger, despite all material considerations; for worry and reflection, in a military man, used to be taken by the theatre public as signs of weakness. Now, the eighteenth-century audience was being encouraged to respect self-questioning and mental disquiet. In this instance it was asked to contrast Frederick's private misery with the fatherly show of confidence he assumes before his soldiers, and to assess his domination over himself as a higher form of courage than blind physical confidence. This play too is meant to illustrate an ideal of judicial objectivity in two directions. We are to admire a just severity in cases where, extenuating circumstances being admitted, tolerance would look more obviously attractive; and we are presented with thoroughness in face of temptations to reach decisions quickly. Frederick's argument in Act III, where he is still laboriously weighing evidence, that a king's unfavourable judgement is respected, even by the victim, so long as he has proved himself willing to examine the whole evidence with an open mind, is an idea which interested the century and which France and Spain did not, as yet, take for granted. Had he been gifted with a more distinguished manner of speech, Frederick's words could have made an important contribution to Spain's political science. The passage is worth quoting for its elaborate meaningfulness:

> *Federico* El Príncipe que camina
> con tiento, cuando un delito
> no está bien justificado
> da a sus vasallos indicios
> de que desea acertar.
> . . . Cuando un Rey
> sigue estos sabios principios,
> la misma pena que impone
> la respeta el reo mismo. . . . (Act III)

The Censor, after swallowing most of the first two Parts out of the belief that they were reasonably good for the soul, rebelled two years later at the treble emphases of Part III, provocatively entitled *Federico II, en Glaatz, o La Humanidad*,[45] and he called Comella's Frederick the pedant that by then he had become:

... El carácter de Federico II, no tanto es propio de un rey, como de un pedante que a cada paso quiere lucir vertiendo a borbotones máximas políticas tan vulgares, y comunes, que se ocurren a cualquiera hombre de menos que mediana educación. ...[46]

Events had moved alarmingly since the year which hailed the experimental Part I. In Comella's zealous hands the political and social innuendos, once mild and tentative, were now, as in his domestic dramas of these years, much more blatant. It was therefore, unfortunately, the most interesting part of *Federico II, en Glaatz* that the Censor was obliged to cut. So if Comella's hero is a sentimental pedant and if the people about him are anaemic, the reason is partly that some of the meatiest speeches have been snatched away before they could be put into their stage mouths. It is only by the practice of eating that the dramatist learns to digest. If these Prussians could not speak in more than harmless generalizations the personality of the figure-head would seem weaker than it really was. This Part in its original form is a complex thesis-drama against the use of torture, raising a difficult question, wrote the Censor repressively, on which Spain has not yet officially pronounced. Consequently while allowing Comella to touch on the subject as far as it was necessary to his plot—indeed the use of torture was as abhorrent to the average Spaniard as to the average Frenchman and as a principle was as much out of date in Spain as elsewhere—he expediently removed those heart-felt speeches on the subject and re-distributed the emphasis over the weak parts.

This play, bringing Frederick to Glaatz, in a revived bustle of anecdote[47] and reasserting his love of examining the state of local affairs at first hand, puts him in touch with Casimiro Thesen, accused wrongly, on very damning circumstantial evidence, of having murdered a man known to have ruined him. Casimiro awaits his final sentence. The thesis-suggestion enters the drama where the exhausted victim, faced

45. It is licensed for 1792 in a manuscript version in the Biblioteca Municipal, Madrid.
46. *Censura*, op. cit.   47. See note 4, page 577.

with torture, makes a false confession out of fear. The chief speeches concerned with propaganda occur in the crucial Act III where the authorities unwillingly decide on torture as a last resort. One speech recklessly attacks the 'barbarous' law itself:

> *Casimiro* No Señor, y de ello hago
> testigo a aquel Dios que todo
> todo lo ve desde lo alto.
> Solio donde mi inocencia
> reclamará su sagrado
> enojo, contra una ley
> que condena a los humanos
> a sacrificar su vida
> a unos bárbaros mandatos,
> ley que ni las fieras mismas
> siendo fieras inventaron. . . .

Another stresses the fact that torture defeats the end of true justice and brings suffering to the innocent:

> *Casimiro* . . . Y que el día
> que Dios descubra el arcano
> de esta puerta, compasivo
> proscriba [el soberano] de sus estados
> un suplicio, a la inocencia
> de los hombres tan contrario.

Yet another is feelingly directed to the Great Frederick in the cause of European enlightenment, urging him to set an example by prohibiting torture:

> *El Barón de*
> *Griefemberg* Y en alas de la piedad
> vine, Señor, a enteraros
> de un hecho que da un ejemplo
> a todos los soberanos
> de Europa para que un uso
> proscriban tan humanos
> que reduce al inocente
> a confesarse culpado.

for the last part of which speech the Censor substituted a more diplomatic plea, receiving, instead of Frederick's definite:

> Desde hoy en mis estados
> el uso de la tortura
> se prohiba.

the more noncommital, and, certainly in expression, the more states-manlike promise:

> Desde hoy en mis estados
> el uso de la tortura
> se mire con el cuidado
> que exige la humanidad,
> no decretando su amargo
> suplicio contra los reos
> por ahora, como el agravio
> no resulte contra Dios
> o contra los soberanos.

Perhaps more drastically still the Censor ordered the removal of the rack which, with the victim in action, was to electrify the atmosphere as the drama mounted in tension. The play, it is true, ought to have been better without it. But one must not ask too much of thesis-experimenters. As regards the cuts outside this thesis-case of innocence misinterpreted, modern sympathy would be entirely with the Censor. He suppressed a few lines of tediously reiterated liberalism, the more exaggerated portions of Frederick's self-conscious objection to praise and etiquette, and the 'noble humility' of his self-estimate as man first and king second. He spared us some of the weeping and wailing in the victim's starving family. He reduced some of the extravagances of speech, and fastidiously cancelled a foolish scene in which Comella arranged for a 'chorus of prisoners' to chant, in marching time, the inane verses beginning:

> Del que protege
> la humanidad
> pasará su nombre
> de edad en edad.

Here the experiment clearly was the healthier for amputation, though some of the more harmless passages, including these verses, were restored in the printed edition of 1795.

But if we can forget Federico's ingenuousness, or, alternatively remember that he was, in his own way, no more priggish or pedantic than Hormesinda's rhetorical brother, and not nearly so empty-headed, we may hope to appreciate the social tension of the times in which the drama was set. This tension present in the public consciousness was a proper phenomenon for the dramatist to exteriorize, not because it could be translated into moral terms of social welfare, but because it was in itself, apart from any of its implications, an aspect of the epoch's mental life. Better artists than Comella had insisted on it with all the emphasis a man gives to the matters that most immediately concern him. Encouraged to remove their gaze from problems of eternity and fix it on their material environment, they had applied their restless logic to their surroundings. They had dealt realistically with, for example, the state of the prisons, and commented on the unfairness of the slow workings of justice, because restless human logic was, just then, fluttering round these subjects. Some of the scenes of *Federico II* . . . , Part III, are broadly reminiscent of scenes in, for instance, Fielding's *Amelia*, not least in their portrayal of misery and humanitarian response. Comella's Prison Governor, Barth, is a compassionate person who allows Casimiro's starving wife and children to take this prisoner's place for stated hours while he goes out to work to keep them; and it is Barth, from his inside standpoint, who tries to bring to the King's notice the lack of proper living conditions in state prisons where, we are told, reforms are impeded because royal inspectors, whose visits are known of beforehand and are carefully prepared for, never see these institutions under normal working conditions. Such themes, however foreign, adjusted themselves effortlessly to Spanish implication.

The atmosphere of Comella's ideas, or borrowings, was enterprisingly true to life. It is the greater pity therefore that poor Federico cannot fit himself into the social atmosphere of pressing realism with artistic maturity. As in Part I, he has a practical awareness of his kingly responsibilities. He is provided with the little personal interests, experiences and relationships meant to give him his proper dimensions as a man: news of his family, of his brother's concerns and his young nephew's mischievousness, come in private letters which he lays aside, with irritating ostentation, that his humbler subjects' interests may be served first:

> . . . atendamos al vasallo
> que en un Rey es lo primero. (Act I)

His exasperated weariness at so many demands on him, a good dramatic idea, should be there to enforce the nervous weight of his responsibilities by implication:

> ... Será forzoso
> que me niegue a responderlos,
> me molestan demasiado,
> para nada tengo tiempo.

but Comella was too unsubtle to imply, and the next lines pompously fuss and elaborate:

> ¿Pero no soy Rey? ¿No puso
> sobre mis hombros el Cielo
> el peso de una corona?
> Si el Cielo le puso, debo
> sostenerlo, y si me pesa
> que me pese; un grande empleo
> siempre de grandes cuidados
> va acompañado. (Act I)

His meeting with a little girl who, thinking he is a doctor, takes him to visit her sick mother, plays on his famous eighteenth-century sensibility and precipitates a highly sentimental scene which chiefly shows how the King's fatherly care for his subjects can be driven to artistic disaster by the force of emphasis. Audiences might justifiably weep with emotion when the child becomes impatient, pulls at the royal sleeve, and baby-ishly takes command:

> *Niña* Conmigo
> venid, vamos, no tardéis.
> *Le agarra, y le lleva hacia la casa.* (Act II)

But if only Comella could have let well alone and spared us the merciless beat of the moral!

> *Federico* Estos encuentros los libros
> son en que estudian los Reyes,
> que gobiernan por sí mismos.

Let it be admitted, however, that the modern reality he was aiming at required much more art and intuition than did Arandan High Tragedy, and that if the unenterprising *literatos* had attempted Comella's difficult feat they would probably have made themselves more laughable than he. As for Frederick II, he continued as a stage model in Spain and elsewhere well into the second decade of the nineteenth century.[48]

Many are the military variants on the theme of the phantom-sovereign, sometimes with women in the title-roles. A very managing woman, with more than her share of Comellan humanitarianism, was María Teresa de Austria who, in a series of three plays, dispensed carefully considered justice, busied herself with first-hand investigations of difficult cases—if necessary disguised as an ordinary townswoman, which led her into all sorts of dramatic ironies—and, in her spare time, attempted to set an example of womanliness by sewing shirts for soldiers and giving personal attention to her children's moral upbringing. One part, *El buen hijo, o María Teresa de Austria*,[49] concentrates heavily on the heroism of a new kind of Déserteur, tortuously derived, it would seem, from Stephanie's *Deserteur aus kindlicher Liebe*,[50] and who allows himself to be accused of treason in order that, by a complicated process, his father, threatened with imprisonment for debt, may get the reward for unwittingly giving information about him. It was a strange angle from which to view the code of honour in Madrid. But that honour could be conceived of even fleetingly on an exclusively humanitarian level, to the detriment of abstract ideals of patriotism and personal integrity, says much for the influence of those disturbed values blowing like autumn leaves before Spain's gate.

In 1791 appeared Comella's *El fénix de los criados o María Teresa de Austria* which the Censor passed with the usual excuse that there was nothing better for the companies to perform. Again María Teresa rides the epoch's hobby-horse of royal responsibility and flogs it unrestrainedly. Since no Spaniard had yet discovered how to illustrate the ideal of justice and equity from a monarch's standpoint except through the ingenuous medium of the audience chamber, she interviews typical subjects in this hallowed manner and from time to time brings up with her advisers burning questions of the Spanish day. Once, for instance, she so tactlessly questions the rightness of a state economy which permits

48. Other plays of foreign origin about Frederick II are, for example: *El Mayor Pálmer*, translated from Pigault-Lebrun by Enciso Castrillón and played in 1803 (Cot. Máiquez, 173); *Caprichos de Federico II, o el Barón de Felchein*, from Pigault-Lebrun, played in 1815; *El panadizo de Federico II, o la petición extraña* (Coe, 174); etc., etc.

49. It was played in 1790.

50. See W. H. Bruford (*Theatre, Drama and Audience in Goethe's Germany*, London, 1950, p. 187), who discusses Stephanie's play as a derivative of Mercier's *Déserteur*.

large sums, in years of bad harvests and general misery, to be spent on royal festivities, that the Censor, his mind on the current policy of the Spanish Court, is obliged to halt her with the remark that she has trespassed upon a delicate subject:

'Omítase porque es punto delicado y muy expuesto a errar.'[51]

Her intervention in public affairs is all too meaningly to the benefit of the common people. She sets an example of magnanimity by inviting children of humble circumstances to dine at her own children's table or by refusing to close her gardens to the public, and an example of conjugal uprightness by urging her unhappy lady-in-waiting to bear her wretched married lot with fortitude while she deplores the iniquity of the lady's parents in having forced her to marry against her will. With the medical and moral debate on inoculation[52] raging in the Spanish press she sets an example of medical and moral enlightenment by submitting her own children to experiment. But apparently her 'Quaker' principles do not exclude a little pomp and military display and at strategically dramatic intervals she reviews troops, watches parades, or poses amid all the palatial grandeur that the theatre's operatic properties could supply.

Another Part, *María Teresa de Austria en Landaw*, notable for its excessive trooping and parading,[53] is also remarkable for its theories on military training. Perhaps because this monarch was the mother of her people and not the father that Frederick was, her views on military discipline were different from his. Despite the smart modern shows of military drill put on at intervals for her greater glory, she could not have known of the Prussian severity which went into the making of these new military mechanics, for her representative, Captain Roht, refuses to allow recruits to be thrashed. In this Part as in the others the Queen pronounces against luxury for the few where many are in want, has views about the harsh extortion of taxes, and busies herself with other topical problems.

The story deals with a cadet, vaguely familiar to us already, who, led astray by wild companions, lifts his sword against his captain; and it introduces the cadet's father saddled with the task of conducting his court-martial. But it is the youth's bad companions, rather unchivalrously denounced by him, who are finally condemned. Comella was

51. *Censura*, MS.   52. See note 5, page 577.   53. See p. 520 above.

putting the moral accent where he thought it should go: not so much on lessons of artificial *pundonor*, as on the unformalized lessons of social cause and effect, in this case on vicious influences in society and their corruption of the innocent. So we are not meant to ask ourselves whether it is or is not right to tell tales in self-defence against one's colleagues. We are asked to observe a social poison and its leavening effect. The unprepossessing cadet, temporarily under sentence of death, makes the moral clear by warning his fellows to obey their superiors, moderate their passions, and give up their vices. Despite his ungentle-manliness, he was of a higher social class than the London Apprentice or the Gamester, but he may well have heard of them through un-English and un-Spanish acquaintances.

An even more thorough-going reformer was Comella's untiring Isabel I of Russia[54] who was given, when praised, to assuming disingenuously that all princes shared her enlightenment, until the Censor, under the irony of the Spanish situation in 1795, was obliged to interfere, turning these words, for instance:

> Como sus almas son grandes
> hay pocos [príncipes] que no la [beneficencia] sepan,
> sino que cada uno sigue
> su camino al ejercerla,
> unos promulgando leyes
> que la justicia sostengan,
> otros aliviando al pobre
> los tributos y gabelas.
> Éstos haciendo dichosos
> prodigando sus riquezas
> aquéllos dando fomento
> a las artes y las ciencias . . .[55]

into the less artful:

> Quiero seguir de mis padres
> en cuanto pueda las huellas,
> fueron grandes en un todo,
> heroicos en sus empresas . . . etc. (Act. II)

54. *El hombre singular* [*o Isabel I de Rusia*], MS., Madrid, 1795.
55. We have had to reconstruct line 8 from another version as in the Censor's copy it is obliterated.

His *censura* of this play was the occasion of one of his outspoken remarks against the Ecclesiastical Censor for 'unintelligently' fussing over harmless trivialities and passing over impertinent opinions on the duties of kings—which subject, though Santos Díez González could hardly say so, would have fallen disagreeably on Bourbon ears—on the empty dignity of titles and scutcheons, on the extravagance of the powerful,[56] and the delegating of kingly authority to unworthy despots, like, any Spaniard would be sure to interpret, the recently ennobled and enriched Godoy. The Literary Censor frankly agreed that there was something in what the playwright said. Like all responsible Spaniards in public positions he would know precisely how the political rot had set in and whom to blame. But, like Jovellanos on the same subject,[57] he was obliged to be discreet; and, as before, he objected to Comella's using the stage as a political platform, still thinking that in the critical times such ideas would do more harm than good.[58] When, therefore, one of the characters set up above his door in the drama, instead of the time-honoured scutcheon of nobility, an enlightened, shield-shaped substitute bearing the legend 'Casa de la Beneficencia en favor de la Humanidad', the Censor wearily took it down with the remark that if he must write words like these above his door, he must write them on a plain board which will not suggest odious comparisons with the gentry's coats-of-arms.

Likewise, in greater or lesser degree, Comella's other military monarchs, male and female, preach to the social susceptibilities in the air and secure their own acceptance by appeal to the mass heart and eye. They address themselves to the family man and woman. If a love story comes into the plot at all it is usually subordinated to the problems of the married characters. Love scenes, even Richardsonian, are rare in military drama: a fact which distinguishes it sharply from the old and new heroic types written by Comella in other moods, where mothers hardly exist and children, if seen, are not heard. Love and sentiment were intended to be of the maturer, the more practical and responsible kinds in which the century was interested. Colour and spectacle were not inspired by the

56. See note 6, page 577.   57. *Diarios*, ed. cit., vol. ii, pp. 24, 171, *et passim*.
58. 'Supongo que la moral sea sana, y que en este drama nos muestre el poeta algunas verdades políticas. Pero dudo si el teatro sea lugar propio para representarlas en unos tiempos en que el mundo malicia demasiado y se halla confuso, y aturdido por una revolución de opiniones.'

ethereal needs of lovers but by the disciplined parade of soldiers symbolizing family security. Kings do not tend, as in the more properly termed heroic drama, to lead the way into a stage fight, or to shout rousing orders while bridges flame and fall and soldiers scale the cardboard battlements. Nor is military drama commonly 'irregular'. Like its domestic relation it often observes the Unities fairly closely, and with more verisimilitude than many regular tragedies, where twenty-four hours can scarce contain the density of catastrophic cause and effect. This too helps to explain why military plays were at first accepted by critics with more seriousness than might have been expected. It was chiefly because Comella so thoroughly repeated and over-reached himself, and because his rivals were doing the same, or worse, that literary critics rebelled. By the time they came to know, in strangely similar circumstances to the aforementioned, a Catalina II, Empress of Russia, determined throughout two Parts[59] to see justice done, not only to poor peasants, but to poor Comellas:

Esta princesa [she reads unblushingly aloud about herself from a history of her reign to date] acostumbrada a premiar los servicios, recompensa los que se hacen a la patria, mucho más que los hechos a su persona: conoce los talentos a primera vista, y protege como princesa ilustrada las ciencias y los artes: su corte es la escuela del buen gusto, de los placeres delicados, y de la política. La verdad proscrita siempre de los palacios encuentra en su corazón el más seguro asilo; su reinado hará la felicidad de la Rusia, así como es la gloria y el ornamento de ella.

a progressive Peter the Great[60] engaged, with occasional military flourishes in uprooting 'ignorance', 'stupidity', 'barbarity', and wrong-thinking generally, or in fomenting the arts and sciences, agriculture, industry, 'wholesome politics', justice, and reason, and receptively pausing now and again in melodramatic style, if only, as in Act II, to give a studied, narrow, regard; a luxury-hating Cristina de Suecia;[61] a Christopher Columbus through whom we are privileged to meet some of nature's philosophers from the Indies whose innocent criticism

59. *Catalina II Emperatriz de Rusia* was played on 4 November 1797, 'en celebridad de los días de nuestro Augusto Soberano'. A *censura* of October 1797 demands various cuts. The quoted passage seems to be one of those affected. Manuscript copies and a printed version exist in B. Mun. There is an edition of a second part, called *Catalina II en Cronstad*, dated Madrid, 1799. It contains some elaborate military parade.

60. See *Pedro el Grande. Czar de Moscovia*. It was played in 1796.

61. There is a manuscript with *Censuras* for 1797, B. Mun.

classifies them as new Citizens of the World;[62] a Louis XIV who was kingly enough, the *Memorial literario* thought, except when he talked about his sonnet-writing:[63] besides various non-Comellan personages,[64] some of them lurching forth in frantic emulation—by this time any predisposition on the part of the discerning to see the 'beauties' in military drama and its associates had long since faded. The critics' views, however, were neither sought nor heard. In fact by this time they themselves were not very sure of what they wanted or what they could believe.

62. *Cristóbal Colón*, (played in 1790).

63. See *Memorial literario*, November 1789. The play is *Pruebas de la virtud. Luis XIV el Grande*, (played in 1789, Bar., n.d.).

64. See note 7, page 577.

The Modernization of Heroic Drama

'El perfecto, el más ínclito heroísmo,
es saber conocerse el hombre mismo;
saber lo que es piedad, lo que es flaqueza'
(From the ode *El verdadero heroísmo*
by González del Castillo)

BETWEEN the performance of *Manolo*, Part I, and *El muñuelo*, Cruz
produced at least one other parody set in Lavapiés. This is *Los bandos
del Avapiés, y la venganza del Zurdillo*, played in 1776.[1] Neither Manolo
nor his relatives figure in this gang-warfare, but the dramatic neighbourhood and atmosphere are the familiar ones of the two parts of
Manolo, *El héroe de la manzana* and *El muñuelo*. There is this interesting
difference, however. *Los bandos del Avapiés* clearly burlesques, not neo-
classical tragedy, but the national heroic drama. It is possible that Don
Ramón in 1776 was re-establishing his reputation as a man of culture
after his successes with the anti-classical *Manolo*. More likely, *Los bandos
del Avapiés* is another instance of the comprehensiveness of his *gracioso*-
mind. At all events this *sainete* makes a good Spanish parallel to Fielding's *Tom Thumb the Great* whose inspiration also derived from national
heroic drama. The tone of *Los bandos del Avapiés* is not satirical and is not
nearly so pointed as that of the semi-polemical *Manolo* Part I. The seedy
disorder of contemporary heroics must have supplied the author with
plenty of practical examples; but in the play he makes no apparent effort
to teach a literary lesson and gives no clear indication as to whether
he laughs at heroic drama in its decadence or in its hey-day. He merely
laughs. It is a matter of comedy for comedy's sake. But the laughter has
historical significance. Modern readers who may not care for too close

1. See Cot. *R.X.*, p. 295. We have used the edition of the *sainete* of Madrid, 1800.

an aquaintance with decadent imitations of the heroic Golden Age can gain a good general impression of what they were like, and an insight into the Spaniard's tolerant affection for them in the days of national depression, from the swollen speeches and the disarmingly playful spirit of *Los bandos del Avapiés*. Cruz's contemporaries made mental reservations as they took their pleasures, just as we do. The tacit normalcy of the spirit of this 'heroic' *sainete* is that of the burlesque tragedies and makes contact with what is fundamentally normal in every generation. *Los bandos del Avapiés* assumes that the Spaniard has a sense of humour; the anxious *Comedia nueva*, directed against the same genre, does not. Cruz's laughter is that of a partner who supposes that his colleague-public makes imaginative allowances for exaggerations attractive to it, as he does himself. Moratín, from a pedagogic height assumes that his public's mind cannot, without instruction, assess what its eyes are viewing.

Though heroic drama in the late seventies was associated most commonly with the battling, incendiary qualities of José Concha, Fermín de Laviano, and their humble compeers, in fact no eighteenth-century heroic drama worthy of the name was complete without at least one battle fully fought out in public under one or more national heroes, for the typical audience, like Mr. Johnson of *The Rehearsal*, loved 'those plays, where they cut and slash one another, upon the stage, for a whole hour together'.[2] Other venerated features, like inset love scenes, the depiction of famous historical incidents, comic relief, considerations of honour and chivalry, and general cloak-and-sword activity, might be used at the convenience of the playwright but the battle must never be omitted. *La comedia nueva* of 1792, referring to the three battles of Don Eleuterio's *Gran cerco de Viena*,[3] does no more than justice to the tradition. Moratín would appear to have taken the idea for satirizing this important aspect of heroic drama from an article fulsomely praising his *El viejo y la niña* in *El Correo*, of June 1790. The writer, who calls himself El Amante del Teatro, relating a dream in which Comellan and Zavalan representatives of bad taste such as Federico II, La Jacoba, Cristóbal Colón, Carlos XII de Suecia, attack the gentlemanly *Viejo*, tells how Carlos XII, like Moratín's Doña Agustina, of *La comedia nueva*, describes the battling breed:

2. *The Rehearsal*, Act V.   3. Act II, i.

538

En mi comedia hay guerras, hay ardides hay bombazos, hay lenguaje, hay
heroísmo, hay cosazas; . . . medios versos, ideas apuntadas . . .[4]

how the *Viejo* silences them with an anticipation of Don Pedro's self-
righteousness:

El dueño de esta mesa me ha hecho agravio en ponerme junta a Vmds.
porque si Vmds. son comedias, desventurada de mí, y si yo lo soy, lo son
Vmds. tanto como las coplas de calainos . . .

and how El Amante del Teatro, after locking up the rabble, turns to the
restrained *Viejo* for the award of his dues:

Ven . . . honor de España y triunfo de la racionalidad y Buen Gusto.

The effect of the *Viejo's* restraint was rather spoilt a month later when
Moratín, accused of inverisimilitude in certain aspects of the play,
answered his critics by a letter to the *Correo* of tedious length.[5] But in
La comedia nueva of 1792 he seems eagerly to have identified his principles with those attributed to him by El Amante del Teatro, and his
satirical voice in this play was echoed, in its turn, by the more tolerant
author of the burlesque *El impresario burlado* which refers to an imagin-
ary heroic play, filled with fighting, and called absurdly *Cerco y asalto
de Guadarrama por Solimán el Primero.*[6]

Cruz's more developed burlesque, *Los bandos del Avapiés*, seizing
upon the battle-essential, unfolds a tale that makes the rivalries of
Benavides and Caravajales, Abencerrajes and Zegríes pale into in-
significance. The source of the trouble, as might be expected, is a particularly sharp point of honour thrust into prominence when one of the
sons of the heroic *barrio* Barquillo is beaten up by the sons of the equally
heroic Lavapiés and left bleeding in the street. At such a crisis the
conservative Barquillo can only revert to another ancient tradition
going far back into the Golden Age—the fine old fury speech, ascending
to its climax of defiance by the steps of rhetorical enumeration,[7] and
here delivered by El Zurdillo, with, one cannot doubt, the fine old
stamping and shouting:

4. Compare Moratín's:
Doña Augustina: Figúrese usted una comedia heroica como ésta, con más de nueve
lances que tiene. Un desafío a caballo por el patio, tres batallas, dos tempestades, un
entierro, una función de máscara, un incendio de ciudad, un puente roto, dos ejercicios
de fuego y un ajusticiado. (Act II, i.)
5. See *Correo* . . ., for 3 and 7 July.
6. See note 1, page 577.   7. See note 2, page 578.

El Zurdillo Soy el furor,
     La ira, la rabia, el veneno
     del invencible Barquillo;
     que aunque ultrajado me veo,
     soy el valiente Zurdillo
     conocido por mis hechos.

Traditional too is the way in which the inhabitants of Barquillo are flattered into action by the liberal use of adjectives like 'noble' and 'heroic'. Noble, heroic matrons are summoned from the sausages and black puddings with which they minister to the capital's needs; a great assortment of heroes is called up from equally vital tasks, with equally lofty apostrophes; and it is only when matrons and heroes appear to have missed their Golden Age cue that the summons turns to an anxiously peevish 'aren't you coming?' But these moderns have not exactly lost their cue. They are merely slow in playing up to the traditional demand on their services and in remembering that to abandon their only means of livelihood is a very minor detail in the logic of heroics.[8] It is unnecessary to recount all the features of this epic struggle which are well up to Cruz's usual standard. But the rallying oration of Zurdillo of Barquillo to his gang, in which Cruz excels himself, cannot be passed over. Calderón's imitators showed that it must start with the simple statement of identity and a self-portrait; features which are also parodied in a 'biographical' speech in *El impresario burlado*.[9] Zurdillo's runs as follows:

Zurdillo Ya sabéis soy el Zurdillo,
    que por mis valientes hechos
    he ido a los cuatro presillos
    . . .

They knew how in a flourish of clichés and Golden Age inversions, it should trace the history of the offence from its remote origins to its present crisis. This orator, at the climax of his retrospection, tells how he

8. The heroic principle is expressed, if a little belatedly, by Zunga:
    aunque una pierda su hacienda
    la honra ha de ser lo primero.
9. Op. cit. See: Mi padre, pues otro ignoro,
    fuel el Nilo, undosa muralla
    que siete bombas de nieve
    por siete bocas dispara.

was left to pay two and a half *reales* in a tavern for what his faithless Zayna and her Lavapiés lover had consumed:

> Piden de beber, bebieron;
> piden pan, piden sardinas,
> y para postres pimientos.

and, not content with his indignant statement, he unflaggingly proceeds to the résumé—peroration:

> Ésta es mi fuerte congoja,
> éste mi duro tormento,
> ésta mi cruel fatiga,
> éste mi gran sentimiento.
> A todos toca el agravio;
> todos vengarle debemos;
> y en Lavapiés con su sangre
> hoy nuestras manos lavemos,
> para cuya gran empresa
> hemos de emplear soberbios
> todos los cinco sentidos,
> aire, agua, tierra y fuego.

Only too familiar also is the *staccato*—dialogue at another tense moment of the drama, pieced together in a jaunty pattern of phrases reflecting conflicts of opinions and anguished divisions of allegiance, in this instance at the very point of the sword:

> *Canillejas* Que es tu enemigo
> *Zurdillo* Bien dices
> *Zayna* Que es mi sangre
> *Zurdillo* Ya lo veo.
> *Canillejas* Derrámala.
> *Zurdillo* Será justo.
> *Zayna* No hagas tal.
> *Zurdillo* Está bien hecho.
> . . .
> *Canillejas* Mátale
> *Zayna* Perdónale.
> *Los dos* Resuélvete
> . . .

541

> *Canillejas* Pues haz lo que digo
> *Zurdillo* Voy
> *Zayna* Pues haz lo que pido
> *Zurdillo* Vuelvo.

Peace on this occasion is restored by the feminine artfulness of Zayna who stages a dying act and delivers a farewell speech of great pathos whenever the situation grows ominous, with the help of which little accomplishment she is able to restrain her lover from further deeds of violence.

Los bandos del Avapiés appears to have been the racketing *sainete* that inspired the *tonadilla El héroe del Barquillo* of which we heard Santos Díez González complaining in 1792 when he deplored the fashion for slum heroics.[10] Some of the *tonadilla's* dialogue showing the gallant's divided mind, is very close to the passage quoted above,[11] and the *tonadilla* itself evidently formed one of the innumerable comedy-turns that Manolo's descendants continued to propagate. The Censor was right in saying that the manners of the real Lavapiés showed no improvement for the ridicule started by *Manolo*. But the inner truth of the situation escaped him. Lavapiés did not figure in parodies in order to receive instruction in morals but to give instruction in the difficult art of acquiring a sense of proportion.

Other traditional features of heroic drama as it had come down in its decadence to the eighteenth century, were mentioned by other parodists and satirists, sometimes with affection, sometimes with contempt. The popular Fermín del Rey in *La comedia de repente*[12] laughed comfortably at the habit of ending speeches with hackneyed vocatives:

> Parlamento hay de sesenta
> versos, y todos acaban
> con 'Brutos, hombres, y fieras.'

and at the poetic exaggeration of love:

> Amor, si mis sentimientos
> no ha de mejorar la suerte
> dale mi vida a la muerte,
> y mi esperanza a los vientos. . . .

10. See p. 271 above.   11. See note 3, page 578.
12. It is a *sainete* licensed for 1788.

542

The not very ingenious parody *El Traidor Tiñitas*[13] is too noisily engaged in backstreet fighting to be coherent. But the serious-minded Cándido María Trigueros, in some notes on the old burlesque *El caballero de Olmedo*, which he presumably meant for discussion in the Academia de Buenas Letras de Sevilla,[14] parallels the unhumorous amusement of Leandro Moratín by solemnly underlining the national characteristics ridiculed amiably in *El caballero de Olmedo*—for instance, the scufflings in the dark and the mysterious conversations 'within', usual in all forms of the *comedia*—and by interpreting them to suit his own views.

No destructive satirist or critic, however, could remedy the situation. Theatres would only relinquish the old battling, the famous old sentiments, and infamous imitations of them, if playwrights could provide them with acceptable substitutes. The efforts of popular dramatists, therefore, to modernize and rationalize the national heroic play have a historical importance out of all proportion to their artistic value.

The word 'heroic' was used so loosely in the eighteenth-century press and in playbills that it leaves the vaguest impression about several kinds of dramas which were very different from each other in effect and represented different ideological impulses. 'Heroic' covered all dramas dealing with the great actions of great men, including all 'historical' dramas not bound by neo-classical precepts, and some lively dramas in which the sensationalism of the action and the mechanical devices thrust all officially heroic thought and feeling into the background. Ramón de la Cruz, for instance, in 1771, described as 'heroic' his arrangement of Metastasio's *Talestre* as *Entre un hijo y el esposo, antes esposa que madre. Talestris, Reina de Egipto*, where, it will be noticed, he used the double title of Spanish Baroque tradition, with its jingling paradox calculated to excite curiosity, and its orientative climax. This kind of title spelt reassurance to the distrustful masses, and it could, if necessary, be broken up later to look like the names of two different dramas. Cruz himself genially burlesqued the tradition of elaborate titles when in an *Introducción* of 1778 he spoke of a play called: '*La*

13. This is an anonymous one-act burlesque of which there is an undated edition in the Biblioteca Nacional, Madrid. It is presumably the same as *Las Tiñitas*, 'tragedia . . . burlesca' in one act, whose publication was advertised by the *Diario* in 1788. The authors initials were given as D. J. A. P. L. See Coe, p. 215.

14. MS. B. Nac.

traición de la piedad es piedad de la traición. El mágico Galalón, y bandos de Leganés';[15] and Antonio Valladares, perhaps less playfully, though from his own glass house he could scarcely afford to throw satirical stones, also parodied the tradition in an *Introducción*, of 1782, when he referred to a play entitled: *'El asombro de la Europa, y a veces hace un engaño que resuciten diez muertos.'*[16] In Cruz's arrangement of Metastasio the double title is used to reassure the masses that this highly Italianate production will be nationally acceptable. Certainly a Spanish audience would have found a Calderonian flavour in the poetic diction and sentiment of *Talestris . . .*, while the Italianate scenery, the marvels, the parading elephants, tigers, and lions, were foreign 'heroic' novelties greatly in demand. The term 'heroic' eventually became almost synonymous with 'de teatro', a term meaning that in the forefront of the play's attractions were its spectacles.[17]

The special group of dramas which we classed as 'military thesis-plays' presented a royal phantom-hero whom, in most respects, the seventeenth-century heroic drama and the eighteenth-century plays which unworthily carried on the national tradition, would have rejected, not merely because he was an inartistic freak, but because his eighteenth-century ideas were incompatible with a chivalresque code of honour. The genre which it is convenient to describe as the new heroic drama, reacting to the same social influences as the domestic and military plays and existing side by side with them, yet without departing so violently from tradition, received this womanish freak of the day but tried, with traditional instruments, to make a modern man of him. The difference between the military thesis play and the new heroic drama is the difference between a dress parade of sociology and active politics on the battle-front. Many names, including those of José Concha, Fermín de Laviano, Fermín del Rey, Luis Moncín, resound notoriously in eighteenth-century heroic story, but for purposes of observing the particular act of conversion referred to, it will be most illuminating to follow the careers of the progressive Zavala y Zamora, Valladares de Sotomayor and Rodríguez de Arellano.

15. *Introducción para la Comedia de 'la Espigadera'*, 1778, MS.
16. See note 4, page 578.
17. See, for example, the anonymous *Berenize en Tesalonica*, Barcelona, n.d.; *No es triunfar saber vencer: Vencerse sólo es triunfar*, by Lucas Alemán y Aguado. There is an undated manuscript in the Biblioteca Nacional.

If Comella were really the author of *La católica princesa, joven la más afligida, y esclava del Negro Ponto*, a play of Turkish colour attributed to him and licensed in 1776,[18] it would mean that one of his earliest bids for popularity took the natural shape of Spanish honour-heroics, with traditional codes of sentiment, crowded incidents, and rallying speeches, and with the new breathless emphasis of operatic spectacle. This would be before Comella had become an addict to full enlightenment. But even later he sometimes struck the old heroic attitude, in the restive *El sitio de Calés*, of 1790, for example, a play which, as has been suggested elsewhere, must have been still fresh in the mind of Leandro Moratín when, in 1792, he presented *La comedia nueva*. Yet the bustle of siege and siege-resistance illustrated by virile men and warring women on their three-dimensional walls and scaling ladders, is for Comella a side-line, and probably appeared in emulation of the sturdy heroics of Zavala y Zamora. The pathos of starving inhabitants, who are reduced in *El sitio de Calés* to eating horses, dogs, or insects, and who, with fanatic heroism, are ready to eat each other rather than yield, differs ideologically from that of the starvation scenes in the domestic and military plays of his enlightenment, and, moreover, is sometimes verbally reminiscent of Mercier's wholeheartedly heroic *La Destruction de la Ligue* or du Belloy's *Siège de Calais*.[19] It figures on the Inquisitorial *Index* for the year 1801, perhaps because of its unbalanced sentiment of honour, its cannibalistic tendencies or its foreign connections.

A curious fact about Comella's investigations of Spanish and foreign heroic positiveness in the nineties, however, was that while he trans-ferred its action, spectacle, and even its manly diction to his own heroic pieces he did not develop the most modern feature of Zavalan heroics: the insistence on complex characterization. Apparently when Comella went outside his new military and domestic field to follow traditional heroics, he took the honour-themes as they had been passed down through the ornamental sixties. Though Comella, Zavala, Valladares, and Arellano severally tried out all possibilities of the times, even attempting to retrieve their sliding reputations with a neo-classical tragedy here or a regular moral comedy there, it is chiefly Comella who is to be regarded as the popular specialist in foreign sensibility, and it is chiefly Zavala y Zamora who may be accounted responsible

18. See note 5, page 578.   19. See note 6, page 579.

for reconditioning the national heroic drama in the light, or glare, of modern Spanish mass ideas.

The manly dramas of the Golden Age were still favourites in the theatre. Many classically minded critics, like Francisco Mariano Nipho, Tomás Sebastián y Latre, Cándido María Trigueros, Enciso Castrillón, or Dionisio Solís, who disapproved of them as they stood, were willing enough to recast them for the public stage.[20] The Spaniard is not by nature effeminate, and the virile, heroic drama was instinctively retained and modernized to meet his need of translating his eighteenth-century experiences, public or private, into a language to which he was accustomed. The phantom-monarchs dominated his outlook, but in heroic drama they were hispanized into persons less calculating than decided. They are mysterious but masculine. Their fears give place to self-control. Families of children do not obtrude in this drama and commonly absent themselves altogether. Lovers, if lacking seventeenth-century balcony and *reja* for their poetic needs, requisition the ramparts, tents and earthworks. The accent lies on incident and intrigue, plot and counterplot. Moratín, who generalized his impressions of popular dramas in *La comedia nueva*, may or may not have been aware of the fact that Comellan and Zavalan reconstructions of reality are of its opposite aspects, and are as different, yet as complementary, as a popular sun and moon.

The national heroic drama that trailed through the dust of the earlier decades of the eighteenth century had been different from the heroic drama of the Golden Age chiefly in artistic degree. Imperturbable soldiers writing their despatches under fire, like Calderón's Marqués de Espínola, noble kings, or princes, or generals, sacrificing their lives in the cause of their country's and their own honour, had grown childish in their eighteenth-century braggadocio; love-scenes lacked the taste of old and depended on fulsome image; intriguing among friends and enemies had reached a point of wearisome excess; incidents bespattered the plot in slatternly disorder. The heroic dramas of the Bazos of the sixties and of the Moncíns and Lavianos of the seventies, eighties, and nineties, were wasted with decay. Their only new feature, the one quality capable of development through the decades to keep them

20. With regard to eighteenth-century performances of Golden Age plays and to the practice of recasting them, see *Origins* . . ., pp, 78, 88–9, 165 ff., 170–6.

popularly alive, was their hysterical concern with spectacular scenery and operatic sound which grew ever more sophisticated with the advance of the technicians. Not 'words' but 'show', says Bayes of *The Rehearsal*, was the current idea of the heroic:

> *Bayes.* Now, Gentlemen, I will be bold to say, I'll show you the greatest scene that ever England saw: I mean not for words, for those I do not value; but for state, show, and magnificence.

The titles of the Spanish equivalents of this grand 'scene' are usually self-explanatory. Moncín's *Como defienden su honor las ilustres Roncalesas*[21] begins with the bland decision of the Spaniards, acting on the maxim 'primero es el honor que la vida', themselves to kill all their own womenfolk before the conquering Moors, seizing the opportunity for rape, can stain their family honour for ever:

> *García de Sesma* Y pues todos convenidos
> estamos ya, sólo falta
> saber el modo: yo digo
> que para que pueda hacerse
> con cautela, y con sigilo
> mañana a la media noche,
> cada uno ejecute altivo
> en las mujeres que tenga
> en casa, este sacrificio.

which was not, mildly said the Censor, perhaps too experienced to be much surprised, the right interpretation of Christian honour.[22] The drama includes, in its clutter of incidental features, a clownish speech of welcome to King Sancho, like a tattered reminiscence of the famous scene in *La prudencia en la mujer*. Among its characters are spirited women, who, instead of submitting tamely to the pious massacre, fling themselves into the fight, ride across the stage on live horses, or, at worst, on the cardboard substitutes[23] which evidently facilitated processions of dramatic beasts, especially elephants, camels, lions, or other

21. We have seen a manuscript copy bearing a *censura* of 1784, in the Biblioteca Municipal.

22. See note 7, page 579.

23. The directions for Act III run: 'Todas las mujeres cristianas van pasando a caballo en las yeguas, y si no puede ser serán pintadas y recortadas en cartón, imitando los vestidos pintados a los que llevan Elvira, Ximena y las damas.'

547

creatures difficult to accommodate in Cruz, Príncipe, or Caños, or even the Retiro, adaptable as was this last to poetic fancy. Properly it is the fighting heroine who at the end brings in the head of the principal Moor.

Moncín's *Sertorio el Magnánimo* of 1784[24] is less unbalanced, and apart from its many 'vulgarities' of phrase and improprieties of amorous declaration, its inverisimilitude, and Sertorio's 'unpolitic' excesses of magnanimity in making his enemy his bodyguard, the Censor, judging relatively, as he must, found it passable. Some of the dialogue, indeed, has a lingering memory of Golden Age vitality. Moreover, Moncín is not afraid of representing faithfully the deliberation of those who have to take important decisions and the discussions are often convincing. If the Roman Captain's wife had said less about her *pundonor* in her otherwise practical argument with her husband in Act III, she would have had the makings of a natural personality. But Sertorio is an old-fashioned hero who does not care to appear in rhetorical undress. The highlights are Metastasian. And in succeeding years Moncín's tendency was to repeat his established scenic excesses. In 1788 Santos Díez González uninterestedly characterized his *Cómo ha de servirse al Rey muestra clemencia de Aubigni*[25] as a piece likely to be popular for its thunder of battle, and cannon-hubbub of alarm. Curiously enough the public, so a note tells us, did not like this blood-and-thunder drama when it was first produced. But that seemingly was not because of the blood or the thunder, but because, as Bayes of *The Rehearsal* would say, of 'the words' which here certainly were of so little value that their loss, when the play was cut down in its expository passages, could pass unnoticed.[26]

Such were the heroic conceptions of Moncín. Laviano's were similar. His fighting men compete with warring women to the clash of

24. In the manuscript copy in the Biblioteca Municipal it is called a 'pieza heroica' and bears a *censura* for 1784. See also Moncín's *Hechos heroicos y nobles del valor godo español*, licensed in 1784 (MS. B. Mun.), and *Restauración de Astorga por D. Alfonso I*, of 1786 (Coe, 194).

25. One manuscript bears the note: 'Esta comedia se hizo en el teatro el Pascua de Espíritu Santo. Ano '88.' There is a *censura* for the same year.

26. The note reads: 'apestó tanto el primer [día] que fue menester atajarla para el 2° de la manera que se ve.' Passages cut include, for example, a long speech in Act II giving military directions to different officers. The directions for the spectacles are not, of course, affected.

arms and the technicians' chemical flames, and, for all the lateness of the day, think none of the thoughts that undermine a reasoner's confidence. Ignacio López de Ayala, who censored the Moorish-Christian *El castellano adalid*[27] in 1785, protested at the vulgar arrogance with which Laviano's heroes spoke,[28] though his own heroes, we may remember, were not the most balanced of men. And when the anxious directions for the battle scene ask for a realistic sprinkling of headless bodies and severed heads, the author of the barbaric *Numancia destruida* does not seem perturbed. Laviano's *La española comandante fiel a su amor y a su patria*, a play about almost equally valiant Englishmen and Spaniards on an island between the Americas, was described by Santos Díez González, in virtually the same terms as he described Moncín's *Como ha de servirse al Rey*, as a noisy play for the masses.[29] To the Censor and to us they are indistinguishably of the 'many' heroic dramas being presented every year. Examples of the same type by others are—to choose at random from an embarrassment of riches—the anonymous *Las matronas catalanas defensores de Tortosa*, licensed in 1783, which speaks in post-Calderonian clichés, of love, honour, and death; stages spectacular fighting, with some singing to relieve the atmosphere; and introduces a bevy of women warriors strangely attired, since their 'virile' battledress, by the Censor's orders, is not to appear mannish. Another anonymous drama, *El gran Visir* of 1789, also displeased the Censor by being neither tragedy nor comedy; further, he testily objected to the inverisimilitude not merely of the Visir's suddenly discovering one day that he was really born a Christian, but of his martyr-like adherence to his new faith which, in defiance of his up-bringing, he observed, without more ado, in all that it entailed, from

27. The full title is *El castellano adalid. Toma de Sepúlveda por el Conde Fernán González*. Ayala tones down such passages of vulgar boasting as:

> Conde . . . Para usurpar mi gloria no concibo
> que hay en tu corazón bastante aliento . . .

28. Other heroic plays by Laviano or adopted by him are: *Al deshonor heredado vence el honor adquirido*, an embattled play about Louis XV, played in 1787; *La afrenta del Cid vengada*, licensed in 1787; *La conquista de Mequinenza por los pardos de Aragón*, played in 1787 (Coe, 175); *Morir por la patria es gloria. Atenas restaurada*, 1785 (Coe, 159).

29. '. . . en mi dictamen es de aquéllas que están acomodadas al gusto del vulgo, con ruidos de batallas, y otras cosas a este tenor que no parecen muy verisímiles en el teatro. Consta de muchos lugares comunes: la dicción tiene algunas impropiedades como también en la trama, y peripecias: y en suma no es tragedia ni propiamente comedia.' The *censura* is dated 1787.

that day forth. Withal the Censor was obliged to remind this author who had ordered a 'full accompaniment of Turkish men and women' as one of his milder sensations, that Turkish women do not appear in public. He reduced some of the swoons, unnecessary exclamations, and Baroque expressions. The Church, for its part, seizing on one clear fact in the confusion, forbade a Christian to kill a Moor even for the pious purpose of borrowing his clothes to help another Christian to escape.[30]

J. Manuel Martínez's *Gustavo Adolfo. Rey de Suecia* of 1789, where we might seem to come nearer to the excitements of the heroic espionage of Zavala y Zamora, beset with military manœuvres, lyrical *amours*, and super-personalities,[31] does not, however, modernize either Gustavo Adolfo or the drama's diction, and the Censor objects to the soliloquies. In the nineties, Calvo de Barrionuevo's *Alexandro en Scutaro*[32] might be said to epitomize the sensation-obsessed heroics of the eighties that sought novelty and found it only in the development of scenic externals. As the Censor suggests, this Alexander passes well beyond historical ken. There are prison scenes, battle-scenes, garden-scenes, moving ships, issues of camels, night adventures, love episodes, and, among other sensations, a real horse. Presumably the camels were cardboard.

In 1790 Santos Díez González received for examination the *Hernán Cortés en Tabasco* of Fermín del Rey who, as First Prompter of the Company of Martínez, had direct knowledge of the kind of blood-and-thunder that spectators enjoyed, the species of meaningless rant, rising at the end of acts to the old chorus-summaries which excited and pleased them without requiring them to concentrate. The Censor was about to write his commentary, he tells us, when he was shown a recent article in the journal *La Espigadera* protesting against the dramatic rubbish passed by Censors in face of the efforts of all cultured critics to raise theatre standards. He therefore took this opportunity to reaffirm, with indignant emphasis, that his sole reason for allowing such rubbish as *Hernán Cortés en Tabasco* to reach the public was that the superior works demanded by the *Espigadera* did not yet exist. In their absence, supply was dictated by demand.

30. See note 8, page 579.
31. See also *El católico Recaredo*, by Valladares, played in 1785.
32. The full title is *Razón, justicia, y honor triunfan del mayor valor. Alexandro en Scutaro*. The *censura* is dated 1792.

Si hubiéramos de reprobar las comedias dando únicamente pase a las primorosas, y ajustadas a las reglas del Arte, en muchos años no se representarían dos nuevas. Son raras, o como el Fénix las excelentes: y entretanto que éstas salen, pasamos (por no haber otras) las que se presentan sin defectos contra la religíon, ni el estado. Y esto mismo se practica en las demás naciones, por más que lo niegue el autor de la *Espigadera*. . . .[33]

Depressing as the prospect seemed, however, it did not bear comparison with the decayed prospect of the sixties. Just as in the flaccid domestic drama and the propagandist themes of militant monarchs, the carefree heroic pieces of the last decades were indiscriminatingly open to everything new, foreign or national; now and again came authors able to select from heroic disarray ideas of living significance for modern times, and techniques capable of artistic development. Zavala y Zamora was one of these.

At first sight Zavalan heroic drama might look much like that of Moncín or Laviano, and at a rough estimate his boastful supermen might be classified as ordinary sawdust Caesars; but a closer examination of the plays reveals qualities which stand above the indiscriminate rant and din of heroic decadence. The supermen are frequently presented in contrast with enemy personalities fully and interestedly developed; now and again they show signs of social or political enlightenment; and they are displayed at crises in spectacular settings which are planned neither just for scenic glamour, nor for the bolstering of phantom-personality, but to bring out dramatic qualities of the plot.

Zavala y Zamora made his name, for what that was worth, with his hero, Charles XII of Sweden, in a three-part *Triunfos de valor y ardid, Carlos XII Rey de Suecia*,[34] published in 1787 after its production a little earlier. This monarch, lauded by Voltaire, by Frederick the Great[35] and, in Spain, by Feijoo,[36] accessible, anecdotally, in many popular places such as *Anecdotes du séjour du Roi de Suède à Bender* by the Baron de Fabrice in 1760, or the English play *The Northern Heroes; or, The*

---

33. MS. B. Mun. Censura, 23 November 1790.
34. The first two parts, *Carlos XII rey de Suecia* and *El sitio de Pultova por Carlos XII*, had been played by 1786. The third part, *El sitiador sitiado y conquista de Stralsundo*, was played in 1787.
35. Voltaire's *Histoire de Charles XII*, Basle, 1731, was frequently reprinted and translated. Frederick II's *Réflexions sur les talents militaires et sur le caractère de Charles XII, Roi de Suède* was published in 1759.
36. *Cartas eruditas* . . ., vol. i, Carta xxix.

Bloody Contest, between Charles the Twelfth . . . and Peter the Great . . .
of 1748,[37] was the less disposed to familiar sentimentality than Comella's heroes in that he was more remote in time. Past prospects may
be conducive to idealism; but sentimentality, which is self-interested,
takes its bearings from the present. The King of Sweden, then, started
his theatre-life in Spain with the advantage of the sublime detachment
of the man of a remoter decade whose little fears and nervousnesses,
whose intimate reactions and embarrassments were not open to the
eighties for direct inspection. Sentimentalists are generally less nauseating when they are forced to invent than when they describe obvious
realities. The artifice of invention covers to some extent the hearts they
unhygienically wear on their sleeves; and while Charles XII is por-
trayed in some of the sentimental colours of the age, these are not the
whey-like shades of the denationalized military drama, but the reds
and yellows of Spanish mass-emotion, positive and bold.

One might suppose that the practical eighteenth century with its
interest in man as he is, and especially as he is 'in the street', would not
find a superman of the supreme nonchalance of Zavala's Carlos XII an
attractive 'phantom'. Yet in addition to the truth that no age, and no
man, is consistent through and through, one must allow for the fact
that the eighteenth century differed ideologically from the mid-
twentieth chiefly in believing that man, as he is, is capable of being
transformed by books, or at least by the logic of bookish men, into the
perfection he was supposed to be before books were invented. If the
worldly Age of Reason could believe in the untutored enlightenment
of the Far East, the natural magnanimity, humanity, and sensibility of
distant potentates so often presented as moral examples, the emergence
of a perfect Émile from properly proportioned circumstance; if,
despite its complicated, everyday experience, it could conceive of
heroic perfection uncomplicated by everyday irregularities, it would
have no difficulty in admitting supermen, so long as they were reasonably remote in time or place. The Zavalan Carlos, as we shall see, was
perfection in process rather than a finished product. But he represents
idealism, not sentimentality.

The eighteenth-century heroic superman usually rose to the climax
of his effect in soldierly circumstances, and for the same reason as

37. It is anonymous and was published in London.

Comella's sentimental monarch. Far from indulging, however, in prolonged emotional scenes with infant pages or misunderstood captains, he behaves in public, for the most part, with restraint, keeping his warmer emotions for illicit, but animated love-adventures. As a leader of men he is notable for his supreme self-confidence, spirited valour, and imperturbability. Most refreshingly he has something of a sense of humour which, though chiefly reserved for dangerous situations when an ironical remark like:

> Ya me conocen las bombas,
> y me tratan con respeto. (Act II)

can testify to the forceful mystery of his personality, contrasts robustly with tears and inhibitions in domestic and military dramas. Theoretically, then, he might seem a mere imitation of the Spanish heroes of old. But the interesting feature of the Zavalan superman is that his mind is worked by modern machinery and that he is kept engaged in a bustle of lifelike reponsibilities.

Carlos XII, objectively discussed by his Russian enemies, is found, according to eighteenth-century standards, to have both virtues and defects. Indeed discussions of character are among the maturer aspects of this dramatic 'thriller'. The Czar's estimate of him is couched in human terms, without either the villainesque prejudice, or the ingenuous obligation to praise that in seventeenth-century drama characterized the enemy. It is true that his defects are such as the average Spaniard would have considered better than virtues. We hear about his overbearing pride. That, in the Spanish view, was the proper quality of a hero. His propensity for amorous adventures was nothing to be ashamed of in eighteenth-century Europe so long as it stopped short of vulgar blatancy. Besides, as Zavala, who may have read Feijoo, or one of Feijoo's disciples on this subject,[38] once explained, it was not Charles' passion but his eventual conquest of himself that qualified him for heroic reputation:

Si al leerlas [the three Parts of *Carlos XII* . . .] extrañases ver en la primera parte amando a Carlos XII, contra la común opinión de los historiadores y la

38. 'En un hombre de genio fogoso, no todo lo que parece valor, es valor. Arrójase, tal vez, a los peligros, no por magnanimidad, sino por ira. Acaso se metió en algunos Alejandro, precipitado de su genio ardiente; lo que no se puede sospechar de Carlos [XII], a quien siempre vieron muy dueño de sí mismo.' *Cartas eruditas*, i, xxix.

severidad de su carácter, mira como esta pasión le hace más heroico, cuando la vence por su gloria: si reparases en las supuestas traiciones del leal Renchild, advierte cuán oportunas las hace el celo de su honor casi perdido: en prueba de lo que aparecerá a tus ojos en la segunda parte con aquel noble carácter que le da la historia.[39]

Piper, his adviser, is allowed to tell him home-truths, with a gruffness and downrightness too self-conscious to be confused with the gruffness and downrightness of the Golden Age, and to advance the theory that birth is inferior to merit. Carlos XII too in his acts of inscrutability, or in the rare contrasting moods of self-revelation, as, for example, on an occasion in Part II when he remembers his shameful conduct with Isabela in Part I and deliberately braces himself to behave like a king:

> *Carlos* Piper, hombre fui una vez,
> porque así el diablo lo quiso;
> yo haré por ser Carlos XII
> mientras viva.
>
> *Piper* Bien, Rey mío,
> que no es fácil cada día
> el vencerse uno a sí mismo.

is a modern exhibitionist rather than the traditional hero who takes himself for granted. Unlike his more illustrious forbears on the heroic stage he is inclined to show himself off by stepping out of the plot. However, when he does step out of the traditional dramatic picture, it is not to preach like that social reformer Frederick. Here or there a character, Czar Peter, in Act I, for instance, may have occasion to discuss the meaning of kingship and pause to visualize a state where peace and justice reign, where artists receive dues, and where taxes are low:

> *Pedro* El Rey en su trono
> poniendo horror al delito,
> dando premio a la virtud,
> fomentando por sí mismo
> las artes, enriqueciendo
> sus reinos con exquisitos
> proyectos, y procurando
> aliviar con mil arbitrios

39. Preface to *Triunfos de valor y ardid. Carlos XII, Rey de Suecia.* Three parts, Madrid, 1787.

> el peso de los tributos
> a sus adorados hijos
> está mejor que en la guerra
> venciendo a sus enemigos:
> el gusto de una victoria
> que vaya siempre es preciso
> con el dolor de comprarla
> con las vidas de infinitos
> vasallos, cuya memoria
> desvanece el regocijo
> de haber triunfado . . .

but missionary talk of this kind never takes first place and never acquires the force of a thesis. Whereas the plot in military drama is loosely constructed, that the monarch may have plenty of time and opportunity for getting to know his humbler subjects, the Zavalan plot is strained with tense public activity. Carlos XII does not try to give the impression of thought. His sole mental effort is in the initiative of his decisions which sometimes are only half communicated to others that their full effect may redound better to his dramatic credit at the crisis. Restraint, the ill learnt lesson of the epoch, is meant to inspire that awe of majesty experienced by Piper on one occasion when he hears his master, just before a tremendous vocal climax, suddenly change the subject to leave his full power powerfully untold:

> *Carlos* . . . y en fin
> sabré, sí, viven los Cielos,
> derribar hasta mis pies,
> las viles almas de aquéllos
> que . . .
> *Piper* Señor . . .
> *Carlos* Vamos a ver
> como trabajan los suecos.
> *Piper* Por Dios, que no habló conmigo,
> y casi le tuve miedo.

The duty of distributing justice he dispatches more briskly than the sensitive Frederick, chiefly because he has so many other pressing things to do, and because he is, after all, usually on campaign. But it provides him with incidental opportunities for displaying his princely qualities of severity with equity, sometimes, though not censurably, to the discomfiture of the nobler classes. Also it gives him the chance to express a carelessness of convention that is a genuine quality of great minds and is always delightful to the general public, worrying as it may be to those who have to deal with the consequences. Usually in Part I, however, he is arrogant, almost with Zavala's conscious consent. He is the man of action, the organizing dictator. His more humane qualities develop in Parts II and III to the pace, perhaps, of Zavala's foreign reading.

Like most popular supermen this Carlos XII depends for his individualism on his eccentricities. The time was past, in one sense, and not yet come, in another, when personality could make itself felt on the stage by the character's inner magnetism of strength in reserve. Carlos, drawing lavishly on anecdote, surprises and startles by outward eccentricity of word and deed. There were the well-known campaigning stories of how he ate the bread his soldiers refused to touch; how he held his wounded leg for the surgeon to make the incision; how he maintained his equanimity under fire[40]—manly incidents all, which did not involve him in scenes of domestic pathos. Moreover history, popular and academic, supplied incidents which might have been invented on purpose to display the newest stage machines. The bridge broke under the escaping Muscovites at Narva; boats were used for a bridge in an engagement with the Danes; a smoke-screen to obscure manœuvres was made by firing wet straw.[41] Espionage, secret meetings, complicated intrigues, were all essential parts of his historical designs. The real Charles XII was by temperament a theatrical figure. In fiction he had merely to be drawn to a larger scale.

Admittedly Zavala y Zamora had a broad sense of design. Though he packed too much into his dramas he did attempt to weave any anecdote used into the pattern of the intrigue. The business of the plot was certainly treated sensationally. At the same time Zavala made an earnest attempt to portray famous incidents—negotiations, sieges, or open battles—fairly from the point of view of all the historical characters

40. These anecdotes are recounted in Voltaire's *Histoire de Charles XII*, ed. cit., and in the translations and adaptations made from it, like the English *The History of Charles XII, King of Sweden*, London, 1734, or *The History of the Remarkable Life of Charles XII, King of Sweden*, London [? 1760].
41. Ibid.

engaged; and it was in this respect that he showed himself at his most mature. In Part I, for example, which centres on Charles's siege of Moscow, Zavala tries to contrast the characters of the two principals and to establish them both as impressive figures that the Tsar, Peter the Great, may not be just a foil to the besieging hero but by his own strength may intensify the strength of his political enemy. The author had enough ability to suggest this by making Peter an individual in his own right and giving him, to occupy his mind, not only the affairs of the siege, but day-to-day business of State. Many more respectable writers than Zavala y Zamora have had poorer dramatic ideas than these. Most neo-classical heroes under siege are empty of all thoughts save that of setting posterity a showy example of heroism. Peter is engaged as well in civil administration. It is, we are to understand, his *forte* for which we must respect him, just as we must respect the author for his dramatic talent in selecting the psychological clash of Peter's quiet preoccupation with home affairs and Charles's dashing initiative in foreign policy, of Peter's defensive righteousness and Charles's sense of power.

There is no denying to Zavala a richness of possibilities. His fault was not in poverty of ideas, it was not even in immaturity, but in lavishness. He had excellent feeling for the dramatic, but none for economy of effect. There is too much to the act. Many imaginative scenes lose their force because they are jostled out of their tense positions by the press of minor incidents. There is more determined planning of events than in the reformist dramas of Comella. But the plot is like Sterling's 'Crinkum-crankum' in *The Clandestine Marriage*—an extensive maze where apparent logic creates bafflement, and where, as Lord Ogle said 'one sees people for half an hour before one can get to them'. Ere the besieging Charles has been sensationally captured in Act III, in time to be released by his rallying army for the *finale*, he is led into complicated relationships both political, with his enemy, the Tsar, and with Augustus, the ex-king of Poland whom he has deposed and whom the Tsar is befriending, and also personal, with the wife of the Field-Marshal, Renchild, who himself is a friend of the Tsarina and is intriguing against Charles. These paths of intrigue lead the spectator into by-ways of mazy variety calculated to keep him from boredom: into the elaborate love scenes closely linked to the political plot by the machinations of eavesdropping enemies, and important in their own right, like the warm reminiscences of Golden Age scenes that in mood and metre they are:

> Carlos   ¿Que en fin sorda a mi favor,
>   que en fin dura a mi querer,
>   ni te vence mi poder
>   ni te persuade mi amor?
>
> Isabela Esto me manda mi honor;
>   pero a tener libertad
>   sin faltar a la lealtad
>   que ya a mi esposo juré
>   para amar . . . Carlos: ¿Qué hicieras?
>
> Isabela ¿Qué?
>   Rendiros mi voluntad,
>   mi vida, mi corazón,
>   mi fe, y cuanto dar pudiera
>   fuera vuestro. Carlos: ¿Mío fuera?
>
> Isabela Ya lo dije. Esta pasión
>   que a pesar de mi opinión
>   por instantes va creciendo
>   me hace . . . Carlos: ¿Qué?
>
> Isabela Ni aun yo lo entiendo:
>   dejadme con mi aflicción.
>
> Carlos   Nada encubras. Isabela: Es forzoso.
>
> Carlos   ¿Quién te lo manda?
>
> Isabela Mi suerte.
>
> Carlos   Que puedo mudarla advierte.
>
> Isabela No podéis, que tengo esposo.
>
> Carlos   Mataréle yo celoso.
>
> Isabela Defenderé yo su vida.
>   . . .
> Carlos   Sabré hasta morir querer.
>
> Isabela Yo querer hasta morir.
>   . . .
> Carlos   Amor, vamos a callar.
>
> Isabela Vamos a callar amor. etc.

into scenes of tense irony like the one in which Charles, *incognito*, and acting as his own ambassador, is interviewed by Augustus pretending to be Peter, while the Tsarina, the only person who knows the identity of all the diplomatic parties, looks on in speaking silence; into scenes of frustrated murder or escape and of tense duelling; scenes of cloak-and-sword-spying and reconnoitring such as González del Castillo parodies in *Los cómicos de la legua*;[42] scenes of military manœuvres, of sinister threat and spirited defiance; scenes of ironic humour, as when Charles calls to the Moscovians who taunt him with the flight of his army:

> *Carlos* Mis Suecos no huyen; irían
> a hacer ganas de reñir;
> pues porque no las tenían
> dejaron por vuestro el campo. (Act III)

or when he imperturbably defies the enemies who capture him, the occasional tableau supplying self-conscious personality by implication:

Al ir [Renchild] a herirle con el puñal, da un golpe Carlos en la mesa, se levanta, le mira airado, y camina hacia la puerta . . .

and a little later:

Va a herirle; Carlos se vuelve, y Renchild deja caer el puñal turbado, y se arrodilla. (Part I, Act III)

and strategically placed battle scenes equipped with modern collapsible walls and scientific fire and smoke. The author was undeniably out to thrill and to hold attention by variety. But he had a talent for arranging urgent activity that many a better dramatist might envy. His handling of scenic material was maturer than that of other popular dramatists and of many of the neo-classicists influenced by Italian opera. His spectacles, for instance, of flaming ships[43] or tower-girt battle, are not unduly frequent in Part I and are not yet included as mere pageantry. A strong feature is dramatic atmosphere; and scenes set in mysterious darkness, or to the accompaniment of lurid shot and shell, have strong dramatic values relating to the development of the plot or the preparation and presentation of the climax, in all of which respects the author

42. See note 9, page 579.
43. See, for example: 'Ensenada larga haciendo margen al río, y al otro lado de éste hacia el foso otra ensenada, levantándose en ella los muros de Moscou con cañones, en el río se verán lanchas incendiadas, cuya luz alumbrará esta escena' (Part I, Act II).

was inspired as much by Spain's old masters as by Italy's new librettists. The love scenes in their traditional word-patterns are genuinely lyrical. Incidental suspense is well manufactured. Nevertheless this is an exhausting play for the literary minded. If it would make a far better film than many films now produced, that is probably the least complimentary thing to be said about it.

Zavala y Zamora in this special field of heroics went on quantitatively from strength to strength. Parts II and III of the trilogy differ from Part I chiefly in name. Charles refrains from giving amorous cause for scandal and love retreats to the underplots; but in Part II he is still playing the single-minded dictator whose strength is his mysterious personality, his shock tactics, and his independence of his ministers. Words like these in real life may sound childishly self-assertive and produce more annoyance than admiration:

> *Carlos* ¿Con que no sois de dictamen
>   que admita yo el desafío?
> *Los dos* No, Señor.
> *Carlos* ¿No? Pues sabed
>   que ya le tengo admitido.
> *Piper* Siempre vos pedís dictamen
>   cuando no podéis seguirlo. (Act I)

Yet though it is true that a Dictator-King can be made more attractive on the stage than in reality, it is also worth remembering that the general Spanish public in the reign of Carlos IV held no brief for ministers or unavailing Cortes and assumed, with some justification, that what Spain needed was a monarch with the bearing of a master. In this real light the unlikely Carlos XII was to become highly suggestive.

Siege and resistance again provide the basic action. Once more the old Numantian rhetoric, calling men to rations of wood and stone, horses and human flesh, resounds within the pasteboard battlements. In Part III Charles is a little more self-conscious and humane, and, appropriating the weary line that had been touring Europe for decades, declares in Act II that he is King first and soldier second. Under the influence of this principle he is drawn momentarily into the ethics of kingship, though only to repeat himself:

> *Carlos* El Rey debe contemplarse
> Rey, para poner el freno
> debido al delito, y dar
> a las virtudes el premio
> solamente: para todo
> lo que es abrazar el riesgo,
> y el trabajo, a que la sola
> conservación de sus reinos
> fuerza a sus vasallos, entre
> él en la cuenta el primero. (Act I)

Nevertheless some of the civil preoccupations of the times press practically on him to the extent of holding him to the fulfilment of his civil duties as law-giver even while his generals call him feverishly to battle, or of filling him with fatherly compassion for a tired sentry whose duty he takes over that the man may sleep. Unlike Frederick he recovers quickly from these moral preoccupations. On the other hand his attention is steadily held by the details of military technique that interested the epoch. In Act III he is to be found demonstrating rifle-drill and cutting a figure neither as kingly nor as masterfully humorous as he imagined:

> *Carlos Atención* . . .
> . . . *Presenten*
> *las armas* . . .
> *Carguen:* Con más brevedad;
> porque en eso ha consistido
> siempre el matar o ser muertos,
> y de nada ha de serviros
> el que hayáis cargado, cuando
> os descargue el enemigo.
> *Apunten: Fuego:* Cuidado
> que yo soy, soldados míos,
> vuestro contrario. . . . (Act III)

The military sights and sounds on a larger scale, which became bigger and better with each new Part, can hardly be said to reflect the same scientific interests. Besides, what Zavala himself knew or had read about military technique was not extensive, and the *Memorial literario* observing his increased tendency in Part III to descend into mere trickery, sarcastically imagined a Fourth Part dealing with Carlos XII at the siege of 'Friderieshall' where, although historically speaking, he was due to die, he would undoubtedly confound historical expectation by a trick-survival:

Y si se ve sitiado en una plaza tan apretadamente que es preciso que se entregue, o la abandone como hizo Carlos XII con la de Stralsundo, ¿de qué modo ha de salvar el poeta a su héroe? dificultades tiene el caso, pero puede mucho la travesura, que halla medio a todo; haga salir de plaza al sitiado, entre a su salvo el sitiador, y sítiele luego el que se halla en mayor peligro y con menos ventajas, y verá qué presto vence; así tomará nuevo y nunca visto aspecto el arte militar, y dejará un ejemplo de heroísmo superior a todos los mortales. De este modo esperamos que en la 4a parte de Carlos XII, que será el *Sitio de Frederieshall* donde murió, quede vivo e inmortal este Gran Rey.[44]

Zavala's plays about other heroes—Charles V,[45] Leopold the Great,[46] or Alexander[47]—repeat the urgent impression of the Swedish intrigue, and some of the exhibitionism of the Spanish superman without further suggestion of interior development. Most of them are frank excuses for introducing pictorial sensations, and these increase at the expense of the superman's character which even in the first of the Swedish series existed mainly in potentiality.

Not that Zavala's spectacles were unpretentious even at the outset of his noisy career. But in some of the early heroic plays—*Leopoldo el Grande* of 1789,[48] for instance—his marvels were in a direct line of descent from the stage marvels of the sixties. They are the live-statue scenes and symbolical or magic features which in the sixties had indiscriminately invaded all forms of drama, until under the sarcasm of Nicolás Moratín and the *Pensador* they had either placed themselves beyond the literary pale altogether or had joined forces with the opera. Zavala's final garden scene for the end of Act II, where Leopoldo and Margarita are seated in a gallery overlooking the ornamental fountains, boasts living statues in niches[49] and speeches to music by Fame and Love. But these operatic incongruities do not appear in heroic dramas

44. See *Memorial literario,* review of *El sitiador sitiado y conquista de Stralsundo,* June 1787.   45. *Carlos V sobre Dura.* It has a *censura* for 1790, MS. B. Mun.
46. Licensed for 1789, MS. B. Mun., and see *Mayor piedad de Leopoldo el Grande.* Bar. undated.
47. *Alejandro en la Sogdiana,* licensed in 1795.
48. It was printed as *La mayor piedad de Leopoldo el Grande,* Bar., n.d.
49. '. . . en cada uno (de los nichos) colocada una estatua, la que cubrirá hasta su tiempo, un lienzo en que habrá pintada otra igual. . . .'

inspired by the Caroline cycle. Even in *Leopoldo el Grande* the Censor cut them down. And the excesses in which Zavalan supermen increasingly indulged were orgies of realism rather than of lyrical fancy. So the Censor in 1793, with *La comedia nueva* accusingly fresh in his mind, condemned *La toma de Breslau* for its excessive battling, and the incendiary *Alejandro en la Sogdiana*, licensed in 1795, for similar features, repeating his strictures in his report on *Selico y Berisa*, a drama which displays a female bodyguard with muskets, four years later:

> . . . aunque no contiene nada contra la religión ni el estado, contiene muchísimas faltas contra la regularidad de la poesía dramática: pues es un tejido de lances y acaecimientos inverisímiles, o es un sueño de una imaginación enferma, y exaltada. . . .

Zavala's non-Caroline plays provide the intrigues and love adventures characteristic of the trilogy and, like this popular favourite, confine their social propaganda to a few remarks about the duties of kings. A portion cut in the acting version of *Leopoldo el Grande*,[50] for example, stresses, in eighteenth-century terms, the fact that kings are men like other men and have no divine right to abuse their power: that, moreover, if anyone is to make material sacrifices, the proper persons to make them are the king and his ministers. The political implication was too obvious to miss, or to risk:

> *Leopoldo* Pero la sabiduría
> del cielo no dio a la tierra
> reyes, a quienes engría
> ni la majestad, ni el mando
> sino hombres que hagan justicia
> a los hombres, y con ella
> su orgullo infame repriman
> pues mirándolo en justicia
> más vale que un soberano
> y sus ministros corrijan
> su vanidad, y modere
> hoy su opulencia excesiva,
> que no que diamantes cuaje
> del sudor del pobre. (Act III)

50. Omission marks in acting versions sometimes may indicate means of shortening the plays. It would rather appear, however, that they indicate a mixture of expedience and practical necessity.

Compared with Comella's thesis dramas isolated scenes like this seem almost inconsequent. The modern cult of homeliness, on the other hand, was zestfully developed by Zavala in season and out of season. Soldiers are manly and heroic, but in the reveille-scene of *La toma de Breslau*[51] the brave soldiers are instructed to be engaged variously in buttoning their waistcoats, putting on their stocks and, combing their hair. The diction, meant to be natural, becomes, if anything, more slipshod than in the trilogy, the dramatist in his haste, and notably during love-scenes, snatching up the hackneyed phrases of national tradition. The Censor's substitution of:

> dedos bellos
> como cristal

for:

> . . . vaya vengan
> esos cinco caños bellos
> de cristal.

in *La toma de Breslau* was the kind of correction that occupied him constantly in Zavalan manuscripts.

The new heroic play as conceived by Zavala y Zamora, then, reflects contemporary aspirations complementary to those reflected in Comellan military drama. It takes the positive features of the practical eighteenth-century phantom, his organizing ability, the dynamism of his mental and material fireworks, and tries to express his humanity in the manly ways normally preferred by Spaniards. It leaves his doubts aside—perhaps Spain was nervous of a doubting king—and it touches sociology gingerly. But Zavala tried to allow for personal faults in the monarch and deepened the characterization by juxtaposing, for example, Carlos and his more complex and self-conscious opposite, Peter of Russia, and encouraging them to respect each other. The result is more Spanish than the Comellan military drama. It is a natural modernization, in topical circumstances and in mental outlook, of the old heroic play. The pity is that it was too easily classifiable with other contemporary forms of heroics and its light touches of modern psychology were obscured by the relentless activity and amorous lyricism of the national tradition in decadence. The character-problems of the promising Carlos-Pedro relationships remained undeveloped and the

51. We have seen a manuscript licensed for 1793.

literary line of evolution for the Spanish heroic drama was blocked by sensation.

Zavala was notably supported in his modernistic battling by Valladares de Sotomayor whose recipe for making drama was to mix together all the successful oddments that he could pick up from home and abroad. His military manœuvres, his scenes of maudlin pathos, his starving children, his magnanimous supermen, and fighting women, might be confused with the products of either Comella or Zavala, but he had fewer missionary tendencies than the first and less interest in character than the second.

Already in 1784 in *Defensa de la Coruña por la heroica María Pita*, his display of modern battleworks was in full swing and provided for a woman member of the cavalry. The Literary Censor was obliged to demand that the lady, instructed to ride in on her charger, should do so with decency, and, in any case, should not ride through the auditorium. This is a ranting play of activity more traditional than modern, though it is possible that the startling first scene of Act III, set in a pantheon, and showing María Pita rising from a winding sheet, may have been inspired by the 'Gothic' mysteries then rampant on the continent. Several of Valladares's heroic pieces are stamped with the Censor's dispirited protests that licence is only given on the grounds that there is nothing else ready for the players to perform. In other words they were sent late to the Censor, who, particularly after the production of *La comedia nueva* in 1792, was sensitive of his own reputation, in the knowledge that they would be distasteful to the refined. In 1796, with Valladares's *El rey es primero*, author and actors timed their arrangements just too finely, for though the rampageous drama was grudgingly passed, the exasperated Censor resorted in this instance to the regulations and, determining to teach the players a lesson, demanded that all copies should be called in immediately after the performance.[52]

Another heroic dramatist of Zavalan calibre was Vicente Rodríguez de Arellano, a man well versed in the Spanish classics, it would seem, for his work is bespattered indiscreetly with reminiscences like the following:

52. Other heroic plays, most of a spectacular type, by Valladares are: *El conde de Werrick*, of which we have seen a verse fragment of 1779; *El católico Recaredo*, played in 1785; *Saber del mayor peligro triunfar sola una mujer*, played in 1785; *La gran victoria de España en los campos de Vitoria*, played and published in 1814, etc.

> *Marco Antonio* ¡Ay dulces prendas por mi mal halladas,
> dulces y, alegres, cuando en otro tiempo
> os ilustró mi esposa![53]

or:

> *Oronte* Campos de Mesopotamia
> ¡qué alegre os pisé algún tiempo!
> ¡y qué triste y afligido
> vuelvo a pisaros de nuevo![54]

which, if ridiculous in these settings, were not meant to be impertinent. His *Palmis y Oronte* of 1797 was agreeable to the Censor, doubtless because its heroics were disciplined and sober.[55] Indeed Arellano made some attempt to present his matter thoughtfully, as is evident in Geroncio's soliloquy on ambition in Act I:

> Abominable ambición
> ¿a qué bárbaros extremos
> conduces al que te hace
> el ídolo de su pecho?
> . . .
> porque es ordinario efecto
> envidiar a el rico el pobre,
> el ignorante al discreto,
> en que sirve al que le manda
> y al virtuoso el perverso.

and in the more serious attempt in Act III to present Oronto in the mood of lofty resignation recalling French and English High Tragedy:

> Para las grandes desdichas
> se hicieron los grandes pechos,
> pero cuando repetidas
> van unas de otras naciendo
> a tan continuado golpe
> desfallece el sufrimiento.
> Ven, pues, horrorosa muerte . . .

But Arellano had not learnt how to convey reflection outside the

53. *Marco Antonio y Cleopatra.* It was produced in 1790.
54. *Palmis y Oronte,* licensed in 1797, MS. B. Mun.
55. He describes it as a play with a 'fábula de bastante interés y una locución castellana propia en versos suaves y corrientes . . .'.

special ground of the soliloquy and the ordered dignity of this play is spoilt by the flurry in Act III of last minute reprieves and rearrangements. He was capable, in other heroic dramas, of dispensing with reflection altogether and abandoning himself uninhibitedly to common riotousness. In this respect his *El sitio de Toro, y noble Martín de Abarca* seemed to cause misgivings even to himself and in a note to this play addressed to the 'Intelligent'[56] he transferred the blame from principle to practical necessity.[57] Unlike Lope's his excuse, however, merely makes him sound ineffectual:

> Bien sé que esta comedia
> nada es de lo que parece,
> y que de unidad carece,
> de lugar, tiempo, y acción.
> Preguntaréis qué ocasion
> hace mi pluma propensa
> a un error tan sin defensa?
> Pero a esto baste que os diga
> que necesidad obliga
> a lo que el hombre no piensa.

The Peninsular War offered a new range of subject-matter to heroic playwrights, but this national experience was too urgent, heartfelt and actual for them to express themselves in more than an impromptu rhetoric of pride, self-encouragement, and glory, as the mere titles of many of the plays will indicate.[58] Patriotism on active service did nothing just then to mature the heroic play and usually developed its defects. Some wars seem to bear literary fruit. But Spain's War of

56. See the manuscript of this play in the Biblioteca Nacional. The note is written at the end.

57. Other plays by Arellano with similar stress are *Jerusalén conquistada por Gofredo de Bullón*, played in 1791, and *Dido abandonada*, played and published in 1795.

Plays of the new heroic type by other authors are, for example, *Gustavo Adolfo*, by Juan Manuel Martínez, played in 1789, and *Los hijos de Nadasti*, an anonymous drama played in 1795.

58. See, for example: *El escarmiento a los traidores o defensa de Valencia* and *La defensa de Gerona*, both by Enciso Castrillón and belonging to the year 1808; *El mejor triunfo de España, la victoria de Baylén, y rendición de Dupont*, by J. J. Aparicio, 1808; *El regocijo militar en los campos de Baylén*, 1808; *Dupont rendido en los campos de Bailén o el triunfo del patriotismo*, by Juan Agustín Poveda, 1813; *Mayor triunfo de España en los campos de Vitoria, la fuga del rey Josef, y prisión de afrancesados*, 1813; *El patriota en Cádiz*, 1815, etc., etc. See Cot. *Máiquez*, pp. 294-5.

Independence was not, from the literary point of view, well timed. It revived the declamatory enthusiasms which had been in the process of dying a natural death but were not yet nearly dead. At least, however, these veteran forms of expression could not long survive the excitement of the war; and the young Romantic generation of playwrights, though sensationally inclined, turned emotion to more subtle account.

NOTES

CHAPTER 10

1.   *Guzmán* En el tropel confuso de encontrados
      afectos y de ideas con que lidio;
      en las arduas y tristes circunstancias
      que más y más estrechan mi conflicto,
      ahora que he logrado libertarme
      de la importunidad de mil testigos,
      esta parte del muro de Tarifa
      menos cercana al militar bullicio
      por algunos instantes, aunque breves,
      sírvame ya de solitario asilo . . .

2. 'Arroja el cuchillo desde el muro al campo. Luego al son de un adagio lento baja los escalones desalentado y con muestras de horror. Da algunos pasos trémulos; y prosigue; variando de tonos según los diferentes afectos de terror, de abatimiento, de valentía, de ternura, o de dolor que expresan los versos.
      . . .
      'Vuelve a subir al muro entretanto que la orquesta toca un largo muy triste con sordinas y flautas. Desde allí con los más expresivos indicios de dolor observa lo que pasa en el campo; baja atónito, y cubriéndose los ojos con ambas manos, déjase caer como postrado de la congoja en el banco; y con voz angustiada y palabras interrumpidas dice, acompañándole la música . . .'

3. See 'O nos entregas la plaza o degollamos tu hijo' dijeron los moros a Guzmán el Bueno que manadaba a Tarifa. Este bravo soldado no les da otra respuesta que arrojarles su propio cuchillo desde el muro al campo. Retírase a comer, oye gritos: levántase de la mesa, acude al muro, ve el sacrificio de su hijo, y se vuelve a continuar la comida, diciendo con serenidad a su esposa: "Creí que asaltaban la plaza." . . .'
      This straightforward Guzmán of history he then compares with Iriarte's irresolute model of sensibility.

4.   Si no es eso,
                  sino porque según dicen
                  todos los semi extranjeros,
                  no hay en España quien sepa
                  tratar con decoro un hecho
                  de estos hombres.

5. For instance the lines:
                  ¿Hay más
                  que buscar un extranjero
                  que con las orejas toque
                  el serpentón; y tenemos
                  función para quince dias?

569

6. Grannis, op. cit., notes the resemblance of certain stage directions in the parody *La Manie des Drames Sombres* with those of Baculard d'Arnaud. M. Prousas of the parody is reading the directions for his new play *Le Brigand Vertueux*:

Prousas 'L'Acte Premier. La Scène représente
Une prison obscure; une lampe mourante,
Par intervale, y jette une pâle lueur,
On voit le criminel étendu sur la paille,
Immobile et couvert d'une froide sueur . . .'
(Act II, iii)

A typical stage direction of Baculard d'Arnaud's lugubrious moods runs as follows: 'À gauche, à peu de distance du mur, est un cercueil, aux pieds duquel se voit une lampe allumée. Du même côté, plus sur le devant de la scène, est un Prie-Dieu surmonté d'un crucifix que soutient une tête de mort . . .'

See *Euphémie, ou le Triomphe de la Religion*, Yverdon, 1768, Act I.

7. '. . . El caso es que pudiera representarse, sin que se siguiese inconveniente, a vista de la necesidad que tienen las compañías de funciones, y poetas. . . . Pero como he visto que en el *Memorial literario* se dan al público los defectos de las comedias, omitiendo las prudentes razones que suelen mediar para permitirlas el Sr. Juez Protector, es preciso hacer presente esta reflexión, para que en vista de ella, o permita el Sr. Juez que se represente, corrigiendo lo más enorme; o niegue la licencia de darse al teatro, para evitar que se de al público una censura de lo mismo que ya está censurado.'

Five days later, in a second *censura* which reports on the corrected script, Santos Díez González still has the *Memorial literario* in mind: '. . . se ha corregido lo más notable . . . y aunque con todo eso queda materia que critique para con el público el *Memorial literario*, en atención a la escasez que hay de funciones nuevas . . . me parece que puede permitirse su representación.'

8. There is an undated edition in the British Museum giving Zavala y Zamora as author. Another composition with the same name, apparently of the operatic kind, and therefore a 'melodrama' in the earlier sense of the word, was also produced in the nineties. As the newspaper reports do not name the authors it is difficult to know if *El amor dichoso* of 1793 (see Cot. *Máiquez*, p. 579) or, as Subirá gives it, 1794 (see *El compositor Iriarte* . . ., pp. 152 ff.) is that of Zavala or if his is the composition produced in 1796. The operatic *libretto* has disappeared. Subirá believes it to be the work of Comella. (See Subirá, loc. cit.)

9. See, for example,

Armida   Dueño querido
duerme mi amado bien, duerme alma mía,
duerme objeto adorado de un cariño
abrasador del más sensible pecho,
pues aunque todo el tiempo que no miro
las luces halagüeñas de tus ojos
estoy considerando que no vivo . . .

CHAPTER II

1. If we can accept Jovellanos's assertion that *El delincuente honrado* was the outcome of a literary discussion in Seville 'at the beginning of' 1773 it would appear that *Le Juge* could not have influenced its composition. *Le Juge* was published, but not played, in 1774, and was in circulation in the November of that year. See Gaiffe, p. 507, n. 1. The Spanish play was performed in 1774 'en el teatro de Aranjuez o de San Ildefonso, y de

570

allí fue trasplantada a los demás de España . . .' (B.A.E. xlvi, p. 77). We have been unable to discover the precise day of its first appearance. See J. A. Cean Bermúdez (op. cit.) who tells of the *tertulia*-contest for which various *drames* were presented, Jovellanos' play being voted the best (pp. 312 ff.).

2. See 'Discurso sobre los duelos leído en la Academia de Jurisprudencia de Barcelona, por su socio D. Antonio Coma, Abogado de aquella Real Audiencia, en el mes de noviembre de 1788', *Memorial literario . . .* , January 1789, pp. 62 ff. Still later, false conceptions of honour were satirized by Alonso Bernardo Rivero y Larrea in *Historia fabulosa del distinguido caballero D. Pelayo, Infanzón de la Vega, Quijote de la Cantabria* (Madrid, 1792, 2 vols.) with special reference to the aristocratic Cantabria. See also J. H. R. Polt in 'Jovellanos', *El delincuente honrado*' (*Rom. Rev.*, 1959, 1, 170–90), where he refers to Montesquieu on honour.

3. Sarrailh, op. cit., pp. 538 ff. See also R. Herr, *The Eighteenth-Century Revolution in Spain*, Princeton, New Jersey, 1958, pp. 61–2. Compare also the comment of *El memorial literario* on *El médico de su honra:* 'El médico de esta comedia es muy ignorante y malvado, y así es una acción de inicuo ejemplo' (*Mem. lit.*, May 1784) and the speech of Don Juan in *Los menestrales*, discussed above (pp. 474 ff.)

¡Cuándo llegará el día alegre y santo,
que olvidemos que hubo en toscos tiempos
estos nombres . . .
de pundonor, venganza, punto y duelo!

4. *Simón:* Pero, decidme, ¿no habrá algún medio de salvar a Torcuato?
Justo: (*Con seriedad*) Esa pregunta es bien extraña en quien sabe las obligaciones de un juez. El órgano de la ley no es árbitro de ella. No tengo más arbitrio que el de representar: y pues habéis oído como pienso, podréis inferir si lo habré hecho con eficacia.
Simón: ¡Oh! pues si habéis representado, yo confío. . . .
Justo: No haréis bien en confiar. Las representaciones de un juez suelen valer muy poco cuando conspiran a mitigar el rigor de una ley reciente. (Act IV, vi.)

5. Calzada's play is translated from a five-act French version in prose of a German play by H. F. Möller. See *Le Comte de Waltron, ou La Discipline Militaire du Nord. Traduit de L'Allemand par M. Eberts, et mis au théâtre par M. Bérard.* We have seen an edition of Rouen, 1789. A three-act arrangement of this exists also in French. See *Le Comte de Waltron ou La Subordination. Arrangée pour le théâtre de Monsieur, frère du Roi, par M. Dalainval, d'après la traduction de J. H. E.* We have seen an edition of Paris, 1789. This was imitated in Spanish in *La subordinación,* a three-act play in prose, by 'J. M. C. B.' published without date in Barcelona. See also *La Discipline Militaire du Nord. Drame en 4 actes, en vers libres, par M. Moline* played in November 1781, and published in Paris in 1782. Moline states in a preface that he has imitated a French play, originally derived from 'Goethe' and called *Waltron, ou la Subordination.*

6. Plays of similar themes, usually of foreign origin, with similar emotional stress, are *Acrisolar el dolor en el más filial amor* by Antonio Rezano Imperiali, a 'pieza militar', of which we have seen an undated edition of Salamanca; and *El culpado sin delito,* a three-act play in verse by Valladares, licensed in 1782 and bearing this note on the censored manuscript: 'Esta comedia con el título de *El reo inocente* es original en prosa de D. Ignacio Planas, escribano de la ciudad de Barcelona.' It appeared also under the title *El inocente culpado* in an edition of Barcelona, 1797. One should be careful not to confuse these titles with *Reo inocente es Clementina y Desormes* which was translated by Rodríguez de Arellano from J. M. Boutet de Monvel's *Clémentine et Desormes* and played in 1784. Fermín de Laviano has a five-act, metrical version, *El reo inocente,* licensed in 1782.

also based on Monvel. See also Valladares's two-act *El preso or amor o el Real encuentro*, played in 1796.

CHAPTER 12

1. The classification is: 'Toda pieza nueva original, de aquéllas a que particularmente se ha dado el nombre de dramas o comedias sentimentales.' For verse translations and recasts authors are awarded 3 per cent for ten years. For operas, *zarzuelas*, etc., the musician is awarded 5 per cent and the librettist 3 per cent, the latter only for a period of ten years if the text has been translated. See *Reglamento General* published in Cot. *Licitud*, p. 701.

2. 'It is, of all others, the most easily written . . . It is only sufficient to raise the characters a little, to deck out the hero with a ribbon, or give the heroine a title; then to put an insipid dialogue, without character or humour, into their mouths, give them mighty good hearts, very fine clothes, furnish a new set of scenes, make a pathetic scene or two, with a sprinkling of tender melancholy conversation through the whole, and there is no doubt but all the ladies will cry, and all the gentlemen applaud.' *An Essay on the Theatre, or, A Comparison between Laughing and Sentimental Comedy*, written for the *Westminster Magazine* of 1773.

3. 'Venerando las censuras precedentes, nostante [*sic*], considerando el encargo que sobre este particular nos manda S.M. a los comisarios de comedias, en su Rl resolución de 6 de febrero de 1758, y traer disfrazado el título, pues esta pieza está conocida por el de *Las cuatro naciones*; no traer firma de quien sea su autor, o traductor, no me conformo en que se ejecute; y se previene al autor de la compañía que en adelante remita las piezas nuevas a lo menos con cuatro días de tiempo, para poderlas reconocer con la reflexión que piden pues de lo contrario no se despacharán', 11 July 1788.

4. She refers to it in these terms:

Luisa   Es
               La Espectadora, una sabia
               mujer, que siempre observando
               va las acciones humanas.
               Examina las pasiones;
               ve cual es buena, y cual mala:
               distingue lo verdadero
               de lo falso; y en fin, trata
               con crítica muy juiciosa
               de hacer bueno al que a esto falta.

5. 'Los seis oficiales de Wilson, salen por la puerta del almacén con delantales, y cruzan la escena para ir a la tienda caminando lentamente, los brazos caídos, las cabezas bajas y en profunda tristeza', Act II. The last details of this stage direction correspond to Falbaire's 'Ces ouvriers . . . passent sur la scène pour s'en aller par la boutique; ils marchent lentement, les bras pendants, la tête baissée, et dans une profonde tristesse.' (Act III, ix.) The Spanish translator gives merely: 'Salen ahora los trabajadores vestidos de jubón y delantal muy afligidos.'

6. *Clarissa* was dramatized in, for instance, R. Porrett's *Clarissa: or The Fatal Seduction* of 1788. See A. Nicoll, *English Drama*, iii, p. 72. A French dramatic version of the novel, Née de la Rochelle's *Clarissa Harlowe*, Paris, 1786, was not acted (see Gaiffe, p. 58) and a Spanish drama, *Miss Clara Harlowe*, in verse, by Antonio Marqués Espejo, appeared only in 1804. The lack of a successful French dramatic link earlier meant that the *Clarissa*-matter reached Spain very indirectly through French dramatic characters vaguely influenced by the heroine of the novel.

7. See *El buen amigo*, 'Sacada de los cuentos morales de Mr. de Marmontel en el que intitula: *L'Amitié à l'Épreuve.*' There is an undated manuscript in the Biblioteca Municipal. A variant title was *La amistad o El buen amigo*. C. S. Favart's *L'Amitié à l'Epreuve*, also from Marmontel, was played in 1770, though it may have been known earlier. See Gaiffe, op. cit., p. 559. Cruz's version appears to belong to the year 1768. See Cot. *R.X.*, p. 247.

The fashionable domestic theme of the good friend runs through innumerable plots of the 'eighties and 'nineties. Another Spanish example is the anonymous *Buen amante y buen amigo*, licensed in 1792.

8. *Thibault* Aprendí desde mi cuna
               de cuanto respeto es digno
               un Rey; aunque de tirano
               tenga los hechos. Quien quiso
               subirle al trono, sabrá
               juzgarle, y dar el castigo
               a sus excesos; que al fin
               los vasallos, no nacimos
               más que para obedecerle
               y venerarle, sumisos
               siempre a sus leyes. (Act II, vi)

9. The manuscript licence extant is for 1792. There is, however, a printed edition of Barcelona, 1778, a date which Cambronero thinks a misprint. He is probably right, as Comella could scarcely have written much before the eighties. (See Cambronero, 'Comella. Su vida y sus obras' in *Revista Contemporánea*, vol. 104, p. 207.)

But there are printed editions of other Comellan plays as early as 1778. So often is this date used in Pamplona and Barcelona editions of various dramas that would seem unnaturally early for their authors that one wonders if it could be artificially adopted for some special reason of the publishers. See Bibliography.

10. 'En lo demás no carece la pieza de mérito, y si no fuera por este defecto, podría pasar entre las dignas de un teatro culto.' *Censura* of Santos Díez González, dated 30 April 1789.

Other examples of the court-martial theme are *Las vivanderas ilustres*, censored in 1781, and *Saber premiar la inocencia y castigar la traición*, censored in 1782, both attributed to Valladares.

11. The free translation of Mme. Molé is the *Misantropie et Repentir Drame . . . du théâtre allemand de Kotz-büe* [sic] *traduit par Bursay, et arrangé à l'usage de la scène française par la citoyenne Molé, artiste du Théâtre français . . .*, Paris [1799]. In 1801 appeared the translation of a one-act continuation from Kotzebue: *La misantropía desvanecida escrito en alemán por – – en continuación al drama intitulado la misantropía*. The translator is anonymous.

12. Later direct versions of the theme outside our period are, for instance, *La cena de Enrique IV, o la pava en la estaca*, anonymous and probably of 1816, and *Una mañana de Enrique IV*, also anonymous, of 1818. Both exist in manuscript versions in the Biblioteca Municipal of Madrid. A *baile* on the theme called *La caza de Henrique IV* was played in 1791 at the Caños. A Spanish play on a related subject is *Los viajes del Emperador Segismundo o El escultor y el ciego* translated by Domingo Botti. We have been unable to trace the original.

CHAPTER 13

1. 'En esta comedia agradó el figurón Pitanzos con la gracia con que hacía burla de los menestrales, las ponderaciones de la nobleza montañesa, y el cuento del borrico cargado de paja que le atropelló; también hallarón agradable el benigno carácter de la esposa de Cortines . . . la bondad de la hija Rufina, y los castos amores y sencillez de Justo. Las quejas de Cortines sobre el mal concepto en que los ricos o nobles tenían a los menestrales, parecieron a muchos bien fundadas; pero no dejaron de conocer, que con las providencias tomadas últimamente por el gobierno, y la protección que nuestro soberano dispensa a las artes y oficios, se ha disminuido tanto el desprecio que casi se ha extinguido. Algunos reconocieron bien pintado el carácter del solapado estafador y embustero Rafa, y el justo castigo de semejantes embaydores, procurado por el alcalde de corte D. Juan, y el descubrimiento que éste hizo para desengaño de Cortines . . .' The report continues with remarks about the audience's enjoyment of the songs and music, and some criticisms on inconsistencies of characterization. See *Memorial literario*, May, 1784.

2. See for example:

> *Don Juan* . . . Todo oficio
> da honor al que le ejerce como honrado:
> sólo en abandonarle está la culpa . . .
> Dejad esos delirios, la nobleza
> se funda en la virtud y en el trabajo.
> Al sudor destinados nacen todos;
> el que busca con él lo necesario,
> cumple con su deber, y es hombre bueno,
> digno por tal de ser reverenciado.
> Si otros que a estar ociosos por fortuna,
> o por desgracia fueron condenados,
> tienen otros caprichos, poco importa;
> quien a razón se opone es temerario.
> Todos de un solo tronco ramas somos:
> no hay más noble que el que es buen ciudadano,
> y el que más útil es, es el más noble
> en bajo esté, o en alto: tales grados
> de las necesidades son seqüela:
> mas tan bueno el alto como el bajo.
> Vivamos donde el cielo nos ha puesto,
> único medio de que bien vivamos,
> y conozcamos ya, pues que no hay duda,
> que lo que siempre es bueno nunca es malo.

3. See, for example:

> *Leandro* Anda tonta,
> vanos escrúpulos deja.
> ¿No he de ser tu esposo?
> *Rosa* ¿Y bien?
> *Leandro* Pues si lo he de ser, ¿qué arriesgas
> en que anticipadamente
> a tu esposo favorezcas? . . . (Act I)

4. See the *Censura* dated 14 November 1788, in the manuscript in the Biblioteca Municipal.
Examples of the Censor's mild alterations are:

for Zavala's:

Ana Hace diez años, Señor,
que di mi mano a otro dueño.

Hace diez años que di
mi blanca mano a otro dueño. (Act I)

or:

Ana parece nacida
para amarte.

for Zavala's:

Ana Ana fue sólo nacida
para amarte.

5. '. . . Y solo reparó en poner *llevan* en lugar de *roban* en la página 11 del primer acto, dejando no sólo las demás palabras, que expresan la idea de un rapto, sino las escenas mismas en que se representa el rapto; el cual sobre ser de mal ejemplo, es un episodio que no tiene conexión con la acción primaria, ni hace falta para la trama. En nada de estas cosas tan de bulto tropieza el citado censor, y tropieza en versos, que corrige echándolos a perder; y ha hecho creer al Sr. Juez Eclesiástico, que nuestras censuras son relajadas porque hacemos ver al Sr. Juez Real, y Protector de teatros que algunos versos tachados están mal tachados, y peor corregidos. La cultura de los teatros públicos, y mi celo por la verdad me hace hablar sin rebozo; y más cuando en mis censuras no hago otra cosa que informar al Sr. Juez, lo que me parece, para que resuelva, como acostumbra, lo más acertado. Y así me parece que la presente comedia se devuelva al Ingenio para que la corrija, y que corregida se presente otra vez a las censuras . . .' (*Censura*, 27 September 1793).

6. '. . . las sentencias y buenas máximas de industria y comercio están sembradas oportunamente por toda la acción. El asunto elegido por el autor no podía ser más a propósito en un tiempo en que se protegen tanto las artes, y se combaten las preocupaciones que hasta aquí alimentaban la ociosidad y desterraban la aplicación. Con todas estas circunstancias no agradó al público el hacerse el robo en el teatro, ni repetir las salidas del niño de mantillas; y la insolencia del vulgo apenas la dejó acabar . . .' *Memorial literario*, February 1790.

7. *Don Alfonso*. . . . Lo que hay es, que nuestros paisanos como tan majaderos, se ríen de Coturnos y de Zuecos; dicen también que dos a lo menos de esas tres unidades son cuentos de viejas inventados para embobar a los niños grandes, que se quedan tan contentitos cuando en un mismo sitio ven enamorarse los amantes, dar batallas, tratar negocios reservados, y conducir reos al suplicio. O cuando en vez de una trama, formada sobre el ridículo de las acciones humanas, les dan diálogos llorones, pesados y más fríos que braseros sin lumbre. Confiesan no obstante, que los extranjeros han tenido y tienen aún, algunos escritores de primer orden que hacen honor al teatro moderno; pero que proporcionalmente les sucede lo mismo que a nosotros, pues en todas partes son raros los buenos poetas, y muchos los copleros (Act I).

8. Miñano may be thinking of the play *Le Dramaturge* by Michel de Cubières played in 1776 and printed in Paris in 1777 with the title *La Manie des Drames Sombres*. There are shadowy resemblances in the situations of the two plays. The particular point referred to occurs in a speech by the dramatist Prousas, disapproving of his daughter's suitor:

Prousas Mais ce qui justement me fait haïr Sainfort,
C'est que je l'ai vu rire aux endroits pathétiques
D'un drame le plus noir de mes Drames Tragiques. (Act I, iii)

9. Additional examples of Spanish Domestic dramas are:

Guillermo de Hanau, a domestic tragedy, by D. I. M. S., published in 1786. *El Amor constante o la Holandesa*, by Zavala y Zamora, played in 1787; *Nunca el hacer bien se pierde, y Dios da ciento por uno*. *La Matilde*, played in 1787; *El hombre agradecido*, by Comella, played in 1790; *De dos enemigos hace el amor dos amigos*, by L. A. J. M. [Moncín], played in 1790; *El egoísta*, by Rosa Gálvez, *Obras poéticas*, Madrid, 1804, vol. i; *La recompensa del arrepentimiento*, by A. Marqués y Espejo, Valencia, 1816.

CHAPTER 14

1. See the undated manuscript: *Tercera parte del Diálogo cómico-trágico-femenino que se tributa a la Sra Polonia*, in the Biblioteca Nacional, which contains the following verses appended as a 'Nota'.

> De ochenta y seis comedias, que escribí
> y se representaron con primor,
> consiguiendo del pueblo el honor
> que jamás esperé ni merecí;
> de éstas, que para hacerlas no atendí
> del arte los preceptos, y el fervor
> con que reprehende Oracio tanto error,
> por dar gusto al oyente, no temí:
> déstas, repito, la que logró más
> aplausos del inmenso pueblo, fue
> la generosa Emilia.

Valladares's first play, he tells us, in a note to a manuscript version of it, was *Nunca el rencor vencer puede a donde milita amor*. *Atis y Erenice*, written in 1758: 'Esta es la primera comedia que hice, año de 1758, de edad de 18 anos. Se representó en la compañía de los Polacos en 1767. La hizo Merino, el padre . . . Me dieron por ella 2 d . . . Duró 12 días y produjo 80 d.' MS. B. Nac.

2. It is referred to as '*Elogio de Federico II* . . . escrito en francés por el Conde de Guibert y traducido en [*sic*] castellano por D. F. A. de E.' See also, for example, a *Frédéric le Grand* . . . , Amsterdam, 1785, which bears on its title-page the note: 'Cet ouvrage peut faire suite aux Mémoires pour servir à la Vie de Voltaire écrits par lui-même.' The Abbé Denina's *Essai sur la Vie et la Règne de Frédéric II* . . . , Berlin, 1788; the *Observations sur la Constitution . . . des armées de S.M. Prussienne* . . . , ed. cit.; C. F. Nicolai's *Anekdoten von König Friedrich II von Preussen* . . . , Berlin and Stettin, 1788–92; Samuel Johnson's *Memoirs of Charles Frederick, King of Prussia*, London, 1786; the *Vida de Federico II*, translated by Bernardo María Calzada, Madrid, 1788. (It was placed on the *Index* in 1792 for its Voltairian sentiments.)

3.

> *Cosme* (*de militar, con reloj*)
> ¿Qué hora tendremos?
> el reloj toca y lo sabremos.
> (*tocan 7 horas* . . .)
> Y pues esto va largo, y son las siete
> mejor será dar fin a este sainete.
>
> *Marquesa* ¡Qué gracioso! Me parece
> composición de Comella.
>
> *Remigio* Me parece que está en prosa.
>
> *Marquesa* Nada menos; que son berzas
>
> *Remigio* Pero él acciona muy bien.

Marquesa Parece una palanqueta
cada brazo, etc., etc.

See *Los cómicos de la legua*. It parodies indiscriminately various aspects of Comella's art but is mainly a burlesque of the 'unipersonal'.

4. A famous anecdote worked into this Part is that of the blunt miller who refuses to sell his mill which occupies land required for reasons of state, and who, to the King's remark that the mill could be taken away from him by force, replies:

Molinero Eso, Señor, fuera cuando
no tuvieseis un supremo
tribunal que hace justicia
a todos.

and wins his case.

5. For example, a book against inoculation on what the author believed to be Christian principles was: *Memoria contra la inoculación, sacada de las dudas y disputas entre los autores . . .*, by Dr. Jaime Menós y de Llena, Manresa, 1785. In support of inoculation see *Memorial literario*, April 1794, which states that inoculation had been known of in Spain since 1771 but, as a practice, was still in its infancy. In fact, Feijoo, as early as 1733 (*Teatro crítico . . .*, vol. v, *Discurso* xi), had advised medical men to consider inoculation seriously and states that there has been much discussion on the subject but little information. It was discussed again for instance in March, 1797. See also Sarrailh, op. cit., pp. 39–41.

6.   *Isabel* que el príncipe que carece
de las necesarias fuerzas
para sostener el peso
de la sagrada diadema,
y se ve en la precisión
de ceder su preeminencia,
no cumple con elegir
personas que las ejerzan
si no cela exactamente
si son déspotas en ella. (Act II)

7. See, for example, Valladares's *El Emperador Alberto I, y la Adelina* (Parts I and II censored in 1781), Part I of which is a free translation of Le Blanc de Guillet's *Albert I ou Adeline*, of 1775; and Valladares's *Saber premiar la inocencia y castigar la traición*, Valencia, 1796 (it was licensed in 1782); an anonymous *La casada con violencia y el doméstico villano*, dealing with Henri IV and played in 1786; *El premio de la humanidad* or *El Czar Iwam*, by Zavala y Zamora, played in 1790; *El carpintero de Livonia* (translated from *Le Menuisier de Livonie*, of Alexandre Duval, see Cot. *Máiquez*, 227, 412), a play about Peter the Great, played in 1806; *El Emperador carpintero*, dealing with Peter the Great, played in 1816 (see Cot. *Máiquez*, 412); *La huérfana de Salzburgo o viaje de José II*, played in 1808 (see Cot. *Máiquez*, 275); *El alcalde de Sardam o los dos Pedros* (*c.* 1820) [see Cot. *Máiquez*, 227], etc., etc.

CHAPTER 15

1. *El impresario burlado* is an anonymous *sainete* licensed in 1793, MS. B. Mun. Like Moratín the author is contemptuous, or affects to be so, of the social class from which the popular playwrights are drawn:

> . . . es de dos Ingenios
> sobresalientes! El uno
> dicen que es aquel botero
> que hay más abajo del puente
> de San Ginés. . . .

Other forms of drama, however, are also parodied, with, it would seem, good-natured impartiality.

2. Compare, for instance:

> . . . Iré
> dando voces como loco
> publicando mis delitos.
> Hombres, fieras, montes, globos
> celestiales, peñas duras,
> . . .
> Yo soy Ludovico Enio.
> Temblad a mi nombre todos.
>
> (Calderón, *El Purgatorio de San Patricio*, Act III, v)

3. See, for example:

> *Prado* ¿Te vas?
>
> *Garrido* Mi honor me llama.
>
> *Prado* ¿Me dejas?
>
> *Garrido* No
>
> *Prado* ¡Qué pena!
>
> *Garrido* Honor, amor ¿qué es esto?
>
> *Prado* Oye
>
> *Garrido* No puedo
> . . .
>
> *Rom* ¡Gran caso!
>
> *Paco* ¡Gran valor!
>
> *Rom* ¡Gran fortaleza!
>
> *Paco* Admítase el partido
>
> *Rom* No se admita.

4. *Introducción para la comedia 'La sangre sin fuego hierve'*, licensed in 1782, MS. B. Mun. One of the characters comments on the '*El asombro de la Europa* . . .' as follows:

> *González* A mí no me gustan esos
> títulos tan abultados,
> que hacen tres, o cuatro versos.
> Me parecen a los años
> secos, que en ellos hay siempre
> mucha paja, y poco grano.

5. We have given an example above (pp. 479 ff.) of a Comellan drama written for private production as early as 1787, and there are doubtless earlier examples. But 1776, when Comella would be about twenty-five, would certainly appear to be early for any drama of his, though certain plays published under his name bear the date, Pamplona, 1778 (see p. 573, n. 9). The Pamplona editions, however, may be wrongly dated with some special intent. See also Cambronero, *Comella* . . ., ed. cit., pp. 309–12. The date 1786 [*sic*] which Cotarelo takes as belonging to a period before Comella started to produce, is probably meant to read 1776, the date of the manuscript licence in the Biblioteca Municipal. Cotarelo states that he possessed a copy with a 'nota del tiempo' referring

to the play as the work of Bruno Solo de Zaldívar. It was a popular play and in Cotarelo's opinion was one of those which inspired Moratín's satire. See Cot. *Máiquez*, p. 38. The same critic states that the first of Comella's dramas to be played—though he refers, of course, to public performances—was *I a buena esposa*, a heroic drama staged in 1786. See Cot. *Tirana*, p. 132. The *Memorial literario* of March 1786, relates the subject matter to a subject treated by Nipho in *El cajón de sastre*.

6. Compare Mercier's *Mlle Lancy (les arrêtant)*: . . . On n'entend que les cris d'une foule féroce, qui se dispute la chair des animaux immondes . . . with Comella's
Margarita. [referring to the food to which the inhabitants are reduced]

> el desabrido caballo
> el can, el inmundo insecto;
> . . . Cuando
> no tengamos más remedio,
> sirvámonos unos a otros
> de alimento, que yo ofrezco
> ser la primera a morir
> para dar a otros ejemplo. (*El sitio de Calés*, Act I)

and with du Belloy's
Saint Pierre: Le plus vil aliment, rebut de la misère,/Mais, aux derniers abois, ressource horrible et chère./De la fidélité respectable soutien,/Manque à l'or prodigué du riche citoyen. (Act I, vi)

7. The Censor, Padre Fr. Ángel de Pablo Puerta Palanco, requires 'que el ingenio (lo que con facilidad podrá hacer) contraiga esta máxima al honor cristiano, y religioso, con que se evitará el escándalo que con otra irreligiosa pueda ocasionarse'.
Moncín's reformed sentiment then produces such speeches as:

> Pues todas las Roncalesas
> blasonan tan de cristianas
> que sabrán perder las vidas
> por no verse profanadas. . . .

which sounds ambiguously bold and brave but does not involve cold-blooded murder by their husbands.

8. Other heroic plays of this period are, for instance, an anonymous *El Rey Eduardo VIII*, staged in 1785; *Defensa de Barcelona por la más fuerte amazona*, by Fermín del Rey, of which we have seen an undated edition; *Hernán Cortés en Tabasco*, licensed in 1790, also by Fermín del Rey; *La escocesa Lambrun*, by Comella, played in 1793 and dealing with a meeting during the chase between Elizabeth of England and one of the Marys who had attended the tragic Mary Stuart.

9. *Cosme* [with cloak and sword, and carrying a light]:

> Por el ojo de la llave
> he visto un hombre en la sala.
> ¡Matarélo, vive el cielo!
> . . . Mas ya
> se apagó la luz . . .

BIBLIOGRAPHY

THIS Bibliography omits eighteenth-century reprints and recasts of Golden Age works unless a writer is specially important as editor or recaster. Of single plays running into several editions, the earlier editions or the censors' manuscript copies only are mentioned. Comedies, *sainetes*, and other short, non-serious plays are not normally given except where they concern this study or except in the case of authors who are generally regarded as minor figures but who are important for historical reasons and whose general range of work it may seem helpful to tabulate. Doubtful authors, attributed works, and other details obtained by deduction or supposition are indicated by square brackets. Anonymous plays referred to in the text are listed under 'Anon.'. Authors publishing under initials only are listed at the end of each letter-section. Pl. (played) refers to date of performance.

1. *Eighteenth-Century Authors, Periodicals, and Earlier Publications*

Actas de la Academia de Buen Gusto. MS. B.Nac.

ADDISON, J. *Cato.* See *Eighteenth-Century Plays.* Ed. Hampden. Everyman. No. 818.

Aduana crítica. M., 1763–4. Hem.

AGAMENÓN, ABATE. *Carta censoria sobre la reforma de los teatros españoles.* M., 1793. B.M.P.

ALEMÁN Y AGUADO, LUCAS. *Índice de comedias raras y no comunes. . . .* MS. 1813. B.M.

— *No es triunfar saber vencer. Vencerse sólo es triunfar.* Com. her. MS. B. Nac. See also *Origins . . .* , pp. 148–50.

ÁLVAREZ DE CIENFUEGOS, NICASIO. *Obras poéticas.* M., 1816. 2 vols. B. Nac.

— *Poesías.* M., 1798. 2 vols. B. Nac.

ÁLVAREZ Y BAENA, J. A. *Hijos de Madrid ilustres . . . Diccionario histórico.* M., 1789–91, 4 vols. B.M.

ANDRÉS, JUAN. *Carta del Abate J. Andrés a su hermano . . . dándole noticia de la literatura de Viena.* M., 1794. B.M.

— *Dell'origine, progressi e stato attuale d'ogni letteratura.* Parma, 1782–9. 7 vols. Also an additional volume published at Parma in 1822. B.M.

— *Lettera dell' Abbate D. Giovanni Andrés al Sig. Comendatore Fra. Gaetano Valenti Gonzaga . . . sopra una pretesa cagione del corrompimento del gusto italiano nel secolo XVII.* Cremona, 1776. B.M.

Aneckdoten und Karakterzüge, aus dem Leben Friedrich des Zweiten. Berlin, 1787–9. B.M.

ANON.

— *Amor conyugal o La Amelia, El.* MS. B. Mun.

— *Andrómaca (La), o Al amor de madre no hay afecto que le iguale.* N.p., n.d. B.M. See Cumplido, José.

— *Ariadna abandonada en Naxos.* Melo. *C.M.C.* vi (1793).

— *Atilio Regulo*. Bar., n.d. (2nd ed.) B.M.

— *Beberley o el jugador inglés (El)*. MS. *Cens*. 1779. B. Mun.

— *Coffee House (The)*. Dramatic Piece. (Adapted from J. B. Rousseau's *Le Café*.) London, 1737. U.L.G.

— *Berenize en Tesalonica*. *Com. her*. Bar., n.d. (2nd ed.).

— *Caton* (Trans. from Addison). 'Le Théâtre Anglais', vol. viii. London, 1749. B.M.

— *Carpintero de Livonia, El:* (From *Le Menuisier de Livonie* of Alexandre Duval) Bar., n.d.

— *Carta de un cómico retirado, a los Diaristas, sobre los teatros*. M., 1788. By 'El cómico retirado, X.E.D.' B. Nac.

— *Casandro y Olimpia* (by Olavide?) MS. *Cens*. 28 Aug. 1781. B. Mun.

— *Celmira, La* (From Du Belloy) N.p., n.d. B.M.

— *Comedia (La) y los dos candiles* . . . *C.M.C*. ii (1790).

— '*Comendador de Ocaña El*. *(Parodia* . . . *del siglo XVII)*' Ed. M. Artigas in *Boletín de la Biblioteca Menéndez y Pelayo*. 1926.

— *Comerciante inglés (El)*. Bar., n.d. B.M.

— *Cuatro días tristes del Sargento Grinedal, Los*. In verse. MS. *Cens*. 1789. B. Mun. B. Nac. has a manuscript prose version called *El reo más inocente. Los cuatro*. . . .

— *Diálogo trágico titulado La Raquel* . . . *intervalos de música*. By 'Un aficionado' [M.], n.d. B.M.

— *Disputa del teatro, La*. *Sain*. MS. *Cens*. M., 24 May 1776. B. Mun.

— *Dos amantes más finos (Los)*. *Hipermenestra y Linceo. La traición más bien vengada y Mágica Erictrea*. MS. *Cens*. 28 Dec. 1774. B. Mun.

— *Esclava del Negro Ponto, La*. *Pieza moderna. C.M.C*. v (1792). See Comella: *La católica princesa*. . . .

— *Esclavo de su dama (El) y Paso honroso en Asturias*. MS. 1749. B. Mun.

— *Es difícil el saber el fin que uno ha de tener. La esclava hallada*. 'Rep. historial y metafórica'. MS. *Cens*. 1772. B. Mun.

— *Esther*. MS. B. Mun.

— *Fanny, or, The Happy Repentance. From the French of M. D'Arnaud*. Dublin, 1767. B.M.

— *Función lugareña (La), o Doña Inés de Castro*. *Sainete*. N.p., n.d., B. Mun.

— *Gran Visir, El*. MS. *Cens*. 1789. B. Mun.

— *Guzmán, El*. Bar., n.d. B.M.

— *Héroe de la manzana, El*. *Sainete*. MS. Licence 1774. B. Mun.

— *Hipermenestra*. Bar., n.d. B. Nac.

— *Inocente culpado, El*. Bar., 1797. B.M.

— *Lacrymanie (La) ou Manie des Drames*. Amsterdam, 1775. B.M.

— *Lealtad al soberano premiada por el amor. La Amelia*. Pl. 1797. See Coe.

— *Majo de Lavapiés, El*. 'Tragedia con gracioso. Su autor Yo.' MS. B. Nac.

— *Manolo. 2a Parte*. *Sain*. M., 1791. B. Mun.

— *Mayor gloria de un héroe es ser constante en la Fe (La), o El héroe verdadero*. MS. *Cens*. 1786. B. Mun.

— *Merope* (From Maffei) MS. B. Mun.

— *Mujer de Padilla (La)*. *Doña María de Pacheco*. MS. B. Mun.

— *Natalia and Menzikof: or The Conspiracy against Peter the Great*. (From Kratter) London, 1790. B.M.

— *No hay amar sin merecer y Más prodigiosa Arcadia*. MS. *Cens*. 1761. B. Mun.

— *Northern Heroes (The); or The Bloody Contest between Charles XII* . . . *and Peter the Great*. London, 1748. B.M.

— *Olimpiada (La)*. MS. *Cens.* 1794. B. Mun
— *Organte, Ejemplo de lealtad* by 'Un aficionado'. M., 1772. MS. B. Nac.
— *Paje, El*. MS. B. Mun.
— *Palmira, (La) Tragedia burlesca. Sain.* MS. Licence, 1779. B. Mun. [? By Lucas Alemán y Aguado].
— *Parodie d'Iphigénie Acte IV*. Boisjourdain: *Mélanges Historiques . . .*, vol. ii. Paris, 1807. B.M.
— *Perder por odio y amor reino, vida y opinión. Mitridates en el Ponto*, MS. *Cens.* 1765. B. Mun.
— *Pérdida de España, La*. MS. *Cens.* 1770. B. Mun.
— *Perico el de los palotes*. M., n.d. B.M.
— *Phedra, La.* (Other copies *La Fedra*.) (From Racine by Olavide.) MS. *Cens.* 1783. B. Mun. See Olavide.
— *Raquel (La). Diálogo trágico.* . . . By 'Un aficionado' [M.], n.d. B.M.
— *Reinar después de morir.* . . . MS. B. Mun.
— *Religión patria y honor, triunfan del más ciego amor. La Hirza*. (From Sauvigny.) MS. *Cens.* July 1786. B. Mun.
— *Richard Cœur de Lion*. 'Hist. Romance' (from Sedaine). London, 1786. U.L.G.
— *Riquimero*. Pl. 1786. See Coe.
— *Rodoguna*. (From Corneille.) MS. *Cens.* M., 1777. B. Mun.
— *Telemaco, El*. Melo. *C.M.C.* xi (1799).
— *Verter (El), o El abate seductor*. Val., 1817. B.M.
— *Viting, El*. Bar., n.d. B.M.
— *Zaida, La*. (From Voltaire's *Zaïre*) Bar., 1782. (2nd ed.) B. Mun.
AÑORBE Y CORREGEL, TOMÁS DE
— *Amantes de Salerno, Los*. N.p., n.d. B. Nac.
— *Caballero del cielo y primer rey de Hungría, El*. N.p., 1735. B. Nac.
— *Como luce la lealtad a vista de la traición. La hija del senescal*. N.p., n.d. B.M.
— *Daniel de ley de gracia (El), y Nabuco de la Armenia*. M., 1733. B.M.
— *Duende de Zaragoza, El*. M., 1734. B.M.
— *Encantada Melisendra (La) y Piscator de Toledo*. M., n.d. B.M.
— *Júpiter y Dánae*. M., 1738. B. Nac.
— *Nulidades de amor*. N.p., n.d. B.M.
— *Oveja contra el pastor, y tirano Boleslao (La)*. M., 1746. B. Nac.
— *Paulino, El*. M., 1740. B.M.
— *Poder de la razón, El*. N.p., n.d. B. Nac.
— *Princesa, ramera y mártir, Santa Afra*. M., 1735. B.M.
— *Tutora de la Iglesia y Doctora de la Ley, La*. N.p., n.d. [1737] B. Nac.
— *Virtud vence el destino, La*. N.p., n.d. B.M.

Apologista universal, El. M., 1786. Hem.
ARELLANO Y EL ARCO, VICENTE. See Rodríguez de Arellano y el Arco, Vicente.
ARMONA (JUEZ PROTECTOR DE TEATROS). *Memorias cronológicas . . . de las comedias en España*. MS. B. Nac. 18. 474–75.
ARNAUD, BACULARD D'. *Fanni, ou La nouvelle Paméla, Histoire Anglaise*. N.p., n.d. B.M.
ASCARGOTA, MANUEL DE. *Las ceguedades del vicio y peligros del rigor. El joven Carlos*. Trans. and versified (from the prose of Mercier's *Jenneval*) by . . . MS. 1776. B. Nac.
ARTEAGA, ESTEBAN DE. *Investigaciones filosóficas sobre la belleza ideal . . .* M., 1789, B.M.
— *Le Rivoluzioni del teatro musicale italiano . . .* Bologna, 1783–8. B.M.

Arteaga, Joaquín de. *Índice alfabético de comedias, tragedias y demás piezas del teatro español.* MS. B. Nac. No. 14698.

(P.D.) A.R.Y. *Acaso, astucia y valor vencen tiranía y rigor, y triunfos de lealtad C.M.C.* iii (1790).

— *Desgraciada hermosura (La) o Doña Inés de Castro. C.M.C.* iv. (1792).

Ayala, Ignacio de. See López de Ayala, Ignacio de.

Barbieri, F. A. *Papeles de* . . . MS. B. Nac.

Baretti, Joseph. *A Journey from London to Genoa, through England, Portugal, Spain and France.* London, 1770. 4 vols.

Bazo, Antonio. *Más que las armas conquista el agrado y la piedad.* MS. B. Nac.

— *Merope y Polifonte.* MS. B. Mun.

— *Paz de Artaxerxes con Grecia.* M., 1763. B.M.

— *Piedad (La) de un hijo vence la impiedad de un padre, y Real jura de Artaxerxes, rey de Persia.* M., n.d. B. Nac.

— *Romance liso y llano.* N.p., n.d. B.M.

— *Sacrificar el afecto en las aras del honor es el más heroico amor. Cleonice y Demetrio.* MS. B. Nac.

— *Sofonisba, La.* MS. B. Nac.

— *Tres (Los) mayores portentos en tres distintas edades.* Val., 1765. B.M.

— *Vencer la propia pasión en las lides del amor es la fineza mayor, y Adriano en Siria.* MS. B. Nac.

Beaumarchais, P. *Œuvres.* Paris, 1876.

Bérard. See Eberts.

[Bernard, Madame]. *Petit Chemin de Potsdam (Le) ou Quelques Anecdotes de la Vie de Frédéric II.* Paris [1793] B.M.

Beyträge zu den Anecdoten und Charakterzügen aus dem Leben Friedrichs des Zweiten. 4 parts. Berlin and Frankfurt, 1788, 1789. B.M.

Bickerstaffe, I. *Lionel and Clarissa.* Com. op. London, 1768. B.M.

— *Maid of the Mill, The.* N.p., 1765. B.M.

— *The Sultan, or, A Peep into the Seraglio.* Com. op. *Modern British Drama*, vol. v, London, 1811.

Botti, Domingo. *Dos amigos (Los), o sea El negociante de León*, Bar., n.d. B.M.

Bourgoing, J F. [*Nouveau Voyage en Espagne*] Paris, 1789. 3 vols. B.M.

— *Tableau de l'Espagne Moderne.* Paris, 1797. 3 vols. 2nd edition. B.M.

Boutet de Monvel, J. M. *Clémentine et Désormes.* Paris, 1781. B.M.

Bueno de Castilla, Patricio [? López de Sedano].

— *Belianís literario, El.* M., 1765. Hem.

Bursay, L. See Molé.

Cadalso, José. *Obras.* M., 1803; 4 vols. M., 1818, 3 vols., etc. See Bibl. in *Noches lúgubres* Publications of *B.S.S.* Plain Text Series, no. 2. Liverpool, 1933, pp. 60–1. See also Valle, Juan del.

Calvo de Barrionuevo, José. *Parricida inocente, El.* MS. Cens. 1786. B. Mun.

— *Razón justicia y honor triunfan del mayor valor. Alexandro en Scutaro. C.M.C.* v (1792).

Calzada, Bernardo María de. *Catón en Útica.* (From Addison) M., 1787. B. Nac.

— *Hijo natural (El), o pruebas de la virtud.* 'Comedia en prosa de Diderot, puesta en verso por . . .' M., 1787. B. Nac.

— *Motezuma*. M., 1784. See *Mem. Lit.* (1784).

— [*Subordinación militar, La.*] Trans. by . . . MS. *Cens.* 1785. B. Mun.

— *Triunfo de la moral cristiana (El) o los americanos*. (From the French.) M., 1788. B. Mun.

CÁNCER Y VELASCO and VÉLEZ Y GUEVARA. *Los siete infantes de Lara* in the collection *El mejor de los mejores*. Alcalá, 1651.

CAÑIZARES, J. DE. *Angélica y Medoro:* Ed. J. A. Molinaro and W. T. McCready. Torino, 1958.

— *Comedias*. B.A.E. xlix.

— *Comedias escogidas*. M., 1829–33. 2 vols. B.M.

CASABUENA, DIEGO. *Ifigenia en Táuride*. Melo. MS. *Cens.* 1797. B. Mun.

CASTRILLÓN, NARCISO. See Enciso Castrillón.

CAVANILLES, ANTONIO, J. *Observations . . . sur l'article 'Espagne' de la nouvelle Encyclopédie*. Paris, 1784. B.M.

CEAN BERMÚDEZ, JUAN A. *Diccionario histórico de los más ilustres profesores de las bellas artes en España*. M., 1800. 6 vols. B.M.

— *Memorias para la vida del Exco. Sr. D. Gaspar Melchor de Jovellanos*. M., 1814. B.M.

Censor, El. M., 1820–2. Hem.

CERDABAR, DAMIÁN L. *Pasajes escogidos de la vida privada de Federico II, Rey de Prusia*. M., 1787. B. Nac

CIBBER, COLLEY. *An Apology for his Life*. Everyman. No. 668.

CIENFUEGOS. See Álvarez de Cienfuegos, N.

[CIFUENTES, JERÓNIMO DE]. *(Fama es la mejor dama, La)* C.M.C. ix (1796).

CLAVIJO Y FAJARDO, J. *Pensador, El* M., 1762–7. 6 vols. B. Nac.

Colección de comedias sueltas, con algunos autos y entremeses de los mejores ingenios de España, desde Lope de Vega hasta Comella, hecha, y ordenada por I.R.C. 33 vols. B. Nac.

Colección de las mejores comedias nuevas que se van representando en los teatros de esta corte. M., 1789–96. 11 vols. B. Nac.

COLOMÉS, JUAN. *Agnese di Castro*. Livorno, 1781. B. Nac.

COLLÉ, CHARLES. *Partie de Chasse de Henri IV, (La)*. Paris, 1766. B.M.

COMELLA Y VILLAMITJANA, LUCIANO FRANCISCO.

— *Obras dramáticas*. Val., 1795.

— *Abuelo y la nieta, El*. Com. mus. Bar., 1778; M., *Cens.* 1792. B. Mun.

— *Aburrido, El*. M.S. With approbation for 1819. B. Mun.

— [*Alcalde proyectista, El.*] Sain. MS. *Cens.* 1790. B. Mun.

— *Alcarreña chismosa, La*. Fin de fiesta. MS. *Cens.* 1795. B. Mun.

— *Alejandro en Oxidraca*. Dr. her. MS. *Cens.* 1794. B. Mun.

— *Ama de gobierno, La*. Sain. MS. *Cens.* 1799. B. Mun.

— *Amantes desgraciados, Los. (or) Los amantes de Teruel*. MS. *Cens.* 1793. B. Mun.

— *Amigos, del día, Los*. MS. *Cens.* 1794. B. Mun.

— *Amor al dote, El*. Pieza de mús. MS. *Cens.* 1798. (First act missing.) B. Mun.

— [*Amor disfrazado, El.*] Op. bufa. MS. Approbation for 1801. B. Mun.

— *Amores del Conde de Cominges, Los*. Part I. MS. *Cens.* 1796. B. Mun. (We have not found a second part.)

— *Andrómaca, La*. Melo. MS. B. Mun. C.M.C. ix (1796).

— *Ardid militar, El*. Fin de fiesta. *Cens.* 1793. B. Mun.

— *Asdrúbal*. MS. *Cens.* 1793. B. Mun.

— *Astucia burlada, La*. Sain. MS. *Cens.* 1794. B. Mun.

— *Astucias amorosas, Las*. Op. (From the Italian.) MS. *Cens.* 1805. B. Mun.

— *Avaro, El. Op. jocosa.* MS. Approbation for 1812. B. Mun. *C.M.C.* ix (1796).

— *Ayo de su hijo El.* MS. *Cens.* 1798. B. Mun.

— *Baile deshecho, (El) y Juan de la Enreda. Fin de fiesta.* MS. *Cens.* 1795. B. Mun.

— [*Bola de gas, La.*] *Sain.* MS. *Cens.* 1784. B. Mun.

— *Buen hijo (El) o María Teresa de Austria.* MS. *Cens.* 1790. B. Mun. Also called *El Fénix de los criados.* . . .

— *Buen labrador, El.* MS. *Cens.* 1791. B. Mun.

— *Buena esposa, La.* MS. Approbation for 1781. B. Mun.

— *Buena nuera, La.* MS. *Cens.* 1794. B. Mun.

— *Burla de las modas, La. Sain.* MS. *Cens.* 1799. B. Mun.

— *Burla graciosa, La. Sain.* MS. *Cens.* 1799. B. Mun.

— *Burlado por sí mismo, El. Sain.* MS. *Cens.* 1790. B. Mun.

— *(Cadetito, El). Tonadilla a solo.* MS. *Cens.* 1782. B. Mun.

— *Cadma y Sinnorosis.* Sal., n.d. B.M.P.

— *Casa de Tararira, La. Sain.* MS. B. Mun.

— *Casado avergonzado.* Sal., n.d. B.M.P.; *C.M.C.* vi (1793).

— *Catalina II, Emperatriz de Rusia. Dr. her.* Val., 1795. B. Nac.

— *Catalina II en Cronstadt. Dr. her.* MS. *Cens.* 1799. B. Mun.

— [*Católica princesa (La) joven la más afligida y esclava del Negro Ponto*] MS. Approbation for 1776. B. Mun.

— [*Cazadorcita, La.*] *Tonadilla a solo.* MS. *Cens.* 1779. B. Mun.

— *Cecilia, La.* Part I. MS. *Cens.* 1786. B. Mun.

— *Cecilia viuda, La.* Part II, *C.M.C.* i (1789).

— *Cecilia viuda, La.* Part III, M., 1787. B. Mun.

— *Celestino, San Papa.* Sal., n.d.

— *Celos aparentes, Los. Sain.* MS. *Cens.* 1793. B. Mun.

— *Cifra, La. Op. arreglada por* . . . . MS. *Cens.* 1799. B. Mun.

— *Coqueta avergonzada de serlo, La. Fin de fiesta.* MS. *Cens.* 1795. B. Mun.

— *Corralón, El. Fin de fiesta.* MS. *Cens.* 1792. B. Mun.

— *Crédulo desengañado, El. Op.* MS. 1801. B. Mun.

— *Cristina de Suecia.* MS. *Cens.* 1797. B. Mun.

— *Cristóbal Colón.* MS. *Cens.* 1790. B. Mun.

— *Cromvel.* MS. *Cens.* 1786. B. Mun.

— *Cuidados ajenos matan al asno. Sain.* MS. *Cens.* 1794. B. Mun.

— *Dama colérica (La) o novia impaciente.* N.p., n.d. B.M.P.

— *Dama sutil, La.* M., 1799. B. Mun.

— [*Dama voluble, La.*] *Op.* MS. B. Mun.

— *Deber y la naturaleza, El.* M., 1806. B.M.P.

— [*Desdeñosa, La.*] *Opereta.* MS. B. Mun.

— [*Desengañado, El.*] *Tonadilla.* MS. *Cens.* 1782. B. Mun.

— *Día de campo (El). Introducción al 'Pueblo feliz'.* MS. *Cens.* 1789. B. Mun.

— *Día de función nueva, El. Fin de fiesta.* MS. *Cens.* 1793. B. Mun.

— *Dichoso arrepentimiento, El.* MS. *Cens.* 1790. B. Mun.

— *Donde menos se piensa salta la liebre. Fin de fiesta.* MS. *Cens.* 1799. B. Mun.

— *Doña Berenguela.* MS. *Cens.* 1793. B. Mun.

— *Doña Inés de Castro. Escena trag. lír.* MS. *Cens.* 1791. B. Mun.

— *Dos amigos, Los.* MS. *Cens.* 1790. B. Mun.

— *Dos comisarios de funciones, Los. Fin de fiesta de mús.* MS. *Cens.* 1803. B Mun.

— *Dos tutores, Los.* Sain. MS. *Cens.* 1791. B. Mun.
— *Duque de Borgoña (El) y los falsos hombres de bien.* (From the Italian.) MS. *Cens.* 1790. B. Mun.
— *Engaño desengaño El.* Sain. M., 1792. B. Mun.
— *Entrada de la función casera, La.* Sain. MS. B. Mun.
— *Error y el honor, El.* (From the French.) M., n.d. B. Nac.
— *Esclavos felices, Los.* Op. seria. MS. *Cens.* 1793. B. Mun.
— *Escocesa Lambrún, La.* Dr. her. MS. *Cens.* 1793. B Mun.
— *Escuela de los celosos, La.* Op. bufa. (From Bertati.) *C.M.C.* xi (1790).
— *Estatuario griego, El.* MS. *Cens.* 1800. B. Mun.
— *Ester.* Dr. sacro. M., 1803. B.M.P.
— *Estudiante en la feria, El.* Fin de fiesta. MS. B. Mun.
— *Estudiantes farsantes, Los.* Fin de fiesta. MS. B. Mun.
— *Familia indigente, La.* MS. *Cens.* 1798. B. Mun.
— *Fanático, El.* Sain. MS. *Cens.* 1794. B. Mun.
— *Federico II en el campo de Torgau.* MS. *Cens.* 1789. B. Mun.
— *Federico II en Glaatz, o la humanidad.* MS. *Cens.* 1792. B. Mun.
— *Federico II, rey de Prusia.* MS. *Cens.* 1788. B. Mun.
— [*Fénix de los criados (El), o María Teresa de Austria*]. MS. *Cens.* 1791. B. Mun. See *El buen hijo.* . . .
— *Fénix de las mujeres (El) o La Alceste* M.S. *Cens.* 1799. B. Mun.
— *Fingida enferma por amor, La.* Pieza de música. (From Goldoni.) MS. *Cens.* 1797. B. Mun.
— *Hércules y Deyanira.* Melo. MS. *Cens.* 1796. B. Mun.
— *Hijo reconocido, El.* M., n.d. (Pl. 1799.) B. Mun.
— *Hijos de Nadasti, Los.* Com. her. MS. *Cens.* 1795. B. Mun.
— *Hombre agradecido El.* Comedia de costumbres. MS. *Cens.* 1790. B. Mun.
— *Hombre de bien El.* N.p., n.d. B.M.P.
— *Hombre sensato por mal nombre (El).* MS. *Cens.* 1797. B. Mun.
— *Hombre singular (El) o Isabel I de Rusia.* MS. *Cens.* 1795. B. Mun.
— [*Hortelanita y el hortelano, La.*] Tonadilla a duo. MS. *Cens.* 1784. B. Mun.
— *Humorada en Nochebuena La.* Sain. MS. *Cens.* 1799. B. Mun.
— *Idomeneo.* M., 1792. B.M.P.
— *Indolente (El) o el poltrón.* MS. *Cens.* 1792. B. Mun.
— *Ino y Neifile.* MS. *Cens.* 1797. B. Mun.
— *Ino y Temisto o Atamante.* MS. *Cens.* 1792. B. Mun.
— *Isabela, La.* Dr. joco-serio. MS. *Cens.* 1794. B. Mun.
— [*Isla de la pescadora, La.*] Zarz. MS. *Cens.* 1778. B. Mun.
— [*Isla del placer, La.*] Op. bufa. MS. *Cens.* 1801. B. Mun.
— *Jacoba, La.* MS. *Cens.* 1789. B. Mun.
— *Jardín del amor de la nación, El.* Loa. MS. B. Mun.
— *Judit castellana, La.* Com. her. MS. *Cens.* 1791. B. Mun.
— [*Lo que puede un desengaño y Elementos de las damas.*] Sain. MS. B. Mun.
— *Locura de las modas, La.* Sain. MS. *Cens.* 1792. B. Mun.
— *Llegar a tiempo.* N.p., n.d. B. Nac.
— *Luis XIV el Grande.* See *Pruebas de la virtud.* . . .
— [*Maja porfiada, La.*] Tonadilla a duo. MS. *Cens.* 1782. B. Mun.
— *Malos lados (Los) o El embrollón castigado.* Sain. MS. *Cens.* 1803. B. Mun.

— *Maragato y el tuno, El. Fin de fiesta.* MS. B. Mun.

— *María Teresa de Austria en Landaw.* Pamplona, 1778. B.M.P. MS. *Cens.* 1793. B. Mun.

— [*Marido avergonzado, El.*] *Sain.* MS. *Cens.* 1779. See *El casado avergonzado* above.

— *Matrimonio por razón de estado, El.* Pamplona, 1778. B. Nac.

— *Matrimonio secreto, El. Dr. en música.* (From Italian.) Pl. 1797. See *Mem. lit.* Aug. 1797.

— *Mayor rival de Roma (El). Viriato.* MS. *Cens.* 1798. B. Mun.

— *Menestral sofocado, El. Sain.* MS. 1798. B. Mun.

— *Moscovita sensible, La.* MS. *Cens.* 1794. B. Mun.

— *Natalia y Carolina.* MS. *Cens.* 1798. B. Mun.

— *Negro sensible, El. Melo.* MS. *Cens.* 1798. B. Mun.

— *Niña, La. Op. joco-seria.* (From the Italian.) MS. *Cens.* 1795. B. Mun.

— *Nina desdeñosa, La. Dr. en mús.* MS. 1794. B. Mun.

— *No ser y parecer. Sain.* MS. *Cens.* 1799. B. Mun.

— *Novio burlado, El. Entremés.* MS. *Cens.* 1798. B. Mun.

— [*Nueva protegida, La.*] *Tonadilla a tres.* MS. *Cens.* 1780. B. Mun.

— *Pedro el Grande, Czar de Moscovia.* MS. Approbation 1796. B. Mun.

— *Pelucas de las damas, Las. Sain.* M., 1799. B. Mun.

— *Perico el de los palotes. Monólogo.* M., n.d. B.M.

— *Petimetre en la aldea, El. Sain.* MS. *Cens.* 1781. B. Mun.

— *Posadero y la criada (El) o Los tres huéspedes burlados. Sain.* MS. B. Mun.

— *Pradera del Canal, La. Sain.* MS. *Cens.* 1799. B. Mun.

— *Premio, El. Fin de fiesta.* MS. *Cens.* 1789. B. Mun.

— *Prueba de los cómicos, La. Sain.* MS. *Cens.* 1790. B. Mun.

— *Pruebas de la virtud (Las) Luis XIV el Grande.* MS. *Cens.* 1789. B. Mun.

— *Psiquis y Cupido. Dr. her.* MS. *Cens.* 1793. B. Mun.

— *Pueblo feliz, El.* M.S. B. Mun; C.M.C. i (1789).

— *Puerto de Flandes, El. Pieza de mús,* MS. *Cens.* 1781. B. Mun.

— *Razón todo lo vence (La) El Duque y la Duquesa.* MS. *Cens.* 1791. B. Mun.

— *Residencia, La. Sain.* MS. *Cens.* 1791. B. Mun.

— *Retrato, El. Zarz.* MS. *Cens.* 1786. B. Mun.

— *Secreto entre vecinas, El. Sain.* MS. *Cens.* 1793. B. Mun.

— *Sedecías o La destrucción de Jerusalem (Sic). Dr. sacro.* MS. *Cens.* 1805. B. Mun.

— *Séneca y Paulina.* MS. *Cens.* 1798. B. Mun.

— *Señorita irresoluta (La) o La función casera. Sain.* MS. *Cens.* 1797. B. Mun.

— *Sitio de Calés, El.* C.M.C. xi (1790).

— *Sofonisba. Melo.* MS. *Cens.* 1795. B. Mun.

— [*Súplica de la Prado, La.*] *Tonadilla a solo.* MS. *Cens.* 1785. B. Mun.

— *Tabernero burlado, El. Sain.* MS. *Cens.* 1790. B. Mun.

— *Teatro antes de empezar, El. Intro.* MS. B. Mun.

— [*Tío Herodes, El.*] *Sain. Cens.* 1783. B. Mun.

— *Tirano de Ormuz, El. Op. seria.* MS. *Cens.* 1793. B. Mun.

— *Tirano Gesler, El.* N.p., n.d. B.M.P.

— *Tornaboda de moda, La. Com de mús.* MS. *Cens.* 1793. B. Mun.

— *Vieja enamorada, La. Sain.* MS. *Cens.* 1793. B. Mun.

— *Violeto universal (El) o el Café. Fin de fiesta.* MS. 1793. B. Mun.

(The Biblioteca Municipal possesses various short pieces such as Introducciones, without titles, also by Comella.)

CONCHA, JOSÉ
— [*A España dieron blasón las Asturias y León. Triunfos de Don Pelayo.*] MS. B. Mun.
— *Accidentes de una fiesta (Los) y El jugador de manos. Sain.* C.M.C. iii (1791).
— *Astucias del enemigo contra la naturaleza. Marta imaginaria, segundo asombro de Francia.* Bar., 1771. B. Mun. (This is Part VII of *Marta la romarantina.*)
— *Buen criado, El.* Cádiz, 1775. MS. B. Nac.
— *Entre venganza y amor, hallar la dicha mayor. Mágico de Cataluña.* (Part III.) MS. *Cens.* 1778. B. Mun.
— [*Honor más combatido (El) y crueldades de Nerón.*] M., 1791. B. Mun.
— *Joven Pedro de Guzmán, El.* C.M.C. VI (1793).
— *Loco en su casa sabe más que en casa ajena el cuerdo (El), El dichoso vizcaíno.* MS. *Cens.* 1791. B. Mun.
— *Manchego en Madrid, (El) o El amigo más a tiempo. Sain.* MS. *Cens.* 1791. B. Mun.
— *Más heroico español, lustre de la antigüedad (Diversión de dos horas, o comedia nueva historial.* C.M.C. iv (1791.))
— *Más puede fina lealtad que dama, padre y crueldad. Antes que todo es el rey.* MS. *Cens.* 1779. B. Mun.
— *Narcete, El.* MS. *Cens.* 1776. B. Mun.
— *Nuera sagaz, La.* MS. *Cens.* 1776. B. Mun.

CORINTEO, EURIDALCO, P. A. (Pastor Arcade: i.e. Gaetano Golt.) *Il Catone in Utica.* (Trans. from Addison) Rome, 1776. B.M.
CORNEILLE, PIERRE. *Théâtre.* N.p., 1776. 10 vols. U.L.G.
Correo de Cádiz. Cádiz (various odd numbers) 1795–8. Hem.
Correo de los ciegos de Madrid (or—*de Madrid y de los ciegos*) M., 1786–91. Hem.
Correo general, histórico, literario y económico de la Europa. M., 1763. B. Nac.
Correo literario de la Europa. M., 1781–7. Hem.
COXE, WILLIAM. *Memoirs of the Kings of Spain of the House of Bourbon.* . . . London, 1813. 3 vols. U.L.G.
CRUZ CANO Y OLMEDILLA, RAMÓN DE LA
— *Sainetes inéditos de* . . . M., 1900.
— *Teatro* . . . *de* . . . M., 1786–91. 10 vols.
— *Bandos del Avapiés, y la venganza del Zurdillo, Los. Sain.* M., 1800. B.M.
— [*Bayaceto*] MS. [1769]. B. Mun.
— *Comedia de Valmojado, La. Sain.* MS. Licence 1776. B. Mun.
— *Despedida de los cómicos. Sain.* MS. B. Mun.
— [*Divorcio feliz.*] *Cuanto destruye un capricho y vale una reflexión. La Matilde.* MS. *Cens.* 1782. B. Mun.
— *En casa de nadie no se meta nadie, o el buen marido.* M., 1770. B.M.
— [*Escocesa, La.*] (From Voltaire, through the prose trans. of Iriarte). 2nd ed. Bar., n.d. B.M.
— [*Eugenia, La.*] Trans. from Beaumarchais. M. 1825. B. Mun.
— *Feria de los poetas, La.* MS. Licence 1777. B. Mun.
— [*Hamleto, Rey de Dinamarca.*] Trans. from Ducis, MS. B. Mun.
— *Inesilla la de Pinto. Sain.* MS. B. Mun.
— [*Introducción para la tragedia de Numancia destruida*]. MS. Licence 1778. B. Mun.
— *Italiano fingido, El.* MS. Licence 1785. B. Mun.

— *Manolo, Tragedia para reír, o sainete para llorar.* M., 1784. B. Nac.

— *Marido sofocado (El) Tragedia burlesca. Teatro . . . de . . .* Vol. iii, M., 1787. B. Mun.

— *Muñuelo* [or *Buñuelo*], *El. Tragedia por mal nombre.* Biblioteca Universal, vol. xxxv, M., 1877.

— *Quien complace a la deidad acierta a sacrificar. Dr. cómico-harmónico.* M., 1757. B. Mun.

— *Severo dictador y vencedor delincuente, (El). Lucio Papirio y Quinto Fabio.* (From Zeno.) *C.M.C.* iii (1791).

— *Soriano loco. V. Sainetes inéditos.* . . .

— *Zara. Teatro . . . de . . .* Vol. vi.

CUBILLO DE ARAGÓN, ÁLVARO. *La más insigne venganza.* Cens. 1775. B. Mun.

CUMBERLAND, RICHARD. *The Carmelite.* London, 1784. B.M.

CUMPLIDO, JOSEPH. *El Astianacte. Tragedia nueva. Por otro título: Al amor de madre no hay afecto que le iguale.* M. 1764. B. Mun. (This is a version of *Andrómaca.*)

DALAINVAL, (CAVANAS, J. B., called) *Le comte de Waltron ou la Subordination. Pièce arrangée pour le théâtre de Monsieur frère du Roi par . . . d'après la traduction de J.H.E.* Paris, 1789. B.M.

DAMA DE ESTA CORTE (UNA). *Posías varias.* . . . M., 1789, B.M.

DEJAURE, JEAN E. B. *Lodoiska.* [Paris, 1791.] B.M.

DENINA, C. G. M. *Essai sur la vie et le règne de Frédéric. II.* . . . Berlin, 1788. B.M.

DESCHAMPS, F. M. C. *Caton d'Utique.* Paris, 1715. B.M.

DESTOUCHES, N. *Œuvres Dramatiques.* 4 vols. Paris, 1757. U.L.G.

DEZÈDE[S]ET (N). *Auguste et Théodore, ou Les Deux Pages.* Paris, 1789. B.M.

Diario curioso, erudito, económico y comercial. M. 1786–8. Hem.

Diario extranjero. See Nipho, F. M.

Diario de los literatos de España. M., 1737–42. 7 vols. B.M.

Diario de las musas. M., 1790–1. Hem.

Diario noticioso. . . . M., 1758. Hem.

Diario noticioso universal. M., 1759. Hem.

DIDEROT, DENIS. *Œuvres,* Paris, 1798. B.M.

DÍEZ GONZÁLEZ, SANTOS. *Casamiento por fuerza, El.* MS. *Cens.* 1795. B. Mun.

— *Informe* (on the petition by Comella in 1789. Published in 'Comella' by Carlos Cambronero in *Revista contemporánea.* 30 June, M., 1896. pp. 578 ff. B.M.

— *Informe* on Comella's protest of libel in *La comedia nueva,* Madrid, 1792. Op. cit. July 1896.

— *Informe* on the state of theatres. Op. cit., 15 Feb. 1896.

— *Instituciones poéticas* [M., 1793]. B. Nac.

DODSLEY, ROBERT. *King and the Miller of Mansfield, The.* London [1737]. B.M.

— *Sir John Cockle at Court.* London [1738?]. B.M.

DUCIS, J. F. *Hamlet.* Nouvelle edition augmentée des variantes. Paris, 1815. B.M.

Duende de Madrid, El. M., 1781–2. Hem.

DU PERRON DE CASTERA. *Extraits de plusieurs pièces du théâtre espagnol.* . . . Amsterdam and Paris, 1738.

DURÁN, FRANCISCO. *Industria madrileña y el fabricante de Olot, La. C.M.C.* ii (1790).

DUVAL, ALEXANDRE. See Anon. *El carpintero de Livonia.*

D.F.M.D.M. and D.A.D.G. [DON ANDRÉS GILABERT]. *Thaléis y Direna.* MS. 1783. B. Nac.

D.F.T.R. *Siempre triunfa la inocencia. C.M.C.* v (1792).

D.I.D.B. *Premio de la constancia (El) o el matrimonio feliz*. MS. *Cens.* 1783. B. Mun.

D.I.M.S. *Guillermo de Hanau.* M., 1786. See *Mem. lit.* Nov. 1786.

EBERTS, J. H. *Le Comte de Waltron, ou la Discipline Militaire du Nord. Traduit de l'allemand* [*of H. F. Möller*] *par . . . et mis au théâtre par M. Bérard.* Rouen, 1789. B.M.

Eighteenth Century Plays. Ed. Hampden, J. Everyman. No. 818.

Encyclopédie Méthodique. Géographie Moderne. Vol. i. Paris, 1782. B.M.

ENCISO CASTRILLÓN, FÉLIX.

— *Abre el ojo, o El aviso a los solteros.* (Recast from Franc. de Rojas.) M., 1814. B. Mun.

— *Amor por el tejado.* (Recast from Álvaro Cubillo.) M. 1833. B. Nac.

— *Batalla de Denain. La. Op. cómica.* Adapted by . . . MS. B. Mun.

— [*Biblioteca de zapatos, La.*] *Op.* MS. *Cens.* 1803. B. Mun.

— [*Carboneros de Holtsback, Los.*] (Trans. from French.) MS. *Cens.* 1807. B. Mun.

— [*Casa en venta, La.*] (Trans. from French.) MS. *Cens.* 1815. B. Mun.

— *Casualidad contra el cuidado La.* (Recast from Antonio Coello.) M., 1807. B. Mun.

— [*Cobrar en vida lo gastado en su entierro, o Lo que puede un apuro.*] MS. *Cens.* 1818. B. Mun.

— [*Comedia de repente, La.*] M., n.d. (Pl. 1814.) B. Mun.

— *Conde de Almaviva, El.* MS. 1818. B. Nac.

— *Cual el padre así es el hijo.* (Trans. from French.) MS. 1804. B. Mun.

— *Distraído, El.* (Trans. from Regnard.) M. 1804. B. Mun.

— *Divorcio por amor, El.* M., 1808. B. Mun.

— *Don Lucas del Cigarral o Entre bobos anda el juego* (Recast from Franc. de Rojas.) MS. 1834. B. Mun.

— *Dorotea, La.* (Recast.) M., 1804. B. Mun.

— *Dos ayos, Los.* (Trans. by . . .) MS. *Cens.* 1816. B. Mun.

— *Elección de esposo, La.* (Trans. from Italian.) MS., *Cens.* 1817. B.M.

— [*Español y la francesa, El.*] MS. *Cens.* 1806; M., 1816. B. Mun.

— [*Esther*] MS. B. Mun.

— *Haber de casarse sin tener con quien, o Los riesgos de la inconstancia.* (Trans. by . . .) MS. *Cens.* 1820. B. Nac.

— *Inquilinos de Sir John (Los) o La familia en la India.* (Trans. from Kotzebue.) MS. *Cens.* 1826. B. Mun.

— [*Intriga por las ventanas, La.*] MS. B. Mun.

— *Joven de sesenta años, El.* (Trans. by . . .) MS. *Cens.* 1815. B. Mun.

— *Marica la del puchero,* (Recast by . . .) M., 1808. B. Mun.

— [*Mayor Pálmer, El.*] MS. *Cens.* 1803. B. Mun.

— *Médico turco, El. Opereta.* (Trans. by . . .) MS. *Cens.* 1805. B. Mun.

— [*Mentira contra mentira.*] MS. 1807. (Trans. by . . .) B. Mun.

— *Mujeres, Las.* (From Demoustier) MS. *Cens.* 1804. B. Mun.

— *Muñecas, (Las) o sea El amor por el tejado.* See *El amor por el tejado.*

— [*Opresor de su familia, El.*] MS. *Cens.* 1800. B. Mun.

— *Pamela casada.* Opera. (From the Italian.) *Cens.* 1806. B. Mun.

— *Pasión secreta, La.* (From Scribe) MS. B. Mun.

— *Persecuciones y amparos del católico príncipe Segismundo.* (Recast from Matos Fragoso and Moreto.) MS. *Cens.* 1816. B. Mun.

— *Reconciliador, El.* (From Demoustier.) MS. *Cens.* 1816. B. Mun. (Also called *El hombre amable.*)

— [*Roberto o El bandolero honrado.*] MS. B. Mun.
— [*Seductor enamorado, El.*] MS. *Cens.* 1803. B. Mun.
— [*Seguir dos liebres a un tiempo.*] MS. *Cens.* 1815. B. Mun.
— *Sordo en la posada, El.* Trans. by . . . MS. *Cens.* 1827. B. Mun.
— [*Sueño, El.*] MS. *Cens.* 1818. B. Mun.
— [*Teatro sin autores, El.*] M., 1814. B. Mun.
— *Tener que casarse sin tener con quien, o Los riesgos de la inconstancia.* (From Caignier by . . .) MS. B. Mun.
— [*Tesoro fingido, (El) o Los peligros de la curiosidad indiscreta.*] Op. MS. *Cens.* 1805. B. Mun.
— *Tippo-Saib o la toma de Seringapatán. Melo.* (From French.) MS. *Cens.* 1805. B. Mun.
— [*Tres maridos, Los.*] MS. *Cens.* 1815. B. Mun.
— [*Una y media, señor Conde, La.*] *Juguete cómico.* MS. 1833. B. Mun.
— [*Vano humillado, El.*] MS. *Cens.* 1802. B. Mun.

ENGEL, J. J. *Dankbare Sohn, Der.* Leipzig, 1773. B.M.
— *Edelknabe, Der.* Leipzig, 1774. B.M.
— *Pagie De,* Trans. in *Spectatoriaale* of Schouwburg. Vol. iv. Amsterdam 1777. B.M.
Espigadera, La. M., 1790–1. Hem.
Espíritu de los mejores diarios que se publican en Europa. M., 1787, etc.
ESTALA, P. *Edipo Tirano.* M., 1793. B. Nac.
— *Pluto, El.* M., 1794. B. Nac.
EXIMENO, ANTONIO. *Dell'origine e delle regole della musica.* . . . Rome, 1774. B.M.
— *Don Lazarillo Vizcardi.* M., 1872–3. B.M.

FACIOLLE, C.A. [*Veuve Généreuse, La.*] Paris, 1788. B.M.
FEIJOO Y MONTENEGRO, BENITO J. *Cartas eruditas y curiosas.* . . . M., 1742–60. 5 vols. B. Nac.
— *Teatro crítico universal o Discursos varios* . . . M., 1726–40. 9 vols. B. Nac.
FENOUILLET DE FALBAIRE DE QUINGEY, C. G. *Fabricant de Londres, Le.* Paris, 1771. B.M.
— *L'Honnête Criminel.* Yverdon, 1767. B.M.
FERNÁNDEZ DE MORATÍN, LEANDRO. *Epistolario.* 'Las cien mejores Obras de la Literatura Española.' Vol. lxxiii. M., n.d.
— *Obras.* B.A.E. ii (1846), pp. 147–631.
— *Obras.* M., 1830–1.
— *Obras dramáticas y críticas.* Paris, 1825. 3 vols.
— See also the list of publications on the centenary of Moratín's death in *B.A.M.* v (1928), pp. 436 ff.
FERNÁNDEZ DE MORATÍN, NICOLÁS. *Desengaño al teatro español, Respuesta al Romance liso y llano y defensa del Pensador.* N.p., n.d. B. Nac.
— *Desengaño II* . . . *sobre los autos sacramentales de* . . . *Calderón de la Barca.* N.p., n.d. B. Nac.
— *Desengaño III* . . . *sobre los autos* . . . *de* . . . *Calderón de la Barca.* N.p., n.d. B. Nac.
— *Hormesinda.* M., 1770. B.M.
— *Lucrecia.* M., 1763. B.M.
— *Obras.* B.A.E. ii (1846), pp. 1–144.
— *Petimetra, La.* M., 1762. B.M.

— *Poeta, El.* M. 1764. B. Nac.

FIELDING, HENRY. *Tragedy of Tragedies (The), or The Life and Death of Tom Thumb the Great.* See *Eighteenth-Century Plays.* Everyman.

— *Works.* London, 1871. 10 vols. U.L.G.

FORNER, J. P. *Asno erudito, El.* Val., 1782. B.M.

— *Corneja sin plumas, La.* M., 1795. B. Nac.

— *Exequias de la lengua castellana.* B.A.E. lxiii.

— *Obras.* M., 1843. B.M.

— *Oración apolegética por España y su mérito literario* . . . M., 1786. B.M.

— *Reflexiones sobre la Lección crítica.* . . . [of García de la Huerta.] M., 1786. B. Nac.

FREDERICK II, KING OF PRUSSIA. *Réflexions sur les talents militaires et sur le caractère de Charles XII, Roi de Suède.* München, 1925. B.M.

Frédéric le Grand, contenant des anecdotes . . . *Cet ouvrage peut faire suite aux Mémoires pour servir a le Vie de Voltaire écrits par lui-même.* Amsterdam, 1785. B.M.

Gaceta de Madrid. 1770 etc. B. Nac.

GÁLVEZ, MARÍA ROSA DE. *Ali-Bek.* M., 1801. B. Nac.

— *Catalina, o la Bella labradora.* (From the French.) M., 1801. B. Nac.

— *Esclavas Amazonas (Las). Hermanos descubiertos por un acaso de amor.* MS. B. Nac.

— *Obras poéticas.* M., 1804. 3 vols. B.M.

— *Safo.* Val. 1813. B. Nac.

— *Un loco hace ciento.* See *Nuevo teatro español.* Vol. v. M., 1801. B.M.

GARCÍA DE LA HUERTA, VICENTE. *Escena hespañola defendida, La.* M., 1786. B. Nac.

— *Fe triunfante del amor y cetro, La. (Xayra)* . . . M., 1784. B. Nac.

— *Lección crítica.* M., 1785. B. Nac.

— *Obras poéticas.* M., 1778-9. 2 vols. B Nac.

— *Obras poéticas.* M., 1786. 2 vols. (2nd augmented edition). B.M.

— *Theatro hespañol.* M., 1785, 15 vols. B.M. See also *Suplemento al Theatro hespañol*, n.d., and *Catálogo alfabético de las comedias y otras obras correspondientes al Theatro hespañol.* M., 1785. B.M.

GARCÍA DE VILLANUEVA HUGALDE Y PARRA, MANUEL. *Manifiesto por los teatros españoles y sus actores.* M., 1788. B. Nac.

— *Origen, épocas y progresos del teatro español.* M., 1802. B. Nac.

GARCÍA MALO, IGNACIO. *Doña María Pacheco, mujer de Padilla.* M., 1788. B.M.

GAY, J. *The Beggar's Opera*, London, 1754. U.L.G.

— *Polly* London 1729. (Ewing Collection.) U.L.G.

GILABERT, ANDRÉS. *La Cristina.* MS. 1782. B. Nac.

GOETHE, J. W. *Die Leiden des jungen Werther.* Berlin-Deutsche Bibliothek Berlagsgesellschaft.

GOLDONI, CARLO. *Tutte le opere.* Milan [1945–54]. 14 vols. U.L.G.

GOLDSMITH, OLIVER. *Poems and Plays.* Everyman. No. 415.

GONZÁLEZ DEL CASTILLO. J. J., *Hanníbal. Scena lírica.* Cádiz, 1788. B. Nac.

— *Obras completas.* M., 1914. 3 vols. B.M.

GONZÁLEZ DE LA CRUZ, J. J. *El delincuente honrado. Tragicom.* MS. 1800. B. Nac.

GUILLEMARD. *Caton d'Utique* [from Addison] Brest, 1767. B.M.

D'HARCOURT, LOUIS FRANÇOIS, Comte de Sézanne. ['Journal de mon voyage en Espagne le 3ᵉ Décembre 1700 jusqu'au 13ᵉ Avril, 1701'] in *Revue Hispanique*, vol. xviii, 1908, pp. 248 ff.

HARVEY, J. *Meditations among the Tombs.* London, 1746. B.M.
HERVÁS Y PANDURO, LORENZO. *Historia de la vida del hombre.* M., 1789–99. 7 vols. B.M.
HIDALGO, MANUEL. *Marta la Romarantina.* Part IV. Bar., 1771. B.M.
History (The) of Charles XII, King of Sweden. [From Voltaire.] London, 1739. B.M.
History (The) of the Remarkable Life of Charles XII, King of Sweden. London, [1760]. B.M.
HOUDART DE LA MOTTE, ANTOINE. *Inès de Castro. Répertoire du Théâtre Français.* Vol. xiv. Paris, 1824.

IMBERT, BARTHÉLEMI. *Historiettes ou Nouvelles en vers.* 2nd ed. Amsterdam and Paris, 1774. B.M.
Índice general de los libros prohibidos . . . por El Sr. Inquisidor General. . . . M., 1844.
Introducciones. MS. Leg. 1-184-1. B. Mun.
IRIARTE, TOMÁS DE
— *Colección de obras en verso y prosa.* M., 1787. 6 vols.
— *Guzmán el Bueno. Escena trágica unipersonal, con música. . . .* Cádiz, 1790. B. Mun.
— *Huérfano de la China, El.* (Trans. by . . .) MS. B. Nac.
— *Mal hombre, El.* (From J. B. L. Gresset's *Le Méchant.*) MS. B. Nac.
— *Malgastador El.* (From N. Destouches's *Le Dissipateur.*) MS. B. Nac.
— *Mercader de Esmirna, El.* (From the French.) M.S. 1773. MS. B. Nac.
— *Música, La.* M., 1779. B.M.
— *Pupila juiciosa, La.* (From the French.) MS. B. Nac.
— *Señorita mal criada, La.* MS. 1788. B. Nac.
— *Señorito mimado, El.* MS. B. Nac.
ISLA, JOSÉ FRANC. DE. *Historia del famoso predicador Fray Gerundio de Campazas. . . .* Paris, 1824. 5 vols. B.M.

JOHNSON, SAMUEL. *Memoirs of Charles Frederick, King of Prussia.* London, 1786. B.M.
JOVELLANOS, G. M. DE. *Delincuente honrado, El.* M., 1787; M., 1793; Bar., n.d.
— *Diarios.* Oviedo, 1953–6. 3 vols.
— *Obras.* B.A.E. Vols. xlvi, l, lxxxv-vii.
Juvenile Dramatist (The), or A Selection of Plays from the most celebrated German Writers upon Education. (Translated from the originals.) Hamburgh, 1801. 3 vols. B.M.
J.M.C.B. *la Subordinación.* Bar., n.d. B.M.
— *Venganza, La.* M., 1785.

Kalendario manual y Guía de forasteros en Madrid. M., 1783. B.M.
KOTZEBUE, AUGUST VON. *Erinnerungen aus Paris im Jahre 1804.* Berlin, 1804. B.M.
— *Theater.* Leipzig, Wien. 1840–1. B.M.

LAMARCA, LUIS. *El teatro en Valencia desde su origen hasta nuestros días.* Val., 1840.
LAMAS, [or LLAMAS] JOSEPH ANTONIO DE. *Primer Horacio héroe, El.* (Pl. 1790.) MS. B. Mun.
LAMPILLAS, FRANC. H. *Saggio storico-apologetico della letteratura spagnuola . . .* Genoa, 1778–81. 6 vols.
LANGLE, MARQUIS DE. *A Sentimental Journey through Spain.* 'Trans. from the Paris edition that was burnt by the common Hangman'. London, 1786. 2 vols. U.L.G.

LANGLET, ABATE J. *Hablador juicioso, El.* M., 1763. B.S.I.

LASERNA, BLAS. *Abusos del teatro de la legua, Los. Tonadilla.* MS. B. Nac.

— *Autora de la legua, La. Tonadilla.* [1770.] MS. B. Nac.

— *Héroe del Barquillo, El. Tonadilla.* MS. *Cens.* 1792. B. Nac.

— *Potagera, La. Tonadilla.* MS. *Cens.* 1774. B. Nac.

LATROBE, B. H. *Characteristic Anecdotes to illustrate the Character of Frederic* [sic]. II . . . London, 1788. B.M.

LAVIANO, MANUEL FERMÍN DE

— *Afrenta del Cid vengada, La.* MS. Approbation 1793. B. Mun.

— *Al deshonor heredado vence el honor adquirido.* (Pl. 1787.) B.M.

— *Bella guayanesa, La.* (From Goldoni.) MS. *Cens.* 1780. B. Mun.

— [*Buena casada, La.*] MS. *Cens.* 1781. B. Mun.

— [*Castellano adalid, El. Toma de Sepúlveda por el conde Fernán González.*] MS. Cens. 1785. B. Mun.

— *Española comandante (La) fiel a su amor y a su patria.* MS. *Cens.* 1787. B. Mun.

— *Reo inocente, El.* MS. *Cens.* 1782. B. Mun.

— *Sigerico, El.* MS. *Cens.* 1790. B. Mun.

— *Sol de España en su oriente y toledano Moisés.* Pamplona. 1778. B.M. *C.M.C.* iii (1791).

— [*Triunfos de valor y honor en la corte de Rodrigo.*] Bar., 1797. B.M.

— *Valor y amor de Othoniel,* MS. B. Nac.

LE BLANC DE GUILLET, A. *Albert I, ou Adeline.* Paris, 1775. B.M.

LECORP, ANT. (ANTONIO PORCEL.) *Merope.* (Versified from Olavide's version of Maffei.) M., 1786.

[LEGRAND, MARC ANTOINE] and 'DOMINIQUE' [BIANCOLELLI, P. F.] *Agnès de Chaillot* in *Les Parodies du Nouveau Théâtre Italien.* . . . Vol. i. Paris, 1731.

LEMIERRE, A. M. *Hypermenestre.* in *Répertoire du Théâtre Français.* Vol. vi. Paris, 1803. U.L.G.

LESAGE, ALAIN RENÉ. [*Théâtre Espagnol, Le.*] La Haye, 1700. B.M.

LESSING, G. E. *Minna von Barnhelm.* Everyman no. 843.

LETOURNEUR, P. P. F. *Méditations sur les Tombeaux.* (From J. Harvey.) Paris, 1770. B.M.

— [*Shakespeare. Traduit de l'Anglais.*] Paris, 1776–82, 20 vols. B.M.

LILLO, GEORGE. *The London Merchant: or The History of George Barnwell.* London, 1731. B.M.

L[INGUET] [S.N.H.]. *Théâtre espagnol.* Paris, 1770. 4 vols. B.M.

LÓPEZ DE AYALA, IGNACIO. *Abides.* MS. B. Nac.

— *Historia de Federico el Grande, actual rey de Prusia.* M., 1768. B. Nac.

— *Numancia destruida.* M., 1775. B.M.

LÓPEZ PINCIANO, ALONSO. *Filosofía antigua poética.* Ed. A. Carballo Picazo. M., 1953. 3 vols.

LÓPEZ DE SEDANO, JOSÉ.

— *Casa de Chinitas, La. Sain.* MS. *Cens.* 1778. B. Mun.

— *Cerco y ruina de Numancia.* MS. B. Nac.

— *Defensa de las damas, La. Sain.* MS. 1779. B. Mun.

— *Deshonra está en la culpa, La.* MS. B. Nac.

— *Huérfano inglés. El.* MS. *Cens.* 1778. B. Mun.

— [*Jahel, La.*] N.p., n.d. 2nd ed. B.M.

— *Misántropo, (El) o El enemigo de los hombres.* (From Molière.) MS. *Cens.* 1771. B. Mun.
— *No hay trono como el honor. Alejandro en Macedonia.* MS. 1778. B. Mun.
— *Paje duende, El. Sain.* MS. B. Mun.
— *Parnaso español.* (Ed.) M., 1768–78. 9 vols. U.L.G.
— *Pasión ciega a los hombres, La.* Sal., n.d.
— *Posadera feliz (La) o El enemigo de las mujeres.* [From Goldoni.] MS. *Cens.* 1779. B. Mun.
— [*Ser vencido y vencedor. Julio César y Catón.*] Cf. Zavala y Zamora.
— *Silesia, La.* MS. *Cens.* 1776. B. Mun.

LUZÁN. IGNACIO DE. *Memorias literarias de París.* M., 1751. B. Nac.
— *Poética, La.* Zar., 1737. B.M.
— *Poética, La. Corregida y aumentada por su mismo autor.* M., 1789. 2 vols. B.M.
L.G.F. *Quien oye la voz del cielo convierte el castigo en premio, o la Camila.* C.M.C. iii (1791).

MALDONADO, FRANC. J. *Triunfos de lealtad y amor. La Cleonice.* C.M.C. xi (1799).
MARMONTEL, J. F. *Contes Moraux.* La Haye, 1765–6 (2nd ed.). 3 vols. U.L.G.
[MARQUÉS DE SAN JUAN] E.S.M.S.J. *Cina. O la Clemencia de Augusto.* (From Corneille.) MS. B. Mun.
MARSOLLIER, B. J. DES VIVETIÈRES. *Richard et Sara.* Geneva and Paris, 1772. B.M.
MARTÍNEZ, J. MANUEL. [*Gustavo Adolfo, Rey de Suecia.*] MS. *Cens.* 1789. B. Mun.
MASDEU Y MONTERO, J. F. DE. *Arte poética fácil.* Val., 1801. B. Nac.
— *Historia crítica de España y de la cultura española.* M., 1783–1805. 20 vols. B.M.
MATOS FRAGOSO, JUAN. *Ver y creer. Segunda Parte de Reinar después de morir.* Val., 1765; (M.) 1795. B. Mun.
MAYÁNS Y SISCAR, GREGORIO. *Rhetorica.* Val., 1757. 2 vols. B.M.
Mejor de los mejores. Libro que ha salido de comedias nuevas. Alcalá, 1651; Alcalá, 1653. B. Nac.
MELÉNDEZ VALDÉS, JUAN. *Bodas de Camacho Las.* M., 1784. B. Nac.
Memorial literario ... M., 1784–1808. Hem.
Memorias de la Academia Española. M., 1870.
MENDÍBIL, P., and SILVELA, M. *Biblioteca selecta de literatura española.* Bordeaux, 1819. 4 vols. B. Nac.
MERAS ALFONSO, JOSEPH M. DE. *Pigmaleón.* M., 1788. B.M.
MERCIER, L. S. [*L'An Deux Mille Quatre Cent Quarante.*] London, 1772; London, 1776. B.M.
— *Jenneval ou le Barnevelt Français.* Paris, 1769. B.M.
— *Théâtre complet.* Amsterdam, 1778–84. 4 vols. U.L.G.
Mercurio literario, o Memorias sobre ... ciencias y artes. M., 1739. B. Nac.
METASTASIO, P.A.D.B.
— *Opere.* Paris, 1780–2. 12 vols; Mantova, 1816–20. 20 vols.
Spanish editions, translations and arrangements:
— *Achille in Sciro.* M., 1744. B. Nac.
— *Adriano en Siria.* M., 1757. B. Nac.
— *Alcides entre los dos caminos.* M., 1765. B. Nac.
— *Alexandro en el Idaspe o en Indias.* [Palma de Mallorca, 1766.] B. Nac.

— *Alexandro en la India.* M., 1792. B. Nac.

— *Alexandro en las Indias.* Trans. by G. Val. M., 1738. B. Nac. Bar., 1762. B. Nac.: Cádiz, 1764. B. Nac.

— *Angélica y Medoro.* M., 1747. B. Nac.

— *Antígono.* Cádiz, 1764. B. Nac.

— *Artaxerxes.* M., 1738. B. Nac.; M., 1749, B. Nac.; Bar. 1767. B. Nac.; Murcia, 1769, B. Nac.; Val., 1769. B. Nac.

— *Asilo del amor, El.* M., 1790. B. Nac.

— *Ciro reconocido.* Cádiz, 1773. B. Nac.

— *Clemencia de Tito.* M., 1739. B. Nac.; n.p., 1747. B. Nac.

— *Demetrio, El.* M., 1738, 1751, 1794. All B. Nac.

— *Demofoonte, El.* M., 1738. M., 1755; M., 1791; Cádiz, 1764. All B. Nac.

— *Dido abandonada.* M., 1752; Bar., 1753; M., 1791; M., 1792. All B. Nac.

— *Endimión y Diana.* [M., 174?] B. Nac.

— *Éroe de la China, El.* M., 1754; Bar., [1755]; M., 1799, etc. All B. Nac.

— *Ezio.,* Bar., 1754. B. Nac.

— *Fiesta chinesca.* M., 1754. B. Nac.

— *Ipermestra, La.* M., 1793. B. Nac.

— *Isla desierta, La.* M., 1765. B. Nac.

— *Niteti, La.* M., 1756. B. Nac.

— *Olimpiada, La.* Cádiz, 1762. B. Nac.

— *Óperas varias.* Bar. [1763] (containing *La isla deshabitada; Ricumero; Adriano en Siria; Catón en Útica* and *La Andrómaca*). B. Nac.

— *Semíramis conocida.* N.p., 1753. B. Nac.

— *Síroe, El.* M., 1739 and 1752. Cádiz [1761]. B. Nac.

— *Sueño de Scipión.* M., 1753. B. Nac.

— *Zenobia de Palmira.* M., 1793. B. Nac.

MIÑANO, ANDRÉS. [*El gusto del día.*] M., 1802; Val., 1802. B. Mun.

MIRA Y PERCEBAL, JORGE. *Bernardo del Carpio en el Castillo de Luna. Soliloquio trágico con música* . . . Orihuela, 1794. B. Nac.

MOLÉ, J. *Misantropie et Repentir.* (Trans. by Bursay from Kotzebue and recast by Molé.) Paris, [1799]. B.M.

MOLINE, P. L. *La Discipline Militaire du Nord.* Paris, 1782. B.M.

[MONCÍN] 'L.A.J.M.'

— *Al maestro, cuchillada.* Sain. MS. 1797. B. Nac.

— *Asturiano aburrido, El. Fin de fiesta.* MS. Cens. 1793. B. Mun.

— *Asturiano en Madrid y observador instruido.* N.p., n.d. B. Nac.

— *Buena madrasta, La.* C.M.C. v (1792.)

— *Como difienden su honor las ilustres Roncalesas.* MS. Cens. 1784. B. Mun.

— *Como ha de ser la amistad.* C.M.C. iv (1792).

— *Como ha de servirse al rey muestra Clemencia de Aubigni.* MS. Cens. 1788, B. Mun.

— *De dos enemigos hace el amor dos amigos.* N.p., n.d., B.M.

— *De un acaso nacen muchos.* C.M.C. iv (1792).

— *Don Rodrigo de Vivar.* MS. Cens. 1781. B. Mun.

— *Embustero engañado, El.* N.p., n.d. B. Nac. C.M.C. vi (1793).

— *Engaño descubierto, El.* M., 1800. B. Nac.

— *Esposos reunidos, Los.* C.M.C. xi (1794).

— *Feliz encuentro, El.* (From Goldoni.) *C.M.C.* iv (1792).
— *Hechos heroicos y nobles del valor godo español.* MS. *Cens.* 1784. B. Mun.
— *Lograr el mayor imperio por un feliz desengaño.* Cádiz, 1777. B. Nac.
— *Más heroica piedad más noblemente pagada, La.* Val. 1767. B. Nac.
— *Montañés sabe bien donde el zapato le aprieta, Un.* N.P., n.d. B. Nac.
— *Mujer más vengativa por unos injustos celos.* N.p., n.d. B. Nac.; *C.M.C.* ix (1796).
— *Olimpia y Nicandro.* MS. *Cens.* 1792. B. Mun.
— *Para averiguar verdades el tiempo el mejor testigo.* Corrected and augmented by ...
    C.M.C. iv (1793).
— *Sertorio el magnánimo.* M.S. Cens. 1784. B. Mun.
— *Virtud premiada (La.) o el verdadero buen hijo, C.M.C.* II (1790).
MONTALVÁN. See Pérez de Montalván, J.
MONTESQUIEU, CHARLES DE SECONDAT, BARON DE. *Lettres Persanes.* See *Œuvres.* Paris,
    1796. 5 vols. Vol. iv. U.L.G.
MONTIANO Y LUYANDO, AGUSTÍN. *Discurso [I] sobre las tragedias españolas.* M., 1750.
    2nd ed. U.L.L.
— *Discurso II sobre las tragedias españolas.* M., 1753, U.L.L.
MOORE, EDWARD. *The Foundling.* London, 1748. U.L.G.
— *The Gamester.* London, 1784. B.M.
MOR DE FUENTES, JOSÉ. *Calavera El.* M., 1800. B. Nac.
MORON, ISABEL, M. *Buen amante y buen amigo, C.M.C.* v (1792).
MUNÁRRIZ, J. L. *Lecciones sobre la retórica y las bellas letras por Hugo Blair.* (Trans. by ...)
    M. 1798–1801. 4 vols. B. Nac.

NASARRE Y FÉRRIZ, B. A. *Comedias y entremeses de ... Cervantes.* M., 1749. B. Nac.
NICOLAI, C. F. *Anekdoten von König Friedrich II von Preussen ...* Berlin and Stettin,
    1788–92. B.M.
NIPHO, FRANCISCO MARIANO
— *Cajón de sastre literato ...* M., 1781–2. 6 vols. 2nd ed. B. Nac.
— *Colección de los mejores papeles poéticos y composiciones dramáticas de ... ofrécela al público
    D. Manuel Nipho, Capitán de los Reales Ejercicios.* M., 1805. 2 vols. B. Nac.
— *Correo general, histórico, literario y económico de la Europa.* M., 1763. 4 vols. B. Nac.
— *Diario extranjero. ...* M., 1763. B.S.I.
— *Estafeta de Londres ...* M., 1762. B. Nac.
— *Idea política y cristiana para reformar el actual teatro de España.* MS. 1769. Arch. Hist. Nac.
— *Nación española defendida de los insultos del Pensador y sus secuaces, La.* M., 1764. B. Nac.
— *Nación española defendida ... La. Discurso II.* M., 1764. B. Nac.
— *Pigmalion. Monólogo patético.* M., 1790. B. Nac.
— *Sátira castigada por los sainetes de moda, La. Entremés.* M., 1765. B. Nac.
— [*Tribunal de la poesía dramática, El.*] MS., n.d. B.Nac. Also entitled *Entusiasmo o sainete
    nuevo. El tribunal ...* M., 1763. B. Nac.
NIVELLE DE LA CHAUSSÉE, *Chefs-d'Œuvres Dramatiques ...* Paris, 1822. See *Répertoire du
    Théâtre Français,* vol. xxi. U.L.G.
— *Œuvres.* Paris, 1762. U.L.E.
NOAILLES, ADRIEN-MAURICE DUC DE. *Mémoires Politiques et Militaires ...* Ed. by L'Abbé
    Millot. Paris, 1777. 6 vols. B.M.
*Observations sur la Constitution ... des armées de S.M. Prussienne, avec quelques Anecdotes
    de la Vie privée de ce Monarque.* Berlin, 1777. B.M.

OLAVIDE, PABLO DE. [*Fedra.*] MS. *Cens.* 1783. B. Mun. Bar., n.d. B.M.
— [*Hipermenestra*] (From Lemierre.) Bar., n.d. B. Nac.
— [*Merope*] MS. B. Mun.
— *Mitrídates.* (From Racine.) MS. B. Nac.
— [*Olimpia (La)*] or *Casandro y Olimpia* (From Voltaire.) MS. 1782. B. Nac. MS. *Cens.* 1781. B. Mun.

Parodies (Les) du Nouveau Théâtre Italien. Paris, 1731. 3 vols. B.M. Also Paris, 1738. 4 vols. B.M.
Pensadora gaditana, La. Cádiz, 1763–4; 2nd. ed., Cádiz, 1786. Hem.
PERCY, THOMAS. *Reliques of Ancient English Poetry.* London, 1765. 3 vols. B.M.
PÉREZ DE MONTALVÁN, J. [*Gitana de Menfis (La). Santa María Egipciaca*]. Vall., n.d. (*Cens.* 1808). B. Mun.
PHILIPS, R. (MRS.). *Poems . . . to which is added M. Corneille's 'Pompez' and 'Horace'.* London, 1667. B.M.
PILOTOS, FERNANDO JUGACCIS (pseudonym). See Postigo, Franc. del.
PISÓN Y VARGAS, JUAN. *Elmira, La.* Mexico, 1788. B. Nac.
— *Perromachia, La.* M., 1786. B.M.
— *Rutzvanscadt (El), o Quijote trágico.* 'Tragedia a secas.' M., 1796. B.M.
— *Sacrificar por la patria la libertad y la vida.* MS. B. Nac. (The title-page of Act III in this copy is dated Cádiz, 1782.)
PIXÉRÉCOURT, GUILBERT DE. *Théâtre Choisi.* Paris, 1841, etc. 4 vols. B.M.
— *Victor, ou L'Enfant de la Forêt.* Paris, 1798. B.M.
PORCEL, ANT. J. *Amante estatua, El.* With music (by 'D.J.A.P. y S.'), MS. B. Nac.
— *Dama doctor* [*sic*] *(La.) o La teología a la almohada.* (From G. J. Bougeant.) MS. 1780. B. Nac.
POSTIGO, FRANC. DEL. *Combates de amor y ley.* (From Voltaire's *Zaïre*) Cádiz, 1765. B. Mun.
PUJAZ, LEÓN. *Hero y Leandro. Monólogo lírico.* (From Florian.) M., 1793. See *Mem. lit.* June 1794.

QUINTANA, MANUEL, JOSÉ. *Obras.* B.A.E. xix.

RACINE, J. *Théâtre Complet.* Ed. F. Lemaistre. Paris, n.d.
REY, FERMÍN DEL.
— *Areo, rey de Armenia. Melo.* N.p., n.d. (Pl. 1797.) B.M.
— *Buena criada, La.* (From Goldoni.) *C.M.C.* vi (1793).
— *Caprichos de amor y celos.* (From Goldoni.) *C.M.C.* iii (1791).
— *Clotilde, La.* M.S. 1784. B. Nac.
— *Defensa de Barcelona por la más fuerte amazona.* N.p., n.d. B.M., *C.M.C.* iv (1792).
— *Faustina, La.* Trans. and arranged by . . . See Napoli-Signorelli, P.
—- *Fiel pastorcita y tirano del castillo, La.* *C.M.C.* iii (1791).
— *Hernán Cortés en Cholula.* MS., 1782. B. Nac.
— *Hernán Cortés en Tabasco.* MS. *Cens.* 1790. B. Mun.
— *No hay poder contra el amor. Scipión en Numidia.* MS. 1779. B. Nac.
— *Policena. Escena trágica* (with *Introducción*). MS. *Cens.* 1794. B. Mun.
— *Valor, constancia y ventura de Aragón y Cataluña. Españoles en Asia.* MS. B. Nac.
— *Viuda generosa. La.* *C.M.C.* v (1792).

REZANO IMPERIALI, ANT. *Acrisolar el dolor en el más filial amor. Pieza militar.* Sal., n.d. B.M.

RICCOBONI, A. F. *L'Art du Théâtre.* Paris, 1750. B.M.

— *Prince de Suresne. Parodie.* With 'Discours sur la Parodie'. Paris, 1746. B.M.

RICCOBONI, LUIGI. *Réflexions historiques et critiques sur les différents Théâtres de l'Europe, avec les Pensées sur la Déclamation.* Paris, 1738; Amsterdam 1740, etc. B.M.

— *Réformation du Théâtre, De la.* [Paris] 1743. B.M.

ROCHON DE CHABANNES. *Amants Généreux, Les.* (1774). See D.G.F.R.

RODRÍGUEZ DE ARELLANO, VICENTE

— *A padre malo, buen hijo. C.M.C.* xi (1791).

— *Amo y criado en la casa de vicios generosos.* M., 1791. B. Nac.

— *Aníbal, El.* MS. *Cens.* 1792. B. Nac.

— [*Armida y Reinaldo.*] Part I: MS. *Cens.* 1797. B. Mun.; Part II: MS. B. Mun.

— *Atenea, La.* (From Metastasio.) MS. *Cens.* 1792. B. Mun.

— *Atolondrado, El.* MS. B. Mun., Pamplona, 1778; N.p., 1789.

— *Augusto y Teodoro o los pajes de Federico II.* M., 1802. B. Mun.

— *Camarerita, La.* (From French.) MS. 1801. B. Mun.

— [*Camino de Portugal.*] MS. Approbation 1849. B. Mun.

— *Cayma y Reba.* MS. *Cens.* 1797. B. Mun.

— *Cayo Fabricio.* MS. *Cens.* 1799. B. Mun.

— *Cecilia y Dorsan.* (From Marsollier.) M., 1800. B. Mun.

— *Celoso Don Lesmes, El. C.M.C.* v (1792.)

— [*Cierto por lo dudoso, La. o La mujer firme.*] (Recast from Lope.) M., 1803. B. Mun.

— *Claris de Florián.* N.p., 1797.

— [*Clementina, La.*] (Trans. from French and originally called *La madrastra.*) MS. 1802. B. Mun.

— *Clementina y Desormes.* (From Monvel.) M., 1801. B. Mun.

— *Consini y Enrique IV.* MS. B. Mun.

— *Dama labradora, La.* MS. 1801. B. Mun.

— *Decámeron español, o Colección de varios hechos históricos, raros y divertidos.* M., 1805. 3 vols. B.M.

— *De padre malo buen hijo y a buen sobrino buen tío.* MS. *Cens.* 1791. B. Mun.

— *Dido abandonada.* M., 1795. B. Mun.

— *Domingo, El. Monólogo.* MS. *Cens.* 1791. B. Mun.

— [*Duque de Pentiebre, El.*] M., 1803. B. Mun.

— *Elfrida, La.* MS. *Cens.* 1798. B. Mun.

— *Elisa y Clearco.* MS. B. Mun.

— *Esplín, El.* MS. *Cens.* 1793. (Also called *El suicida enmendado.*) B. Mun.

— *Extremos de lealtad y valor heroico navarro.* Pamplona, 1789.

— *Fatme y Selima.* Val., n.d. B.M.P.

— *Fuerza de la amistad, La.* MS. *Cens.* 1798. B. Mun.

— *Fulgencia, La.* M.S.; M., 1801. B. Mun.

— *Gran Seleuco, El.* MS. *Cens.* 1799. B. Mun.

— *Himeneo.* MS. *Cens.* 1799. B. Mun.

— [*Inquilino, El.*] *Op.*, MS. B. Mun.

— *Jerusalén conquistada por Gofredo de Bullón.* [M., 1791.] B.M.

— [*Lealtad (La) o La justa desobediencia.*] (By Don Gil Lorena de Arozar. ? Anagram of Arellano. M.) 1803. B. Mun.

— *Mal hermano (El) o Sofía y Ricardo*. (From French.) MS. 1802. B. Mun.
— *Marco Antonio y Cleopatra*. C.M.C. vi (1793).
— [*Marinerito, El.*] MS. Approbation 1815. B. Mun.
— *Mirena y Sinifredo*. MS. Cens. 1799. B. Mun.
— [*Muerte de Héctor, La.*] MS. Cens. 1798. B. Mun.
— [*Mujer de dos maridos, La.*] MS. Approbation 1815. B. Mun.
— [*Negro y la blanca, El.*] Melo. MS. Cens. 1797. B. Mun.
— [*Noche de Troya, La.*] Melo. MS. Cens. 1797. B. Mun.
— *Ópera cómica, La.* (Trans. by . . .) MS. 1801, B. Mun.
— *Palmis y Oronte.* MS. Cens. 1797. B. Mun. (Also attributed to Zavala y Zamora.)
— *Parmenia, La.* MS. Cens. 1797. B. Mun.
— *Paz, La.* ('En celebridad de la paz general'.) MS. 1801. B. Mun.
— *Pintor fingido, El.* M., 1800. B. Mun.
— *Pirro y Casandro.* (Trans. by . . .). MS. Cens. 1798. B. Mun.
— *Reconciliación (La) o Los dos hermanos.* (Trans. from Kotzebue.) M., 1800. B. Mun.
— *Reo inocente es Clementina y Desormes* (Trans. from Boutet de Monvel.) Pl. 1784. See
   Clementina y Desormes.
— *Sitio de Toro, (El) y Noble Martín de Abarca.* MS. Cens. 1790. B. Mun.
— [*Soliman II.*] C.M.C. vi (1793).
— *Temístocles.* Melo. (From Metastasio.) MS. Cens. 1800. B. Mun.
— Also Loas without titles.

ROJO, JUAN DIEGO. *Pigmalión Escena lírica, traducida del francés al castellano por* . . . M.,
   1788. B. Nac.
ROMEA Y TAPIA. *Escritor sin título, El.* M., 1790. B. Nac.
ROUSSEAU, J. B. *Café, Le.* See *Œuvres.* Brussels and Paris, 1753. Vol. iv. U.L.E.
ROUSSEAU, J. J. *Œuvres Complètes.* Paris, 1825. U.L.G.

SALAZAR, JUAN CLIMACEO DE. *Mardoqueo.* M., 1791. B. Mun.
SALCEDO, PEDRO DE. *Dorinda.* MS. (Dedication: Málaga, 1776.) B. Nac.
SALVINI, ANTON MARIA. [*Il Catone.*] (From Addison.) Florence, 1715. B.M.
SALVO Y VELA, *Mágico de Salerno, El.* 5 Parts. M., 1733, etc. See *Origins* . . ., p. 190.
SAMANIEGO, FÉLIX, MARÍA DE. *Obras críticas* . . . In 'Biblioteca vascongada de Fermín
   Herrán.' Vol. xxiii. Bilbao, 1898.
— *Obras inéditas de.* . . . Vitoria, 1866.
SÁNCHEZ BARBERO, F. *Principios de retórica y poética.* M., 1805. B. Nac.
SARMIENTO, MARTÍN. *Memorias para la historia de la poesía y poetas españoles.* M., 1775.
   B. Nac.
SATURIO IGUREN. See Trigueros, Juan.
SAURIN, B. J. *Beverlei.* Répertoire du Théâtre Français. Second Ordre, vol. xxv. Paris,
   1824. B.M.
— *L'Orpheline Leguée.* Paris, 1765. B.M.
SAUVIGNY. See *Religión, patria y honor* . . . *La Hirza.* Anon.
SAVAGE, RICHARD. *Tragedy of Sir Thomas Overbury. The.* London, 1724. B.M.
SEBASTIÁN Y LATRE, TOMÁS. *Británico.* (From Racine.) A versification of the prose trans-
   lation by Saturio Iguren (J. Trigueros.) Zar., 1764. B. Mun.
— *Ensayo sobre el teatro español.* Zar., 1772. B.M.
— [*Progne y Filomena.*] MS. B. Mun.

SEDAINE, MICHEL JEAN. *Philosophe sans le savoir, Le.* Paris, 1825. Répertoire du Théâtre Français . . . Vol. xxxi. U.L.G.
— *Roi et le Fermier, Le.* Paris, 1777. B.M.
SEMPERE Y GUARINOS, JUAN. *Ensayo de una biblioteca española de los mejores escritores del reinado de Carlos III.* M., 1785–9. 6 vols. B. Nac.
SHERIDAN, R. B. *Dramatic Works.* London, Cassell. N.d.
SIGNORELLI, P. N. *Discorso storico-critico . . . da servire di lume alla Storia critica de' teatri* . . . Naples, 1783. B.M.
— *Faustina., La.* Parma [1778]. B.M. See Fermín del Rey.
— *Storia critica de'teatri* . . . Naples, 1777. B. Nac.
SILVA, PEDRO DE. *Fedra.* (From Racine.) MS. B. Nac.
SOLÍS, DIONISIO. *Misantropía y arrepentimiento.* M., 1800. B. Nac.
— [*Delirio, o las consecuencias de un vicio, El.*] (From St. Cyr.) Val., 1816. B.M.
SOLO DE ZALDÍVAR, BRUNO. [*Satisfacer por sí mismo y venganza sin vengarse. La Efigenia.*] 2a. Parte. MS. *Cens.* 1769. B. Mun.
SOULAS D'ALLAINVAL, L. J. C. [*Anecdotes du règne de Pierre I, dit le Grand.*] 2 Parts. [Paris?] 1745. B.M.
SUÁREZ, GABRIEL. *Asombro de Jerez y Noble Agustín Florencio.* MS. *Cens.* 1734. B. Mun.
SUÁREZ DE LANGREO, DON TORIBIO. See G. M. de Jovellanos (*El delincuente honrado*).
SWINBURNE, HENRY. *Travels through Spain in the years 1775 and 1776.* London, 1779. B.M.

TALMA, F. *Quelques Réflexions sur Lekain et sur l'Art Théâtral.* Paris, 1856. Reprinted from *Mémoires de Lekain* by Talma in the collection *Mémoires sur l'Art Dramatique.* 1821–5.
Teatro nuevo español. M., 1800–1. B.M.
Teatro selecto antiguo y moderno . . . compiled by F. J. Orellana. Bar., 1866–8. 6 vols. B. Nac.
THIÉBAULT DE LAVEAUX, J. C. (*Vie de Frédéric II, Roi de Prusse*). Strasbourg and Paris, 1788–9, 7 vols. B.M.
TOWNSEND, JOSEPH. *A Journey through Spain in the years 1786 and 1787.* London, 1791. B.M.
TRIGUEROS, CÁNDIDO MARÍA.
— *Baccanales, (Los) Ciane de Syracusa.* MS. 1767. B. Nac.
— *Buscona (La) o el anzuelo de Fenisa.* (Recast from Lope.) MS. 1803. B. Mun.
— *Cándida, o la hija sobrina.* MS. B. Nac. (Written 1774.)
— *Don Amador o El indiscreto.* MS. B. Nac.
— [*Egilona (La) Viuda del rey D. Rodrigo*] 1ª Parte, Bar., 1801. B. Mun.
— *Electra, La.* (From French. 'Corrected' by . . .) MS. *Cens.* 1788. B. Mun.
— *Entremeses* . . . (Collection of 6.) MS. B. Nac.
— *Ifigenia en Aulide* ('Corrected' by . . .) MS. 1788. B. Mun.
— *Ilustres salteadores (Los).* MS. 1774. B. Nac.
— *Melindrosa (La) o Los esclavos supuestos.* (Recast from Lope.) M., 1803. B. Mun.
— [*Menestrales, Los.*] MS. 1784. B. Mun.
— *Mísero (El) y El pedante o Duendes hay, Señor D. Blas.* MS. 1763. B. Nac.
— *Moza de cántaro, La.* (Recast from Lope.) Val., 1803. B. Mun.
— [*Pleito del cuerno, El.*] MS. B. Nac.
— *Poeta cómico, El. Sain.* MS. B. Nac.
— *Precipitado, El.* [Sev.] 1785. B.M.
— *Sacrificio de Efigenia, El.* (From Calderón.) B.M.

— *Sancho Ortiz de las Roelas*. (Recast from Lope.) MS. B. Mun.
— *Teatro español burlesco, o Quijote de los teatros*. Por el Maestro Crispín Caramillo. [Trigueros.] M., 1802. B.M.
TRIGUEROS, JUAN. *Británico*. (From Racine by 'Don Saturio Iguren'.) M., 1752. B. Nac.
TWISS, RICHARD. *Travels through Portugal and Spain in 1772 and 1773*. London, 1775. U.L.G.
T.M.G. [GONZÁLEZ GARCÍA, TADEO MORENO.] *Axtianacte, El*. MS. 1788. B. Nac.
— *Pelindango (El), o Desagravio de Manolo, 2a parte de éste*. Sain. MS. 1784. B. Nac.

URGUIJO, MARIANO LUIS DE. *Muerte del César, La*. (From Voltaire.) MS. B. Nac. Also printed with a Discourse by translator. M., 1791. B. Nac.

VALLADARES Y SOTOMAYOR, ANTONIO
— *A suegro irritado, nuera prudente*. M.S. Approbation 1817. (Pl. 1775.) B. Mun.
— *A una grande heroicidad, pagar con otra más grande*. Also entitled *Eduardo III*. MS. Approbation 1782. B. Mun.
— *Aben-Said. Emperador del Mogol*. (Trans. by . . .). MS. B. Nac.
— [*Adivinador, El*.] Sain. MS. B. Nac.
— *Adivino, El*. (Trans. by . . .). MS. B. Nac.
— [*Amigo verdadero, El*.] Sain. MS. 1791. B. Nac.
— *Amistad es lo primero, La*. MS. Cens. 1785. B. Mun.
— [*Apoderado de Indias, El*.] MS. 1780. B. Nac.
— *Boda a la moda, La*. Sain. MS. Cens. 1782. B. Mun.
— *Bodas de Camacho, Las*. Zarz. MS. 1777. B. Nac.
— [*Bodas de los manchegos, Las*.] Sain. MS. B. Nac.
— *Caldereros, Los*. Sain. MS. 1780. B. Nac.
— [*Cándida o amante precipitado, La*.] (1st act only.) MS. B. Nac.
— *Carbonero de Londres, El*. MS. B. Mun.
— [*Carpintero burlado, El*.] Sain. MS. 1787. B. Nac.
— *Castigo del avaro, El*. Sain. MS. 1777. B. Mun.
— *Católico Recaredo, El*. MS. B. Mun. (Pl. 1785.)
— *Cómicos de repente, Los*. Sain. MS. Cens. 1782. B. Mun.
— *Conde de Werrick, El*. MS. 1779. B. Nac.
— *Constantino y Maximiano*. MS. B. Nac.
— *Criados embusteros, Los*. Sain. M., n.d. B. Mun.
— [*Cuál más obligación es, la de padre o la de juez*.] MS. Cens. 1777. B. Mun.
— [*Cuatro naciones (Las) o la viuda sutil*.] (From Italian.) MS. Cens. 1788. B. Mun.
— *Culpado sin delito, El*. M.S. Cens. 1782. (A note on this copy reads 'Esta comedia con el título de El reo inocente*, es original en prosa de D. Ig. Planas, Escribano en la ciudad de Barcelona'.) B. Mun.
— *Curar los males de honor es la física más sabia. Médico holandés*. (From Goldoni.) MS. B. Nac.
— *De la más fiera crueldad sabe triunfar la virtud . . . Adelaida*. (From Italian.) MS. B. Nac.
— *Defensa de la corona por la heroica María Pita*. MS. Cens. 1784. B. Mun.
— [*Desdicha la más dichosa, La*.] MS. B. Nac.
— [*Diálogo (Tercera parte del) cómico lírico femenino . . .*] MS. B. Nac.
— [*Dichoso por la suerte (El) y también por la elección*]. MS. Cens. 1782. B. Mun.
— *Dos famosos manchegos, y máscaras de Madrid, Los*. MS. B. Nac.
— [*Edubige en Persia (La) o Sólo vence la traición un constante corazón*.] MS. B. Nac.

— [*Efectos de la virtud y consecuencias del vicio.*] MS. *Cens.* 1781. B. Mun.
— *Egilona (La), viuda del Rey Don Rodrigo.* Bar., n.d. B.M.P.
— [*Elmira americana, La.*] MS. *Cens.* 1788. B. Mun.
— [*Emperador Alberto I o La Adelina.*] Part I. MS. B. Mun. Part II. MS. *Cens.* 1781. B. Mun.
— *Encantador, El. Sain.* MS. B. Nac.
— *Escuela de las mujeres, La.* MS. B. Mun.
— [*Español afrancesado, El.*] *Sain.* MS. *Cens.* 1777. B. Nac.
— *Exceder en heroísmo la mujer al héroe mismo, La Emilia.* MS. *Cens.* 1781. B. Mun.
— [*Fabricante de paños, El.*] MS. *Cens.* 1783. B. Mun.
— *Falsa cordera, La.* MS. B. Nac.
— *Faltar a padre y amante por obedecer al rey. La Etrea.* MS. 1778. B. Mun.
— [*Fiesta de novillos (La) y la novillada.*] *Sain.* 1768. B. Nac.
— *Franceses generosos, Los.* MS. B. Nac.
— [*Galeote cautivo, El.*] MS. B. Mun.
— *Golondra, La. Sain.* 1a and 2a Parte. MS. B. Nac.
— *Gran victoria de España en los campos de Vitoria.* M., 1814. B. Nac.
— *Gratitud, La.* MS. B. Nac.
— [*Grito de la naturaleza, El.*] MS. *Cens.* 1784. B. Mun.
— *Guzmán el Bueno.* MS. B. Nac.
— [*Hija fingida (La) y Enredos de Papagayo.*] (By D. Valerio Llamas Dávalos y Resa ? Anagram.) MS. B. Nac.
— *Hombre de buena fortuna, El. Sain.* MS. B. Nac.
— *Lacayo, paje y marido. Sain.* MS. B. Nac.
— *Lealtad, traición e inocencia o Sifiro y Etolia.* MS. 1782. B. Mun.
— *Locuras amorosas, Las.* (From Regnard.) MS. B. Nac.
— [*Madrastra (La) o El padre de familias.*] MS. B. Nac.
— *Magdalena cautiva, La.* Bar., 1784. B.M.P.
— [*Mágico del Mogol, El.*] MS. 1788. B. Mun.
— *Mágicos de Tetuán, Los.* MS. B. Nac.
— [*Maleta, La.*] M., 1804. B.M.P.
— *Marido de su hija, El.,* Bar., 1790. B. Nac.
— *Más altiva arrogancia (La) postró unida España y Francia y Grande triunfo de Roma.* MS. B. Nac.
— [*Matrimonio interrumpido, El.*] (Trans. by . . .). MS. B. Nac.
— *Máximas de un buen padre (Las) para probar un mal hijo.* MS. *Cens.* 1777. B. Mun.
— *Niña inocente, La. Sain.* MS. 1779. B. Nac.
— *No hay cosa que no se sepa.* MS. *Cens.* 1779. B. Mun.
— *No hay trono como el honor. Alejandro en Macedonia.* (By López de Sedano and . . .) MS. 1778. B. Mun.
— *Nuestro Rey Fernando VII en el complot de Bayona.* MS. 1814. B. Nac.
— *Nunca el rencor vencer puede adonde milita amor.* MS. 1769. B. Mun.
— *Obrador de los sastres, El. Sain.* MS. B. Nac.
— *Perfectos comerciantes, Los.* MS. *Cens.* 1782. B. Mun.
— [*Por esposa y trono a un tiempo, Mágico de Serbán. Tirano de Astracán.*] MS. Approbation 1815. B. Mun.
— *Por defender a su rey derramar la sangre es ley. La Dircea.* MS. B. Nac.
— [*Posada feliz, La.*] MS. *Cens.* 1780. B. Mun.

— *Premiar con una corona a la lealtad de un vasallo.* MS. B. Nac. *C.M.C.* ix (1796).

— *Preso por amor o el Real encuentro, El.* N.p., n.d. B.M.

— *Rey Eduardo el VIII, El.* MS. *Cens.* 1783. B. Mun.

— *Rey es primero, El.* MS. 1796. B. Mun.

— *Rufino y Aniceta.* N.p., n.d. B.M.P.

— *Saber del mayor peligro triunfar sola una mujer. La Elvira.* MS. *Cens.* 1781. B. Mun.

— [*Saber premiar la inocencia y castigar la traición.*] MS. *Cens.* 1782. B. Mun.

— *Sainete de repente, El.* MS. B. Nac.

— [*Samir y Nircea.*] (By D. Anselmo Tovalina Ordaso de Tiroa.) MS. *Cens.* 1793. B. Mun.

— *Semanario erudito,* M., 1787–91. 34 vols.

— [*Sitio de Calatayud por el Marte Empecinado.*] (By Atanasio Valderrosal y Montedoro.) MS. *Cens.* 1814. B. Nac.

— *Tener la fama de fiera y en las acciones no serlo, Laomedón.* MS. *Cens.* 1778. B. Mun.

— *Trapero de Madrid, El.* MS. B. Mun.

— *Usurero celoso (El) y la prudente mujer.* MS. B. Nac.

— *Vanidad corregida, La.* (From Destouches *Le Glorieux.*) MS. 1781. B. Nac.

— *Vinatero de Madrid, El.* MS. B. Mun.

— *Vivanderas ilustres, Las.* [M.] 1792. B.M.

— (Also Introducciones and loas without titles. B. Mun.)

VALLE, JUAN DEL. [CADALSO]. *Don Sancho García, Conde de Castilla.* MS. *Cens.* 1771. B. Mun.

Variedades de ciencias, literatura y artes. M., 1805. Hem.

VELA, EUSEBIO DE. [*Pérdida de Espana, La.*] MS. *Cens.* 1770. B. Mun.

VELÁZQUEZ, LUIS JOSÉ, MARQUÉS DE VALDEFLORES. See Actas de la Academia de Buen Gusto, 'Examen' [*of Virginia*].

VÉLEZ Y GUEVARA. See Cáncer y Velasco.

VILLARROEL, LORENZO MARÍA DE, MARQUÉS DE PALACIOS Y VELÁZQUEZ. ('D.L.M.D. V.M.D.P.') *Ana Bolena.* M., 1778. B. Nac.

— *Conde Don Garci-Sánchez de Castilla, El.* Bar., n.d. B.M.

— *Padre de familias, El.* M., 1785. B. Nac.

Vie de Frédéric II . . . Strasbourg and Paris, 1788–9. 7 vols. B.M.

VOISENON, C. H. FUSÉE DE [and C. S. FAVART]. *Petite Iphigénie, La. Parodie de la grande.* (With music.) Pl. 1757. See *Œuvres* . . ., Paris, 1781. Vol. ii. B.M.

VOLTAIRE, F.M. AROUET DE. *Histoire de Charles XII, Roi de Suède.* Basle, 1731, etc. 2 vols. B.M.

— *Histoire de l'Empire de Russie sous Pierre le Grand.* [Geneva] 1759–63; 2 vols. B.M. [Geneva] 1775. B.M., etc.

— *Théâtre.* Amsterdam, 1764. 5 vols. B.M.

— See also *Répertoire Général du Théâtre Français.* Vols. 10–13. 1813, etc.

WEAVER, JOHN. *The History of Mimes and Pantomimes.* London, 1728. B.M.

ZAMORA, ANTONIO. *Comedias nuevas* . . . M., 1722. B.M.P.

— *Obras.* M., 1744. 2 vols. B.M.

ZAVALA Y ZAMORA, GASPAR. (Also, rather less commonly, spelt ZABALA Y ZAMORA.)

— *Academia de música, La. Loa.* (Also entitled: *La academia cómica.*) MS. *Cens.* 1796. B. Mun.

— [*Acmet el Magnánimo.*] MS. *Cens.* 1792. B. Mun. (Also entitled *Los desgraciados felices.*)

— *Adriano en Siria.* MS. *Cens.* 1797. B. Mun.

— *Alejandro en la Sogdiana.* MS. *Cens.* 1795. B. Mun.

— *Alianza, La. Alegoría cómica.* MS. *Cens.* 1808. B. Mun.

— *Amante generoso, El.* MS. *Cens.* 1794. B. Mun.

— *Amante honrado, El.* MS. *Cens.* 1793. B. Mun.

— *Amor constante (El) o La holandesa.* MS. B. Mun.

— *Amor dichoso, El. Melo.* N.p. n.d., B.M.

— [*Amor perseguido (El) y la virtud triunfante.*] MS. B. Mun; M., 1792. B.M.

— *Aragón restaurado por el valor de sus hijos* . . . M., 1790. B. Nac.

— [*Belorofonte en Licia.*] MS. B. Mun; *C.M.C.* ix (1796).

— *Besugueras, Las. Sain.* Val., 1813. B. Nac.

— *Bueno y el mal amigo, El, C.M.C.* viii (1793).

— *Calderero de San Germán (El) o El mutuo agradecimiento.* MS. *Cens.* 1790. B. Mun.

— *Carlos V sobre Dura.* MS. *Cens.* 1790. B. Mun.

— *Clemencia de Tito, La.* MS. B. Mun.

— *Confidente casual, El.* (From French.) MS. 1803. B. Mun.

— *Confitero y la vizcaína, El. Sain.* MS. *Cens.* 1786. B. Mun.

— [*Constitución y su significado, La.*] *Pitipieza jocosa.* MS. B. Mun.

— *Czar Iwan (El). Haz bien sin mirar a quien, o El premio de la humanidad.* MS. *Cens.* 1790. B. Mun.

— *De un acaso mil enredos.* MS. B. Mun.

— *Defensa de Ciudad Rodrigo, La.* Bar., 1817.

— *Destrucción de Sagunto, La.* M., 1800. B. Nac.

— *Día de campo, El.* MS. *Cens.* 1793. B. Mun.

— *Don Chicho, Sain.* MS. B. Mun.

— [*Eduardo y Federica.*] MS. *Cens.* 1811. B. Mun.

— *Elvira portuguesa, La.* M., 1804. B.M.P.

— *Eumenia (La) o la madrileña. Teatro moral.* M., 1805. B.M.

— [*Exteriores engañosos, Los.*] (From de Boissy.) MS. Licensed 1804. B. Nac.

— *Imperio de las costumbres, El.* (From Lemierre.) M., 1801. B. Mun.

— [*Justina, La.*] MS. *Cens.* 1788.

— *Leopoldo el Grande.* MS. *Cens.* 1789. B. Mun.

— [*Llegar a tiempo.*] MS. 1803. B. Mun.

— *Más heroica espartana, La.* M., 1800. B.M.

— *Matilde de Orlein.* M., 1804. B. Mun.

— *Mayor piedad, la de Leopoldo el Grande.* (Pl. 1789.) Val. 1795. B.M.

— *Naufragio feliz, El.* MS. *Cens.* 1782. B. Mun.

— *No hay poder contra los hados. Píramo y Tisbe.* MS. *Cens.* 1793. B. Mun.

— *Novelas nuevas.* (From Florian.) M., 1799. B.M.

— *Padre criminal, El.* MS. Approbation 1825. B. Mun.

— *Palmis y Oronte.* M., 1798. B.M.P.

— *Patriotas de Aragón, Los.* M., 1808. B.M.

— *Perfecto amigo, El.* MS. B. Mun.; M., 1790. B.M.

— *Por amparar la virtud olvidar su mismo amor. La hidalguía de una inglesa.* MS. *Cens.* 1790. B. Mun.; [Pamplona, 1778] B. Nac.

— *Por salvar al delincuente acusarse la inocente.* (From Mme B. Hadot and . . .) MS. Approbation 1816. B. Mun.

— *Por ser leal y ser noble dar puñal contra su sangre.* See *Toma de Milán.*
— *Premio de la humanidad, El.* See *Czar Iwan.*
— *Rey Eduardo, El.* MS. Cens. 1803. B. Mun.
— *Segundas nupcias (Las) o La condescendencia.* Also called *Los efectos de la condescendencia.* MS. 1825. B. Mun.
— *Selico y Berisa.* MS. Cens. 1799. B. Mun.
— *Semíramis.* N.p., n.d., B.M.P.; *C.M.C.* i (1789).
— [*Ser vencido y vencedor. Julio César y Catón.*] (From Metastasio.) [M.] 1801. B. Mun. Also attributed to J. López de Sedano.
— [*Soldado exorcista, El*] Sain. MS. Cens. 1818. B. Mun.
— *Sombra de Pelayo, o el día feliz de España.* M., 1808. B. Nac.
— *Tamara (La) o el poder del beneficio.* MS. B. Mun.
— *Tener celos de sí mismo.* N.p., 1790. B.M.
— *Tienda de joyería.* MS. B. Mun.
— *Toma de Breslau, La.* MS. Cens. 1793. B. Mun.
— *Toma de Hay, poi Josué, La.* MS. Licensed 1801. B. Nac.
— [*Toma de Milán, La.*] MS. (Prohibited 1814). B. Mun.
— [*Tramas de garulla, Las.*] MS. Cens. 1806. B. Mun.
— *Triunfo del amor, (El).* MS. Cens. 1793. B. Mun.
— *Triunfo del amor y la amistad, o Jenwal y Faustina,* MS. Licensed 1804. B. Nac.
— *Triunfos de amor y ardid. Carlos XII, rey de Suecia.* 3 Parts. (Part I. *Carlos XII, rey de Suecia.* Part II. *El sitio de Pultov por Carlos XII.* Part III. *El sitiador sitiado, y conquista de Stralsundo.*) M., 1787. B.M.
— *Víctimas del amor. Ana y Sindham.* MS. Cens. 1788. B. Mun.
— *Zenobia y Rhadamisto.* M., 1799. B. Mun.

II. *Critical Works Relating to the Period*

ALCALÁ GALIANO, ANTONIO. *Historia de la literatura española, francesa inglesa, e italiana en el siglo XVIII.* M. 1847.
— *Recuerdos de un anciano.* M. 1907.
ALONSO CORTÉS, NARCISO 'El teatro en Valladolid.' *B.R.A.E.* 1920, vii, 234–48; 318–31; 482–95; 633–53. 1921, viii, 226–63; 570–84. 1922, ix, 366–86; 471–87; 650–65. 1923, x, 55–71.
AMADOR DE LOS RÍOS, JOSÉ. *Historia de la villa y corte de Madrid.* Vol. iv, M., 1864.
ARMSTRONG, MARTIN. *Spanish Circus.* London, 1937.
ATKINSON, W. C. 'Hernán Pérez de Oliva'. *Rev. Hisp.* 1927, lxix and lxxi.

BARRERA Y LEIRADO, CAYETANO A. DE LA. *Catálogo ... del teatro antiguo español.* M., 1860.
BAYNE-POWELL, R. *Eighteenth-Century London Life.* London, 1937.
BERLEN, I. *The Age of Enlightenment.* N.Y., 1958.
BOUSSAGOL, G. 'Montiano et son *Ataulfo*' in *Mélanges ... Bataillon.* pp. 336–46.
BRANCA, V., and MANGINI, NICOLA. *Studi Goldoniani.* Venezia-Roma, 1960. 2 vols.
BRENNER, CLARENCE D. *Dramatizations of French Short Stories in the Eighteenth Century.* University of California Press, Berkeley and Los Angeles, 1947.

SPANISH DRAMA OF PATHOS

BROWN, R. F. *La novela española. 1700–1850.* M., 1953.
BRUFORD, W. H. *Theatre, Drama and Audience in Goethe's Germany.* London, 1950.
BUCHANAN, MILTON A. 'Some Aspects of Spanish Journalism before 1800'. *Rev. Hisp.* 1938, 81. Part II, 29 ff.
BURNET, MARY SCOTT. 'Marc-Antoine Legrand' in *Bibliothèque de la Société des Historiens du Théâtre.* Vol. xiv. Paris, 1939.

CABAÑOS, PABLO. 'Moratín y la reforma del teatro de su tiempo'. *Rev. Bib. Nac.* 1944, v, pp. 63–102.
— 'Un nuevo dato sobre Isidoro Máiquez'. *Rev. Fil. Esp.* 1943, xxvii, 424–5.
CAMBRONERO, CARLOS. 'Apuntes para la historia de la censura dramática.' *Rev. comp.* 1899, cxvi, 594 ff.
— 'Comella, su vida y sus obras.' *Rev. comp.* 1896, cii, etc.
CANBY, H. S. 'Pamela Abroad'. *M.L.N.* 1903, xviii, no. 7, 206–13.
CANFIELD, D. F. *Corneille and Racine in England,* N.Y., 1904.
CANO, J. L. 'Una "poética" desconocida del XVIII'. *B. Hisp.* 1961, 1–2.
CARMENA Y MILÁN, LUIS. *Crónica de la ópera italiana en Madrid desde . . . 1738 hasta nuestros días.* M., 1878.
CARRETER, FERNANDO LÁZARO. *Cotejo de las églogas que ha premiado la Real Academia de la Lengua,* by Juan Pablo Forner. Ed. by . . . C.S.I.C. Sal., 1951.
— *Ideas lingüísticas en España durante el siglo XVIII, Las.* C.S.I.C. M., 1949.
CASTAÑEDA, V. 'Un curioso bando sobre representación de comedias en Valencia en el siglo XVIII.' In *Homenaje . . . a Menéndez Pidal.* M., 1925. 3 vols. See vol. i, 577–82.
CASTRO, AMÉRICO. 'Algunos aspectos del siglo XVIII'. *Lengua, enseñanza y literatura.* M., 1924, 281–334.
CHARPENTIER, J. *Rousseau.* London, 1931.
CHASTENET, JACQUES. *Godoy. Master of Spain, 1792–1808.* (Trans. by J. F. Huntington.) London, 1953.
CIAN, VITTORIO. *Italia e Spagna nel secolo XVIII . . .* Torino, 1896.
COE, ADA M. 'Additional notes on Corneille in Spain in the eighteenth century.' *Rom Rev.* 1933, xxiv, 233–5
— *Carteleras madrileñas.* Mexico, 1952.
— *Catálogo bibliográfico y crítico de las comedias anunciadas en los periódicos de Madrid desde 1661 hasta 1819.* Baltimore, Maryland, and London, 1935.
— *Entertainments in the Little Theatres of Madrid 1759–1819.* N.Y., 1947.
— 'Richardson in Spain.' *Hisp. Rev.* 1935, iii, 56–63.
COLOMA, LUIS. *Retratos de antaño.* M., 1895.
COOK, J. A. *Neo-Classic Drama in Spain.* Dallas, 1959.
COTARELO Y MORI, EMILIO.
— *Bibliografía de las controversias sobre la licitud del teatro en España.* M., 1904.
— [*Catálogo abreviado de una colección española, hasta fines del siglo XIX y de obras relativas al teatro español.*] M., 1930.
— *Don Ramón de la Cruz y sus obras.* M., 1899.
— *Estudios de historia literaria de España.* M., 1901.
— *Estudios sobre la historia del arte escénico en España.*
  I. *María Ladvenant y Quirante.* M., 1896.
  II. *María del Rosario Fernández. (La Tirana.)* M., 1897;
  III. *Isidoro Máiquez y el teatro de su tiempo.* M., 1902.

— *Historia de la zarzuela, o sea el drama lírico en España.* M., 1934.
— *Iriarte y su época.* M., 1897.
— *Orígenes y establecimiento de la ópera en España.* M., 1917.
— 'Traductores castellanos de Molière' (in *Homenaje a Menéndez y Pelayo,* M., 1899, Vol. i, 69–141.
— *Un gran editor español del siglo XVIII. Biografía de D. Ant. de Sancha* . . . M., 1924.
CUESTA, LIBRERÍA OF. *Catálogo de comedias antiguas y modernas* . . . [M.] n.d.

DALSÈME, R. *Beaumarchais.* London, 1929.
DANVILA Y COLLADO, MANUEL. *Reinado de Carlos III.* M., 1893. M., 6 vols.
DEFOURNEAUX, MARCELIN. *Pablo de Olavide ou L'Afrancesado.* Paris, 1959.
DELPY, G. *L'Espagne et L'Esprit Européen. L'Œuvre de Feijoo.* Paris, 1936.
DEMERSON, G. *Don Juan Meléndez Valdés et son temps.* Paris, 1962.
DESDEVISES DU DÉZERT, G. *Les Institutions de l'Espagne au XVIIIe Siècle. Rev. Hisp.* 1927, lxx, 1–554.
DÍAZ DE ESCOVAR, N. *Intimidades de la farándula.* Cádiz. n.d.
— *Teatro en Málaga* . . . *siglos XVI, XVII, XVIII, El.* Málaga, 1896.
DÍAZ DE ESCOVAR, N., and LASSO DE LA VEGA, F. DE P. *Historia del teatro español.* Bar., 1924. See Vol. i.
DÍAZ-PLAJA, GUILLERMO. *Historia general de las literaturas hispánicas.* Bar., 1949, etc. See Vol. iv.
DÍAZ-PLAJA, F. *La vida española en el siglo XVIII.* Bar., 1946.
DOBSON, A. *Eighteenth-Century Studies.* Dent, n.d.
DOMÍNGUEZ ORTIZ, A. 'Don Leandro Fernández de Moratín . . .' in *R.U.M.* 1960, ix, 35, pp. 607–42.
— *La sociedad española en el siglo XVIII.* M., 1955.

ENCISO RECIO, L. M. 'Actividades de los franceses en Cádiz, 1789–90.' *Hisp.* 1959, xix, no. 75.
ENTRAMBASAGUAS, JOAQUÍN DE. *El Madrid de Moratín.* M., 1960.

FERNÁNDEZ Y GONZÁLEZ, F. *Historia de la crítica literaria en España desde Luzán hasta nuestros días.* M., 1867.
FERRER DEL RÍO, ANTONIO. *Historia del reinado de Carlos III en España.* M., 1856. 4 vols.
FORD, RICHARD. *Gatherings from Spain.* London, 1846.
— *A Handbook for Travellers in Spain.* London, 1845. 2 vols.

GAIFFE, F. *Le Drame en France au XVIII Siècle.* Paris, 1910.
GARCÍA MARTÍN, LUIS. *Manual de teatros y espectáculos públicos.* M., 1860.
GATTI, JOSÉ FRANC. 'La fuente de Inesilla la de Pinto.' *Rev. Fil. Hisp.*, 1943, v, 368–73.
GAYA NUÑO, J. A. 'El arte en la época de Moratín' in *R.U.M.* 1960, ix, 35, pp. 703–28.
GLENDINNING. O. N. V. *Vida y obra de Cadalso.* M., 1962.
GLENN, R. F. 'Leandro F. de Moratín in England'. *Hisp.* 1965, xlviii, no. 1.
GÓMEZ DE ARTECHE, JOSÉ. *Reinado de Carlos IV.* 3 vols. M., 1893.
GONZÁLEZ PALENCIA, ÁNGEL. *Eruditos y libreros del siglo XVIII.* M., 1948.
— 'La fonda de San Sebastián.' *B.A.M.* ii, 549–53.
— 'Nuevas noticias sobre Isidoro Máiquez.' *B.A.M.* iii, 73–128.
— 'La Tonadilla de Garrido.' *B.A.M.* iii, 241–45.
— 'Tonadilla mandada recoger por Jovellanos.' *B.A.M.* i, 138–42.

GONZÁLEZ RUIZ, NICOLÁS. *La Caramba*. M., 1944.

GONZÁLEZ RUIZ, NICOLÁS, and GÓMEZ DE ORTEGA, R. 'Juan Ignacio González del Castillo y el teatro popular del siglo XVIII.' *B.S.S.* 1924, i, 135–49.

GRANJEL, LUIS S. 'Panorama de la medicina española durante el siglo XVIII' in *R.U.M.* 1960, ix, 35, pp. 675–702.

GRANNIS, VALLERIA B. *Dramatic Parody in Eighteenth-Century France*. Publications of the Institute of French Studies, N.Y. 1931.

GUINARD, P-J. 'Le Règne de Charles III vu par ses contemporains in *Mélanges Bataillon*, pp. 81–3.

HAMILTON, ARTHUR. *A Study of Spanish Manners (1750–1800) from the Plays of Ramón de la Cruz*. Urbana, 1926 (University of Illinois Studies in Language and Literature, vol. ii, no. 3.

[HARTZENBUSCH] MAXIRIARTH. *Apuntes para un catálogo de periódicos madrileños desde el año 1661 al 1870*. M., 1894.

— *Unos cuantos seudónimos de escritores españoles*. M., 1904.

HARTNOLL, P. (Ed.). *The Oxford Companion to the Theatre*. O.U.P., 1951 and 1967.

HAZARD, PAUL. *La Pensée Européene au XVIII*ème *Siècle*. Paris, 1946. 2 vols.

HELMAN, EDITH F. *Noches lúgubres* (with Introduction). Santander, M., 1951.

— 'Moratín y Goya'. in *R.U.M.* 1960, ix, 35, pp. 591–605.

HERR, RICHARD. *The Eighteenth-Century Revolution in Spain*. Princeton, New Jersey, 1958.

— 'The Twentieth Century Spaniard Views the Spanish Enlightenment'. *Hisp.* 1962, xlv, no. 2, 183–93.

Homenaje ofrecido a R. Menéndez Pidal. M., 1925.

IACUZZI, ALFRED. *The European Vogue of Favart*. N.Y., 1932.

Índice General de los libros prohibidos . . . por El Sr. Inquisidor General. M., 1844.

JIMÉNEZ SALAS, M. *Vidas y obras de Juan Pablo Forner y Segarra*. M., 1944.

JOUCLA-RUAU, ANDRÉ. 'À Propos d'une Correspondance inédite du Prince de la Paix' in *Mélanges . . . Bataillon*, pp. 91–112.

Jovellanos su vida y su obra. Homenaje del Centro Asturiano de Buenos Aires . . . Buenos Aires, 1945.

JOURDAIN, E. F. *Dramatic Theory and Practice in France. 1690–1808*. London, 1921.

JULIÁ MARTÍNEZ, E. 'Preferencias teatrales del público valenciano en el siglo XVIII.' *Rev. Fil. Esp.* 1933, xx, 113–59.

— 'El teatro en Valencia' in *B.R.A.E.* 1917, iv, 56–83; 1926, xiii, 318–41.

KANY, C. E. *Life and Manners in Madrid. 1750–1800*. Berkeley, California, 1932.

— 'Plan de reforma de los teatros de Madrid aprobado en 1799.' *B.A.M.* vi, 246–84.

— 'Theatrical Jurisdiction of the *Juez Protector* in XVIII*th* Century Madrid.' *Rev. Hisp.* 1933, lxxxi, ii, 382 ff.

LAGRONE, G. C. *The Imitations of 'Don Quixote' in the Spanish Drama*. Publication of th. Series in Romanic Languages and Literatures. No. 27. University of Pennsylvaniae Philadelphia, 1937.

LEA, K. M. *Popular Italian Comedy*. Oxford, 1934. 2 vols.

LEE, VERNON. *Studies of the Eighteenth Century in Italy*. London, 1907. (2nd ed.)

LEWIS, W. *The Hooded Hawk*. London, 1946.
LLINARES, ARMAND: 'Un Aspect de l'antilullisme au XVIII Siècle' *in Mélanges* . . . *Bataillon*, pp. 498–506.
LOPEZ PELÁEZ, A. *Los escritos de Sarmiento y el siglo de Feijoo*. La Coruña, 1901.

MCCLELLAND, I. L. 'Comellan Drama and the Censor.' *B.H.S.* 1953, xxx, 20–31.
— 'Comentario sobre *La Disputa del teatro*. Sainete anónimo de 1776' in *Homenaje a J. A. Van Praag*. Amsterdam, 1956.
— 'Concerning the Dramatic Approach to the Eighteenth Century.' *B.H.S.* 1950, xxvii, 72–87.
— 'The Eighteenth-Century Conception of the Stage and Histrionic Technique' in *Estudios Hispánicos. Homenaje a Archer M. Huntington*. Wellesley, Mass., 1952. 393–425.
— *The Origins of the Romantic Movement in Spain*, Liverpool, 1937.
— 'Tirso de Molina and the Eighteenth Century.' *B.S.S.* 1941, xviii, 182–204.
MADOL, H. R. *Godoy the First Dictator of Modern Times*. London, 1934.
MARÍAS, J. *La España posible en tiempo de Carlos III*. Madrid, 1963.
Mélanges offerts á Marcel Bataillon par les Hispanistes Français. B. Hisp. Bordeaux, 1962.
MENÉNDEZ Y PELAYO, MARCELINO. *Biblioteca de traductores españoles. Obras completas.* Vols. 54–7. C.S.I.C. 1952.
— *Estudios de crítica literaria*. M., 1893–1908.
— *Historia de las ideas estéticas en España*. M., 1923.
— *Historia de los heterodoxos españoles*. M., 1911–27.
MÉRIMÉE, PAUL. 'El teatro de Leandro Fernández de Moratín' in *R.U.M.* 1960, ix, 35, pp. 729–61.
MESONERO ROMANOS, R. DE. *El antiguo Madrid*, M., 1881. 2 vols.
— *Nuevo manual histórico-topográfico-estadístico y descripción de Madrid*. M., 1854.
MOLL, J. 'Catálogo de comedias sueltas conservadas en la Biblioteca de la Real Academia Española'. *B.R.A.E.* 1964, xliv, nos. 171–2; xlv. nos. 174–5.
MORALES DE SETIÉN, FELIPE. 'El Hato de las compañías cómicas a fines del siglo XVIII.' *B.A.M.* i, 106–8.
MOREL-FATIO, A. *Études sur l'Espagne*. Paris, 1895–1925. 4 vols. See vol. ii. Paris, 1890.
MUNTANER, J. *La colección teatral de Don Arturo Sedó*. Bar. 1951.

NICOLL, J. R. ALLARDYCE. *British Drama*. London, 1951.
— *The English Theatre*. London, 1938.
— *A History of Early Eighteenth-Century Drama. 1700–50*. Cambridge, 1925.
— *A History of Late Eighteenth-Century Drama. 1750–1800*. Cambridge, 1927.
— *World Drama*. London, 1951.
NOVALES, ALBERTO G. *Las pequeñas Atlántidas*. Bar., 1959.

OLIVER, A. 'Verso y prosa in Leandro Fernández de Moratín'. in *R.U.M.* 1960, ix, 35, pp. 643–74.
OMAN, C. *David Garrick*. Hodder and Stoughton, 1958.
OZANAM, DIDIER. 'L'Idéal Académique d'un Poète Éclairé: Luzán et son Projet d'Académie Royale des Sciences, Arts . . .' in *Mélanges . . . Bataillon*. pp. 188–208.

PALAU Y DULCET, ANTONIO. *Manual del Librero Hispano-Americano* . . . Bar., 1923–7. 2nd ed. Bar., 1948 etc.

PAR, ALFONSO. *Contribución a la bibliografía española de Shakespeare.* Diputación Provincial de Barcelona. Publicaciones del Instituto de Teatro Nacional, No. 7, 1930.

— 'Representaciones teatrales en Barcelona durante el siglo XVIII.' *B.R.A.C.* 1929, xvi. 326–46; 492–513; 594–614.

— *Shakespeare en la literatura española.* Bar., 1935. 2 vols.

PASCUAL DE GAYANGOS. *Catalogue of the Manuscripts in the Spanish Language in the British Museum.* London, 1875–93.

PAZ Y MELIA, A. (Ed.). *Catálogo de las piezas de teatro que se conservan en el departamento de manuscritos de la Biblioteca Nacional.* M., 1934. (2nd ed.), vol. i.

PEERS, E. A. 'The Influence of Ossian in Spain.' *Phil. Q.* 1925, iv, 121–38.

— 'The Influence of Young and Gray in Spain.' *M.L.R.* 1926, xxi, 404–18.

— 'The Vogue of Alfieri in Spain.' *Hisp. Rev.* 1933, i, 122–140.

PELLICER, CASIANO. *Tratado histórico sobre el origen y progresos de la comedia y del histrionismo en España.* M., 1804.

PELLISSIER, R. E. *The Neo-Classic Movement in Spain during the XVIII Century.* California, 1918.

PÉREZ BUSTAMENTE, C. 'La España del P. Feijoo.' *Boletín de la Biblioteca de Menéndez y Pelayo, Santander.* 1964, xl, no. 1.

POLT, J. H. R. 'Jovellanos' *El delincuente honrado.*' *Rom. Rev.* 1959, l, 170–90.

PRICE, L. M. *The Vogue of Marmontel on the German Stage.* University of California Press, Berkeley and Los Angeles, 1944.

QUALIA, C. B. 'The Campaign to substitute French Neo-Classical Tragedy for the Comedia, 1737–1800.' *P.M.L.A.* 1939, liv, 184–211.

— 'Corneille in Spain in the Eighteenth Century.' *Rom. Rev.* 1933, xxiv, 21–9.

— 'Racine's Tragic Art in Spain in the Eighteenth Century.' *P.M.L.A.* 1939, liv, 1059–76.

REGLÁ, JUAN, and ALCOLEA, SANTIAGO. *El siglo XVIII.* Bar., 1957.

RICARD, R. 'Jovellanos y la nobleza.' *Atlántida,* M., Sept.–Oct. 1965.

RODRÍGUEZ CASADO, V. *La política y los políticos en el reinado de Carlos III.* Madrid, 1962.

ROGERS, P. P. *Goldoni in Spain.* Oberlin, Ohio, 1941.

— *The Spanish Drama Collection in the Oberlin College Library. A Descriptive Catalogue.* Oberlin, Ohio, 1940.

ROSSI, GIUSEPPE, CARLO. 'La teórica del teatro in Juan Pablo Forner.' *Filologia Romanza,* no. 18, 1958, 210–22.

— 'La teórica del teatro en Tomás de Iriarte' in *Filologia Romanza,* no. 17, 1958. 49–62.

RUBIO, JERÓNIMO. 'José Ant. de Armona. El buen Corregidor de Madrid.' *B.A.M.* xvi, 3–89.

RUMEU DE ARMAS, ANTONIO. *Historia de la censura literaria gubernativa en España.* M., 1940.

SAINZ DE ROBLES, F. C. *Antiguos teatros de Madrid, Los.* M., 1952.

— *El teatro español. Historia y Antología.* M., 1942–3. 7 vols. See vol. v.

SAINZ Y RODRÍGUEZ, P. *La evolución de las ideas sobre la Decadencia española.* M., 1925.

SALVA, JAIME. 'La Fragata del Buen Retiro.' *B.A.M.* xviii, 209–59.

SÁNCHEZ AGESTA, LUIS. 'Moratín y el pensamiento político del despotismo ilustrado.' *R.U.M.* 1960, ix, 35, pp. 567–89.

— *El pensamiento político del despotismo ilustrado.* M., 1953.

SÁNCHEZ RIVERO, A. MARUTTI DE. 'Un ejemplo de intercambio cultural hispano-italiano en el siglo XVIII' in *R.U.M.* 1960, ix, 35, pp. 763–808.

SAN JOSÉ, DIEGO. *El Madrid de Goya.* M., [1929.]

SARRAILH, JEAN. 'Á Propos du *Delincuente honrado* de Jovellanos' in *Mélanges d'Études Portugaises offerts à M. Georges Le Gentil.* Instituto Para A Alta Cultura. [Lisbon], 1949.

— 'La Crise Religieuse en Espagne a la Fin du XVIIIᵉ Siècle.' The Taylorian Lecture for 1951. Oxford, 1951.

— *L'Espagne Eclairée de la Seconde Moitié du XVIIIᵉ Siècle.* Paris, 1954.

SAZ, AGUSTÍN DE. 'Moratín y su época.' *B.A.M.* 1928, v, 411–16.

SCHACK, ADOLFO FEDERICO, CONDE DE. *Historia de la literatura y el arte dramático en España.* M., 1887. Vol. v.

SCOTT, W. S. *The Georgian Theatre.* London, 1946.

SEELEY, L. B. *Mrs. Thrale.* London, 1908.

SIERRA CORELLA, ANTONIO. *La Censura en España. Índices y catálogos de libros prohibidos.* M., 1947.

SIMÓN DÍAZ, J. *Bibliografía de la literatura hispánica.* M., 1950, etc.

— 'Documentos sobre Comella.' *Revista de Bibliografía Nacional.* M., 1944, v, 467–70.

SITWELL, E. *Alexander Pope.* London, 1930.

SMITH, S. HARCOURT. *Alberoni or the Spanish Conspiracy.* London, 1943.

SPELL, J. R. *Rousseau in the Spanish World before 1833.* Texas, 1938.

STEEN, M. *The Lost One.* (A Biography of Mary [Perdita] Robinson). London, 1937.

SUBIRÁ, JOSÉ.

— 'Bajo el imperio de la tonadilla.' *B.A.M.* iii, 371–5.

— 'La canción y la danza populares en el teatro del siglo XVIII,' *B.A.M.* vi, 87–90.

— *El compositor Iriarte y el cultivo español del melólogo.* Bar., 1949.

— 'Críticas teatrales en el repertorio tonadillesco.' *B.A.M.* x, 419–23.

— 'Dos tonadillas cortesanas.' *B.A.M.* viii, 91–5.

— 'En pro de la tonadilla madrileña.' *B.A.M.* vi, 205–14.

— 'La escena trágica *Policena* . . .' *B.A.M.* v, 360–4.

— 'Estampas madrileñas en el teatro tonadillesco.' *B.A.M.* x, 255–9.

— 'El estreno de *La Serva Padrona* de Paisiello en Madrid.' *B.A.M.* ii, 559–62.

— 'Evocaciones en torno a las *óperas madrileñas.*' *B.A.M.* xxiii, 85–129.

— 'García, Manuel, "El Malo" Un Actor y autor madrileño del siglo XVIII.' *B.A.M.* ii, 433–6.

— *El gremio de representantes españoles y la cofradía de Nuestra Señora de la Novena.* C.S.I.C. M., 1960.

— 'El idioma como elemento satírico en la literatura tonadillesca.' *B.A.M.* ix, 449–53.

— 'Iriarte y otros autores. Los melólogos de Rousseau.' *B.A.M.* v, 140–61.

— 'La Junta de reforma de teatros.' *B.A.M.* ix, 19–45.

— 'El *Malbru* de Valledor. Una tonadilla extraordinariamente aplaudida.' *B.A.M.* v, 87–91.

— 'Los melólogos de Rousseau, Iriarte y otros autores'. *B.A.M.* v, 140–61.

— 'La participación musical en las comedias madrileñas durante el siglo XVIII.' *B.A.M.* vii, 109–23; 389–404.

— 'Los petimetres en el campo tonadillesco.' *B.A.M.* xi, 434–8.
— 'La Tirana . . .' *B.A.M.* xi, 105–9.
— 'Un fondo desconocido de tonadillas.' *B.A.M.* xi, 338–42.
— 'Un sainete olvidado: *La academia de Bolero.*' *B.A.M.* iii, 500–3.
— 'Una tonadilla de costumbres filarmónicas.' *B.A.M.* x, 113–16.
— Varias *Medeas* musicales en el antiguo teatro madrileño. *B.A.M.* x, 429–38.

TOMPKINS, J. M. S. *The Popular Novel in England, 1770–1800.* London, 1932.
TRENAS, JULIO. 'Periódicos madrileños del siglo XVIII.' *G.P.E.* 1951, no. 46, 25–31.
TUDELA, M. *La Caramba.* Bar., 1959.

UHAGÓN Y GUARDAMINO, F. R. DE (MARQUÉS DE LAURENCÍN). *Don Agustín de Montiano y Luyando, primer director de la Real Academia de la Historia. Noticias y documentos.* M., 1926.

VALBUENA PRAT, A. *Historia del teatro español.* Bar., 1956.
VALLADARES Y SAAVEDRA, RAMÓN DE. *Nociones acerca de la historia del teatro desde su nacimiento hasta nuestros días.* M., 1848.
VAREY, J. E. *Historia de los títeres en España.* M., 1957.
VÁZQUEZ-MACHICADO, H. 'Un código cultural del siglo XVIII' in *Revista interamericana de Bibliografía.*' Washington, 1958. No. 4.
VEGA, JOSÉ. *Luis I de España.* M., 1943.
VON BOEHN, MAX. *Modes and Manners.* London, 1935.
VULLIAMY, C. E. *Aspasia.* London, 1935.
— *Voltaire.* London, 1930.

WILLIAMS, M. *Lady Luxborough goes to Bath.* Oxford, 1946.

ZABALA, ARTURO. *La ópera en la vida teatral valenciana del siglo XVIII.* Val., 1960.

Note. Some works which have appeared during the production of these volumes have been included in the Bibliography, but it has not been possible to discuss them in the text.

GENERAL INDEX

REFERENCES are not given to the Bibliography or to the works of modern critics, though the names of modern critics are included. Short dramatic pieces are grouped under their generic names: Introducciones, *Sainetes, Zarzuelas,* etc., unless any one piece has some special bearing on the text. An eighteenth-century drama usually has several long titles and sub-titles. Reference here is made to the commonest and most orientative of such titles. Names in brackets are of authors or translators of the works concerned, or of writers to whom those works are most commonly ascribed. Names consisting of initials only are listed at the end of the letter-sections.

The alphabetical order is English; ñ follows n.